Living Bread, Saving Cup

Edited by R. Kevin Seasoltz O.S.B.

Living Bread, Saving Cup

Readings on the Eucharist

The Liturgical Press

Collegeville, Minnesota

Cover by Frank Kacmarcik.

Nihil obstat: Robert C. Harren, J.C.L., *Censor deputatus*.
Imprimatur: † George H. Speltz, D.D., Bishop of St. Cloud. March 15, 1982.
 For information, address The Liturgical Press, Collegeville, Minnesota 56321.
Printed in the United States of America.

Library of Congress Cataloging in Publication Data

Main entry under title:

Living bread, saving cup.

Includes bibliographical references and index.
1. Lord's Supper — Catholic Church — Addresses, essays, lectures. 2. Mass — Addresses, essays, lectures. 3. Catholic Church — Doctrinal and controversial works — Catholic authors — Addresses, essays, lectures. I. Seasoltz, R. Kevin.
BX2215.2.L57 264' .02036 81-20813
ISBN 0-8146-1257-1 AACR2

Contents

The Contributors

JEROME MURPHY-O'CONNOR is professor of New Testament at the Ecole Biblique in Jerusalem.

AIDAN KAVANAGH is professor of liturgics in the Divinity School at Yale University.

ROBERT J. LEDOGAR was formerly professor of liturgy at Maryknoll Seminary, Maryknoll, New York.

THOMAS J. TALLEY is professor of liturgics at The General Theological Seminary in New York City.

JAMES DALLEN is professor of religious studies at Rosemont College, Rosemont, Pennsylvania.

PHILIPPE ROUILLARD is professor of sacramental theology at the Collegio di Sant' Anselmo, Rome.

DAVID POWER is professor of liturgical studies at The Catholic University of America, Washington, D.C.

EDWARD SCHILLEBEECKX is professor of theology at the Catholic University of Nijmegen, Netherlands.

DONALD GRAY is professor of religious studies at Manhattan College, Bronx, New York.

HERVÉ-MARIE LEGRAND is professor of theology at the Institut Catholique, Paris.

JEAN LECLERCQ, from Clervaux Abbey in Luxembourg, is a specialist in the spirituality of the early Middle Ages.

JOHN QUINN is professor of Church history at Mt. St. Mary's Seminary, Emmitsburg, Maryland.

ROBERT TAFT is professor of Eastern liturgies at the Pontifical Oriental Institute, Rome.

R. KEVIN SEASOLTZ is professor of liturgical studies at The Catholic University of America, Washington, D.C.

KENNETH SMITS is professor of liturgical theology at St. Francis School of Pastoral Ministry, Milwaukee.

M. FRANCIS MANNION is rector of the Cathedral of the Madeleine, Salt Lake City, and diocesan director of theological affairs.

JOHN M. HUELS is professor of canon law at Catholic Theological Union in Chicago.

Introduction

During the summer of 1981 I taught a course on eucharistic liturgy in the School of Theology at St. John's University in Collegeville, Minnesota. While preparing bibliographies for the students, I noticed that a number of the most useful articles were taken from back issues of *Worship*. Since some of the issues have gone out of print and are no longer readily available to students, it seemed a worthwhile project to bring the articles together under one cover in book form. The editors of The Liturgical Press agreed. Since the first printing of this collection, a number of other articles on the Eucharist have appeared in *Worship* which have aroused special interest among readers. Three of these have been added in this second printing.

Jerome Murphy-O'Connor's article on "Eucharist and Community in First Corinthians" was first published in two parts in 1976–1977. In some ways it summarizes the main themes of the author's book *Becoming Human Together*, but those themes are specifically related to the Eucharist and Paul's teaching on the subject in his First Letter to the Corinthians. That teaching is characterized above all by its realism and its foundation in Paul's understanding of the Church as a community of faith. The collection of essays presented here would have been strengthened if it had been possible to include an article on the Johannine understanding of the Eucharist in which the emphasis is more on the union of the individual person with the risen Lord. In that way the scriptural foundations for both the communal and personal aspects of eucharistic liturgy would have been set out.

The collection includes a number of articles on the eucharistic prayer. Although basic information is sometimes repeated, the articles generally complement one another and present distinctive points of view. Aidan Kavanagh's lengthy piece on the Roman anaphora, published in two parts in 1965–1966, sets out the basic vocabulary and themes which must be grasped by any student working in the area of eucharistic liturgy. The article clarifies the main areas of concern that were considered in reforming the anaphora after the Second Vatican Council; it likewise provides the primary criteria for evaluating new eucharistic prayers. A number of the questions raised by Kavanagh are further explored by Robert Ledogar in his article "The Eucharistic Prayer and the Gifts over

Which It Is Spoken." The piece is based on his excellent doctoral dissertation, *Acknowledgement: Praise Verbs in the Early Greek Anaphoras*, published in Rome in 1968. Thomas Talley has for years been interested in the structure of the eucharistic prayer and its relationship to the Jewish *berakah*. While noting similarities in the two prayer forms, his scholarly article clearly establishes that the two forms are not the same; it likewise highlights the complexity of the relationship between Jewish and Christian prayer forms.

In his "Thoughts on the New Eucharistic Prayers," Kavanagh applies his technical knowledge of the morphology and content of the eucharistic prayer to the three new anaphoras provided for official use by the Roman Church in 1968. James Dallen's article, published in 1978, is a consideration of the congregation's role in the eucharistic prayer. The author confines his attention to the official contemporary prayers of the Roman rite; he has not attempted to set out other possible forms which would enable the congregation to have more involvement in the eucharistic prayer. Use of the official canons for Masses with children and various unofficial texts have in fact shown how some of the questions Dallen raises might be solved to pastoral advantage.

The meal aspect of the Christian Eucharist is treated in a beautiful article by Philippe Rouillard. His piece, reminiscent of the work done by Edmond Barbotin in *The Humanity of God*, is a study of the successive stages which led from the human meal to the Christian Eucharist. Since the article considers only one aspect of the Eucharist, it is effectively complemented by David Power's article on "The Uses of 'Sacrifice' in Eucharistic Discourse." Certainly the theme of sacrifice is one which continues to exercise passions in ecumenical discussions, so much so that the imagery of sacrifice is sometimes consciously avoided. Robert Daly has discussed the Judaeo-Christian background to Christian sacrifice before the time of Origin in his monumental work published in 1978. Power's conclusions are generally consonant with Daly's work; his reflections, however, on the use of metaphor in the New Testament and early Christian language shed useful light on the subject of Christian sacrifice from another point of view.

Edward Schillebeeckx' article on "Transubstantiation, Transfinalization, Transignification" is basically the substance of the latter part of his book *The Eucharist*, originally published in Dutch in 1967. After analyzing the meaning of transubstantiation in the documents of the Council of Trent, the author shows how the philosophies of personalism and phenomenology can complement the expression of the eucharistic mystery in terms of Aristotelian metaphysics. Although the debate on the nature of the Real Presence which was waged in the years after the Second Vatican Council has subsided, the article is still very useful in setting out the strengths and weaknesses of the traditional teaching on transubstantiation and how that teaching might well be complemented rather than contradicted by more contemporary terms such as transfinalization and transignification.

Donald Gray's note on "The Real Absence" is a reminder that the presence of the risen Lord in the Eucharist is always mysterious and can never be adequately expressed in human language. Certainly his presence is not object-like or physical; if that were so his presence in the Eucharist would exhaust his presence with his people. As Gray states, "The real presence is accompanied by a real absence which summons the people of God into the future promised by the resurrection. The purpose of this real absence is to call the people of God to greater intimacy of presence in the immediate future and to definitive presence in the ultimate future."

The presidency of the Eucharist is a much-debated topic these days. Discussion is stimulated above all by the contemporary interest in the ordination of women to the priesthood and the declining number of ordained ministers in many parts of the world. Hervé-Marie Legrand's article is a carefully researched investigation of eucharistic presidency according to the ancient tradition. His conclusion, based on the legacy of the ancient tradition, is that it pertains to those who preside over the upbuilding of the Church to preside over the sacraments, including the Eucharist, which for their part build up the Church. In light of that conclusion, Legrand raises significant questions concerning the contemporary pastoral practice and the way it relates to the tradition: (1) If the bond between the Church and Eucharist is so strong that the local community is not conceived without the Sunday Eucharist, how do we justify pastoral situations in some churches where Mass is celebrated only a few times a year? (2) If the Eucharist has become rare in some churches today, it is because there is no one to preside. The ancient tradition indicates that in the pre-Nicene period local churches regularly provided themselves with presidents. Does that mean that today once Christians are competent to preside over the upbuilding of their local churches they are likewise competent to receive ordination which entitles them to preside at the Eucharist? (3) The lack of presidents of the Church and consequently of the Eucharist today is said to be due to a lack of vocations. If as the early Church practice indicates, a vocation is objective in the sense that it is the call which the community addresses to one of its members, is our modern understanding of vocation too subjective? Is it balanced theologically and ecclesially? Although Legrand does not answer his provocative questions, he does show that in our modern approach to the presidency of the Eucharist we have in fact separated ourselves from what he describes as "the best founded and best assured tradition."

Not only are parishes often without priests in various parts of the world today, but convents of women religious, especially nuns, are often without regular chaplains. In his article on "Eucharistic Celebrations without Priests in the Middle Ages," Jean Leclercq shows how various medieval communities maintained a eucharistic tradition without daily celebration of Mass. He does not advocate a simple return to these medieval practices, but he does stress that the earlier tradition "can provide ideas about what can be done today and tomorrow, differently to be sure, but in continuity with the same tradition."

John Quinn's article on "The Lord's Supper and Forgiveness of Sin" was published in 1968. Baptism and penance were acknowledged for centuries to be the primary sacraments of pardon. Since the Second Vatican Council, however, liturgists have stressed baptism more as a sacrament of Christian initiation than as the sacrament which forgives original sin. Penance is a pastorally problematic sacrament at the present time due to complex unresolved theological and canonical questions. Certainly few contemporary Christians feel a compulsion to receive the sacrament of penance before receiving the Eucharist unless there has been a serious sin. In practice, many Christians experience the Eucharist itself as a meal of reconciliation. Quinn's article provides a sound theological foundation for that appreciation of the sacrament.

Robert Taft's article on concelebration grew out of a discussion of the topic by a study group at the North American Academy of Liturgy's annual meeting in 1980. In the last ten years there has been a growing dissatisfaction with the restored Roman rite of eucharistic concelebration. Taft's article does not pretend to solve any of the contemporary problems. However, it does clarify the state of the question, correct misinterpretations of early eucharistic discipline, and dispel misconceptions concerning the normative value of Eastern usage of concelebration.

My own article on "Monastery and Eucharist" is an attempt not only to set out the tradition but to specify the strengths and weaknesses of what in fact are various traditions. It would seem that many aspects of the article bear not only on monastic life but also on religious life in general, especially as it is lived in this country.

Kenneth Smits' discussion of "A Congregational Order of Worship" is especially useful in light of the ongoing evaluation of the revised Order of Mass. It is advisable, however, not simply to attend to the congregation's order of worship but to evaluate the order in light of the whole assembly's celebration of the Eucharist. The missal promulgated after the Council of Trent set out the rubrics for the celebration of Mass as though the Mass were the priest's Mass. The General Instruction of the Roman Missal, issued by the Congregation of Rites in 1969, envisions Mass with a congregation as the normative form of celebration. More recent studies, however, have stressed the liturgical assembly as the primary celebrant of the Eucharist since all Christians are baptized to priesthood. The distinctive roles of those who are ordained to the presbyterate and so commissioned to preside at the Eucharist and those who make up the congregation are thus viewed as complementary within the unity of the assembled community. An evaulation of the Order of Mass within that context naturally raises questions not envisioned by Smits' more limited concerns.

The relationship between the Eucharist and social justice is a matter of growing concern among committed Christians because many of them have become increasingly conscious of the widespread poverty and injustice in the world. An article which I wrote in 1984 has been included in this second printing because it seeks to promote a spirituality which is authentically liturgical and at the same time demonstrates that Christian involvement in efforts to establish a reign of justice and peace in the world is not optional but imperative for those who celebrate Eucharist.

Many non-Catholic Christians are scandalized by the Roman Catholic practice of taking Mass stipends. It is indeed a practice that is open to abuse and one that seeks an alternative arrangement for supporting ordained ministers. The two articles on the subject by M. Francis Mannion and John M. Huels have been very much appreciated by *Worship* readers and have been widely circulated. Their inclusion in this second printing certainly strengthens the collection.

Since the Second Vatican Council approximately one hundred articles on the Eucharist have appeared in the pages of *Worship.* Another editor might well have selected other articles than those included here, but these are presented with the hope that they will be useful to those whose interest or training leads them to seek a more informed understanding of the eucharistic liturgy.

R. Kevin Seasoltz
School of Religious Studies
The Catholic University of America
Washington, D.C.

Jerome Murphy-O'Connor

Eucharist and Community in First Corinthians

Paul's allusions to the eucharist are concentrated in Chapters 10–11 of First Corinthians. His silence regarding this central sacrament in other letters is due to the "occasional" character of his communications with the churches for which he was responsible. He was not a speculative theologian principally concerned with the interrelationship of concepts within an ideal structure, but a pastor whose attention was focused by the real problems of Christian living in a concrete situation. In the oral preaching which led to the foundation of communities, Paul presumably followed a pattern which ordered the basic themes in such a way as to demonstrate their relative importance, and the eucharist certainly had a significant place in this type of exposition (11:23). In his letters, on the contrary, the attention given to particular doctrines is related to the degree of misunderstanding or confusion that Paul perceived among the recipients. The fact that he devotes so much space to the eucharist in the Corinthian correspondence is a clear indication that there was something radically wrong with the Corinthians' approach to this sacrament. The fact that he does not touch on the topic in other letters signifies only that the same problem did not arise in other communities.

In order to determine what so disturbed Paul in the Corinthian attitude towards the eucharist, we must begin by establishing the links between the various paragraphs that make up 1 Corinthians 10–11.

Paul opens with a reference to the Exodus (10:1–13) in which we find an allusion to eating and drinking (vv. 3–4). Its function, however, is not to establish a relationship between the paschal meal and the eucharist, but to underline the fact that the privileges of the Israelites did not protect them from the consequences of their errors. They were punished for disobedience, and Paul holds up this experience as a lesson to the Corinthians (v. 11). If the Israelites had been privileged by gifts similar to baptism and the eucharist (vv. 2–4) and had nonetheless been excluded from salvation, then the same fate could well befall the Corinthians unless they came to a correct understanding of what being a Christian involved. Paul was concerned to disabuse them of their belief that "every sin which a man commits is outside the self" (6:18). The overwhelming experience of conversion has bred in them the conviction that no action could alter their status because every action of the "saved" was self-authenticating.

One domain in which the overconfidence of the Corinthians manifested itself was the assiduity with which some maintained their association with the environment which they had left, namely, by continuing to take part in pagan ritual meals (10:14–22; cf. 8:10).

From the thought of pagan ritual it is but a short and natural step to the question of participation in private banquets offered by nonbelievers (10:23–30). The issue with which Paul deals, however, concerns the type of food that was likely to be offered on such occasions, namely, meat that had been offered to idols. His solution is that proposed in Chapter 8. A believer may eat such meat provided that his so doing does not scandalize a brother Christian. Effective concern for the other, even if he be in error, must be the decisive factor in the moral judgment of a Christian.

This leads Paul into a brief digression in which he evokes the example of his own behavior (10:31—11:1). In all that he does he seeks to be of service to others with a view to their salvation. He translates this into the injunction, "Be imitators of me, as I am an imitator of Christ" (11:1), and the context makes it clear that it is question of behavior that will make it possible for Jews and Greeks to accept the gospel and for believers to maintain their commitment. This brief paragraph, which comes between his two evocations of the eucharist, is a highly condensed presentation of Paul's vision of Christian life. It is a digression only in terms of the specific topics under discussion. On a deeper level it reveals the consistent principle that governs his approach to the issues.

Having dealt with social occasions involving pagans, Paul next turns his attention to the social occasion of the Christian community, its liturgical celebration. His treatment falls into two parts. The first (11:2–16) is an extremely complicated text which has given rise to much discussion. Claims that the section is a post-Pauline interpolation are demonstrably untrue. The point at issue is not the subordination of women to men. It is taken entirely for granted that both sexes can take a leading role in both prayer and prophesy. Paul's concern is that the difference between men and women should be proclaimed by their modes of dress. His motive for asserting this obvious point is never brought to light, but there is some justification for the hypothesis that his secret fear was an outbreak of homosexuality and/or lesbianism. He considered relationships of this type to be destructive (1 Cor 6:9–10) because they rejected the pattern established by the Creator (cf. Rom 1:24–27). They embodied what Paul saw as the fundamental attitude of the "world," an egocentric drive towards self-gratification.

In the second part (11:17–34) Paul takes up a different manifestation of selfishness, the refusal of some Corinthians to share their food when they assemble for the Lord's Supper.

From this brief survey of the contents of 1 Corinthians 10–11 it is evident that there was a deep-seated malaise in the Corinthian community which manifested itself in different facets of its existence. The problem did not lie on the level of theoretical understanding. The Corinthians had assimilated the words that had been proclaimed to them, but they faltered in the process of translating those words into a pattern of practical living. Paul's insistence on the primacy of love and his absolute refusal to condone any form of selfishness point unambiguously to the root of the problem. The Corinthians had not succeeded in achieving an adequate grasp of the basic postulate in Paul's theology, the true nature of Christian community. Hence, in order to appreciate fully what Paul says about the eucharist it is imperative to have a clear understanding of his vision of authentic community.

CHRISTIAN COMMUNITY

All the basic components of Paul's understanding of Christian community appear in First Corinthians and these will constitute the armature of the presentation. Some elements, however, are expressed more fully or more clearly in other epistles and where it is appropriate these texts will be introduced in order to fill out the picture.

The Community Is One. Despite centuries of hostile division sincere Christians still retain a sense of the oneness of the Church. They pray that the barriers of mistrust may be torn down so that those who belong to Christ may live in harmonious peace. Very often this goal is conceived in terms of fellowship, as is only natural, given the fact that believers have been long conditioned by the individualism of the Renaissance. Almost inevitably we tend to give Paul's concept of the Church as the body of Christ the status of a metaphor or image.

Starting with the conception of the Church as a society we see the multiplicity of its members, and frequently that aspect dominates to the point where we give merely notional assent to their unity. We permit the vision of faith to be distorted by our perception of reality where fragile hope has received so many brutal shocks, and we drag the ideal down to our estimate of what is possible. In the last analysis we equate unity with union. Paul's perspective is so radically different that we need to make a very conscious effort to assimilate it.

When we reflect on the Church as the body of Christ we do so in the light of the parallel provided by the human body, as Paul himself did (12:12). But where we are tempted to see the point of the parallel in terms of coordination and cooperation, for Paul it was a question of *coexistence* in the strict sense of that much abused term. The limbs of the human body all share a common existence, since they are infused by the same life. Their very reality as limbs is conditioned by their being part of the body. An amputated limb may look like an arm, but in fact it is something radically different because the mode of existence proper to an arm demands vital participation in the life of the body. In its very essence an arm is not a whole but a part. When given the status of a whole, as by amputation, it is no longer what it was destined to be. The animation of life has given place to the stillness of death.

In precisely the same perspective Paul conceived the body of Christ as an *organic* unity. This is implicit in his consistent emphasis that believers "belong" to Christ (3:23; 15:23) or are "members" of Christ (6:15; 12:27), and it comes to formal expression in his exhortation to the Colossians to hold fast to the head "from whom the whole body, nourished and knit together through its joints and ligaments, grows with a growth that is from God" (Col 2:19). Only this concept of a shared life derived from a single vital principle can explain the apostle's understanding of the Christian community as "the new man" (Col 3:10–11), an idea that goes back to the period of the great epistles, for we read in Galatians, "In Christ Jesus you are all sons of God, through faith, for as many of you as were baptized into Christ have put on Christ. There is neither Jew nor Greek, there is neither slave nor free, there is neither male nor female, for you are all *one man* in Christ Jesus" (Gal 3:26–28). Terms indicative of metaphor are completely lacking in this statement, and it is wrong to interpret Paul as if a living organism were merely a rather farfetched parallel to the Christian community. He is making a fundamental assertion concerning Christian being. The statement is one that no philosopher could make, and it stands over all philosophical insights. The unity of Christians is that of a living person. No one possesses, but each one participates in a shared life.

Only if we keep this in mind is it possible to appreciate the full force of such statements as, "You are the body of Christ and individually members of it" (1 Cor 12:27). The individuality of Christians is not that of independent agents. It derives from the diversity appropriate to a living organism. "If all were one member, where would be the body?" (12:19). As parts within the whole, believers are individuated, not by the assertion of autonomy, but by the uniqueness of their contribution to the common life which sustains all. "Let all things be done with a view to building up [the community]" (14:26). The idea of an autonomous Christian is a contradiction in terms. Believers are what they are because they belong to something greater than themselves. They are renewed because they *belong* to the "new man." They are Christians because they *belong* to the body of Christ. The vitality of this relationship is constitutive of their new mode of being. We think of individuals as coming together to create community. For Paul it is precisely the reverse. The community is a radically new reality (1:28) which makes the believer a new creation (2 Cor 5:17). We consider unity as something to be created, whereas Paul saw this unity as primary and envisaged individuals as being changed by absorption into that unity.

The Community Is Christ. This might seem to be at best a meaningless paradox and at worst an unwarranted denigration of the role of Christ. Does it not attribute to the community a function that properly belongs to Christ? Paul would answer in the negative because, for him, the community is Christ. Thus, for example, he begins his exposition of the need for diversity within the community with the words, "For just as the body is one and has many members, and all the members of the body, though many, are one body, *so also Christ*" (1 Cor 12:12). In order to express the same idea we should say: Just as the diversity of the physical body is unified by sharing a common life, so also the body of Christ. Paul is not speaking of the individual Jesus but of the community of believers. In speaking of "Christ" rather than the "body of Christ," it cannot be claimed that he made an accidental slip, because precisely the same idea appears in the question, "Do you not know that your bodies are members of Christ?" (6:15). The question form of this verse is highly significant because it is generally understood to connote a doctrine with which Paul felt his converts should be familiar. The application of the name "Christ" to the community must, in consequence, be considered to have formed part of Paul's habitual vocabulary.

It would be absurd to imagine that he intended to identify the community with the individual body of flesh of the historical person, Jesus Christ. In a later epistle he makes explicit the distinction between the "head" and the "body" (Col 1:18) which is implicit in the earlier letters. If an explanation in "static" terms is thereby excluded, we are forced to consider an explanation in terms of "function." In this perspective the name "Christ" could be predicated of the community if it is possible to conceive Christ and the community as functionally identical, that is, as performing the same identical function. Once the problem has been posed in this way it is easy to see how Paul's mind worked.

The community mediates the salvation won by Christ. The word that he spoke is not heard in the contemporary world unless it is proclaimed by the community. The power that flowed forth from him in order to enable response is no longer effective unless it is manifested by the community. This conviction is clearly attested in Paul's very first letter, "You became imitators of us and of the Lord, for you received the word in much affliction, with joy inspired by the Holy Spirit, so that you became an example to all the believers in Macedonia and in Achaia. For not only has *the word of the Lord* sounded forth from you in Macedonia and Achaia, but *your faith in God* has gone forth everywhere, so that we need not say anything" (1 Thes 1:6–8; cf. Phil 2:14–16; Rom 10:14–15). This passage underlines the importance, not only of verbal proclamation ("the word of God"), but also of the existential affirmation ("your faith in God") without which the other is powerless. Both, moreover, are presented as being in imitation of the Lord who is Christ. The community, therefore, is the incarnational prolongation of the mission of the saving Christ. What he did in and for the world of his day through his physical presence, the community does in and for its world. In terms of the reality of salvation the community is the physical presence of Christ. It is hardly surprising, therefore, that the name "Christ" is given to the community which he founds (1 Cor 3:11) and in which his power is effective.

Jerome Murphy-O'Connor

Given the situation at Corinth it is highly appropriate that Paul should insist on this aspect. The position taken by his opponents is not without ambiguity, but it seems that there was a tendency to divorce the Christ of faith, the "Lord of glory" (2:8), from the Jesus of history.[1] This approach was no more acceptable to Paul than it would be later in his career (cf. Col 2:6; Eph 4:21) because his understanding of the structures of human existence demanded that salvation come from within the human situation. Strictly speaking God cannot save humanity. In view of the decision-making capacity that is integral to human dignity, all that he can do is offer a genuine alternative to the inauthentic existence in which man is imprisoned and at the same time empower him to make that choice. Christ as the instrument of salvation must have been part of the human situation. Equally, in his risen state he must be effectively represented within the framework of real existence by a mode of being endowed with a power which makes its imitation possible. If this representation is to go beyond mere theory, there must be those who authentically live in imitation of Christ, who exist as other Christs, or in Paul's own words, who have "put on Christ" (Gal 3:27). In order to maintain his extremely realistic concept of salvation Paul was virtually forced to designate the community as "Christ."

Once this dimension of Paul's thought has been grasped, a number of passages appear in a new light, and notably those in which we find the enigmatic expression "in Christ." This has been seen as the summit of Pauline mysticism, and elaborate theories have been built upon it. Evidence for Paul's mysticism, however, is slight and always ambiguous. In the light of the above observations it seems both easier and more natural to understand "in Christ" as meaning "in the community which is Christ." Confirmation of this view is provided by the statement, "you are all one man in Christ Jesus" (Gal 3:28). By entering the community, "Christ," through faith and baptism (Gal 3:26–27) believers are absorbed into the organic unity which is "one man."

Alive in Christ. Paul draws a fundamental distinction between "those who belong to Christ" (1 Cor 3:23; 15:23) and all others. "The word

[1] Cf. B. Pearson, *The Pneumatikos-Psychikos Terminology in 1 Corinthians. A Study in the Theology of the Corinthian Opponents of Paul and its Relation to Gnosticism* (Cambridge: Society of Biblical Literature 1973).

of the cross is folly to those who are perishing, but to us who are being saved it is the power of God" (1:18). The most authoritative commentary on this verse is provided by the apostle himself. "We [the preachers] are the aroma of Christ to God among those who are being saved and among those who are perishing, to the latter a fragrance from death to death, to the former a fragrance from life to life" (2 Cor 2:15–16).

The two states — being saved and perishing — are contrasted as "life" and "death." Both of these terms can be predicated of those who are "alive" in the physical sense ("You who were dead . . . God has made alive," Col 2:13) and in consequence can only be interpreted as modes of being. The same individual can exist in a mode which Paul qualifies as "death" or in another which he qualifies as "life." The criterion Paul uses in making this judgment in particular cases is a relationship to Christ. Those who accept Christ are "alive," whereas those who reject him are "dead." Acceptance of Christ, however, has a very specific meaning for Paul. Over and above explicit confession (Rom 10:9–10), he demands a lived realization of the attitude manifested in the death of Christ. "He died for all, that those who live might live no longer for themselves" (2 Cor 5:15). It is question of the total commitment to others that is realized in the unity of the body of Christ, as is manifest in the priority given to "building up" the community (1 Cor 14:17, 26) and in the exhortation, "Let all you do be done in love" (16:14).

Paul's use of the categories "life" and "death" in this context might seem to be merely striking symbols. They appear in a different light if we take seriously his stress on the *organic* unity of the body of Christ. An arm is truly an arm only as part of the body. Only as part of an organic whole does it "live." Detached from the body it may look the same but it is in fact "dead." If the human creature is "alive" only as a member of the body of Christ, then when separated from the body he/she can only be classified as "dead." Here we touch the very kernel of Paul's anthropology, because it implies a very precise vision of what God intended the human condition to be. His choice of categories can only be explained on the assumption that he believed God to have intended his human creatures to exist in the reciprocity of parts within a whole.

This could be rephrased to say that they should live united in the bonds of love, but this formulation is open to a superficial interpretation which would fail to grasp Paul's intention. Nonetheless, the formulation is exact if we give love the profound sense of "letting-be" that John Macquarrie has proposed as the only adequate definition of this much abused term. "Love, in its ontological sense, is letting-be. Love usually gets defined in terms of union, or the drive towards union, but such a definition is too egocentric. Love does indeed lead to community, but to aim primarily at uniting the other person to oneself, or oneself to him, is not the secret of love, and may even be destructive of genuine community. Love is letting-be, not of course in the sense of standing off from someone or something, but in the positive and active sense of enabling-to-be. When we talk of 'letting-be' we are to understand both parts of this hyphenated expression in a strong sense — 'letting' as empowering, and 'be' as the maximal range of being that is open to the particular being concerned."[2]

To love in this sense involves accepting responsibility for the very being of the other. It is a creative function which brings the other within the sphere that constitutes the existence of the agent. Without the other, man cannot be himself. He needs to love and to be loved, to empower and to be empowered. In the divine intention this vital reciprocity is constitutive of his being. Consequently, man is as God intends him to be only when he forms part of an organic unity. Those who isolate themselves from others violate the will of the Creator. Viewed precisely from the perspective of the divine intention they are nonexistent, "dead" in Paul's terminology.

Paul's insight into the divine intention is rooted in his understanding of the humanity of Christ "who loved me and gave himself for me" (Gal 2:20). He refused to derive his anthropology from the observation of fallen humanity. Contrary to many of our contemporaries, he recognized that that approach could only result in a distorted picture. As the embodiment of authentic humanity, Christ was what all human creatures were intended to be from the beginning. The divine plan for humanity having been distorted by sin, God had to intervene in order to restore "life." We are now in a position to see the wealth of meaning that Paul has compressed into the brief statement, "From him [God] you are in Christ Jesus" (1 Cor 1:30). The verb "to be" has the pregnant sense of fully authentic existence which the believers enjoy because of a divine decision to

[2] *Principles of Christian Theology* (New York: Charles Scribner's Sons 1966) 310.

bring into existence "the things which were not" (1:28). This decision was executed through Jesus Christ, and the power which he disposed of remains effective in the community of faith. Hence, if the believers are as God intended them to be it is because they are "in Christ Jesus."

Sin. It now becomes easy to see why Paul considers the state of sinful humanity to be characterized by division. The "world" is divided into blocks opposed by deep-rooted suspicion and hostility — Jew and Greek, slave and free, male and female (Gal 3:28; Col 3:11). Within themselves, however, these blocks do not manifest the cohesiveness that one might expect. This can be deduced from the lists which enumerate the dominant attitudes of fallen humanity.[3] The technique of the vice-list was well known to Paul's contemporaries, but while the apostle may have borrowed the literary form he nonetheless introduced a significant modification into the content. Whereas the lists of his contemporaries are heavily weighted with personal vices, the vast majority of the forty-four distinct vices recorded by Paul are antisocial. In other words, he deliberately broke with the current convention in order to highlight attitudes which made genuine communication impossible. He envisioned the "world" as riven into a multitude of isolated units whose relationships were founded on self-interest.

Only in this perspective can we understand the rather curious phraseology of a passage addressed to the Corinthians (3:3–4), which I translate literally, "While there is jealousy and strife among you, are you not fleshly, do you not walk according to man? For whenever anyone says, 'I belong to Paul,' and another, 'I belong to Apollos,' are you not men?" "Walking" is a common Semitic synonym for a pattern of behavior, and in Paul's lexicon "according to man" (cf. 1 Cor 9:8; 15:32; Rom 3:5; Gal 3:5) means "according to the common estimation." By accepting jealousy and strife as part of their habitual pattern of behavior the Corinthians simply conformed to the common estimation of what was normal. Hostile divisions were taken for granted as an integral part of human existence. In consequence, the formation of opposed parties within the Corinthian community was not considered a problem. That was the way men lived, and there was no justification for being either shocked or

[3] 1 Cor 5:10–11; 6:9–10; 2 Cor 12:20–21; Gal 5:19–21; Rom 1:29–31; 13:13; Col 3:5–8.

surprised. Paul's reaction, however, was to classify this attitude as "fleshly," that is, typical of the mode of being that believers had in theory abandoned in committing themselves to Christ. In his view, the Corinthians were using an outmoded standard in their judgment of what was "normal." "Are you not men?" is equivalent to, "Are you not like the vast majority of men?" Their criterion was not derived from Christ, the model of authentic humanity, but from popular opinion.

This passage also provides us with the clue to a correct understanding of the reality that Paul terms "sin." "The sting of death is sin, and the power of sin is the law" (1 Cor 15:56). The way that this verse is phrased clearly distinguishes sin from the personal sins that each individual commits. It is personified in a way that appears much more clearly in Romans. Sin "came into the world" (5:12) where it "reigns" (5:21; 6:14), "enslaving" humanity (6:6, 17, 20) or buying them into its service (7:14), and paying wages (6:23) to those who submit to its law (7:23). What reality stands behind this symbol? First Corinthians 3:3–4 shows us that we inherit our way of looking at ourselves. We are conditioned by the attitudes that we have received. By acting in conformity with that conditioning we reinforce those attitudes and pass them on to those who come after us. When we realize that this process has been going on for untold ages — since the Fall — we begin to appreciate the tremendous pressure of the orientation to which the individual is subject. The point has been made with great effectiveness by John Macquarrie in words which offer the best description of what Paul means by sin.

"When we think of sin as not merely a particular action, and not merely even the attitude of an individual, but a massive disorientation and perversion of human society as a whole, we begin to perceive the really terrifying character of sin. For the 'world,' or *kosmos*, the collective mass of mankind in its solidarity, is answerable to no one, and has a hardness and irresponsibility that one rarely finds in individuals. These individuals are, as it were, sucked into the world and carried along with it, being deprived of their own responsibility and swept along by forces beyond their control. . . . The individual, or again the small group, may be utterly helpless and impotent within this anonymous mass, and there can take place a kind of 'escalation' of evil as collective standards and patterns of behaviour establish themselves and irresistibly carry everyone along. . . . The sense of helplessness in the face of some movements or situations for which no one seems directly responsible and which no one seems able to control has led to the thought of sin as somehow superhuman."[4]

It is very easy to reduce this description to concrete terms. In a society in which various forms of dishonesty are considered acceptable behavior they become virtues which are inculcated as a matter of course. In a society which puts a premium on independence and self-sufficiency everything concurs to impress the individual with the desirability of these attitudes. In a society which measures success by the ability to acquire material goods everyone will desire such possessions. The individual who rejects the value system of his society is treated as an outsider and deprived of any real capacity to effect change. Virtually insurmountable obstacles are put in the way of his living out the values he cherishes. His existence is absorbed in struggle against an all-pervasive and relentless pressure. Only the very strong can even think of opposing any resistance, the majority quietly acquiesce and most frequently are not even conscious of how they are manipulated.

Freedom. Once these facts of experience are admitted it appears in no way exaggerated to speak of sin, a false value system, as "reigning" or "enslaving." It is a toxic pollution pervading all dimensions of society. No one is immune because it is absorbed below the level of consciousness from the very earliest age. The realism of this view of the "world" is equalled by the apostle's realistic approach to the problem of freeing men from sin. If sin is the toxic pollution of a corrupt environment, the individual can be freed from the necessity of absorbing this pollution only by being transferred to a different environment into which toxic elements do not penetrate. A person with a respiratory condition which is aggravated by the high level of industrial pollution in his area can be given the chance to recover and to live a normal life only by going to live in another area where the air is clean and pure. Paul saw his task, therefore, as involving the creation of an alternative environment. If he recognized that "bad company ruins good morals" (1 Cor 15:33), he was forced to envision an environment in which the individual would not only be exempt from the destructive pressure of bad example but would be subject to the inspiration of good example, a group in which all

[4] *Op. cit.* (n. 2 above) 240–241.

could say, "Imitate me as I imitate Christ" (11:1).

At this point we begin to perceive another reason for Paul's inexorable emphasis on community as the basic Christian reality. Not only is it the mode of existence willed by the Creator, but it is the only practical and concrete means whereby an individual is rescued from the false orientation of a fallen world. Only in an authentically Christian community is the individual free to be as God intended. Protected from pressures hostile to authentic development, he is inspired and supported in his efforts to appropriate the mode of existence that Christ lived to the full.

Christian freedom is not an individual thing. It is not an internal power that operates within the believer under any and all circumstances. Those, and they are many, who profess this understanding of freedom, operate only on the level of value perception. Paul, more realistically, was concerned with the actualization of values over the span of a lifetime. Inevitably, therefore, he saw freedom as a quality of community which benefited individuals. Without a vital community totally committed to the living of Christian values there is no genuine freedom. The reality of freedom is founded exclusively on the effectiveness of the protection against the compulsion of sin afforded the believer by the community.

This intrinsic relationship between freedom and community is given its most forceful expression in a context where the word freedom does not appear. It occurs when Paul is dealing with a question on marriage proposed by the Corinthians who felt that a believer married to a pagan should be forced to divorce. Paul disagreed. As long as the unbeliever consented to live with the convert, they should not be forced to separate, "for the unbelieving husband is sanctified through his wife, and the unbelieving wife is sanctified through her husband. Otherwise your children would be unclean, but as it is they are holy" (7:14).

Paul's concern here is to capitalize on the goodwill shown by the unbeliever. His hope is that it will lead to conversion (7:16; cf. 1 Pt 3:1–2). But he goes further by saying that the unbeliever is "sanctified," because this is a term that he elsewhere reserves to describe the state of believers. This letter, for example, is addressed "to the church of God which is at Corinth, to those sanctified in Christ Jesus" (1:2). The justification for his claim is provided by the practice of the Corinthian Church of not baptizing their children. We have to assume that this was the case because otherwise there would be no parallel with the situation of the unbeliever. Despite the lack of baptism, that is, the sacrament of formal admission into the community, the Corinthians considered their children to be "holy" and not "unclean." This is comprehensible only if they believed (and Paul finds no fault with their attitude) that their children had never been enslaved to sin. They had never belonged to the "world." They were born free, because they were born into a Christian community which protected them from influences that would have made them unclean. Equally, Paul felt that even association with the community through marriage would provide a counterbalance to the false orientation of the "world," and one which he hoped would prove increasingly effective.

Selfishness. Given this realistic understanding of the nature of Christian freedom, Paul could not but be highly sensitive to the ways in which this freedom is endangered. Conversion had been an overwhelming experience for the Corinthians. It brought them to a state of exaltation which was intensified by the profusion of charismatic gifts. This they interpreted as a complete take-over by the Spirit. Because they now were different, they had to feel different. They were "new," and "old" values and customs were irrelevant. Hence the pride they took in the fact that a man was living with his stepmother, a form of incest "that is not found even among pagans" (5:1). Paul's objection was immediate and violent, and he expressed himself in a metaphor derived from the Jewish Passover ritual. "Do you not know that a little leaven ferments the whole lump [of dough]? Cleanse out the old leaven in order that you may be a new lump [of dough], as you should be, unleavened" (5:7).

Ideally, the community should be "unleavened," completely free of sin, and the rhetorical question indicates that Paul expected the Corinthians to have assimilated this point. It was part of Jewish tradition that the messianic community would be sinless. "Then shall wisdom be bestowed on the elect, and they shall all live and never again sin, either through ungodliness or through pride. . . . And they shall not again transgress, nor shall they sin all the days of their life" (1 Henoch 5:8–9). A sinner, therefore, makes the community a living lie. More seriously, the barrier erected against sin is thereby penetrated and influences inimical to authentic development are once again operative. The presence of sin dilutes and obscures the inspiration of authenticity. All, in consequence, suffer loss through the failure of one. "If anyone has caused pain [through sinning], he has caused it, not to me, but in some measure — not to put it too severely — to you all" (2 Cor 2:5).

The fundamental error of the Corinthians was to exaggerate their freedom. They had failed to recognize that freedom has two aspects which, though intimately associated, must be carefully distinguished. Basic to the notion of freedom is the lack of restraint or compulsion, and founded on this is a capacity to act. These two facets can be termed "freedom *from*" and "freedom *to*" respectively. "Freedom *from*" is absolute. In Christ the believer is totally liberated from the compulsion of sin. From this, however, the Corinthians drew the erroneous conclusion that their "freedom *to*" was also absolute, and that they could do precisely what they wished. Hence their slogan, "All things are lawful to me" (1 Cor 6:12; 10:23).

In Paul's view they should have seen that this could not possibly be a correct attitude for Christians. To adopt this slogan is to proclaim that in the ultimate analysis others do not really matter. It betrays an attitude that is totally incompatible with genuine community, because those who profess it in effect isolate themselves from others. In destroying community they thereby remove their only protection against the compulsion of sin, and negate the very basis of their "freedom *from*." The practical effect of the slogan, therefore, is to put them back into the condition of slavery from which they had been redeemed. Hence, to the slogan Paul opposes the injunction, "Let no one seek his own good but the good of the other" (10:24).

The question of the propriety of Christians eating the superfluous meat from pagan sacrifices which was sold on the public market affords a striking illustration of how seriously Paul took this principle. Arguing that "an idol has no real existence," that "there is no God but one" (8:4), and that "the earth is the Lord's and everything in it" (10:26), some Corinthians reached the theoretically correct conclusion that there could be no objection to believers eating such meat. Paul approved this initiative in a delicate moral issue, and concurred in the solution (10:25). Yet at the same time he found fault with the Corinthians for acting on it. "Not all possess this knowledge. Some, through being hitherto accustomed to idols, eat food as really offered to an idol, and their conscience, being weak, is defiled. . . . . And so by your knowledge this weak man is destroyed, the brother for whom Christ died" (8:7–11). The reaction of the "weak" was objectively wrong, but because it was a facet of a concrete situation it should have been taken into consideration. Genuine concern for others demanded that their needs should be given the first priority. "If food scandalizes my brother I will never eat meat, lest I scandalize my brother" (8:13).

Paul was fully aware that speculative truth can cast a cloak of respectability over attitudes that are fundamentally selfish. Hence, his insistence that the decisive factor in the moral judgment of Christians must be the probable effect on others of the proposed line of action. It would have been surprising had he taught anything else, given what we have seen of his understanding of the organic unity of the Christian community. If believers do not exist save as members of the body, they cannot judge as if they were entirely independent. To make knowledge, however accurate, the exclusive basis of judgment is inappropriate to the believers' mode of being in Christ. Since without love they are nothing (13:2), the knowledge out of which they act must spring from love. Because "knowledge puffs up whereas love builds up" (8:1), Paul prays that "your love may abound more and more in knowledge and all discernment so that you may choose the things that really matter" (Phil 1:9–10).

Conclusion. The Christian community is an organic unity in which the members are vitally related to each other through participation in a common life. By love they are bound together in a mode of existence which is the antithesis of the individualistic mode of existence that constitutes the "world." Only in this mode do they exist as the Creator intended humanity to exist. They are protected from the compulsion of sin conceived as the false value system of a disoriented society, and thus are free to become what God destined them to be. This community is Christ in that it prolongs incarnationally the power of love that was the essence of his mission. It represents the saving force of Christ because in the world it demonstrates the reality of an alternative mode of existence in which humanity is not dominated by the egocentricity that provokes possessiveness, jealousy and strife. To enter this community is to abandon the individualism of self-affirmation. In a group which possesses "the mind of Christ" (1 Cor 2:16) the individual is distinguished only by different Spirit-given gifts of service (12:6).

EUCHARIST

Having surveyed Paul's understanding of the nature of Christian community, we are now in a position to investigate in greater depth his treatment of the central act of this community, the celebration of the Lord's Supper.

The Words of Institution. In addition to Paul (1 Cor 11:24–25) the words used by Jesus to institute the Eucharist are recorded by the three Synoptics (Mt 26:26–29; Mk 14:22–25; Lk 22:15–20). It is now generally recognized that these four accounts are derived from liturgical versions. What Jesus actually said and did was preserved with minor variations in different churches, and when the gospels were given their definitive form the words actually in use in the various eucharistic celebrations were inserted into the narrative of the Last Supper. Paul's version is most closely related to that of Luke, and it has been suggested that it records the usage of the church of Antioch. The plausibility of this hypothesis, which is impossible to prove or disprove, rests exclusively on the fact that Paul's closest association was with the church of that city (Acts 11:25–26), even though he also had contacts with the churches in Damascus (Acts 9:19) and Jerusalem (Acts 9:26–30). Antioch was the home to which he invariably returned after his journeys.

In 11:23 we find the technical terms "to receive" and "to pass on" which place Paul as an intermediary in a chain of tradition. The same verbs appear apropos of the kerygmatic creed in 15:3, but there is a significant variation in that here he explicitly designates the one from whom he received that which he transmitted, "I received *from the Lord*" (11:23). The formula in question, however, betrays characteristic signs of liturgical usage in a Greek-speaking community. In what sense, then, can Paul say that he received it from the Lord? For some exegetes Paul simply intended to evoke Jesus as the origin of the tradition that he had actually received from other men. Others understand the phrase as a claim that the words of institution were communicated to him in a vision of the risen Christ. Both of these views present obvious difficulties. If the first respects the characteristics of the institutional formula, it does violence to the words of Paul. The second, while doing justice to the apostle's statement, ignores the liturgical coloring of the formula. A much more satisfactory solution is suggested by a point noted in the first part of this article. Christ is not only the founder of the community of believers, but in a real sense *he is the community* (6:15; 12:12) because it is through the community that the saving reality of Christ is made effective in the world. What Paul has received from the community, therefore, he has received from the Lord. This interpretation is the only one to do full justice both to Paul's words and to the liturgical character of the formula of institution, and it underlines once again the radical realism of the apostle's understanding of salvation.

The formula of institution can be broken down into two parts, the statements concerning the bread and the cup, and the injunctions concerning repetition.

The Bread and the Cup. The meaning of the statements, "This is my body" and "This cup is the new covenant in my blood" (11:24–25), is not unambiguously settled by their structure, because the identity established by the verb "to be" can be understood either symbolically (cf. Mt 13:37–38) or realistically. In order to determine which sense Paul intended we have to have recourse to another factor, namely, the Jewish comprehension of "covenant." There could be no covenant without a real relationship to the victim sacrificed to seal the covenant. Thus we read with reference to the Sinai covenant, "And Moses took the blood, and threw it upon the people, and said, 'Behold the blood of the covenant which the Lord has made with you in accordance with all these words'" (Ex 24:8). It would have been inconceivable to have used a substitute designed to symbolize the blood. The reality of the blood gave reality to the covenant.

Nothing emerges with greater clarity from the whole of the Pauline correspondence than the apostle's belief that the death of Christ inaugurated a new form of relationship between God and humanity, a relationship that is renewed for each individual through personal appropriation. This suggests that he understood the words, "This cup is the new covenant in my blood," in a nonsymbolic sense. What the believers drink seals them into the new covenant. If the drinking is thought of in purely symbolic terms, then the new covenant must be conceived in the same way. It would have been impossible for an individual formed in the Jewish tradition as Paul was to have made a distinction between these two elements. A purely symbolic cause would not produce a real effect. Hence, from the reality of the effect (new covenant) we are led to infer the reality of the cause (what is contained in the cup is the blood of Christ). This interpretation of the cup necessarily imposes a parallel understanding of the statement regarding the bread.

Even though 10:14–22 is encountered first in the perusal of the epistle, this passage in fact represents the consequence of Paul's understanding of the words of institution. In it he draws a parallel between Christian participation in the Eucharist (10:16–17) and the participation of Jews (10:18) and pagans (10:19–20) in their ritual meals. It is often assumed that Paul is arguing from the implications of such rituals to the meaning of the Eucharist, but the very structure of the text makes it much more probable that the reverse is true. The principal point that Paul is concerned to get across is, "You cannot drink the cup of the Lord and the cup of demons. You cannot partake of the table of the Lord and the table of demons" (10:21). To this end he argues that if a certain thing happens as a result of participation in the Eucharist, then it must be assumed that both Jews and pagans assume something similar to be effected by their rituals. In consequence, a believer who participates both in the Eucharist and in pagan rituals involves himself in contradictory commitments. Why this impossible situation should be avoided will be evident from what has been said above regarding Paul's vision of the nature of Christian community.

The premise on which Paul builds his argument is clearly stated. "The cup of blessing which we bless, is it not *koinonia* in the blood of Christ? The bread which we break, is it not *koinonia* in the body of Christ?" (10:16). The rhetorical interrogative form clearly indicates Paul's belief that this doctrine is nothing new to the Corinthians. He regularly uses this technique to introduce points to which his converts have given notional assent without fully grasping the implications (e.g., 3:16; 5:6; 6:16; 19; 9:24). The problem is to determine the precise meaning he gives to *koinonia*. The term appears frequently in both the Septuagint and profane Greek, but Paul uses it for the first time in this letter. Two instances precede its use in the present context. "God is faithful, by whom you were called into the *koinonia* of his Son Jesus Christ our Lord" (1:9); "I do all things for the sake of the gospel in order that I may become a *syn-koinonos* of it" (9:23).

In 1:9 the term is normally translated "fellowship," but in the light of the first part of this article it will be recognized that this rendering gives only a superficial glimpse of what Paul has in mind. When accepted, the saving call of God brings the believer into a new mode of existence whose dominant characteristic is the sharing of a common life in an organic unity. Fellowship is only an expression of the communal participation that takes place on the level of being. Within the framework of Paul's thought, therefore, *koinonia* in 1:9

must be given its root meaning of "common share or participation in." This is confirmed by the use of the cognate term *koinonos* in 9:23 to which Paul has added his cherished particle *syn*. The basic idea of this verse is that Paul hopes to share in the blessings of the gospel with those whom he has saved. The communal element is again to the fore, and the preceding discussion has underlined the extreme realism of this aspect of the apostle's thought. Hence, only the literal translation "joint-partaker" or "joint-sharer" is appropriate here. "Full partner" would be a more elegant rendering, but it is susceptible of the same weak interpretation as "fellowship" in 1:9.

If the apostle's understanding of the nature of Christian community demands that *koinonia* in 1:9 and *koinonos* in 9:23 be understood as connoting "real participation" on the level of being, then there is a strong presumption that Paul intended the same connotation in 10:16. The eating of the bread (10:17) and the drinking of the cup (11:27–28) is a real participation in the body and blood of Christ. This is possible only if the bread and wine are in fact the body and blood of Christ. The concept of spiritual communion was unknown to the Jews, and a share in the sacrifice was possible only through physical consumption of the flesh of the victim.

Remembrance. The statements concerning the bread and the cup are both followed by the injunction, "Do this in remembrance of me" (11:24–25). "Do this" is a rubric which covers the taking of the bread/cup, the giving of thanks, and the pronunciation of the word of institution. The motive behind the desire of Jesus that these should be repeated in the community he founded is revealed by the second part, "in remembrance of me."

Joachim Jeremias attempted to show that the meaning is "that God may remember me," but this interpretation has been shown to be without foundation.[5] One of the reasons why Jeremias felt himself obliged to maintain this position was his conviction that it was inconceivable that the Lord should fear that his disciples would forget him. This, however, is to misunderstand the type of remembrance that is envisioned. To remember Jesus authentically is to become aware, not merely of his historical existence, but of the meaning of his life and in particular of his death. By this gesture Jesus offered an opportunity which the believer has grasped. Remember-

[5] Cf. D. Jones, "Anamnesis in the LXX and the Interpretation of 1 Cor. XI.25," *Journal of Theological Studies* 6 (1955) 183–191.

ing, therefore, involves an element of gratitude, but more especially it incorporates an acceptance of the responsibility of prolonging the saving mission of Christ (11:26). Christian remembrance is concerned with the past only insofar as it is constitutive of the present and a summons to the future. In the active remembrance of total commitment to Christ the past is made real in the present and its power is released to shape the future.

Death the Proclamation of Life. The relationship between remembrance and mission is clearly indicated in the words, "For as often as you eat this bread and drink this cup, you proclaim the death of the Lord until he comes" (11:26). In this commentary appended to the traditional formula Paul reveals his comprehension of what happens when the gestures of Christ are reproduced.

The view that Paul saw the broken loaf and the outpoured wine as a symbolic declaration of the death of Jesus is without foundation. A number of scholars insist, at first sight justifiably, that the verb "to proclaim" necessarily involves a verbal element and, in consequence, claim that the verse must be understood as an allusion to the retelling of the passion, or at least that section concerning the Last Supper, during the celebration of the Eucharist. Nothing seems more natural than that the passion should be evoked on such an occasion, but when viewed objectively this seems to be the only justification for the proposed interpretation. It is not a very strong argument, and it is countered by a number of considerations. The wording of the verse — in particular the present tense of the verb "to proclaim" and the terminal phrase "until he comes" — rather suggests that Paul is concerned with the implications of the sacramental act. This impression is strengthened by the commentary found in 10:17 to which we shall return in a moment. Finally, we have already noted a number of passages (1 Thes 1:8; Phil 2:14–16; 1 Cor 4:16–17, 11:1) which disqualify any attempt to limit "proclamation" to the purely verbal level. Paul was fully conscious of the importance of the existential affirmation that is manifested by quality of life, and this dimension would seem to fit the context here perfectly. The eating of the bread and the drinking of the cup are a statement, and what is "said" is the death of Christ.

The death of Christ is, of course, a central Pauline theme which has given rise to a variety of interpretations. In great part this is due to the fact that death can be looked at from different perspectives. It can be viewed negatively as putting an end to any further possibility of achievement. From another point of view death can be seen as being in itself an achievement, e.g., when it is accepted for an end judged more valuable than survival. A third way of looking at death is to see it as focusing to exceptional clarity the dominant quality or characteristic of a life. Which perspective was that of Paul? His consistent emphasis that Christ died "for others" (e.g., 1 Cor 8:11; 1 Thes 5:10) immediately directs our attention to the second possibility, but the third is not thereby to be excluded. For Paul the self-giving which animated the whole existence of Jesus came to its highest expression in his death (cf. Gal 2:20), and provided the most radical demonstration of the way God desired his creatures to live. "He died for all, that those who live might live no longer for themselves" (2 Cor 5:15).

Because he had thoroughly assimilated this lesson Paul was able to say of his own mode of existence, "We are afflicted in every way . . . always carrying in the body the dying *(nekrosis)* of Jesus, so that the life of Jesus may also be manifested in our bodies. For while we live we are always being given up to death for Jesus' sake, so that the life of Jesus may be manifested in our mortal flesh" (2 Cor 4:8–11). The paradoxical tone of this statement is due to the fact that "life" is used in two distinct senses. By "while we live" Paul means his ordinary physical existence which is continually threatened by persecution. Yet that ordinary existence is capable of manifesting the "life of Jesus." Both terms in this phrase are charged with significance. "Jesus" is Paul's way of formally underlining the historicity of him who is now the risen Lord, and "life," as we have seen, is his shorthand designation for authentic existence. The authenticity of the humanity of Jesus is reproduced in the person of Paul because he carries in his body (=the self) the "dying of Jesus." The term *nekrosis* is not attested prior to Paul, and it seems likely that he invented it in order to bring out a specific dimension. "Dying" evokes both life and death, or more specifically life as culminating in death. The way in which Jesus died was in perfect harmony with the way he had lived. His whole existence, therefore, was "for others." His death only brought to unambiguous expression what was always there during his lifetime. If Paul carries in his person the "dying of Jesus," it can only be because his whole being is dedicated to the same mission, the salvation of others (10:33). The apostle's existential attitude is identical with that of

Jesus and so "manifests the life of Jesus." In other words, the saving love of Jesus is made concrete and real in the loving of Paul.

Once the apostle's vision of the death of Christ as the decisive clue to the quality of his existence is clearly grasped, it becomes possible to understand the proclamation of the death of the Lord that takes place in the Eucharist. The realism of Paul's approach needs to be kept clearly in mind. This forces us to go behind the sacramental gestures to the disposition of the participants. The attitude of those who eat and drink is essential to the proclamation because if their imitation of Christ (11:1) is defective, then, as Paul expressly insists, "it is not the Lord's Supper that you eat" (11:20). Only if the participants have truly put on Christ (Gal 3:27), which is equivalent to putting on love (Col 3:14), is there an authentic Eucharist. In remembering they acknowledge the demand implicit in the death which makes their new mode of being possible. By their comportment they keep that possibility alive for others. What they are is focused to brilliant clarity in the sacramental gestures, and Christ becomes a reality in the "world." They incarnate the saving love expressed in his death, and will continue to exercise this function until it is rendered unnecessary by his return, "until he comes." This evocation of the physical presence of Christ in the eschaton reinforces the above interpretation of the proclamation of his death in existential terms. Love gave substance to the words of institution, and only loving can continue to do so.

Bread and the Body. If 11:26 reveals one facet of Paul's understanding of the Eucharist, another appears in 10:17. We have already discussed the previous verse which speaks of *koinonia* in the blood and body of Christ, but at this point it is important to underline that 10:16 represents a traditional formulation recognized and acknowledged by the Corinthians.[6] They, however, had failed to grasp the practical implication of his *koinonia*, and so Paul inverts the traditional order (bread — cup) in order to facilitate the transition to his authoritative statement, "Because the bread is one, we who are many are one body because we all partake of the one bread" (10:17).

The immediate impression given by this formulation is that the Eucharist is constitutive of the body of Christ. It is through the

[6] For details, cf. E. Käsemann, "The Pauline Doctrine of the Lord's Supper," in his *Essays on New Testament Themes* (Studies in Biblical Theology, no. 41; London: SCM 1964) 109.

eating of the bread that the body comes into being. An immediate objection to this interpretation is provided by what Paul himself says of the relationship of baptism to the body, "By one Spirit we were all baptized into one body" (12:13). In other words, the body exists prior to the incorporation of the believers, as Käsemann has perceptively noted: "If we put on the Body of Christ or are baptized into it, this Body is therefore already there before our faith and baptism, just as Christ is present prior to our faith. Nor is the unity of this Body based on baptism. According to 1 Cor 12:13 we are baptized into the unity of the Body. Unity therefore is not the result of our coming together, but the sign manual of Christ. Hence, unity does not grow out of the members of the Body, as if it could be thought of quantitatively as the sum of them, but it is qualitatively the identity of Christ with himself in all his members."[7]

Käsemann, of course, has in mind the gnostic myth of the Archetypal Man which, for him, constitutes the preexistent unity. This is neither obvious nor necessary. After his conversion Paul came into an already existing community, and it was natural for him to consider his converts as doing the same. As we saw in the first part of this article Paul conceived the community as the effective channel of saving grace which transformed the individual by absorbing him into its organic unity. It is within this perspective, therefore, that we must try to understand the formative force of the Eucharist relative to the body of Christ. The limitation thus imposed necessarily directs our attention to the category of "growth."

The Pauline letters are replete with indications that the new mode of existence that the believers enjoy in Christ is not a static state. The participle, "those being saved" (1:18), unambiguously suggests a process which 3:7 qualifies as "growth" (cf. Col 2:19). The primary emphasis is not on the quantitative extension of the Church but on the qualitative improvement of those who are already members. There is always room for ever greater perfection. Nowhere perhaps was this more evident than at Corinth, and particularly in the attitude of the Corinthians towards the Eucharist. It is hardly surprising, therefore, to find Paul insisting on the contribution of the Eucharist to the intensification of the unity of the body.

As a true pedagogue he begins with the simple and obvious fact that one loaf is used in the liturgical celebration. As such it is a

[7] *Art. cit.*, 111.

symbol of unity. But it is more than a symbol because this bread is the body of Christ (10:16). Yet for the power of Christ to become active, human involvement is necessary. Unity, or more precisely a greater unity, is achieved only when "we all partake." For all to eat a common loaf is already a sharing, but because of the particular nature of this loaf Christ is directly involved. The participants share with each other but they also "participate" (*koinonia*) in Christ. Just as bread sustains physical existence, they draw from the source of their common life (cf. Col 2:19). In the action of partaking they commit themselves anew in faith and love not only to Christ but to each other. They again recall (11:24–25) the root of their new being and the obligation of genuine concern that Christ's example imposes. The already existing unity (12:13) is thereby deepened, and the body acquires a new and more profound reality. The Christ who is present under the sacramental species becomes more effectively present in the body which incarnates more intensely the creative love which animates his being. That love which alone empowers authentic transformation is released into a divided world in a lived demonstration which "holds forth the word of life" (Phil 2:16).

Christ Divided. Thus far we have been discussing what might be termed Paul's theoretical approach to the Eucharist. The underlying assumption was that the Eucharist was celebrated in an ideal community. The real situation that Paul had to deal with was in fact very different. The Corinthians were far from perfect, not merely in the sense that they had not yet attained the ideal, but in the sense that their overconfidence had led them to misunderstand the way in which the Eucharist achieves its effect. They imagined themselves to be in a definitive state of salvation whereas in reality they were only part of a process which could be aborted. This is why Paul begins chapter 10 by drawing a parallel between their situation and that of the Israelites in the desert. The relevance of his reaction to our contemporary situation where many so-called communities have no organic life can hardly be overemphasized.

The situation at Corinth is described in explicit detail. "In the first place, when you assemble for a church meeting, I hear that there are divisions among you" (11:18). There is no "secondly" in the continuation of the text, and it seems likely that Paul has in mind other unsatisfactory features of the Corinthian assemblies (cf. 11:34) with perhaps particular emphasis on their attitude towards charismatic gifts. Hence, the divisions are not the parties mentioned in 1:12 and 3:4 but the subgroups created by the selfishness of the participants. "For in eating, each one goes ahead with his own meal, and one is hungry and another is drunk. What! Do you not have houses to eat and drink in? Or do you despise the church of God and humiliate the have-nots?" (11:21–22).

From this attitude Paul draws the conclusion, "When, therefore, you assemble together it is not to eat the Lord's Supper" (11:20). In this literal translation the verse gives the impression that Paul is referring to the intention of the Corinthians. They come together, not with a view to eating the Lord's Supper, but with some other purpose in mind. It is obvious, however, that the Corinthians assembled with the intention of celebrating the Lord's Supper, because what Paul criticizes is the way they go about it. Hence, the apostle must be referring to the consequences of their attitude. The only viable interpretation is that found in the paraphrase of the Revised Standard Version [RSV], "When you meet together it is not the Lord's Supper that you eat." No matter what the Corinthians think they are doing, they are not in fact eating the Lord's Supper, because their attitude precludes it. The shared being that is the new mode of existence in Christ should come to expression in the practical concern which sees that no one is in want. The selfishness of the Corinthians is the antithesis of what should be, and so makes the celebration of the Lord's Supper impossible. Although the perspective is slightly different, H. Conzelmann's paraphrase is equally accurate, "When you assemble for a meeting, it is not possible to eat the Lord's Supper."[8]

Since the Lord's Supper involves the transformation of bread and wine into the body and blood of Christ, it would seem that for Paul the attitude of the Corinthians robbed the words of institution of validity. This is entirely congruent with the apostle's existential identification of the community of believers with Christ. In theory the community is Christ, but Paul was not concerned with this speculative aspect. His function as pastor was to ensure that the community was in fact Christ, i.e., truly animated by his life, fully penetrated by his spirit. As such the community could act with the power of Christ, and could speak with the authority of Christ. In an

[8] *1 Corinthians.* Hermeneia: A Critical and Historical Commentary on the Bible (Philadelphia: Fortress 1975) 192.

inauthentic community, such as that of Corinth, Christ is not present. The words of institution may be his but the voice which speaks them is not. The transforming authority is lacking and in consequence nothing happens. The words of institution do not effect what they signify.

It is impossible to prove apodictically that this was Paul's view, but it must be noted that nothing he says contradicts this interpretation. As translated by the RSV, 11:27 appears to do so. "Whoever, therefore, eats the bread or drinks the cup of the Lord in an unworthy manner will be guilty of profaning the body and blood of the Lord." The implication of this rendering is that the unworthy participant in the Eucharist commits a sacrilege by consuming the body and blood of Christ which are there under the sacramental species in virtue of the words alone and without reference to the attitude of the community. This interpretation, however, depends on the participle "profaning," which does not appear in the Greek text, which says simply, "will be guilty of the body and blood of the Lord." These words suggest a quite different explanation because "to be guilty of the blood of someone" is most naturally understood as meaning, "to be responsible for the death of that person" (cf. Dt 19:10). In consequence, the import of this verse is to range the unworthy participant among those responsible for the killing of Jesus (cf. Heb 6:6; 10:29). In this perspective the relationship to the preceding verse becomes perfectly clear. Ideally, participation in the Eucharist should be "a proclamation of the death of the Lord" (11:26), but because of the participant's attitude it can become an act which places him among those responsible for his death. The antithesis could hardly have been formulated with more graphic force. Failure to proclaim the death of the Lord authentically is equivalent to persecution. Far from being an allusion to the real presence, this verse rather underlines the crucial importance for Paul of the existential attitude of Christians. As always, his concern is with reality not with theory.

Hence, in the next verse it is natural to find the exhortation, "Let a man examine himself, and so eat of the bread and drink of the cup" (11:28). Respect for the Eucharist demands that participation be preceded by self-examination. Such testing, however, presupposes a standard against which believers must measure themselves. This gives rise to the crucial question: what standard or criterion does Paul have in mind? On general principles we could immediately answer, Christ (cf. 2 Cor 5:15). A more specific answer is provided by the next verse, "Anyone who eats and drinks without discerning the body eats and drinks judgment upon himself" (1 Cor 11:29).

The difficulty of determining the precise meaning of this verse is attested by the variants in the manuscript tradition, and which highlight the attempts to come to grip with it. In the Western Text the verse is given as, "Anyone who eats and drinks *unworthily*, without discerning the body *of the Lord*, eats and drinks judgment upon himself." The italicized words are universally recognized to be scribal additions designed to bring out the generally accepted meaning, which is that Paul condemns a failure to distinguish the Eucharist from common food. The secondary character of the interpolations, however, does not necessarily mean that the interpretation is to be rejected. Among modern commentators it is maintained by E. B. Allo,[9] C. K. Barrett,[10] and H. Conzelmann.[11] Such arguments as they offer are far from convincing. Conzelmann sees the verse as a variation of verse 27, and Barrett speaks of the parallelism between verses 27 and 29. Given the interpretation of verse 27 adopted above, these suggestions can only appear as forced in the extreme. They derived from a preoccupation with the problem of the real presence which is not Paul's concern in the present context.

It seems worthwhile, therefore, to explore the alternative possibility, namely, that "the body" is an allusion to the community as the body of Christ. In a eucharistic context Paul has already stated that "we who are many are one body" (10:17), so the terminology poses no difficulty. It is not as if the apostle were introducing the concept for the first time. The community interpretation is also recommended by the structure of 11:17–32. It has often been remarked that in this epistle Paul frequently organizes his material in a three-part structure in which the first and third parts correspond (e.g., 1:18—2:5; 3:5—4:5; 12—14). There can be no doubt about the threefold structure here. In 11:17–22 Paul deals with the actual situation at Corinth where divisions mean that the Lord's Supper is not in fact celebrated. In the center section (11:23–26) he is concerned with the Eucharist in itself as the proclamation of the

[9] *Première épître aux Corinthiens.* Etudes Bibliques (Paris: Gabalda 1934) 282–283.

[10] *The First Epistle to the Corinthians.* Harper's New Testament Commentaries. (New York: Harper & Row 1968) 174–175.

[11] *Op. cit.*, 202.

death of the Lord. In the third and final part (11:27–32) the admonitory character of his discourse coupled with his use of the second person clearly indicates that he has the concrete situation at Corinth again in view. The first and third parts are in fact related as problem and solution. The Corinthians' acceptance of divisions is a sign that the "body" character of the community has not been understood. The organic unity that should bind the believers together has been neither recognized nor affirmed. Hence, anyone who dares to participate in the Eucharist without adverting to the body is guilty of perpetuating the divisions which make the Lord's Supper impossible (11:20), and in consequence eats and drinks to his own condemnation. The community interpretation of 11:29, therefore, accentuates both the unity of Paul's thought and its relevance to the Corinthian situation.

Barrett, however, objects that this interpretation strains the meaning of the verb *diakrinein*. This would be difficult, for the verb has a wide spectrum of meaning, "to quarrel, to doubt, to arrange, to separate, to differentiate, to judge." In fact, the usage here is very close to that in 4:7, "Who discerns you?" i.e., who singles you out? The Corinthians had given notional assent to the concept of the community as the body of Christ, but their behavior revealed all too clearly that they had no real grasp of the implications of what they had accepted. They accepted jealousy and strife as part of the normal pattern of existence even for those in Christ (3:1–4). It seems entirely natural that Paul should insist on the communal dimension of the Eucharist. Only the profound conviction that all believers shared the common life of the body could restrain and eventually destroy the centrifugal tendencies that were the residue of their previous self-centered mode of existence. It is on this precise point that believers must examine themselves (11:28) and discern themselves (11:31) before they participate in the Eucharist. Since the authentic community is Christ (6:15; 12:12), we thus rejoin Paul's basic criterion, the historical Jesus (2 Cor 5:15).

Conclusion. The dominant characteristic of Paul's treatment of the Eucharist is its extreme realism. There is no exalted poetry, no flights into mysticism. It is firmly rooted in his concept of the community of faith as the basic reality of the New Age introduced by the death of Christ. Christ remains incarnationally present in and to the world through the community that is his body. The organic unity which is integral to this body is reinforced and intensified by the Eucharist. Not by the Eucharist in itself, because Paul would energetically repudiate any mechanical approach to the sacrament. The person of Christ is really present under the sacramental species only when the words of institution are spoken by "Christ," an authentic community animated by the creative saving love which alone enables humanity to "live." The power of Christ is released and becomes effective only when the participants demonstrate a lived realization of the demand implicit in the organic unity of which they are members. The reality of the body is presupposed if the sacramental elements are to become the body and blood of Christ, but in the lived remembering of the supreme act of love the body develops with a growth that is from God.

Aidan Kavanagh

Thoughts on the Roman Anaphora

In its section devoted to the principles of reform the Constitution on the Sacred Liturgy states that the liturgy is made up not only of immutable elements divinely instituted, but also of elements that are subject to change. Of these latter the Constitution says: "These not only may but ought to be changed with the passage of time if they have suffered from the intrusion of anything out of harmony with the inner nature of the liturgy or have become unsuited to it. In this restoration, both texts and rites should be drawn up so that they express more clearly the holy things which they signify; the Christian people, so far as possible, should be able to understand them with ease and to take part in them fully, actively, and as befits a community" (CL 21). The methodology for such reform is, furthermore, to be carried out in such a way "that sound tradition may be retained, and yet the way remain open to legitimate progress": thus, a "careful investigation is always to be made into each part of the liturgy which is to be revised. This investigation should be theological, historical, and pastoral," stemming both from the overarching laws of liturgical morphology and from the data gathered as results from foregoing liturgical reforms already in effect come in

(CL 23). The Constitution is definite in this, that newly evolving forms should as far as possible "grow organically from forms already existing" (CL 23) in a certain continuity so as to preserve the essential genius of the Roman rite from formless syncretism.

As the reforms already undertaken by the Consilium go forward it is inevitable that the question of what is to become of the eucharistic prayer, or anaphora, of the Roman rite will be raised with increasing frequency. Already one suggestion has been publicly made that, since the Roman anaphora is a "Gallican hodgepodge" and a "latecomer to the Roman Mass" (reasons that are breathtaking in their historical naiveté), it should be wholly replaced with a simpler one, such as that of Hippolytus.[1] And one hears rumors of other proposals, such as the use of several different anaphoras, or of the composition of new ones for children's Masses and other special occasions.

While such proposals surely exhibit a commendable pastoral concern for the present, it may be questioned whether they are adequately responsible in terms of the past development and use of the specifically Roman-type of eucharistic anaphora, of the present and future pastoral role that could be exercised by a better form of such an anaphora, and of the Constitution's concern for organic growth in continuity with forms already existing. This is not to say that the Roman-type anaphora must be regarded as inviolable. It is certainly not, in all its details, one of those "immutable elements divinely instituted" that cannot be subject to change: it has constantly been undergoing change ever since it attained its present general form by the fourth century, as witnessed by the additions made to it by Leo I,[2] Gregory I,[3] Alcuin, others who have composed many of the later prefaces and whose identity is unknown, John XXIII by his addition

[1] Leo T. Mahon, "What is to be Done," *Commonweal* 82 (1965) 590–597, esp. 591. For more solid suggestions cf. H. A. Reinhold, *Bringing the Mass to the People* (Baltimore 1960) 63–71; K. Amon, "Reformwünsche zum innersten Bereich der eucharistischen Feier," *Bibel und Liturgie* 35 (1961/62) 107–109; H. Küng, "Das Eucharistiegebet: Konzil und Erneuerung der römischen Messliturgie," *Wort und Wahrheit* 18 (1963) 102–107; K. Amon, "Wünsche an die künftige Messliturgie," *Bibel und Liturgie* 38 (1964/65) 208–217; *ibid.*, "Gratias Agere: zur Reform des Messkanons," *Lit. Jahrbuch* 15 (1965) 79–98.

[2] Who seems to have added *sanctum sacrificium immaculatam hostiam* to the *Supra quae:* cf. *Liber Pontificalis* (ed. Duchesne) I, 239.

[3] Who added *diesque nostros in tua pace disponas, etc.*, to the *Hanc igitur*: cf. *Liber Pontificalis* I, 312.

of the name of St. Joseph, and by the Consilium itself in its alterations of some manual gestures and later rubrical additions. Nevertheless, its extreme antiquity is a precious witness of the wholly Roman tradition of eucharistic prayer, and because of this its modern revision should be carried out with exceptional care and understanding based not only on immediate pastoral concern, but on thorough theological and historical investigations as well (CL 23).

What follows is not an attempt to lobby for certain reforms or to prejudice the work of the Consilium in this area. Rather, it is intended only to inform by presenting some of the relevant technical data and to spur responsible discussion of the problem by asking some central questions that seem to be at issue, leaving to others the opportunity for criticizing these efforts and thus furthering a solution of the present difficulties.

THE TERMINOLOGY OF *EUCHARISTIA*

According to J. P. Audet it has been agreed among most lexicographers that the primary and principal meaning of the verb *eucharisteo* in classical and koine Greek is "to give or return thanks."[4] In its substantive form it thus would mean "thanksgiving." The psychological state indicated by these terms would then seem to be one of "gratitude": the gift received (*charis, charisma*) calls for an interior acknowledgment of that gift (*eucharisteo*) through a corresponding exterior statement of gratitude (*eucharistia*). On these suppositions " . . . the *eucharistia* becomes normally a returned offering (*prosphora, anaphora*) of actions and words of gratitude, or . . . in a fuller form, an offering of a gift considered beforehand as acceptable to God (bread and wine, body and blood of the Lord) — a gift which is, on the part of the one who offers it, spontaneously accompanied by words and gestures primarily expressing gratitude."[5]

There are, to be sure, some grounds for holding this lexicographical view,[6] and it would seem that this sort of thing lies behind a majority of systematic theological treatments of the Eucharist until

[4] "Literary Forms and Contents of a Normal εὐχαριστία in the First Century," *Studia Evangelica: Papers Presented to the International Congress on 'The Four Gospels in 1957,'* eds. K. Aland et al. (Texte und Untersuchungen zur Geschichte der altchristliches Literatur 73) Berlin 1959, 643–662. Cited hereafter as Audet. This essay also appeared in French in *Revue Biblique* 65 (1958) 371–399, and in English again in *The Gospels Reconsidered* (Oxford 1960) 16–35.

[5] Audet, 643–644.

[6] This view seems especially valid of classical Greek usage, which seeps into both

recently. This view has a certain logic and justice-tone to recommend it: one receives a gift, is moved to gratitude, and gives back a gift in return with words of thanks. But such presuppositions as these will be productive of a *theology* that is not only static, but is unable to evaluate other pertinent data that cannot be fitted readily into such a schematization. Audet points out, for example, the proximity and equivalence of *eulogeo* ("to bless") with *eucharisteo*; the positive semantic relationship, through *eulogeo*, of *exomologeomai* ("to give praise to") with the *eucharisteo-eucharistia* group; and finally the connection shared by all these terms, in both Septuagint and New Testament Greek, within a literary genre, the normal function of which seems to determine their meaning. The terms do not just wander, cropping up here and there capriciously. They cluster to form a constellation indicative of the literary genre from which they spring. Proper methodology will be to observe the effect, ". . . not only of the proximate content, but of the literary genre as a whole, on the meaning of the related words *eucharisteo-eucharistia, eulogeo-eulogia, exomologeomai-exomologesis*."[7] What is this literary genre, and in what component parts does it consist?

THE LITERARY GENRE OF *EUCHARISTIA*

In this discussion the relationship between Jewish and Christian modes of liturgical expression cannot be over-emphasized. The very originality of the Christian eucharistic prayer can hardly be grasped apart from its development out of the literary genre of Jewish prayers of blessing or benediction. Many recent works have studied this development,[8] and in so doing have revealed that in the elab-

the Septuagint and the New Testament: for example, compare 2 Macc 12:31 with Lk 17:16 and Rom 16:4 where simply a "return of thanks" is indicated; also compare Acts 24:3 with Sir 37:11 and 2 Macc 2:27 indicating simple "gratitude." Cf. Audet 644.

[7] Audet, p. 645.

[8] In addition to Audet, cf.: I Elbogen, *Der jüdische Gottesdienst in seiner geschichtlichen Entwicklung* (Leipzig 1913); W. O. E. Oesterley, *Jewish Background of the Christian Liturgy* (Oxford 1925); G. Dix, *The Shape of the Liturgy* (Westminster 1945); J. A. Jungmann, *The Mass of the Roman Rite* I (1950) 7–22; L. Bouyer, *Liturgical Piety* (Notre Dame 1956) 115–128 *passim; ibid., The Spirituality of the New Testament and the Fathers* (London 1960) esp. 23–26; *ibid.*, "Jewish and Christian Liturgies," *True Worship*, ed. L. Sheppard (London 1963) 29–44; B. Fraigneau-Julien, "Éléments de la structure fondamentale de l'eucharistie: bénédiction, anamnèse et action de grâces," *Rev. des Sciences Religieuses* 34 (1960) 35–61; J. Daniélou, *The Theology of Jewish Christianity* (London 1964) *passim*; C. W. Dugmore, *The Influence of the Synagogue upon the Divine Office* (Westminster 1964); J. Godart, "Aux origines de la célébration eucharistique," *Les*

oration of the Christian from the Jewish genre, certain aspects must be considered primary and others secondary or tertiary; also that in this same elaboration certain elements came to be emphasized which, although primitive, are nonetheless still secondary at best to the intrinsic structure of the prayer-form — for example, prayers of intercession or supplication. It must suffice here simply to state that such emphases by other than primary elements have exerted pressure upon subsequent generations' understanding of the whole form of this type of prayer. Thus, so as to establish an adequate perspective in dealing with the structure, content, and meaning of the Christian prayer of eucharistic benediction, it will be necessary to concentrate on those elements *primary* in the structure of this type of prayer and, by consequence, upon the *mistress concepts* that flow from them and should govern our understanding of the prayer as a whole. We shall then be in a position to discuss more dispassionately those elements that are less than primary.

THE JEWISH PRAYER OF BENEDICTION

The Christian *eucharistia*, as a literary genre, is the natural offspring of the older Jewish *eucharistia*-form known as the *berakah* (plural = *berakoth*). Already the older form had developed the primary elements of its structure and had attached to them very definite meanings and equally specific worship values in the area of content.[9] Two forms of *berakah* are to be noted. The first was what might be called a spontaneous or "informal" *berakah*, and it was made up of two elements: the benediction or opening doxological blessing proper, and then a short statement of the motive for which benediction is being made. This motive is always a divine wonder, an act either directly or indirectly touching the person making *berakah*. The Old Testament is strewn with such spontaneous *berakoth*; they express the

Questions Liturgiques et Paroissiales 46 (1965) 8–25 and 104–121. Also helpful is C. Stuhlmueller's "Old Testament Liturgy," *Studies in Salvation History*, ed. C. Luke Salm (Englewood Cliffs, N.J. 1964) 81–91.

[9] *Berakah* derives from *brk-barak*, used almost always (some 370 times in the Old Testament) to mean "bless": only once is it used to denote simple "thanks" (2 Sam 14:22), and even then it appears that "to thank" and "to bless" are closely allied in their psychological import for the Jew. The more usual Old Testament term for "to bless" is *yadah*: yet even here it is translatable in this manner 64 times, as "to praise" 55 times, and as "to confess" some 18 times. Thus in the Hebrew terms themselves we can detect a closeness of association that continues to show through in the Greek *eulogeo, eucharisteo*, and *exomologeo*. Cf. C. E. B. Cranfield, "Thank," *A Theological Book of the Bible*, ed. A. Richardson (New York 1960) 254–257.

natural manner in which a Jew reacted to some marvelous act of Yahweh in his regard. Thus in Genesis 24:27 Abraham's servant breaks forth spontaneously upon finding in Rebekah a suitable wife for Isaac: "Blessed be the Lord, the God of my master Abraham, who has not forsaken his steadfast love and his faithfulness toward my master. As for me, the Lord has led me in the way to the house of my master's kinsmen." Such simple *berakoth* were especially associated with the taking of food. Thus Deuteronomy 8:10 commands concerning the food that Israel will partake of out of Yahweh's wondrous mercy: "And you shall eat and be full, and you shall bless the Lord your God for the good land he has given you." It was forbidden, according to the Talmud, to taste of this world without first blessing him who made all things. Because the motive for benediction is thus the *mirabilia Dei,* we may affirm with Audet that the psychological pattern underlying the *berakah* is ". . . above all that of admiration and joy, not of gratitude, which remains subordinated, in fact, to the fundamental feeling of admiration, and is therefore secondary."[10]

This insight holds good also for the second kind of *berakah.* This was essentially the same as the first except that it was more developed in detail, more formal, and is associated usually with some cultic act. Here we find a threefold structure. First there occurs the initial doxology or benediction proper, just as in the spontaneous form already mentioned. This is usually brief, somewhat stereotyped in form, and rather "invitatory," being an enthusiastic call to the hearers to enter into the act of blessing God. There then follows, as before, a statement of the motive for which praise and thanksgiving are being offered — the *mirabilia Dei,* except that in this case the statement of motive is much more protracted and detailed, centering much less on some discrete "wonder" of a particular circumstance than upon the permanent wonder of all that Yahweh has done for his chosen people *as perceived and remembered above all by the consciousness of that community itself.*[11] This section is thus not only a proclamation to the community of its divinely directed past and its messianic (in the broad sense) destiny; not only a narrative listing of the wonders that have made Israel a people of predilection (*haggadah*); not only a psychological calling to mind of all these things so that Israel might thereby be humbled and charged once again with a

[10] Audet 646.
[11] *Ibid.*

sense of its mission. In addition to all this, the statement of motive for blessing *within a cultic action* is a veritable kerygmatic annunciation to the assembly that this same *mirabile* is present here, active now, accomplishing its purpose still within the life of each and every member of the worshiping people. By reason of its immediacy and its grandeur, the proclamation of it as fact is more than just joyful and full of admiration: it is *ecstatic*. Witness the famous text of the Mishnah on the Passover celebration, in which the narrative of the exodus-wonder is recited together with repeated *berakoth* on this theme over bread, cups of wine, and food: "It is therefore incumbent on every person, in all ages, that he should consider as though he had personally gone forth from Egypt, as it is said, 'and thou shalt explain to thy son in that day, saying, "this is done because of what the Lord did for *me* in Egypt"' (Ex 12:27). We are therefore in duty bound to thank, praise, adore, glorify, extol, honor, bless, exalt, and reverence Him who wrought all these miracles for our ancestors and for us; for He brought *us* forth from bondage to freedom, He changed *our* sorrow into joy, *our* mourning into a feast. He led *us* from darkness into a great light, and from servitude to redemption — let *us* therefore say in His presence, 'Hallelujah.'"[12]

Furthermore, not infrequently one finds within the solemn cultic form of a *berakah's* statement of motive either one or several explicit statements of *response* to the *mirabile* that is being proclaimed. Because Yahweh has done this or that in the past, and because he continues to create his people down to this very moment, *therefore* the assembly states its purpose of doing this action now. Thus in 1 Chronicles 29:10–22 David "blesses God" in the midst of a great assembly of the people by narrating God's goodness to him and the nation throughout his lifetime, injecting into the narrative, "And now we thank thee, our God, and praise thy glorious name" (v. 13), and concluding the narrative with a command to the assembly, "Bless the Lord your God" (v. 20). The people do so, bow down to the Lord, do obeisance to the king, and offer sacrifice. The same sort of structure is also found in the account of Solomon's *berakah* for the dedication of the temple (2 Chron 6:3–7:11), and of Nehemiah's *berakah* rededicating the people after the exile (Neh 9:5–38).[13]

[12] See *The Mishnah*, trans. and ed. H. Danby (London 1933) 150–151.

[13] See also the narrative-*haggadah* given in Deut 26:5–11 which concludes: "And behold, now I bring the first of the fruit of the ground which thou, O Lord, hast given me."

With the inclusion of this latter element of response to the narrated *mirabilia* on the part of the worshiping assembly we may now be able to view something of the richness of this second section in the solemn, cultic form of *berakah*. This section is *anamnesis* in the fullest and most objective sense of the term: that is, it is an ecstatic recounting, in a proclamatory manner before the assembly, of the wonders of God's goodness that stretch from the past down into the present moment. Here the mystery of that goodness is not only recognized as being present, but is celebrated as an accomplished fact in an act of worshipful joy and astonished admiration. This event is seen as the cutting edge of salvation history.[14]

The third and final section in the cultic *berakah* is a brief concluding benediction that takes the form of an inclusive "doxology." This is often colored by the manner in which the *anamnesis*-narrative has been developed in a given instance.[15]

CHRISTIAN *BERAKOTH*

The literary genre of the *berakah* was still very much alive at Jesus' time. We can detect this in the continuing elaboration of the great Jewish prayer (*tefillah*) par excellence of the "Eighteen Benedictions" (*Shemoneh 'esre berakoth*),[16] in the codification of the tractate "*Berakoth*" of the Mishnah around the first century after Christ, and we can see the same forms present in some of the Qumran literature — especially in the collection of psalmodic *Blessings and Thanksgivings (Berakoth we-Hodayoth)*.[17] The *berakah* remains, indeed, a living tradi-

[14] On the full Judaeo-Christian tradition of *anamnesis* cf. O. Casel, *Das Gedächtnis des Herrn in der altchristlichen Liturgie* (Freiburg 1918); *ibid.*, "Das Mysteriengedächtnis der Messliturgie im Lichte der Traditon," *Jahrb. für Liturgiewissenschaft* 6 (1926) 113–204; N. Dahl, "Anamnesis: mémoire et commémoration dans le christianisme primitif," *Studia theologica* (Lund) I (1948) 69–95; B. Botte, "Problèmes de l'anamnèse," *Journ. of Eccl. Hist.* 5 (1954) 16–24; M. Thurian, *The Eucharistic Memorial*, trans. J. G. Davies (London 1960) 2 vols.; B. S. Childs, *Memory and Tradition in Israel* (Naperville, Illinois 1962) esp. 81–89.

[15] See Psalms 103 and 104 (RSV) for clear and classic examples of this benediction-*anamnesis*-benediction structure.

[16] These prayers are individually dated in the time of their composition from the pre-Maccabean period to about 117 A.D. by L. Finkelstein in the *Jewish Quarterly Review*, new series, 16 (1925) 1–43 and 127–170.

[17] For a convenient text of these see *The Dead Sea Scriptures in English Translation*, ed. Theodor H. Gaster (New York 1956 Doubleday Paperback) 123–202; note also the directions for *berakoth* to be said at the time of new members' initiation into the community, *ibid.*, 40.

tion in Judaism to this day, having proved to be one of the most deep-rooted literary forms to which the oldest stratum of semitic religion gave birth. There is no reason to suppose that Jesus and his disciples broke with this literary tradition in which they were immersed, nor is there any reason to suppose "that a partial transposition into Greek of literary forms sanctioned by so constant a practice had already implied a perceptible alteration of their fundamental meaning in Christian communities still dominated by their Jewish component."[18] Such an alteration can only be expected, it would seem, at a later date, after the split of church from synagogue and the domination of the former by gentile converts without an appreciable Judaic background.

EXAMPLES OF BERAKOTH IN THE GOSPELS

It would be impossible to cite all occurrences of *berakah* forms in the New Testament, but certain examples stand out and may be used to illustrate the data so far presented. The first such example is the *berakah* of our Lord recorded in Matthew 11:25–26 and Luke 10:21. This *eucharistia* is a benediction (*eulogia*) and a proclamation (*exomologesis*) as well, coming after an apocalyptic statement concerning the destruction those bring upon themselves who reject his good news of salvation (*euangelion*). The *berakah* spoken by our Lord here is, in form, a typical example of the spontaneous, short, and "informal" type of benediction-prayer we have already noted in Genesis 24:27, containing the two elements of that type — namely, a brief opening blessing of God followed by a statement of motive for the blessing. Thus:

1) I praise thee (*exomologoumai soi*) Father, Lord of heaven and earth,
2) that thou didst hide these things from the wise and understanding and revealed them to little ones; yes, Father, for such was thy gracious will.

In John 11:41–43 we find an even shorter formula in the *berakah* recorded as having been said by Jesus just prior to his raising of Lazarus:

1) Father, I thank thee (*eucharisto soi*)
2) that thou has heard me. I knew that thou hearest me always, but I have said this on account of the people standing by, that they may believe that thou didst send me.

[18] Audet 648.

In the statement of motive we should notice the proclamatory and "confessional" value of his *eucharistia*: he is blessing God in order to proclaim to those present the wondrous good news (*euangelion*) not of some past event done by God *but of the present and actual "wonder" of himself and his saving mission*. Then he calls out "Lazarus, come forth" — and the action of a resurrection stands as a sign of the "wonder" he has publicly proclaimed by commemorating it audibly in this short benediction.

In these two forms of short and non-cultic *berakah* spoken by Jesus we may then with confidence affirm two notes that are of the very core of this literary genre. The first note is common to both Old Testament and New Testament *berakoth*, and it is that the benediction opens with a *proclamation* of the divine name. The second note is rather more specifically New Testament: the motive of Jesus' benediction is none other than the astonishing *mirabile* of himself in the process of being totally actualized. This process is identical with the progress in proclaiming the "kingdom" he began at the opening of his public ministry and will consummate only in that baptism wherewith he is to be baptized, his passion-glorification. And the wonder is intensified in this, that, as Audet puts it, the coming of the "kingdom" is being announced to, and is finding a place in the hearts of, ". . . the little ones, that is, the simple, the meek and the 'poor'."[19]

JESUS' FORMAL BERAKOTH

Even in such short forms of benediction as those just mentioned it is not too difficult to see how they are perfect examples of "evangelical eucharists" (thus Audet). It is thus even more the pity that we do not possess records of Jesus' more extended *berakoth* in detail: usually only the fact of his having "prayed" is noted in passing (e.g., Lk 3:21; 5:16; 6:12; 9:18, 28–29; 11:1), but sometimes we know more specifically that he "made benediction." This latter instance is the case with the accounts of the feeding of the multitude with loaves and

[19] *Ibid.*, 649. He calls attention to Is 61:1f as the background of Jesus' marveling and rejoicing. In him this prophetic promise of good news brought to the poor, the afflicted, the broken-hearted, captives, and those who mourn is being fulfilled. In this light the beatitudes must be seen. Also notice Eph 1:3–3:21, where the "gospel to the poor" becomes with Paul the "gospel to the gentiles." What formerly had been a mystery in God's heart has now become "good news" proclaimed at last, wisdom rendered available to men.

fishes, where the terms used are forms of *eulogia* and *eucharistia.*[20] But no details are given concerning the content of his prayer. It is sometimes suggested that he would have used rather a set form or stereotype that was customary for ordinary meal-use. If we recall what we know of Jesus and of the literary genre of the prayer he would have been using, however, this seems less than likely. Our Lord was fully conscious of the role he bore in proclaiming the gospel-kingdom by way of words and such event-signs as the common meal, and the very elasticity of the narrative-*anamnesis* section in the *berakah* form of prayer would have allowed him ample scope in which to proclaim by way of kerygmatic thanksgiving the wonders being performed by God *now* in this event. This same elasticity within the prayer-form was surely a main factor contributing to what Audet calls the extraordinary vitality of the literary genre of benediction.[21] In such circumstances it is hard to think that Jesus would have fallen back on a "common formula" of *anamnesis,* independent of the good news of the kingdom ". . . at the very moment when, through him as a 'sign' of these 'good tidings', God was about to revive on behalf of the crowds the 'wonders' which had of old cast such a radiance of divine power, faithfulness and loving-kindness on the people's march across the desert."[22]

This too would help explain why the disciples at Emmaus recognized him in the "breaking of bread" (Lk 24:35) — i.e., they recognized his own "personal *anamnesis,*" that style of proclaiming the good news in *berakoth* he must have developed, and with which they had become familiar during their association with him in his public ministry. They had perhaps heard him do this many times — at Passovers and at repeated fraternal meals (*chabburoth*).

JESUS' PASSOVER BERAKOTH: THE LAST SUPPER PROBLEM

We have no explicit details of Jesus' major *berakoth* at the Last Supper except the fact that he said them, plus the three explanatory sentences: 1) "This is my body," 2) "This is the cup of my blood," and 3) "Do this for the *anamnesis* of me" (only in Lk and 1 Cor).[23]

[20] The Greek terms used are *eulogesen* (Mt 14:19; Mk 6:41; 8:7; Lk 9:16) and *eucharistesas* (Mt 15:36; Mk 8:6; Jn 6:11).

[21] Audet 650.

[22] *Ibid.*

[23] See Mt 26:26–29; Mk 14:22–25; Lk 22:19–20; Cor 11:23–25. In these accounts the terms used for his having "blessed" are both *eucharistesas* and *eulogesas.*

Subsequent consideration has given rise to a eucharistic theology based on these three sentences: formerly the main concentration was on the first and second, but more lately increased attention has been given to the third, the "precept of reiteration."[24] As a result of this type of attention being given to the few explicit details of Jesus' Last Supper *berakoth*, it is hardly surprising that the eucharistic theology resulting from such attention was not adequately prepared to maintain all aspects of the equilibrium we have noted in the structure and content of the literary genre of the *berakah-eucharistia*. And to this must be added the other negative factor already mentioned, namely, that the Judaic literary genre tended to become more and more obscured within the gentile churches, the members of which did not have the same tradition of and familiarity with the genre as did their Jewish predecessors.

This situation has perdured to our own time, and it would seem to be responsible in large measure for certain inabilities, endemic in our conventional theology of the Eucharist, for coping with crucial areas of evidence concerning the *eucharistia* and its meaning. Audet points out, for example, that theological consideration has not devoted much effort toward an evaluation of the fact that the *liturgical name* which the Lord's Supper has been given — in preference to any other — has been taken from that *eucharistesas* (= *eulogesas*) of the Greek narratives. Theological consideration has rather emphasized the ontological consideration of what *is* this bread (body) and this wine (blood); it has done somewhat less in seeking to penetrate the *dynamic* matter of what the action of giving thanks or, better, of "doing eucharist" might entail. But this latter must be of considerable importance if the action is indeed one of celebration, and if the consecrated elements are indeed the sacred signs and causes of the "wonder" that transpires *in* that celebration. In this connection Audet also points out that our conventional theology has not taken quite adequate account of the fact that, from the earliest times, the Eucharist has been linked *liturgically* with the day of resurrection — Easter, "the Lord's day," Sunday — rather than with the night of his betrayal or the day of his death. Good Friday has indeed been *the* day on which the *eucharistia* itself is not said, although communion might be given. In a crucial sense, Easter is the sacred time-sign of the whole *euangelion* and the cause of the Church's *eucharistia* whereby she proclaims that "wonder" in kerygmatic, joyful admira-

[24] See note 14.

tion. She has always been liturgically aware that her Lord related the breaking of the bread, the giving of the cup, and the command to keep on doing this for his *anamnesis* within the context of the *eucharistia-berakah*. Thus in her own *anamnesis* of him, she proclaims his death (his "breakthrough" into glory which is entered into at baptism) until he comes, in a modality that is ecstatic, wondering, exultant — in short, eucharistic.[25] It need hardly be suggested that this should be a primary datum not only for a theology of the Eucharist, but also for any future reform of the present eucharistic prayer itself.[26]

SUMMARY OF RESULTS

We have observed that every *berakah* formula included a statement of motive for blessing God by praise. In the formal, cultic *berakoth* prayers this statement of motive was expanded into a narrative (*haggadah*) of God's wonderful mercies produced in Israel's favor in the past and continued on into this particular instance. The object of this narrative, which we have called the *anamnesis* section of the prayer, was none other than this wonderful work of God; thus we have, for example, St. Stephen's testimony before his judges taking the form of a veritable *haggadah-anamnesis* which becomes not only a narration of the *mirabilia* but also a public "confession" (*exomologesis*) and proclamation (*kerygma*) of them (Acts 7:2–53).

Thus in the Last Supper *berakoth* of Jesus, according to the structure of the literary genre and the practice of Jesus himself, the *anamnesis* that formed the substance of his benedictions would certainly have amounted to a final and plenary proclamation, in joyful praise, of the many wonders that the Father had performed and would bring to completion in and through the Son. In that particular context, the greatest of these wonders would loom large, namely, the crowning wonder of the Son's glorification in his passover from death to life. This wonder would be, as the resurrection of Lazarus had been, the action that would stand as the *sign* par excellence of all that Jesus had proclaimed and praised in his *anamnesis*, as well as the *cause* of his will to do the same in and for his people for all time to come.

[25] See Audet 652–653.

[26] Note, for example, the principles stated in CL 2, 5–8, 10, 47–48, and also that stated concerning the baptismal "ontology" of the celebrating community in the first paragraph of 14.

In this perspective, then, it is hardly surprising that we detect not gloom, but a pervading mood of the deepest joy, in admiration for the Father's mysterious design for the ultimate salvation of men, running throughout the final conversations of Jesus with his companions in John 13–17. This is especially noteworthy in the final great prayer recorded in 17:1–26, "Father, the hour has now come; glorify thy Son. . . . " This prayer bears so close a resemblance to the form and psychology of the *eucharistia-anamnesis* that one might not be too far wrong in hazarding that it may contain some elements of the Last Supper *berakoth* actually said by Jesus and set down in something of a paraphrased, synthetic form by the author of the fourth gospel. If this is true, then we have glimpses of the *anamnesis*-content proclaimed by him in the most plenary way on that night — proclaimed so fully, indeed, that the apostles could be recorded as exclaiming "Ah, now you are speaking plainly. . . . Now we know that you know all things, and need none to question you; by this we believe that you came from God" (16:29–30).

Be this hypothesis as it may, it remains nonetheless true that, as Audet observes, Jesus' command to his apostles to perpetuate his action over the bread and the cup must necessarily have been at the same time an invitation to do it for the *anamnesis* of him. "The distinctive element of any *eucharistia* being its motive, or its anamnesis, it was simply normal that, within the 'gospel', or rather, to be true, at its summit, the anamnesis of the *eucharistia* left by Jesus for his disciples should have been properly 'evangelical'."[27] Our Lord was thus inviting his own to take up — within the limits of the good news proclaimed and consummated by him — his own *eucharistia* in their turn and to carry it on. As had been done once for the people of Israel at Sinai, here is being set a cultic criterion that would assure a future continuity of awareness concerning the final and decisive order of values his own exodus from death into life had effected, consummated, and exhausted. For the new people of God, this awareness would always remain the tap-root of their faith and hope, as these are channeled *through* the eucharistic proclamation-function belonging to any *anamnesis,* and *into* that mode of life he knew to be the final term of the good news he came to bring. The "final term" of the good news is a life of reconciliation, of integration between God and man as accomplished through the Son alone. It is the heart

[27] Audet 654.

of the one great commandment he gave us, and it is — not fortuitously — what St. Thomas calls the *res eucharistiae*.[28] Let us spell out in greater detail what this implies.

First it implies the closest natural links between *anamnesis* and "gospel" within the very heart of the *eucharistia*. These links mean that the "gospel" is "confessed" (*exomologesis*) in the narrative-commemoration (*anamnesis*) of the eucharistic *berakah*. This insight not only brings to light the actual indissolubility of the *kerygma* and the Christian *eucharistia*,[29] but it also reveals the ideal balance that should obtain between the *kerygma*, baptism, and Eucharist in all areas of Christian life and worship. Thus the *kerygma* is the call to hope and faith in the wonders God has worked, and continues to work in Jesus; baptism is the actual incorporation of a person into that order of wonders which constitute the "gospel" and brings to completion the wonders both of creation and the whole of salvation history; and the Eucharist is simultaneously the "confession" (*exomologesis*) and the celebration, in marveling and joyful praise, of that wonder's dynamic presence within individuals and their communities as well — "until the Lord comes."

Secondly it implies that the *eucharistia* expresses, or should express, what Audet calls the general equilibrium of the evangelical event itself.[30] Thus Jesus, in his public ministry of announcing and effecting the "good news," does not merely forgive sins, but he does so in such a free and open-handed way, and with such authority, that it was itself "wonderful" in the eyes of his beholders. We notice the marveling, "eucharistic" attitude of the witnesses to his forgiveness of sins and his cures ("And amazement seized them all, and they glorified God and were filled with awe. . . ." See Lk 5:26; Mt 9:8; Mk 2:12, etc.) These attitudes and reactions are the same as those underlying the literary genre of *berakah-eucharistia*, and they reach their summit in the great act of cure and forgiveness that was accomplished through the wonder that crowned them all — Jesus' death and resurrection, the key-stone of the "good news."[31]

[28] See Lev 19:18; Mt 22:37–40; Gal 5:14, 16, 22–25, etc.; also *Summa Theol.* III 65, 3 and 4; III 73, 1, 2 and 3.

[29] In this light see CL 10. At the heart of the whole sacramental economy this prayer stands as the primordial type of Christian proclamation — to which the homily, rightly understood, is closely analogous.

[30] See Audet 654–655.

[31] Note Paul's "eucharistic" reaction to the wonder of our utterly gratuitous salvation by Christ in Eph 1:3–10; see Rom 3:21–26, 5:1–11, etc.

Thirdly it implies that, because the people of God are aware in this celebration of praise and thanksgiving of their reconciliation with God through integration into the mystery of the Son, some explicit expression of this awareness will naturally be made in the *eucharistia*-prayer itself. In this the Christian prayer would be following the pattern set by Jesus himself in his own *anamnesis*: "may they all be one, even as thou, Father, are one in me and I in thee . . . that they may be one even as we are one, I in them and thou in me, that they may become perfectly one . . . " (Jn 17:20–24). This nuance in the *eucharistia*-prayer is peculiarly Christian; it is also radical and strong. On this basis, then, we would suggest that perhaps it is in this perspective that what has come to be called the *epiclesis*, or "invocation," should be viewed — that is, basically as the intra-anaphoral prayer-statement of assimilation or integration with God above all things and with our neighbor as ourselves. Our hypothesis goes far in explaining, in our opinion: 1) how in the Roman anaphora the *Supra quae* and *Supplices te rogamus* can be regarded as an "epicletic" unit in the sense advanced above; 2) how the Holy Spirit will come to be associated in most liturgies with the prayer-statement of total integration, for he is the bond of unity and the source of *koinonia* in the Holy Church, which is itself the *unitas Spiritus Sancti* of frequent doxological use in all liturgies;[32] 3) how there naturally comes to be allied with this prayer-statement intercessory prayer for members of the community, our brethren through Christ in the Spirit, and commemoration of the saints, our brethren now in complete unity in the bosom of the Father; 4) and in what place within the structure of the anaphora such intercessory and commemorative prayer-statements should best be made, especially in any future revision of the eucharistic prayer of the Roman rite.

Three areas render primary data concerning the spirit and form of a eucharistic anaphora. First, the psychological attitude underlying it is one of joyful admiration, not merely one of gratitude. Secondly, this prayer-type is liturgically resurrectional, being linked from the earliest times with Easter and Sunday rather than with the night of Jesus' betrayal or the day of his death. The church has always been aware that Jesus related the breaking of bread, the giving of the cup, and the command to keep on doing this for his *anámnesis* within the context of his own *berakah-eucharistía* said within the form of a sacred

[32] See S. Bendo's assembly of data on this point in *The Meaning of Sanctorum Communio* (Naperville, Ill. 1964).

banquet. Thus, thirdly, the church not only celebrates but also proclaims his death and resurrection until he comes in a modality that is "ecstatic," wondering, exultant and, in short, eucharistic. This final datum is, as we have noted, primary both for a theology of the Eucharist and for any future reform of the present Roman anaphora itself.

MAIN AREAS OF CONCERN IN REFORMING THE ANAPHORA

According to these criteria, together with those concerning the structure of the Judaeo-Christian *berakah-eucharistía* already examined, one may suggest that the present Roman anaphora is rendered unclear by two main factors. The first of these is comprised of two extrinsic emphases that create high points of audible and visual interest, namely, the Sanctus hymn and the elevations during the institution account or "consecration." The Sanctus is the elder of these two by far, appearing within an anaphora at least by the time of Serapion in the fourth century.[33] At present it is already being better integrated into the whole cursus of the Roman anaphora, especially through the linguistic unity it will soon have with the "preface" (the vernacular).[34] The elevations during the institution account, on the other hand, date only from the twelfth century and did not become common usage until well into the thirteenth or even later.[35]

The second main factor is more intrinsic to the structure of the anaphora, and thus more serious. It is the hiatus created in the

[33] See E. Ratcliff, "The Sanctus and the Pattern of the Early Anaphora," *Journ. of Eccl. Hist.* 1 (1950) 29–36, 125–134. Ratcliff's hypothesis that the anaphora may originally have ended with the Sanctus, although carefully worked out, seems not to have won more than limited acceptance.

[34] The oldest Sanctus melody appears to be that of Mass XVIII. Patterned closely upon the ferial tone of the "preface," the musical unity of the two suggests that originally the hymn was meant to be sung by all, clergy together with ministers and people. See A. Couratin, "The Sanctus and the Pattern of the Early Anaphora: a Note on the Roman Sanctus," *Journ. of Eccl. Hist.* 2 (1951) 19–23.

[35] See E. Dumoutet, *Le désir de voir l'hostie* (Paris 1926); P. Browe, *Die Verehrung der Eucharistie im Mittelalter* (Munich 1933); G. G. Grant, "The Elevation of the Host a Reaction to Twelfth Century Heresy," *Theol. Stud.* 1 (1940) 228f; V. L. Kennedy, "The Moment of Consecration and the Elevation of the Host," *Med. Stud.* 6 (1944) 121f; *ibid.*, "The Date of the Parisian Decree of the Elevation of the Host," *Med. Stud.* 8 (1946) 87f; J. A. Jungmann, *The Mass of the Roman Rite* I (New York 1950) 118f; S. J. P. van Dijk and J. Hazelden Walker, *The Myth of the Ambry* (London 1957) 87–92; D. R. Dendy, *The Use of Lights in Christian Worship* (London 1959) 89–91.

narrative sequence of the *mirabilia Dei* by the presence of commemorative, intercessory, and petitionary prayers, together with oblatory material, in the five-fold *Te igitur-Quam oblationem* group. Structurally, this group acts rather as an anticlimactic enclave and a psychological interlude between the moments of high intensity in the Sanctus before, and in the institution account's conclusion of the narrative sequence after. In view of the classic structure of the *berakah-eucharistía*, this group interrupts the narrative sequence of the *mirabilia Dei* far more than does the Sanctus, and it produces a situation that obscures the major point of textual transition from narrating the main wonders done by God throughout salvation history to the statement of the assembly's decisive response thereto in the *Unde et memores . . . offerimus*.

This group thus affords, in our opinion, the most serious problem both to an adequate exegesis of the anaphora's content and to its reform. The only proper methodology for solving this problem will be to keep in mind the primary structure-sequence of biblical *berakoth*[36] and of the classic Christian *eucharistía* developing from them — as can be seen in the outline of an anaphora found in Hippolytus' *Apostolic Tradition*, in the full anaphora given in the *Apostolic Constitutions*, and in other early sources. The faults of archaeologism and historicism must be avoided in favor of an authentic concern for the clarity of the eucharistic proclamation itself. Thus one would hope to secure for the anaphora the council's design for the liturgy generally when it states that "the rites should be distinguished by a noble simplicity; they should be short, clear, and unencumbered by useless repetitions" (CL 34).

In the five prayers of the *Te igitur-Quam oblationem* group, however, one finds an involved repetition and anticipation of content — that God might remember persons, unite the church, accept, bless, hold as blessed, worthy, approved, "reasonable,"[37] and acceptable this offering. Such accumulation of terminology was a rhetorical device in public speech used to emphasize the solemnity of a statement or petition. But it may be doubted whether such a device today produces more than tedium — especially in English — and an unwarranted religiosity of language that could more surely be a pas-

[36] See CL 24 concerning scriptural orientation as a condition *sine qua non* for liturgical "restoration, progress and adaptation."

[37] On *rationabilis* see B. Botte, *Le Canon de la Messe romaine* (Louvain 1935) 60; *ibid.*, *L'Ordinaire de la Messe* (Louvain 1953) 117–122.

toral barrier than an aid.[38] It may be asked further whether this content does not obscure the meaning of the *Unde et memores*, with its major statement of offering and petition for acceptance occurring in the classic sequence *memores-offerimus-petimus.*[39]

The *Te igitur-Quam oblationem* group is, admittedly, very old within the Roman anaphora,[40] and it presents a coherent line of thought. *Te igitur* recommends the gifts and those for whom they are offered to God; *Memento* prays for those who offer, being perhaps a rather formalized reading of the diptychs done originally by the deacon while the celebrant quietly named his own particular intentions in the *Hanc igitur*;[41] in this context a commemoration of the major saints, with whom the offerers enjoy communion — *Communicantes* — may be explained as an expression of the offerers' awareness that they are one with the whole universal church.[42] Yet this very coherence puts this group of prayers once again in competition with the *Unde et memores-Supplices te rogamus* group. The purpose of the latter is anticipated by the former and interposed within the narrative sequence, disrupting that sequence's purpose of stating the motive for thanksgiving. Thereby, the structure of the narrative sequence is harmed, as is that of *Unde et memores* group.[43] The secondary growth of oblatory and petitionary matter in the *Te igitur* group thus causes a dislocation within the Roman anaphora: and the effects this has had on the eucharistic theology, piety, and practice in the Roman rite have been considerable.

In view of the classic structure of the *berakah-eucharistía* genre of prayer and of the general liturgical tradition of the church, it would seem desirable that the oblatory and petitionary matter now contained in the *Te igitur* group be assimilated 1) into the restored prayer of the faithful as regards persons mentioned, and 2) back into the *memores-offerimus-petimus* sequence begun with the *Unde et me-*

[38] See Edmund Bishop's essay on the terse sobriety of the Roman sort of prayer, "The Genius of the Roman Rite" (1899), in *Liturgica Historica* (Oxford 1918) 1–19.

[39] This sequence is already found in Hippolytus' *Apostolic Tradition* and in Ambrose's *De Sacramentis.*

[40] It is in place by the time of Leo I (d. 461), and may be alluded to already by Innocent I (d. 417). See Botte, *L'Ordinaire,* 21–23.

[41] This is the hypothesis of Botte, *Le Canon,* 59.

[42] This is the sense of *communicantes* as used by Cyprian in *De Lapsis* 33, *Ep.* 59:13. See Botte, *Le Canon,* 56.

[43] Later the same matter would be anticipated even earlier, in the celebrant's private prayer *Suscipe sancta Trinitas,* during the preparation of the elements.

mores as regards the rest. Several desirable results could ensue from the latter reform. First, the narrative sequence would be clarified by having the institution account rejoined to the other *mirabilia Dei,* and the institution account would be revealed once more as the greatest of these wonders (the "mystery of faith" par excellence), summing up in itself the whole motivation for praising and giving thanks to the Father. Secondly, this reform would emphasize the major textual transition of the anaphora as initiated in the *Unde et memores,* which is the statement of the church's response to the wonders recounted in the narrative sequence. This would, thirdly, enhance the importance of the *Unde et memores* for a theology of the Eucharist, inasmuch as it states the church's response as one of offering in a modality that is eucharistic, commemorative, and communal in its realization: and, indeed, Christian petitionary prayer in its highest form (*Supra quae* and *Supplices te rogamus*) is the same. Fourthly, by thus clarifying the anaphora's structure and shortening its length, its pastoral and catechetical effect would be improved — especially once the whole prayer comes to be spoken in the vernacular. This structure would then be as follows:[44]

1. Opening doxology (*Vere dignum . . . nos tibi gratias agere, Domine*)
2. Narration of the *mirabilia Dei* (preface, Sanctus, institution account)
3. Statement of the church's response to the wonders narrated, the "good news" (*Unde et memores*)
4. Petition that the divine acceptance of this response may result in union between God and the offering community (*Supra quae-Supplices te rogamus*)[45]
5. Closing doxology (*Per ipsum, et cum ipso, etc.*)

THE "UNDE ET MEMORES-SUPPLICES TE ROGAMUS" GROUP

With the excision of the *Te igitur* group from section 2 of the above outline, and the insertion of some transitional sentence leading from the Sanctus directly into the institution account,[46] attention must next be given to sections 3 and 4. These sections will be expected to

[44] Compare with the biblical *berakah* structure mentioned in *Worship* 39 (1965) 519–523.

[45] See *ibid.*, 528–529.

[46] Such transitional sentences are numerous in Spanish and Gallican anaphora prayers, where they are usually termed *Post sanctus*.

resume their original purposes of stating the response of the community and begging its acceptance by the Father.

The *Unde et memores* is a single unified prayer of commemorative offering.[47] It is the original textual offertory of the Roman eucharistic rite. This being the case, it would seem anachronistic to elaborate either a theology of eucharistic sacrifice solely from the institution account, or a pastoral catechesis of the same too exclusively from the action of preparing the elements (the rather misnamed "offertory"). Both these efforts appear to arise from too constricted a notion of "consecration" and "oblation." Western theology has tended perhaps too much to view these matters as brought about in the recitation of the institution account — a convention not wholly shared by other rites of the church, and arising both out of a failure to interpret adequately the content and structure of the eucharistic prayer itself and out of a gradual demise in regard for the whole anaphora as consecratory.[48] The institution account stands last in the list of *mirabilia* narrated as the total motive for giving thanks, and it is essential for the confection of the sacrament. Yet it is not textually a "prayer for consecration"; rather, it is comprised of words of the Lord that are cited in course. As Sebastian Moore has observed, "Temporal limitation [of consecration] to a prayer excludes the surrounding prayer: limitation to the words of our Lord, which are not a prayer but are cited by the Prayer, does not."[49]

More is involved in "consecration" than the transformation of bread and wine into the sacramental body and blood of Christ. Considered liturgically, in terms of the whole eucharistic prayer, "consecration" is a processive offering to the Father of the whole assem-

[47] See G. Dix, *The Shape of the Liturgy* (Westminster 1945) 243–247. K. Amon, "Gratias Agere: zur Reform des Messkanons," *Lit. Jahrbuch* 15 (1965) 89, calls it "die Kurzanamnese" (short anamnesis), but it is not clear why he would have the prayer broken into two separate parts in his suggested reform of the anaphora; see *ibid.*, 97.

[48] Ambrose, in *De Sacramentis* 4, speaks of "Christ's creative word" as that which turns the elements into his body and blood. He then goes on to say *Accipe, quae sunt verba. Dicit sacerdos . . .* and the substance of the anaphora follows. The same concept is expressed in the oath Berengarius was required to swear in 1079 concerning the real presence of Christ in the sacrament: "I, Berengarius, believe in my heart and confess with my mouth that the bread and wine placed on the altar are substantially changed by the mystery of sacred prayer *and* the words of our Redeemer . . . and that they are, after consecration, the true body of Christ" (Denz. 355).

[49] "The Theology of the Mass and the Liturgical Datum," *Downside Rev.* 69 (1951) 41, note 1.

bly — Christ's body which is the church. This is the import of the *Unde et memores*: its *offerimus* refers essentially to the action (*hostiam puram, hostiam sanctam, hostiam immaculatam*) done here in Christ by the whole hierarchically assembled community. "We your servants, together with your holy people . . . offer." The offering-sacrifice is conceived of as being made not "with" the sacrament after it has been confected; rather, the offering-sacrifice of the body of Christ which is the church *makes* the sacramental body of Christ — under the forms of food for Christian nourishment (*panem sanctum vitae aeternae, et calicem salutis perpetuae*).[50] The whole anaphora is the prayer of eucharistic offering, but the *Unde et memores* makes this textually explicit in view of the command, "Do this for the *anamnesis* of me."

Following upon the *Unde et memores* come *Supra quae* and *Supplices te rogamus*. In the earliest extant citation of these two sections — that quoted by Ambrose in *De Saramentis* — they are one single prayer. It forms a petition that the offering of the church may be accepted by the Father. We have suggested earlier that this petition seems to be a prayer for the community's assimilation or integration with God above all things and the members one with another through this action of thanksgiving in Christ.[51] Thus the Holy Spirit, as the bond of unity and the source of *koinonía* in the holy church, will come to be invoked in this prayer; and the prayer itself then comes to be known as "the invocation" or *epíclesis*. Thus Hippolytus' anaphoral *epíclesis* reads: "And we pray thee that thou wouldest send thy Holy Spirit upon the offerings of thy holy church; that thou, gathering them into one, wouldest grant to all thy holy ones who partake to be filled with Holy Spirit, that their faith may be confirmed in truth, that we may praise and glorify thee."[52] The fact that the Roman

[50] See H. de Lubac's *Corpus Mysticum: l'Eucharistie et l'Église au moyen âge* (Paris ²1948), in which the shift from the earlier concept of the eucharistic sacrament as *corpus mysticum* (= sacramental body) to the church as the *corpus mysticum*, with the sacrament becoming *corpus verum*, is discussed at length. The theology presupposed by and contained in the Roman anaphora antedates this shift.

[51] See pp. 30–45 of this article.

[52] See G. Dix, *The Treatise on the Apostolic Tradition of St. Hippolytus of Rome* (London 1937) 9, 75–79, on the difficulties of the text. Note too the form in *Testamentum Domini* of the 4th-5th century and its Hippolytan influence: *Da deinde, Deus, ut tibi uniantur omnes qui participando accipiunt ex sacris [mysteriis] tuis, ut Spiritu sancto repleantur ad confirmationem fidei in veritate* . . . (in Rahmani, *Testamentum Domini Nostri Jesu Christi*, Mainz 1899, 45).

equivalent of this prayer is couched not in pneumatic but in Old Testament sacrificial terms (Abel, Abraham, Melchisedech, the altar of the heavenly tabernacle) should not confuse the issue that, in both types of this prayer, what ultimately is being prayed for is oneness with the Father — that oneness he has made available in Jesus and extends to all men through Jesus' body, the church.

In this perspective it is significant that this prayer of petition (*proseuché*)[53] occurs where it does within the *eucharistía*. Having narrated the *mirabilia Dei* and having then responded to the "good news," the assembly finally prays that the reconciliation of all with the Father through Jesus may be appropriated by all who share in this action — *ex hac altaris participatione*. An expression of this same concept may be seen in the eucharistic *proseuché* in the *Didache*, 9: "As this broken bread was scattered upon the mountains, but was brought together and became one, so let thy church be gathered together from the ends of the earth into thy kingdom." This type of intra-anaphoral petition can thus be understood as one of a deeply eschatological consciousness of the church, opening upon man's union with God both presently in this celebration of the mystery and ever more fully in the future. The church is seen as being achieved after the manner in which Jesus unites all to the Father (Jn 17).

There would, therefore, seem to be strong reason for making mention at this point of those with whom the assembly is in *koinonía* or for whom it may want especially to pray. This is the place for solemn commemorations and intercession, particularly in those eastern liturgies deriving from the West Syrian tradition — such as that of St. John Chrysostom. It might be possible for the substance of the *Communicantes* to be located here after the petition for unity; and it may also be possible to have at this point the prayer for the departed, except that this might be employed only at requiems rather than at every celebration.[54]

THE VARIABLE PREFACE

The Roman anaphora is special in this, that it has a structural stability nonetheless admitting of elastic variety. In this it differs from the

[53] See Phil 4:6; Col 4:2 and compare Acts 4:24–30; 16:25. Note also the two *proseuché* of Paul's great *eucharistía* in Eph 1:3–3:21 (1:17–23 and 3:14–19).

[54] There seems to be precedent for such a restriction of the *memento defunctorum* in Roman usage prior to the eighth century: see Botte, *Le Canon*, 67–68.

completely set eastern forms of anaphora on the one hand, and from the almost wholly variable Spanish and Gallican anaphora prayer-sequences on the other. The variety admissible within the Roman type occurs mainly in the narrative of the *mirabilia Dei* (section 2 of the outline above), that is, in the variable "prefaces." Several advantages are obvious in this arrangement, but in general one may note that the Roman anaphora can thus remain relatively brief while yet incorporating over the course of a year considerable richness of detail in its narration of the motive for which thanksgiving is made. It thus possesses the potential richness of matter one may see in the "Anaphora of St. Basil," but it is not encumbered by Basil's great length — a pastoral disadvantage.

A thorough reconsideration of the proper prefaces used in the Roman anaphora should be made. Many more prefaces could be added, either as fresh compositions or as redactions of the many prefaces to be found in the various Roman and non-Roman sacramentaries (the Leonine Sacramentary alone contains more than two hundred). From the eleventh century it became the rule to restrict the number of prefaces to nine; but this restriction was based on a decree of Pelagius II since recognized to have been spurious.[55] In the last hundred years this number has been slightly expanded, and there seems little reason why growth should not continue. At the same time, existing prefaces should be reviewed and rewritten where necessary in a truly narrative style. For example, the preface of the apostles is a petitionary prayer that has little to narrate concerning the apostolic office as a divine mercy for which the church gives thanks; the preface of the Holy Trinity tends to become a credal disquisition; and the common preface is nothing more than two formulas, the first leading out from the opening dialogue and the second leading into the Sanctus, with no content in between.

A somewhat more adequate common preface might follow the Logos-narrative formula given by Hippolytus:

> We thank you, Father, through Christ
> Whom you sent . . .
> Who is your Word,
> Through whom you created all things,
> Who became man in order to suffer, and thus triumphed . . .

[55] See N. M. Denis-Boulet, "Analyse des rites et prières de la messe," *L'Église en prière,* ed. A. G. Martimort (Paris 1961) 388–399.

[Holy, holy, holy . . . . Truly holy and blessed is he,]
Who took bread and cup, gave them, and commanded:
"Do this for the commemoration (*anámnesis*) of me."

Such a narrative sequence could serve as a good regular foundation that would support more specific proper prefaces detailing the motive for thanksgiving in terms of various feasts, seasons of the year, and special occasions (such as the celebrations of jubilees, baptism, confirmation, first communion, times of distress, etc.). It would also be helpful in this connection to revise the typographical format in future liturgical books so as to make clear the unity and the proper sequence of parts in the anaphora.[56]

SECONDARY AREAS OF CONCERN IN REFORMING THE ANAPHORA

Several other lesser areas open to possible clarification should be mentioned. First, it would be helpful to have the role of the deacon written into the rubrics of the anaphora now that the diaconal office is in process of being restored. This would at least to some degree assure the diaconate's remaining before the eyes of all as a major liturgical office in its own right and not solely dependent upon the whim of a given celebrant. Such a rubrical recognition of the deacon's proper "liturgy" would also help rescue his rightful functions from their being shared out between the celebrant and the "master of ceremonies." This latter office should be reabsorbed once more by the deacon. Special mention could be made of the deacon's role in speaking the commemorations and sharing in the action of the great elevation at the end of the anaphora. Thus the constitution's stipulations concerning the distinction of liturgical roles would be realized in an important area (see CL 28, 29, and 32).

Secondly, greater clarity and consistency can be given to the various manual gestures in the anaphora. The gesture of the celebrant's praying with extended hands is the basic norm for the whole prayer. The various subordinate gestures whereby he indicates the gifts should be emphasized by their fewness, and they should not be made to look like "blessings." The same principle touching the frequency of gestures would seem to apply also to reverences and to the elevation of the gifts. It is in this area that repetitive accumulation has gradually built up, even to the point of obscuring visually

[56] A possible design for this, revised from Amon, *art. cit.*, 95–98, will be found in the anaphora example below.

the meaning, structure, and coherence of the anaphoral act as a whole (CL 21).

Thirdly, the section immediately preceding the final great doxology of the Roman anaphora (*Per quem haec omnia . . .*) seems originally to have been a formula for blessing other things offered at the time of Mass. This formula could be included to be used only at such times when an actual blessing is in fact to be given. This would provide a point at which the various seasonal blessings of things (wine on St. John's day, bread and eggs at Easter, candles at Candlemas, foodstuffs at Thanksgiving, money offerings at any time, etc.) could be made, thus bringing these things visually and audibly within the ambit of the *eucharistía* itself.

And lastly, it is to be hoped that such a reformed anaphora might be somewhat shorter length than at present. This will allow it to be spoken more slowly and distinctly while avoiding the charge of too much time being required. Brevity is not a sin, providing irreverence is avoided and tradition is not pauperized (CL 23): it can, indeed, coupled with clarity, be a real pastoral advantage (CL 34).

An adequate procedure for serious reform of the anaphora might be provided in view of the necessity for catechesis to keep abreast with such reform on the parochial level. Moving too fast in so sensitive an area as this has nothing to recommend it. An untried adaptation, originating from authority by fiat and without enough time for adequate experimentation and assimilation of data, or permitting a plurality of anaphoras from differing traditions of prayer to be used, or simply putting the present anaphora directly into the vernacular as it stands — all these are less than what seems to be required. An adequate procedure might follow something like this sequence: 1) a preliminary revised form of the anaphora in Latin for experimental use in some places where special competence for judgement is at hand; 2) extension of this program to include certain parishes; 3) use of the further revised form throughout the church, at least on certain days or during certain seasons such as Eastertide; 4) vernacularization of the revised anaphora according to the same stages, but now carried out within areas of linguistic unity; 5) vernacular anaphora for all according to the Latin typicum. The following may illustrate, as a single theoretical example, the type of anaphora that could initiate the foregoing process.[57]

[57] I must express my debt to Amon's article, already cited, and I hope that my revisions of his first suggestion may be of help as a mark of appreciation for his work.

PREX EUCHARISTICA

Sacerdos, iunctis manibus ante pectus, dicit dialogum ante Precem eucharisticam. Cum autem dicit: Vere dignum et iustum est, *manus disiungit, et disiunctas tenet per totam Precem eucharisticam, nisi aliter notetur. Dum ab omnibus cantatur vel dicitur* Sanctus, *celebrans iungit manus, si cantus adhibeatur prolixior.*

C. Dominus vobiscum.
P. Et cum spiritu tuo.
C. Sursum corda.
P. Habemus ad Dominum.
C. Gratias agamus Domino Deo nostro.
P. Dignum et iustum est.

GRATIARUM ACTIO

Vere dignum et iustum est, aequum et salutare, nos tibi semper et ubique gratias agere: Domine, sancte Pater, omnipotens aeterne Deus, per Christum Dominum nostrum:

NARRATIO: FORMULA COMMUNIS

Quem in ultimis temporibus misisti nobis salvatorem et redemptorem et angelum voluntatis tuae;

Qui est verbum tuum per quem omnia fecisti et beneplacitum tibi fuit, voluntatem tuam complens ut populum sanctum tibi per passionem suam acquireret;[58]

Qui, ascendens super omnes caelos sedensque ad dexteram tuam, promissum Spiritum Sanctum in filios adoptionis effudit;[59] Spiritum veritatis, qui a te procedit, et ipsum clarificat,[60] ut omnes gentes, linguis diversas, in unius fidei confessione sociaret.[61]

Unde laetantes coram te, Domine virtutum, hostias tibi laudis offerimus, per Christum Dominum nostrum:[62]

Cum Angelis et Archangelis, cumque omni militia caelestis exercitus, sine fine dicentes:

Sanctus, sanctus, sanctus Dominus Deus Sabaoth.
Pleni sunt caeli et terra gloria tua.

[58] Adapted from Hippolytus.

[59] Pentecost preface.

[60] Adapted from Jn 15:26; 16:14 by Amon.

[61] Adapted from a Pentecost Monday formula in the Gregorian Sacramentary.

[62] Adapted from a *vere dignum* formula for the vigil of Pentecost in the Gelasian Sacramentary (Mohlberg no. 627).

Hosanna in excelsis.
Benedictus qui venit in nomine Domini.
Hosanna in excelsis.

Vere sanctus, vere benedictus Dominus noster Iesus Christus filius tuus:

Qui venit de caelis, ut conversaretur in terris, homo factus, habitaret in nobis, et hostia effectus nos faceret sacerdotes:[63]

Qui pridie quam pateretur, *iungit manus, et accipit hostiam ambabus manibus inter indices et pollices, et elevans ipsam ante pectus dicit*: accepit panem in sanctas ac venerabiles manus suas, *elevat oculos* et elevatis oculis in caelum ad te Deum Patrem suum omnipotentem, tibi gratias agens, benedixit, fregit, deditque discipulis suis, dicens: Accipite et manducate ex hoc omnes. Hoc est enim Corpus meum. *Deponit hostiam consecratam super patenam, et genuflexus adorat.* Simili modo postquam cenatum est, *ambabus manibus accipit calicem, et elevans ipsum ante pectus dicit*: accipiens et hunc praeclarum calicem in sanctas ac venerabiles manus suas: item tibi gratias agens, benedixit, deditque discipulis suis dicens: Accipite, et bibite ex eo omnes. Hic est enim Calix Sanguinis mei, novi et aeterni testamenti: mysterium fidei: qui pro vobis et pro multis effundetur in remissionem peccatorum. Haec quotiescumque feceritis, in mei memoriam facietis. *Deponit calicem super corporale, et genuflexus adorat. Deinde, disiunctis manibus, ut antea, prosequitur*:

COMMEMORATIO ET OBLATIO[64]

Unde et memores, Domine, nos servi tui, sed et plebs tua sancta, eiusdem Christi Filii tui, Domini nostri, tam beatae passionis, nec non et ab inferis resurrectionis, sed et in caelos gloriosae ascensionis, offerimus praeclarae maiestati tuae de tuis donis ac datis hostiam puram, hostiam sanctam, hostiam immaculatam, *iungit manus, et dextera hostiam ostendit, dicens*: Panem sanctum vitae aeternae, *calicem*

[63] *Post sanctus* formula from the *Missale Gothicum* for Sundays (Mohlberg no. 482).

[64] In view of what we have seen of the structure of the *berakah-eucharistía,* might it not be possible in cases of concelebration to have the *collegium* join with the main celebrant in speaking the Prayer at this point? All would thus say the *commemoratio et oblatio,* the *deprecatio ad unitatem,* and the *doxologia magna* together. By the *Unde et memores* the concelebrants could express their collegiate sacrificial intent, and indeed this is the very nature of this prayer. The advantage of this arrangement would be to leave the presiding celebrant alone throughout the narrative section, thus fulfilling the unique role of Christ liturgically: also the transition between the narrative section and the response thereto would be rendered more clear and decisive.

ostendit, dicens: et Calicem salutis perpetuae. *Disiunctis manibus, prosequitur*:

DEPRECATIO AD UNITATEM

Et petimus et precamur, ut hanc oblationem suscipias in sublime altare tuum per manus angelorum tuorum, sicut suscipere dignatus es munera pueri tui iusti Abel, et sacrificium Patriarchae nostri Abrahae, et quod tibi obtulit summus sacerdos tuus Melchisedech,[65] sanctum sacrificium, immaculatam hostiam:[66] *profunde inclinatus, iunctis manibus super altare positis, dicit*: ut quotquot, ex hac altaris participatione[67] *osculatur altare: deinde, erigit se, manu dextera ostendit hostiam, dicens*: sacrosanctum Filii tui Corpus *calicem ostendit, dicens*: et Sanguinem sumpserimus, *seipsum cruce signat, dicens*: omni benedictione caelesti et gratia repleamur: *extensis manibus, prosequitur*:

Communicantes, et memoriam venerantes, in primis gloriosae semper Virginis Mariae, Genetricis Dei et Domini nostri Iesu Christi, et omnium Sanctorum tuorum:

Pro Communicantes *supra posito, diebus Dominicis et festis I et II classis dicitur formula haec longior a diacono, si ministret, iunctis manibus, aliter a celebrante, extensis vero manibus*: Communicantes, et memoriam venerantes, in primis gloriosae semper Virginis Mariae, Genetricis Dei et Domini nostri Iesu Christi, beati Ioannis Baptistae, et beati Ioseph, eiusdem Virginis Sponsi; sed et beatorum Apostolorum ac Martyrum tuorum Petri et Pauli, Andreae, Iacobi, Ioannis, Thomae, Iacobi, Philippi, Bartholomaei, Matthaei, Simonis et Thaddaei, Clementis, Polycarpi, Ignatii et Cypriani, Hippolyti, Stephani, Laurentii et Iustini; Perpetuae et Felicitatis, *hic includuntur nomina patroni seu patronae ecclesiae, vel loci, vel dioecesis, vel ordinis, sed et diei, si nondum nominantur*: et omnium Sanctorum tuorum:

[*In missis* de Requiem *dicitur in hoc loco Commemoratio Defunctorum a celebrante vel a diacono, ut supra*: Memento etiam, Domine, famulorum famularumque tuarum *N.* et *N.*, qui nos praecesserunt cum signo fidei, et dormiunt in somno pacis. Ipsis, Domine, et omnibus in

[65] This united form of the present *Supra quae* and *Supplices te rogamus* is given in Ambrose, *De Sacramentis* 4:6 (Quasten, *Monumenta*, 161–162).

[66] See *Liber Pontificalis* I, 239.

[67] Note 1 Cor 10:16–18: "Calix benedictionis, cui benedicimus, nonne communicatio [*koinonía*] sanguinis Christi est? et panis, quem frangimus, nonne participatio [*koinonía*] corporis Domini est? Quoniam unus panis, unum corpus multi sumus, omnes qui de uno pane participamus [*metéchomen*]. Videte Israel secundum carnem; nonne qui edunt hostias, participes [*koinonoí*] sunt altaris?"

Christo quiescentibus, locum refrigerii, lucis et pacis, ut indulgeas, deprecamur:]

Cum quibus te laudamus, et glorificamus, per dilectum Filium tuum Iesum Christum.

BENEDICTIO RERUM

Si aliqua res, necnon pecunia, benedicenda allata sit, celebrans manus iungit, et versus rem benedicendam dicit: Per quem haec omnia, Domine, semper bona creas, sanctificas, [vivificas, *si vivat*] bene + dicis et praestas nobis. *Et iunctis manibus iterum se vertit ad altare.*

DOXOLOGIA MAGNA ET ELEVATIO

Accipit hostiam inter pollicem et indicem manus dexterae, sinistra autem calicem, et elevans eum ante pectus cum hostia, quam tenet super calicem [diacono adiuvante, si ministret], dicit: Per ipsum, et cum ipso, et in ipso, est tibi Deo Patri omnipotenti, in unitate Spiritus Sancti, omnis honor et gloria, per omnia saecula saeculorum.

P. Amen.

Deponit hostiam in patena, et calicem super altare, genuflectit, surgit, etc.

A SELECT BIBLIOGRAPHY ON THE EUCHARISTIC ANAPHORA

K. Amon, "Gratias Agere: zur Reform des Messkanons," *Lit. Jahrbuch* 15 (1965) 79–98.

J. P. Ander, "Literary Forms and contents of a Normal Εμχαριστία in the First Century," *Studia Evangelica, etc.*, eds. K. Aland et al. (Berlin 1959) 643–662. For a fuller notice on the publication history of this paper, see *Worship* 39 (1965) 516, note 4.

J. Blomfield, *The Eucharistic Canon* (London 1930).

B. Botte, *Le Canon de la messe romaine* (Textes et études liturgiques 2) Louvain 1935. A good critical edition with notes, reprinted in 1962.

——— and C. Mohrmann, *L'Ordinaire de la Messe* (Études liturgiques 2) Louvain 1953, especially 15–27, and 72–85.

L. Bouyer, *Liturgical Piety* (Notre Dame 1954) 23–37, 115–128, 129–142.

———, *The Spirituality of the New Testament and the Fathers* (History of Christian Spirituality 1) London 1960, especially 3–34 on the *berakah.*

F. Cabrol, "Canon," DACL 2 (1910) cols. 1847–1905.

N. M. Denis-Boulet, "La liturgie eucharistique: le canon," *L' Église en prière*, ed. A. G. Martimort (Paris 1961) 380–412.

G. Dix, *The Shape of the Liturgy* (Westminster 1945).

G. Every, *Basic Liturgy: a Study in the Structure of the Eucharistic Prayer* (London 1961).

W. H. Frere, *The Anaphora: or Great Eucharistic Prayer* (London 1938).
J. Godart, "Aux origines de la célébration eucharistique," *Les Questions Liturgiques et Paroissiales* 46 (1965) 8–25 and 104–121.
A. Hamman, *Early Christian Prayers* (Chicago 1961). Some sources in English.
J. A. Jungmann, *The Eucharistic Prayer* (Chicago 1958).
E. Kilmartin, *The Eucharist in the Primitive Church* (Englewood Cliffs, New Jersey 1965) 154–159, passim.
H. Küng, "Das Eucharistiegebet: Konzil und Erneuerung der römischen Messliturgie," *Wort und Wahrheit* 18 (1963) 102–107.
T. Maertens, *Pour une meilleure intellegence de la prière eucharistique* (Collection de pastorale liturgique 42) St. André ²1963.
E. J. Sutfin, "An Inquiry About Mass for People Today," *Liturgical Arts* 33 (1965) 81–89. On pp. 86–88 of this article a vernacular anaphora is given with suggested reforms, not all of which would be acceptable. But this is the type of study that badly needs to be done.
G. G. Willis, *Essays in the Early Roman Liturgy* (London 1964) 107–133.

Robert J. Ledogar

The Eucharistic Prayer And the Gifts over Which It Is Spoken

A strange dichotomy seems to exist today between the writings of theologians and those of liturgiologists on the subject of the eucharist. A glance at the six-page index of J. M. Powers' very useful *Eucharistic Theology*[1] shows no entry for such key concepts as anamnesis or memorial, anaphora, praise, confession, thanksgiving, nor any mention of such important names as Audet, Lietzmann, Dix, Baumstark, or Hippolytus, Chrysostom, Serapion. This is not Father Powers' fault. It simply reflects the fact that the many authors whose thought he has made accessible tend to elaborate their theologies of the eucharist with relatively little regard for what should be their primary source, the liturgical texts themselves. For one thing, they seem to be very little concerned with the fact that the great eucharistic prayer which accomplishes the "transubstantia-

[1] New York 1967.

tion," "transignification," or "transfinalization" they write about is an act of praise.

On the other hand, historians of the liturgy sometimes display a kind of academic detachment from the real concerns of the theologians and a mild disdain for any theorizing that ventures a step beyond textual evidence. In this there is a certain basic respect for the transcendence of the mystery which is quite healthy. But the desire of the theologian to express the mystery in contemporary terms, even if they are only highly poetic terms, is also healthy.

It is indeed dangerous to try to interpret the facts of history in the light of a modern theological problem. But theology can at least suggest to the historian that he re-examine his facts to see if his original statement of them might not have been subtly influenced by one of those unconscious attitudes which we all bring to any investigation.

In this article I would like to suggest to both theologians and liturgiologists a re-examination of the motive of praise which prompts the eucharistic prayer. Just what does it mean to praise God? What is the basic attitude from which Christians offer praise, and what is the relationship of this praise-act to the bread and wine over which it is made? I will try to show that the essential element in all praise is that of a public acknowledgment; that the Christian eucharist is basically an acknowledgment prompted by gratitude; that it is precisely this notion of gratitude which relates the bread and wine of the offertory to the memorial meal at which they are transformed. In doing this I will also try to show how ancient texts and modern theories can be mutually helpful in achieving a deeper understanding of what we are about when we celebrate the Lord's supper.

WHAT DOES IT MEAN TO PRAISE GOD?

Most dictionaries define praise by giving synonyms like glorify, extol, commend, magnify, which is not really very helpful. One basic distinction that can make the notion clearer is the difference between praise offered to a person in private and praise offered to a person in public. In both cases the words and/or gestures used may be exactly the same, but the personal stance of the one offering the praise can be vastly different. If I were invited to a private dinner with President Johnson, for instance, and had little hope of influencing his policies, I would probably spend my time saying nice things to him, if only for the sake of making the occasion as painless as possible. But if I were invited to deliver a public testimony to him, I would have second thoughts. In private nothing is at stake but his feelings and my relationship to him as a person. In public I would be engaging my whole moral position, my right to speak, my reputation. Public praise demands much more of the one praising. It is much more significant because a man's integrity, fidelity, and willingness to risk all for what he believes in are put to the test in a way which is usually not true of the private conversation. As an individual I am too insignificant to be taking a moral stance before the President, but I must take a moral stance before my peers in relation to the President. Public praise is a statement of what I believe in.

I think it can be shown that the basic meaning of the notion of praise as found in the Bible and in the earliest eucharistic texts is precisely *public* praise. To document this claim thoroughly I will have to refer the reader elsewhere,[2] but a few illustrations may be sufficient.

In the first book of Samuel, chapter 15, we have the story of King Saul's disobedience in failing to destroy the Amalekites completely as God had commanded. Samuel reproaches Saul and tells the king that God has rejected him. But Saul pleads with him: "I have sinned; yet honor me now before the elders of my people and before Israel, and return with me, that I may worship the Lord your God" (1 Sam 15:30). Samuel accepts the request and returns to appear with Saul in the sanctuary, thereby confirming, for the time being, his authority. The word used for "to honor" here is the Hebrew verb *kbd* which the Septuagint translated by *doxázein* — "to glorify." The word obviously does not stand for any interior attitude on Samuel's part, for he has just written Saul off the books. But it does imply an exterior public stand in his favor. In this case there is no need of words. Samuel "glorifies" Saul simply by being seen with him in the right place at the right time.

The psalms bear abundant witness to the public nature of praise as understood by the Hebrews:

I will tell of thy Name to my brethren
In the midst of the congregation I will praise thee (Ps 22:22 [21:23]).

Praise the Lord, call upon his Name
Proclaim his deeds among the peoples (Ps 105 [104]:1).

[2] R. Ledogar, "Verbs of Praise in the LXX version of the Hebrew Canon," *Biblica* 48 (1967), 29–56. My doctoral dissertation, *Acknowledgment: Praise Verbs in the Early Greek Anaphora,* will be published shortly by Herder in Rome.

Robert J. Ledogar

This basically public meaning of praise continued in the New Testament, the early Fathers, and the first eucharistic prayers. I do not mean to imply that no one ever praised God in private. When anyone speaks to him personally in prayer there may clearly be elements of praise, but this is by derivation from the public act.

Public praise can obviously be insincere ("This people honors me with their lips, but their heart is far from me"), but praise uttered in private can be even more so. Publicly at least, the one who praises acknowledges a relationship to the one being praised, takes a stand in favor of that person in the eyes of others. It is an act of commitment. This is why the epistle to the Hebrews can exhort its recipient to take a stand for Jesus and call this stand a "sacrifice of praise": "Let us go forth to him outside the camp, bearing abuse for him. For here we have no lasting city, but we seek the city which is to come. Through him then let us continually offer up a sacrifice of praise to God, that is, the fruit of lips that acknowledge his name" (Heb 13:13ff). This kind of praise is an act of faith — if you understand faith as basically a commitment rather than an intellectual assent. It is a confession. Just as the early creeds were called confessions, so were acts of praise.[3] The goal of such praise is "to give glory to God," not in the sense of pleasing him or satisfying some desire of his for recognition, but in the sense that others come to know God better and to relate to him more deeply in faith (cf. II Cor 9:11–13).

It is as a public acknowledgment, then, that the act of praise must be understood, and this applies to the eucharistic anaphora. It is a statement of the church's faith, not in the form of credal propositions but in the form of joyous proclamation of a faith experience.

Next we must ask *why* we offer praise.

THE PRAISE OF CHRISTIANS: THE THANKSGIVING

One may praise God for many reasons. The beauty or grandeur of nature may inspire praise. Meditation upon certain manifestations of God in history may inspire praise. In such cases wonder or admiration are the dominant motives. When one offers praise on account of something God has done for him, we understand the praise offered to be an act of thanksgiving. Thanksgiving is a specific kind of praise. If praise is essentially public, then the act of thanksgiving

[3] Cf. Günther Bornkamm, "Das Bekenntnis im Hebräerbrief," *Studien zu Antike und Christentum* II (Munich 1959), pp. 188–203; St. Basil, *De Spiritu Sancto* 193c (ed. Pruche, Paris 1945, p. 239).

is a public acknowledgment of gratitude. The Christian celebration which Paul called the Lord's supper has been known, at least since the second century, as the eucharist, the thanksgiving.

Very few theologians have ever taken this fact seriously enough to base their entire theology on it, but more recently even the specialists in liturgical history have questioned the validity of the notion of thanksgiving as adequate to express the meaning of the eucharist. In the past several years, while the importance of praise in the eucharistic act has come to the fore, liturgists have tended to speak of the eucharistic *blessing* rather than of thanksgiving. There seems to be considerable agreement among historians of the liturgy that the eucharistic prayers of the many Christian traditions are all closely linked in their origins to a Jewish literary and cultic form called the *berakah*, or "blessing." In this they more or less follow the work of Father Jean-Paul Audet, O.P., who emphasized the importance of the *berakah* in connection with his studies on the *Didache*.[4]

According to Audet, the *berakah*, in its more ample shape, usually contains three elements: a) the introductory formula of praise, usually beginning with some form of the word *berakh*, "to bless"; b) the "anamnesis of the *mirabilia Dei*," i.e., the more or less prolonged development of the motives of praise: wonderful acts that God has performed in creation or in the history of his people; and c) the concluding formula or "doxology." It is the central elements, the recall of the wonderful works of God, that he considers the most important. He further insists that the essential note in this "anamnesis" is the sentiment of admiration and praise rather than that of appreciation and gratitude. He says that the eucharist should not be understood in the first instance as thanksgiving "if by that one means 'gratitude' for the 'benefits' received in the gospel event."[5]

"A religious consciousness dominated by admiration and praise is not the same thing as a religious consciousness dominated by appreciation and thanksgiving. Where admiration is predominant there is a going-out of oneself and, at best, movement toward the other as he is in himself. Where gratitude dominates there is on the contrary,

[4] For a statement of Audet's views in English, see J.-P. Audet, "Literary Forms and Contents of a Normal *Eucharistia* in the First Century," *Studia Evangelica* (Texte und Untersuchungen 73) (Berlin 1959), pp. 643–662. In French he has stated his position most recently in: "Genre littéraire et formes cultuelles de l'Eucharistie, 'Nova et Vetera,'" *Ephemerides Liturgicae* 80 (1966), 353–385.

[5] "Genre littéraire . . . ," p. 373.

by the very force of things, preoccupation with self and, at best, appreciation of the other for the benefit he can bring. Spiritually and pastorally we may surely choose one or the other way. But we should tell ourselves at the beginning that the end result will be somewhat different according as we give conscious or unconscious primacy to admiration or to gratitude. In any case, there is no doubt, in our opinion, that the "benediction," the veritable summit of cultic expression in Jewish antiquity, invites us to choose unequivocally for the primacy of admiration."[6]

Unfortunately there is no space to develop Father Audet's position in full. It is based on a good deal of research and contains many valid insights. But his tendency to depreciate the validity of gratitude is unfortunate. It comes partly from a failure to emphasize the basically public character of praise, and partly from certain inaccuracies in his analysis of the *berakah* as a cultic form.

To correct this picture there are some fairly technical points which must be discussed, first as regards the *berakah* itself, second as regards the vocabulary of praise in the primitive Christian community, and third as regards the presence of the offertory theme in the earliest eucharistic texts. (The reader who is willing to take my word for it can skip to the conclusions of the next three sections.)

THE BERAKAH

The meaning given by various authors to this term is not always clear. Perhaps we may begin by stating the two extreme possibilities. A *berakah* may be considered as: 1) any formula, however short or long, whose initial or principal verb is the Hebrew *berakh;* or 2) the very standardized form of praise-enunciation for which the Rabbis of the third century (Amoreans) established hard and fast rules. For them every *berakah* required: a) the mention of the name of God; b) the mention of his kingship; c) *barukh* at the beginning when it was a one-sentence formula, or at the end, at least, when longer; d) when several *berakoth* followed one another, only the first begins with *barukh;* e) when, in a longer *berakah,* the thought-content departs from that of the first phrase, the final sentence is to bring the thought back to that of the beginning.[7]

As for the first of the above definitions, it is worth remarking that

[6] *Ibid.*, p. 367.

[7] Elbogen, *Die jüdische Gottesdienst in seiner geschichtlichen Entwicklung,* third edition (Frankfurt 1931), pp. 4ff.

in the Old Testament the noun *berakah* is used primarily to signify a blessing bestowed on men.[8] The word does not appear in the sense of an act of praise prior to Nehemiah 9:5.[9] It is true that the word could have had this meaning at a much earlier date, and 1 Kings 8:14–15 would seem to indicate that it did. But there is no indication in the Old Testament that the noun *berakah* had any meaning more specialized than that of a public act of praise, probably introduced by the participle *barukh* and containing quite naturally a mention of God's name. For the use of the word in any more precise way we must wait until the Mishna.

Obviously the later form of *berakah* was not born with the Rabbis of the third century. They were simply giving fixed rules to a prayer-style that had been current long before them. But, as Elbogen notes,[10] there are numerous exceptions to the rules of the *berakah* in Jewish prayer, and he interprets this to mean that the fixed form cannot be very ancient. One has only to consider the blessings *'ahavah rabbah* and *'emet w^e yasiv* which surround the Shema in the Jewish Prayerbook and are admitted by all to be very ancient.[11]

The only thing that can be said for certain about the berakah in a general sense in New Testament times is that it was at a stage in its evolution somewhere between the two extremes defined above. A more precise determination can be made only by analysis of specific forms of prayer.

The *barukh*-participle as an opening formula was particularly common to prose-prayers in the Old Testament. The prose-prayers of the post-exilic period, whose text is given us, generally begin with *barukh* and the name of God followed by a relative clause whose content may be either God's qualities (Dan 4:34; Neh 9:5), or his interventions in favor of men (Dan 3:28; Ezra 7:27; Ruth 4:14ff). The shorter ones among them generally limit themselves to praise-affirmations but do not as yet have any particular type of conclusion. They usually appear as cultic acclamations.[12] The longer ones

[8] It also means a gift (Prov 11:25); a truce (II Kings 18:31; Is 36:16).

[9] The only other time it occurs in this sense is II Chron 20:26.

[10] *Die jüdische Gottesdienst*, p. 5.

[11] The presence of later elements in these texts as we now know them makes no difference to the argument. Cf. Mishna Tamid V, 1; Berakot II, 1; Elbogen, *Studien zur Geschichte des jüdischen Gottesdienstes* (Berlin 1907), p. 29; L. Blau, "Observations sur l'histoire du culte juif," *Revue des Etudes Juives* 73 (1921), 141.

[12] On the notion of "Acclamation" see E. Peterson, *EIS THEOS* (Göttingen 1926), p. 141ff; T. Klauser, "Akklamation," *Reallexikon für Antike und Christentum* I, 216–233.

usually pass over into petition, confession of sin, protestations of unworthiness and faithfulness, etc.[13] They terminate in different ways: 1 Chronicles 29:10ff ends with a *barukh*-acclamation but Nehemiah 9:6ff does not.

Among the shorter *berakoth* in the Old Testament, Nehemiah 9:5 contains the one most closely allied to the practices of the synagogue as we know them. After confession of sin and reading of the Law, the levites shout out a call to praise and this call is answered[14] by the acclamation "Blessed be thy glorious Name which is exalted above all blessing and praise." Thereafter Ezra commences a long prayer of praise, confession of sin, and petition. This prayer has no special introduction or conclusion.[15]

No doubt such short acclamations beginning with *barukh* were quite common in Palestinian Judaism at the time of Christ. A similar acclamation was the regular temple response of the people: "Blessed His Name, whose glorious kingdom is for ever and ever."[16] And it is probably from such acclamations that the Christian "doxology" developed.[17] In this sense it is perfectly acceptable to talk of the *berakah* as a forerunner of Christian prayer-forms. But it must be noted: these are one-sentence declaratory formulas, lacking both an explicit finite verb and, in most cases, any recital of what God has done for man. The affirmation is often extended into eternity by expressions such as "for ever and ever," and is answered by a response of at least an "Amen." Such acclamations have their proper setting in community worship, but as we see from their use in the epistles of Paul, doxologies were used also outside the liturgical assembly.

This *berakah*-doxology is something quite different from the "literary genre" which Audet calls a "benediction" and seems to be the forerunner of the Christian eucharistic prayer.[18] Among other things,

[13] See the summary in *Theologische Literaturzeitung* 83 (1958), 644–646, of a dissertation(Barbara Hornig, *Das Prosagebet der nachexilischen Literatur* (Leipzig 1937).

[14] The text does not say this. The acclamation may have been pronounced by the Levites themselves.

[15] Cf. Leon J. Leibrich, "The Impact of Nehemiah 9:5–37 on the Liturgy of the Synagogue," *Hebrew Union College Annual* 32 (1961), 227 237.

[16] Mishna Yoma IV, 2. This acclamation was reserved for the temple precincts; outside it was replaced by "Amen" (Talmud Ta'anit 16b).

[17] Compare Rom 9:5 and 11 Cor 11:31 with Rom 11:36 and Gal 9:5. See A. Stuiber, "Doxologie," *Reallexikon für Antike und Christentum* IV, 211.

[18] See J.-P. Audet, "Esquisse historique du genre littéraire de la Bénédiction juive et

it generally does not contain the "anamnesis" of the "mirabilia Dei" which he considers an essential feature. Audet's analysis cuts across the lines that distinguish prose and poetry and other literary forms in the Old and New Testaments, but selects in each of them only that which fits the pattern he describes. This is legitimate and useful for the sake of isolating the trends that will eventually crystalize into the fixed *berakah* of the Talmudic period, but it does not justify fitting all the praise formulas of the first century into a single mold. And, most important of all, it does not justify translating the word *eucharisteîn* as "to bless," which Audet does in his edition of the *Didache*. The fact is that there were numerous forms of praise being used in New Testament times and the verbs used often retained their particular nuances. Some, such as the "Nunc dimittis" of Simeon, used no special praise-verb at all. The one thing they all have in common is the basic notion of praise as a public proclamation of God's qualities or deeds in history, and this notion is quite sufficient to account for the elements of anamnesis often encountered.[19]

If we study just what it meant to praise and thank God in Jewish culture, I think we will find that the proclamation of the "mirabilia Dei" is essential to the very notion of praise. It is not just a matter of literary or cultic form. To praise God *meant* to tell his wonderful works. Praise was essentially a public act, and this fact is sufficient.

It is quite right to insist — and for this we can only be grateful to Audet — that the essential element in the body of our canon is the verbal recall of the basic events in salvation history (including that of creation).[20] It is quite right to appreciate the cultic forms assumed by this concept of praise in Judaism and early Christianity. But it is important to realize that Christians today can make public acknowledgment of a eucharistic faith that is essentially one with that of the apostles without necessarily having to do so according to a Jewish literary form. A truly contemporary eucharistic prayer might safely break away from the *berakah*. It could not cease to be an acknowledgment of gratitude.

de l'Eucharistie chrétienne," *Revue Biblique* 65 (1958), 371–399; *La Didache: Instruction des Apôtres* (Paris 1958), pp. 377–398.

[19] This element is not limited to praise formulas which are Jewish. It is also found in pagan "aretalogy" accounts. See G. Delling, *Worship in the New Testament* (Philadelphia 1962), p. 82.

[20] When speaking of "essential elements" one should also include the notion of epiclesis.

Robert J. Ledogar

Whatever one may think of gratitude as a religious sentiment, the fact that the central act of Christian worship is known as the eucharist and has been called that since very early times is inescapable. All the anaphoras of the church[21] begin with the invitation, "Let us give thanks." Basic to all this is the Greek word *eucharisteîn*, the meaning of which, despite claims to the contrary, is "to thank," or "to be thankful."

It is true that this Greek word, like many others, took on connotations when spoken by Jews that it did not have for Greeks. By being frequently associated with other more traditionally Jewish words for praise like "to bless" (*eulogeîn*), "to glorify" (*doxázein*), "to confess" (*exomologéomai*), its meaning was influenced by them. It did not, however, lose the meaning of thanksgiving which it had. It took on the connotation of a public testimony which was already common to these other words. Henceforth, in Jewish circles, it meant: to acknowledge one's gratitude before others.

The semitic languages did not have a word for gratitude or thanksgiving. They had to use more general words like "praise," "blessing," "confession," or else speak in sentences like, "What shall I return to the Lord for all he has given to me?" (Ps 116). They were certainly no more lacking in the sentiment of gratitude toward God than their Greek neighbors. Their language simply lacked the specific word, just like English lacks equivalents for the Spanish *simpatico*, the French *engagement*, or the German *Gemütlichkeit*. When Jews first began to translate their Bible into Greek they made very little use of the verb *eucharisteîn* for the good reason that it was not the equivalent of any Hebrew word. But when they began composing directly in Greek, as in Wisdom and Maccabees, they used the word just as the great Alexandrian Jew Philo used it, to signify thanksgiving. Later, under Greek influence, both Hebrew and Syriac developed their own compound words to express thanksgiving.

New Testament writers like Paul make frequent use of the word *eucharisteîn* and *eucharistía*, and in all cases the notion of thanksgiving or gratitude gives perfect sense to their translation. In cases like 1 Thessalonians 3:9 the context will admit of nothing else.

[21] One exception is the liturgy of the Nestorian Church. See J. M. Hanssens, *Institutiones liturgicae de ritibus orientalibus*, vol. 3 (Rome 1932), pp. 375ff. The present phrase, "This offering is being offered unto God the Lord of all," may well be a later replacement.

It is reasonable to suppose, though it cannot be proved, that by the time of Jesus the Greek-speaking Jews of the diaspora regularly used the word *eucharisteîn* instead of the more Hebraic *eulogeîn* when they said the blessing over bread at meals.[22] This makes very good sense, since the natural motive for words of praise spoken over one's food is gratitude. The Hebrew-speaking Jews "blessed" God for their bread simply because they did not have a specific word for thanks, and the more conservative Palestinian Jews preferred to retain the notion of blessing contained in the Greek word *eulogeîn*. That word had its advantages because one who "blessed God" before taking bread was also considered to have "blessed the bread"; indeed "nothing is to be rejected if it is received with thanksgiving; for then it is consecrated by the word of God and prayer" (1 Tim 4:4).

So it is that our eucharist is called the "thanksgiving" and not the "blessing" for the good reason that it has its origin in a formula that was essentially a thanksgiving.

That Jesus (or the apostles) may have improvised when pronouncing the blessing over the bread and may have added motives from salvation history, or *mirabilia Dei*, as Father Audet suggests, is quite possible. But these motives of praise can be perfectly well understood as motives of thanksgiving, since all the *mirabilia Dei* happened *for our salvation*. Everything for which we praise God in the eucharist, even the creation of the sun and moon and stars, is seen as having been done "for us men." Our response *must* be one of gratitude. That wonder or admiration should accompany this gratitude and draw us out of ourselves toward our creator and saviour "as he is in himself," is granted. But such wonder, such admiration, has its firmest basis in the discovery by faith of the marvel that is man. After all, God has been revealed to us not primarily as he is in himself, but in what he has done for us.

It is remarkable how often the phrase "for us" (*propter nos homines*) occurs in the most ancient eucharistic prayers. We find examples in the *Apostolic Tradition* of Hippolytus: "*Gratias tibi referimus deus per dilectum puerum tuum Iesum Christum, quem in ultimis temporibus misisti nobis salvatorem et redemptorem . . .*";[23] in the Syrian anaphora of

[22] Cf. Rom 14:6; 1 Cor 10:30; 1 Tim 4:3f; Philo, *Special Laws* II, 175.

[23] No. 4 (B. Botte, *La Tradition Apostolique de Saint Hippolyte, Essai de Reconstruction* [Muenster 1963], p. 12).

the apostles Addai and Mari: "And for all this wonderful dispensation *toward us*, we confess . . .";[24] in the anaphora of the Twelve Apostles: "And so, Lord, while we recall your salutary command and the whole of your economy which was established *for us* . . .";[25] and in the concluding doxology of another Syriac anaphora: ". . . so that in us, and for us, and because of us, your most honored and blessed name may be glorified and praised and magnified with that of Our Lord Jesus Christ, as it was. . . ."[26]

EUCHARIST AND OFFERTORY: HISTORICAL CONSIDERATIONS

If the original and fundamental spirit of the eucharistic anaphora is to be described in terms of admiration, it is difficult to see what specific relationship there is between the anaphora and the gifts over which it is said. The fact of the meal accounts for the presence of bread and wine upon the altar during the eucharistic prayer, but among all the motives of praise listed in the various ancient anaphoras, bread and wine are seldom if ever singled out for specific mention, even when the enumeration of the *mirabilia Dei* begins with the details of creation. When the anaphora alludes to the bread and wine it mentions them either in the institution narrative ("he took bread . . .") or in the anamnesis and epiclesis portions as *dona, sacrificia, prosphorá*.

This word *prosphérein* has been consistently linked with the eucharist ever since Clement of Rome said (c. 96 A.D.) that it was the bishop's office to "offer the gifts." And at least since the time of Hippolytus (early third century) it has been clearly used to refer to the gifts of bread and wine *prior to* their "consecration" in the anaphora.[27] It is very interesting that his *Apostolic Tradition* uses the words *offerre* and *oblatio* not only in reference to the eucharistic gifts but also in reference to the bread and the cup shared in the non-eucharistic community meal described in numbers 26 and 27 of that work.[28] Now it is precisely the notion of thanksgiving which links the action of offering with the proclamation of praise. We can see

[24] W. F. Macomber, "The Oldest Known Text of the Anaphora of the Apostles Addai and Mari," *Orientalia Christiana Periodica* 32 (1966), 335–371.

[25] *Anaphorae Syriacae* quotquot in codicibus adhuc repertae sunt cura Pontificii Instituti Studiorum Orientalium editae et latine versae, vol. I, fasc. 2 (Rome 1940), p. 219.

[26] *Ibid.*, p. 252.

[27] No. 20 & 21 (ed. Botte, pp. 45, 55).

[28] Cf. H. Lietzmann, *Mass and Lord's Supper*, trans. Dorothea H. G. Reeve (Leiden, n.d.), pp. 148–151.

this very clearly in the same *Apostolic Tradition* in a prayer prescribed for the bishop when the faithful bring to him the first-fruits of the harvest: "*Gratias tibi agimus, deus, et offerimus tibi primitiuas fructuum, quos dedisti nobis ad percipiendum. . . .*"[29] The gifts of bread and wine can be referred to as oblations or sacrifices or offerings even prior to the eucharistic prayer for the good reason that any food taken with grateful acknowledgment of its source is an offering to God. This means, it seems to me, that the offertory of the mass should be seen basically as a rite of thanksgiving.

Now we know that the offertory rite as such is, in its different forms, a somewhat secondary development in the history of the eucharist.[30] But if the fundamental spirit of the most primitive anaphoras is recognized to be one of thanksgiving, it is possible to understand the introduction of the offertory rite as a positive organic development. If not, it must appear to be a kind of relapse into pre-Christian ways.

The primitive church's grateful acknowledgment of all that God had done for us in Christ Jesus was concentrated on the event of the paschal mystery, the *Pascha Domini*. This, in a way, summed up everything. It was a marvelous, wonder-inspiring fact which happened *for us*. The Christian reponded in praise, a praise which arose from the consciousness of being the beneficiary of this event, and from the sense that this must be acknowledged.

There was at first a certain reluctance to relate any notion of "offering" to the eucharist. The second-century apologists repeatedly insist upon the futility of all offerings since God needs nothing and can be given nothing by man. And yet St. Justin himself (c. 135 A.D.) does speak of the gifts of bread and wine and does link their presence on the table to the motive of gratitude.[31] Already with Irenaeus (c. 185 A.D.) we see the possibility of offering God a material gift explicitly entertained, but only in terms of thanksgiving. Irenaeus understands the bread and wine which are brought for the eucharist to be representative of God's creation.[32] Man owes thanks

[29] No. 31 (ed. Botte, p. 76).

[30] See N. M. Denis-Boulet, "La liturgie eucharistique: L'offertoire," in *L'Eglise en Prière*, ed. A. G. Martimort, third edition (Paris 1965), pp. 370ff.

[31] Dial. 41, 1–3; 117 (J. Quasten, *Monumenta Eucharistica et Liturgica Vetustissima* [Bonn 1935–37], pp. 337ff.).

[32] *Adv. Haer.* IV, 17, 5 (*Sancti Irenaei Episcopi Lugdunensis libros quinque adversus Haereses*, ed. W. Wigan Harvey, vol. II, pp. 197f.).

for creation and rightly offers back the first fruits of creation, not as though God needed them, but as signs of his own gratitude.

There was no need to make this thanksgiving for creation explicit as long as the eucharist was celebrated in the context of the Jewish meal. The blessing or *berakah* pronounced over the bread and wine were themselves a thank-offering. The eucharistic recall of the paschal mystery was simply inserted into this thank-offering context. St. Justin makes this quite clear, even while avoiding the word "offering": "[You say that] prayers and thanksgivings accomplished by worthy persons are the only perfect and acceptable sacrifices to God. I say the same. For this alone is what Christians learned to do even in the *anamnesis* of their solid and liquid food, in which the passion which the Son of God suffered for them is also recalled."[33] As the relationship of the eucharist to the blessing at meals became less evident, the need to express the thank-offering context grew stronger. Irenaeus expressed it in the pithy phrase: *prosphéromen de autô ta ídia*: "We offer him that which is his."[34]

This phrase sounds very much like one which we find in the anamnesis of the Byzantine anaphoras of St. John Chrysostom and St. Basil as well as in the Alexandrian anaphoras of St. Basil and St. Mark. The phrase is *ta sa ek ton son dóron*, and is apparently taken from 1 Chronicles 29:14 where we read: *hoti sa ta pánta kai ek ton son dedókamén soi*. The context of this phrase is most enlightening. King David has gathered an enormous donation of materials for the construction of the temple and, apparently for the sake of forestalling any false pride in the greatness of their gift to God, acknowledges that what they have contributed is already God's own gift to them: "But who am I, and what is my people that we should be able thus to offer willingly? *For all things come from thee, and of thy own have we given thee*" (RSV). This collection of materials for the building of the temple thus becomes an acceptable free-will offering because it is acknowledged as gift. Any idea that the people should be giving to God something that he doesn't already have is ruled out, and it is ruled out precisely by the act of acknowledgment (in the form of a *berakah*).

The Roman liturgy expresses this same idea in the phrase *de tuis donis ac datis* of the *Unde et memores*. It expressed it in a way peculiar to its own culture. In contrast to the tradition of pagan inscriptions

[33] Dial. 117, 2–3 (Quasten, p. 338f).
[34] *Adv. Haer.* IV, 31, 3 (ed. Harvey II, p. 203).

which read *N. de suo fecit*, a Christian's monument is identified with the phrase *ex donis Dei*.[35] But the thought is the same: God, not man, gets the credit for whatever man has made, and in everything man does he must acknowledge the true source.

Now these phrases do not go back to the earliest eucharistic texts. They have no equivalent in Hippolytus or the *De Sacramentis* of Ambrose, nor in the anaphora of Addai and Mari, nor in the Syriac anaphora of the Twelve Apostles which represents an earlier stage of the anaphora of St. John Chrysostom. Such explicitly biblical phrases frequently turn out to be later additions to the eucharistic prayer, and such is the case here as well. But we can see how naturally the phrase fitted the context into which it was placed. The anamnesis of the Syriac anaphora of the Twelve Apostles concludes: "And we, Lord, with gratitude, praise you for all and on account of all. . . ."[36] The phrase "with gratitude" here translates the Syriac *kad mquabblinan taybutok*, which very literally means "receiving thy graciousness" and is comparable to the Greek *chárin échein*.[37] The fact that gratitude is the motive of praise could not be more clearly expressed.

Now it is precisely as a reworking of this passage in the anaphora of the Twelve Apostles that the expression *ta sa ek ton son* enters into the anaphora of St. John Chrysostom, where the anamnesis concludes: "For all this, and because of all this, offering to you gifts which are already your gifts to us, [People:] we praise you. . . ."[38] Here we see the offertory theme (*prosphérontes*) being inserted quite naturally into what is already a context of thanksgiving. It is simply a spelling-out of the earlier phrase "with gratitude we praise you."

The eucharistic prayer is an acknowledgment of gratitude offered to God in the context of a meal. This gratitude is primarily for man's deliverance from sin and death achieved by Jesus in his paschal mystery. But the context of this gratitude is itself one of gratitude for the elements of the thanksgiving meal. We first offer bread and wine in thanksgiving to acknowledge that the very elements used to celebrate our salvation are themselves gifts of God. This is the sense of the offertory as seen from the liturgical texts. It was originally

[35] See *Dictionnaire d'Archaeologie Chrétienne et Liturgie* IV, 1507–1510.

[36] *Anaphorae Syriacae* I, 219.

[37] C. Brockelmann, *Lexikon Syriacum*, second edition (Halle 1928), pp. 270, 641.

[38] F. E. Brightman, *Liturgies Eastern and Western*, Vol. I: *Eastern Liturgies* (Oxford 1896), p. 329.

implicit in the meal context out of which the eucharist developed. After the eucharist became completely separated from the meal, this thanksgiving aspect of the offertory was made explicit in the eucharistic prayer itself by simply drawing out what was virtually there already.

EUCHARIST AND OFFERTORY: THEOLOGICAL CONSIDERATIONS

The eucharist is a meal and a celebration, but it is also something which we *offer*. And it is not sufficient to say with St. Cyprian, "the passion is the Lord's sacrifice which we offer,"[39] because this does not explain the offering of bread and wine *for* the sacrifice. This offering of bread and wine can easily be exaggerated in a very Pelagian sense. But it need not be. Ignoring it, in any case, is no solution.

If we are to get away from the idea that at the offertory we place our little daily sacrifices on the paten and offer them up so that at the consecration Jesus can swoop down and make them part of his passion and death, we must give the offertory some other significance, secondary as this must be. I am suggesting here that it is fundamentally a thanksgiving for the gifts of creation or, better perhaps, an acknowledgment of the material universe as gift to man.

This means, of course, that the bread and wine are seen as symbolic realities prior to their transformation in the eucharistic blessing. What do they symbolize? They can symbolize a number of things according to the cultural context; but, precisely as the elements of a thanksgiving meal of discipleship, they signify that whatever man uses as sign and source of communion with God and his brothers is already God's gift to him. They signify, in other words, that everything is gift. Life is a gift, self is a gift, existence is a gift. We do not take all this for granted and look for salvation to come from somewhere outside the created order. We see and acknowledge "the goodness and kindness of God our Saviour" already in the universe at the root of matter itself, waiting to "come into the world" not as though from outside but as gradually manifested, as an epiphany.

Why could we not include the order of creation in an understanding of the eucharist that emphasizes admiration rather than thanksgiving? Certainly there is a note of admiration to our acknowledg-

[39] Epist. 63, 17 (*PL* 4, 387).

ment, but I think it is important to specify that Christians look upon creation not just as an objective reality in itself but as an anthropological reality. Creation is for man and has meaning precisely in its relation to man. He can view it correctly only if he sees it as a gift of God to him. And therefore his attitude must be one of thanksgiving.

There are two modern approaches to the eucharist which, it seems to me, stand or fall upon this anthropocentric view of creation. One is that of Teilhard de Chardin.[40] "It is first by the Incarnation and next by the Eucharist that (Christ) organizes us for himself and imposes himself upon us. . . . Although he has come above all for souls, uniquely for souls, he could not join them together and bring them to life without assuming and animating along with them all the rest of the world. By his Incarnation he inserted himself not just into humanity but into the universe which supports humanity, and he did so not simply as another connected element, but with the dignity and function of a directing principle, of a Centre towards which everything converges in harmony and in love."[41] The relationship of Christ to the evolving universe, in the vision of Teilhard, is possible because this universe exists for, and culminates in, man. "As our humanity assimilates the material world, and as the Host assimilates our humanity, the Eucharistic transformation goes beyond and completes the transubstantiation of the bread on the altar. . . ."[42] Such a perspective must see the bread and wine as anthropocentric realities and must treat them not merely with admiration but, as gifts, with gratitude.

In similar fashion the notion of gratitude is essential to that personalist approach which speaks of the eucharistic transformation as "transignification" or "transfinalization." For if there is to be a transignification of bread and wine, these elements must have a signification to start with, and that initial signification must come from their relationship to man.

Again, it is possible to view all creation as a sign of the grandeur, splendor, wisdom, and goodness of God and to respond to it by an attitude of wonder and admiration. But then we are caught wondering what special merit there is to bread and wine as signs of these divine qualities and as sources of wonder. As food, on the other

[40] See Christopher Mooney, *Teilhard de Chardin and the Mystery of Christ* (New York 1966).

[41] *La Vie cosmique,* 1916. As translated in Mooney, p. 70f.

[42] *The Divine Milieu* (New York 1960), p. 104.

hand, they make sense precisely in their relationship to man who eats them.[43]

The eucharistic gifts of bread and wine are fundamentally (and, yes, ontologically) transformed in their signification or finality precisely because they already are gifts which man receives with gratitude, because they are seen by him already as signs of the creator's concern for man. This is why the eucharistic anaphora grew so naturally out of the *berakah* spoken over the bread and cup at the Jewish meal. The Christian faith of the eucharistic assembly, embodied in that act of praise which is the eucharistic prayer, transposes this signification to a higher level so that these elements of bread and wine relate to man in an entirely new way, no longer merely as gifts of the creator but as the Saviour's gift of his own flesh and blood unto eternal life.

It seems that historians and theologians will not get together on their way of talking about the eucharist unless both recognize a place for the offertory as an act of thanksgiving, as precisely the equivalent of the thanksgiving-blessing at the meal, which was the original setting of the eucharistic prayer.

Bread and wine of themselves are just bread and wine. Bread and wine over which thanks is offered become signs. They must first become signs of God's presence in the universe and his ordering of it toward man before they become signs of his self-emptying, redeeming love for man. This double signification is given to the elements by the community's act of acknowledgement. In the first instance it acknowledges bread and wine as gifts by the gesture of the offertory. In the second it acknowledges them as signs of the paschal mystery by the eucharistic anaphora. This concords well with Hippolytus' description of the eucharist celebrated at baptism: "Then the *oblatio* will be presented by the deacons to the bishop and he will give thanks, over the bread that it might be the symbol of the Body of Christ, over the cup of mixed wine that it might be the image of the blood which was poured out for all those who believe in him."[44]

Jesus does not "come down upon" the altar at the utterance of a magic word to change one chemical substance into another. He, the Christ, in whom and for whom all things were created, is radically present to the entire universe as its ultimate fulfilment. Creation is a

[43] Cf. *ST* III, 60, 2 ad 1.

[44] No. 21 (ed. Botte, p. 54).

part of salvation history. Faith enables the Christian to recognize this finality in creation. Bread and wine are chosen and presented as signs by which we publicly acknowledge our vision of this finality in creation, this being-for-man and ultimately being-for-Christ.

Jesus does not "come down upon" the altar at the consecration precisely because he is already present. Jesus is progressively manifested at the eucharist through the acknowledgment of his saving presence in the act of praise. This *manifestation* is a true *becoming* just as the incarnation was, just as the manifestation of a man's fundamental self in a moment of heroic crisis leaves that man a changed person. The gifts of creation become the material of Christ's life-giving sacrifice because that is the only thing which ultimately gives them any meaning. They become what they are.

Is this not double-talk, "becoming what they are"? Here we touch upon the mysterious transforming power of faith. If there is a finality to what exists and if the consummation of that finality is the risen Lord, then faith is the "pull" exercised by him not only upon our minds but upon the material universe which has being for our sakes. This faith is not just the faith of the individual participant; it is the faith of the whole church as shared in by the assembled members of the community. "It is in the church's sacramental confession of faith," says Schillebeeckx, "that the risen Christ can make an earthly element or a human action into a sacramentally visible manifestation of his heavenly act of salvation."[45] We need only add that this "sacramental confession of faith" is a "confession of praise" or an acknowledgment-in-fath.

This concept of manifestation is strong in the epicleses of the Syrian tradition. The liturgy of the *Apostolic Constitutions* prays: "Send your Holy Spirit upon this sacrifice, the witness of the sufferings of the Lord Jesus, that he might show (*apophaínein*) this bread to be the Body of your Christ and this cup to the Blood of your Christ. . . ."[46] The epiclesis of the Syriac anaphora of the Twelve Apostles is much the same, and the Byzantine Liturgy of St. Basil shows the trace of a similar notion using the word *anadeîknymi*.[47]

This manifestation of the Lord takes place on a number of levels. The Lord of creation is manifested in the gifts. The same Lord is

[45] E. Schillebeeckx, *Christ the Sacrament of the Encounter with God* (New York 1963), p. 99.

[46] VIII 12, 38–39 (Quasten, *Monumenta*, pp. 45f).

[47] Brightman, *Eastern Liturgies*, p. 329.

present in the faith-lives of the participating members. He it is who, through his Spirit, enables them to "offer spiritual sacrifices" or "spiritual service" in their day-to-day witness of God's saving love to the world.[48] This Spirit-filled living becomes manifest in the community through the "sacrifice of praise," which recalls to the faith of all that it is the Lord's paschal mystery which is the prototype and source of all Spirit-filled living. This faith that proclaims and acknowledges the victory of Jesus over death is itself the work of the Holy Spirit, so that "in all" Christ alone is the person acting, the one offering sacrifice, the one whose paschal mystery is accomplished in each celebration. Through him all grace comes to us; through him, in the Spirit, all glory is given to God.

All of this makes some kind of sense when we speak of the eucharist as "thanksgiving" or public acknowledgment of gratitude. Father Audet says that where gratitude dominates there is a "preoccupation with self and, at best, appreciation of the other for the benefit he can bring," whereas "where admiration is predominant there is a going-out of oneself and, at best, movement toward the other as he is in himself." I would suggest that God is not merely an "other" outside of man, and that only when man truly looks to himself in faith and acknowledges with his whole being what he sees in his whole being will he come to a true admiration of God as a transcendence that is his to share.

[48] 1 Pet 2:5. Cf. J. H. Eliot, *The Elect and the Holy* (Leiden 1966); Rom 12:1. Cf. P. Seidensticker, *Lebendiges Opfer* (Muenster 1954).

Thomas J. Talley

From *Berakah* to *Eucharistia*: A Reopening Question

One of my earliest encounters with serious liturgiological study came in the summer of 1949, the summer following my first year in seminary. Then, under a blazing Texas sky, I gathered with an enthusiastic crowd of clergy and laity at a summer camp in the diocese of Dallas to hear a series of lectures by Dom Gregory Dix whose "fat green book," as he loved to call it, had appeared four years earlier.[1] I can still remember (verbatim, it seems) his opening sentence: "Our understanding of our forms of worship underwent a radical transformation some forty years ago when it finally occurred to someone that Jesus was a Jew."

Certainly, it cannot be said that the years since then have lost sight of that fact. Indeed, one may say that studies in the early eucharistic prayer in recent years have been dominated by the consideration of the relation of that central Christian cult act to Jewish liturgical tradition, especially as that tradition manifested itself in table prayers and in the liturgy of the synagogue. More particularly, research has focused on the relation of the eucharistic prayer to that prayer form which has been identified as the structural unit of Jewish euchology, its *Grundform* (to use Elbogen's term[2]), viz., the *berakah* or "benediction." Signalled already by the third of Dr. Frank Gavin's lectures on *The Jewish Antecedents of the Christian Sacraments*[3] delivered at the S.P.C.K. House in London in September 1927, fascination with the *berakah* as parent of the eucharistic prayer received new and stronger impetus from an essay of Jean-Paul Audet read before the International Congress on the Four Gospels held at Oxford in 1957.[4]

[1] Gregory Dix, *The Shape of the Liturgy* (London 1945).

[2] Ismar Elbogen, *Der jüdische Gottesdienst in seiner geschichtlichen Entwicklung* (Frankfurt am Main 1931) 4.

[3] F. Gavin, *The Jewish Antecedents of the Christian Sacraments* (London 1928) 59–114.

[4] J.-P. Audet, "Literary Forms and Contents of a Normal *Eucharistia* in the First Century," *Studia Evangelica*. Paper presented to the International Congress on "The

Audet sought to examine the broad literary genre of the *berakah* rather than to examine particular *berakoth* in Jewish liturgy. Nonetheless, he accepted as the starting point for his thesis the established regulations for the form of the *berakah* set forth in the third century A.D. by the Amoraim. He presents these regulations, however, only in part and without careful examination of particular examples, and especially without examining these benedictions in the liturgical groupings in which they are most significantly encountered. This limitation of evidence was consistent with Audet's purpose which was to consider the benediction as a genre, the sort of consideration which virtually requires generalization.

Audet describes the two well-known forms of the *berakah* as these were seen by the Amoraim, but in so doing he uses a terminology which is, to one degree or another, his own. The short form consists of two parts: [1] the *baruch* formula — "blessed art Thou, JHWH, our God, King of the Universe," — and [2] the briefly stated and variable body of the prayer which gives the particular motive of the praise. This short form he wishes to designate "spontaneous," although a great many are found in the liturgy. It is the longer form that Audet wishes to call "cultual," a form which he describes as follows: "[a] the 'benediction' proper, always rather short, more or less stereotyped in its form, leaning toward the invitatory genre, an enthusiastic call to divine praise; [b] a central element which I would call the anamnesis of the *mirabilia Dei* . . . a more or less protracted development of the motive as it already existed in the original spontaneous 'benediction'; its proper object, thus, is much less the transient 'wonder' of a particular circumstance . . . than the permanent and universal 'wonder' as perceived and remembered . . . above all by the conscience of the community itself . . . ; [c] lastly, the return of the initial 'benediction' by way of *inclusio*, or doxology, oftentimes colored in different shades according to the particular theme which prevails in the anamnesis."[5]

For the actual phraseology of the "benediction proper" as encountered in Christian texts, Audet treats three Greek verbs as being

Four Gospels" held at Christ Church, Oxford 1957, Texte u. Untersuchungen 73 (Berlin 1959) 643–662. [An expanded version of the essay appeared in *Revue Biblique* 65 (1958) 371–399.]

[5] *Ibid.*, 646.

equivalent to *barak: eulogein, exomologeisthai,* and *eucharistein*. The first of these is, of course, the normal rendering of "to bless" and is thus immediately equivalent to *barak.* Audet's treatment of the other two as equally equivalent to *barak* raises serious problems, however. It is true that these and still other Greek verbs belong to a genre of praise. The difficulty comes in moving from such a broad genre to the precisions of the constitution of the *berakoth*, precisions which were, at least in part, already established in the time of Christ.

Although Audet's essay was accorded wide and positive or even enthusiastic reception, a reaction to its problems appeared in the thesis presented by Robert Ledogar to the *Institut Supérieur de Liturgie* at Paris in 1964, the eighth chapter of which is given to praise verbs in rabbinic literature. There Ledogar wrote: "Before bringing this chapter to a close we must give consideration to what everyone these days is calling 'the berakah.' It is difficult to discover just what this or that author means when he uses this term."[6] Noting that the term could mean any formula whose principal verb is *barak*, or could, at the other extreme, refer to the formulae ruled by the precise patterns laid down by the Amoraim in the third century, he concludes that while little can be said about the *berakah* in general in the New Testament period, there is a probability that Christian doxological forms grow out of the one sentence declarative *baruch* formularies common in Palestinian Judaism. He then adds: "This berakah-doxology is something quite different from the 'literary genre' which Père J. P. Audet calls a 'Benediction' and sees to be the forerunner of the Christian Eucharistic Prayer. Among other things, it generally does not contain the 'anamnesis' of the 'mirabilia Dei' which he considers an essential feature. . . . And, most important of all, it does not justify translating the word *eucharistein* as 'to bless.'"[7]

Ledogar's thesis is a splendid treatment of its proper subject, *Praise Verbs in the Early Greek Anaphora*, but as the first of these two quotations from it reveals, his treatment of the position of Audet and those who have followed him really was incidental to his purpose. He did not find it to his point to examine in detail the findings of Jewish liturgiology. While serious use of those findings must be

[6] Robert J. Ledogar, *Acknowledgment: Praise Verbs in the Early Greek Anaphoras* (Rome 1968) 121.

[7] *Ibid.*, 124.

left to those more qualified than I, it would seem that this matter of the role of the *berakah* (or, better, the *berakoth*) in shaping the Christian anaphora has achieved a sufficient prominence in our recent literature to require some closer examination. With some temerity, therefore, it seems necessary to make at least a few observations.

BERAKOTH IN SERIES

My own rather extensive dissatisfaction with Audet's position flows from the very nature of his intention, and is twofold: [1] he focuses all attention on the interior structure of a single and artificial *berakah* and thus misses the relations of real *berakoth* to one another (a procedure which strikes me as somewhat analogous to seeking to explain the structure of a Gelasian mass from a description of the interior structure of a single collect); [2] this same fault, when compounded by the identification of significantly different Greek verbs with the "benediction proper," the *baruch* formula, has the effect of not only ignoring the relations between *berakoth* but of actually obscuring them. Specifically, it obscures relations that are important for our immediate concern, those between *barak* forms and *yadah* forms, between blessing and thanksgiving. We will suggest, on the contrary, that it is at least possible that it is the relation of Jewish prayers to one another that *produces* (around the time of the fall of Jerusalem) the pattern of that individual *berakah* described by Audet.

While it may prove necessary to refer to other groups of *berakoth*, I would like to focus especially upon that group whose influence on the eucharistic prayer is most frequently urged, the grace after meals, *Birkat Ha-Mazon*. Of this group of prayers, Louis Finkelstein wrote: "In the liturgical service of the Jewish home it occupies much the same outstanding position that the *Amidah* holds in the synagogue service. Together these prayers helped to make possible the continuance of a full and complete Jewish life after the destruction of Jerusalem."[8]

Before examining this particular group of prayers, however, some general definitions derived from the third century regulations may prove helpful, though it must be borne in mind that here (as in most matters liturgical) exceptions can be found. First of all, as has already been mentioned, the short *berakah* consists of a benediction of

[8] Louis Finkelstein, "The Birkat Ha-Mazon," *Jewish Quarterly Review* 19 (1928–29) 212.

God for or with regard to some particular motive. It must begin with "blessed" and, for the Amoraim, must name God and refer to his Kingdom. While this latter requirement remained fluid longer than the others, the standard form for the Amoraim was nonetheless: *baruch atta JHWH Elohenu Melek ha-olam*, "blessed art Thou, O Lord, our God, King of the universe." To this is attached, most frequently as a relative clause, the motive, e.g., "who hast not made me a slave," or, "who hast sanctified us by Thy commandments and commanded us to wrap ourselves in the fringed garment."

If, however, this motive becomes extended into a longer praise, the *berakah* must take the long form, which means that it must also end with "blessed." What this actually entails is that another short *berakah* with a somewhat simpler and perhaps more primitive *baruch* phrase and a summary, brief motive is appended to the extended motive of the original. This short concluding *berakah* is what Audet calls the "doxology," but Jewish liturgiologists today usually call it the *chatimah*, "seal." We will be concerned to examine its function more closely in a moment.

What Audet neglected to consider is that when a number of *berakoth* occur in series, only the first begins with *baruch*, but all conclude with a *chatimah*. In the case of those after the first, therefore, this concluding *chatimah* is the only occurrence of the *baruch* formula, and thus is that by virtue of which the prayer can be called a *berakah*. This leads to a tolerable but persistent ambiguity in the meaning of *berakah*: it can mean a formula which begins with *baruch*; or a formula which, joined to one which begins with *baruch*, concludes with a *chatimah*; or the concluding *chatimah* itself (since, of course, it begins with *baruch*). These complex distinctions can be illustrated (and, it is hoped, made more clear) in the example of *Birkat Ha-Mazon*.

BIRKAT HA-MAZON

Although the *Mishna* speaks of a grace after meals of only three benedictions, the tractate *Berakoth* of the Babylonian Talmud already knows the four whose text is given in one form or another by the *siddurim* (prayer books or *ordines*) of the ninth and tenth centuries. The fourth of these, according to R. Nachman (b. Berakoth 48b), was added only in A.D. 132, but Louis Finkelstein gives reason for believing that it might have been somewhat earlier in the second century.[9]

[9] *Ibid.*, 215–216.

This would emphasize still more strongly the antiquity ascribed by Nachman to the other three. Along with his candor about the late institution of the fourth benediction, he says that the first was instituted by Moses at the feeding with manna, the second by Joshua when they entered the land, and the third by David, with Solomon supplying the reference to the temple. This same supposition of great antiquity is indicated by the grace after eating which the author of the *Book of Jubilees*, around 100 B.C., ascribes to Abraham:

"5. And Isaac, too, sent by the hand of Jacob to Abraham a best thank-offering, that he might eat and drink. 6. And he ate and drank, and blessed the Most High God, Who hath created heaven and earth, Who hath made all the fat things of the earth, and given them to the children of men that they might eat and drink and bless their Creator. 7. 'And now I give thanks unto Thee, my God, because Thou hast caused me to see this day: behold, I am one hundred three score and fifteen years, an old man and full of days, and all my days have been unto me peace. 8. The sword of the adversary has not overcome me in all that Thou hast given me and my children all the days of my life until this day. 9. My God, may Thy mercy and Thy peace be upon Thy servant, and upon the seed of his sons, that they may be to Thee a chosen nation and an inheritance from henceforth unto all the days of the generations of the earth, unto all the ages.'"[10]

While the content of these prayers has required serious alteration to avoid obvious anachronism in the second and third pericopes (the equivalent to the benediction for the land in verses 7–8 and that to the benediction for Jerusalem in verse 9), the three prayers of Abraham's grace are nonetheless the same forms as those found in the traditional Birkat Ha-Mazon, viz., a benediction (in the strict sense), a thanksgiving, and a supplication. A formal difference, and a significant one, is that these prayers in *Jubilees* lack the concluding *chatimah*. This poses a question regarding the use of the *chatimah* in 100 B.C. As we shall see, there is further reason to doubt that the author of *Jubilees* would have known of a *chatimah* attached to the opening *berakah* at least.

While the *seder* of R. Amram, the ninth century Gaon of Sura, is

[10] R. H. Charles, ed., *The Book of Jubilees or The Little Genesis* (London 1902) 138. [Ch. xxii, vv. 5–9.]

the earliest document to give us the text of *Birkat Ha-Mazon*,[11] this Babylonian version has undergone more expansive development than the shorter text preserved in the *seder* of R. Saadia from the following century. Finkelstein's critical study has shown this latter to be nearer the early Palestinian version, and it is this that we reproduce here in Finkelstein's translation.[12]

"I. Blessed art Thou, O Lord, our God, King of the Universe, Who feedest the whole world with goodness, with grace, and with mercy. Blessed art Thou, O Lord, Who feedest all.

II. We thank Thee, O Lord, our God, that Thou hast caused us to inherit a goodly and pleasant land, the covenant, the Torah, life and food. For all these things we thank Thee and praise Thy name for ever and ever. Blessed art Thou, O Lord, for the land and for the food.

III. Have mercy, O Lord, our God, on Thy people Israel, and on Thy city Jerusalem, and on Thy Temple and Thy dwelling-place and on Zion Thy resting-place, and on the great and holy sanctuary over which Thy name was called, and the kingdom of the dynasty of David mayest Thou restore to its place in our days, and build Jerusalem soon. Blessed are Thou, O Lord, who buildest Jerusalem."

As can be seen clearly, only the first of the three pericopes begins with what Audet called, "the 'benediction' proper." This first part extends the opening "blessed" (*baruch*) through the reference to the Kingdom required by the Talmud (b. Ber. 40b). There follows the motive for the benediction, "who feedest the world with goodness," etc. It is this part of the *berakah*, variable according to function or cultic context, that Audet wishes to call, "anamnesis of the *mirabilia Dei*." In this instance such a designation seems appropriate enough, although it would be a rather elaborate one for so modest a phrase. It would be quite inapplicable, however, to such a supplication as the final pericope of the present group.

After this motive, the pericope closes with the *chatimah* which is but a short-form *berakah*. Finkelstein's careful analysis of this whole initial benediction, however, has convinced him that much of the development it received in the Tannaitic period was by way of enlargement rather than refinement. Indeed, he believes that this, like the opening *berakah* of the *Amidah*, was but a short form *berakah* prior to the

[11] David Hedegård, *Seder R. Amram Gaon* (Lund 1951) 147–148.

[12] Finkelstein (n. 8 above) 215–216.

destruction of the temple. While his note is somewhat more guarded with respect to the first benediction before *Shema* in the morning and evening services, he still offers the general opinion that prior to the destruction of A.D. 70 (i.e., prior to the period of the Tannaim) all "benedictions" which begin with *baruch* were short-form *berakoth*, and thus lacked the *chatimah*.[13] In such a case, the *chatimah* would have been a feature only of those prayers which did not begin with *baruch* and were joined to one which did. Thus, rather than being a purely formal return to the opening theme (such as we see in a dance movement's return to the opening scherzo after the trio), the *chatimah* would seem to have the function of making *berakoth* of prayers that otherwise would not be. It is this which accounts for the ambiguity referred to above. The *berakah* in the strict sense always begins with *baruch*, but when it is affixed to the end of some other sort of prayer, such as a thanksgiving, the entire pericope comes to be known as *berakah*. Remembering the complete absence of the *chatimoth* from the grace of Abraham in *Jubilees*, one might conjecture that it is in the century or two before the destruction of Jerusalem that the *berakah* achieves its dominance as the *Grundform* of Jewish euchology, and that the assimilation of other prayer forms to the *berakah* through the addition of the *chatimah* is an index to that development, a development which is finally completed by the addition of the *chatimah* to the *berakah* itself, evidently from the beginning of the Tannaitic period. Such an interpretation of the age and function of the *chatimah* seems to be consistent with its particular formal characteristics: it lacks the reference to the Kingdom which was still a matter of controversy in the early third century, while it is much more consistent in the use of the tetragrammaton than are some of the very ancient *berakoth*.[14]

However this may be, if Finkelstein is right about the absence of the *chatimah* from the first pericope of *Birkat Ha-Mazon* before the fall of Jerusalem, then there could have been at the institution of the eucharist no such "cultual benediction" as Audet describes. The initial *berakah*, being a short form, could not have received such an expanded "anamnesis of the *mirabilia Dei*" as he envisages. That expansion appropriate to the immediate situation (which, with Audet,

[13] *Ibid.*, 227 and n. 36.

[14] Louis Finkelstein, "The Development of the Amidah," *Jewish Quarterly Review* 16 (1925–1926) esp. pp. 3ff.

I would expect) could only come in the second pericope, the thanksgiving.

This second pericope opens with *nodeh lekah*, "we thank Thee." Here, more richly than in the opening *berakah*, the body of the prayer refers to the *mirabilia Dei*, but now especially to God's redemptive action rather than to creation. There are many indications that this prayer would have been quite alive and flexible in its content in our Lord's time. The Talmud records some of the additions, and a comparison of the texts of Saadia and Amram show that such development continued in the Gaonic period. Indeed, this prayer receives regularized embolisms on Purim and Chanukah. A further indication of such frequent expansion of the body of the thanksgiving is the rule, attributed to Rab (third century), that there must be a return to the theme of thanksgiving before the *chatimah*, implying that the body of the prayer was becoming so developed as to wander from the basic thanksgiving mode. The *chatimah* of the thanksgiving pericope is called *Birkat Ha-Aretz*, a name that is commonly used today to refer to the entire thanksgiving.

The original series concluded with the supplication for Jerusalem. As was mentioned above, it is difficult to see in what sense such a supplication could qualify as that "anamnesis of the *mirabilia Dei*" which Audet took to be an essential feature of every *berakah*. Remembrance in quite a different sense does figure in the embolism inserted into this supplication on festivals, but this is again a supplication that God will remember us, not a praise which remembers God's acts.[15] Of such praise there is in this third pericope only the *chatimah, Birkat Ha-Yerushalayim*, which is again commonly used to refer to the entire prayer.

THE BERAKOTH AT THE LAST SUPPER

Such, then, is the *Birkat Ha-Mazon* whose structure has proved so suggestive for many students of Christian eucharistic texts. What is most suggestive is the blessing-thanksgiving-supplication pattern of the series, a pattern quite different from the blessing-anamnesis-doxology structure which Audet saw in his single ideal *berakah*. While Audet and those who have followed him in taking *eucharistia* as translation of *berakah* have been unable to take adequate account

[15] As will be noted below, the anamnesis in the third *gehanta* of the Maronite *sharar* will perhaps connect with this supplication for divine remembrance, but nothing of that sort is evident in the festal embolism in *Birkat Ha-Yerushalayim*.

of the difference between the initial benediction and the following thanksgiving, it should be remembered that Audet was only expanding here upon an existing tradition which had long sought to identify *eulogein* and *eucharistein*. Karl Völker in 1927 had disposed of the two words as *beide identisch*, evidently thinking of the occurrence of the former (*eulogēsas*) in reference to the bread and the latter (*eucharistēsas*) in reference to the cup in the first two synoptic accounts of the supper.[16] Having taken a closer look at *Birkat Ha-Mazon*, however, we are in a better position to appreciate the precision of the Marcan and Matthean narratives. Over the bread our Lord recites an *eulogia* (or, as the Peshitta says, *barek*), i.e., the short *berakah* still prescribed. But over the cup at the conclusion of the meal, having recited another probably short *berakah*, he entered upon that prayer which distinguished the grace after meals from the simple benediction before, the prayer which could accept (as the short *berakah* could not) the expansion — yes, the anamnesis of the *mirabilia Dei* — demanded by that most pregnant moment of their common life and ours, and in that prayer, whose opening *yadah* verb proved determinative for Paul and Luke and Justin and the entire tradition, *he gave thanks*.

In the Tannaitic period the entire *Birkat Ha-Mazon* underwent significant development: the probably very early extension of the first *berakah* to the long form, the enrichment of the body of *Birkat Ha-Aretz*, but especially the addition (Finkelstein thinks before A.D. 132) of a fourth pericope which, interestingly, begins with *baruch* but does not conclude with a *chatimah*, although an attempt was made to add one and so to bring this new *berakah* into conformity with the accepted structure by R. Jose the Galilean.[17] The major alteration to the pattern itself made by this added pericope suggests that it was a very early form of *Birkat Ha-Mazon* which would have affected very early Christian prayers, of which — in spite of all the problems of dating — we must regard the prayers of *Didache* as examples.

THE REORGANIZATION OF THE GRACE IN DIDACHE

At the important liturgical week of the Institut Saint-Serge in 1965, the papers of which were published in 1970 as volumes 46 and 47 of Lex Orandi under the title *Eucharisties d'Orient et d'Occident*, Dr. Willi

[16] Karl Völker, *Mysterium and Agape* (Gotha 1927) 21, n. 2.

[17] See n. 13 above.

Rordorf argues, following Audet and a prestigious company including Baumstark,[18] that these prayers of *Didache* 9 and 10, which seem to frame a meal, cannot be such a true eucharist as that sacrificial action referred to in chapter 14. What he regards as the decisive point of his argument is the "close link" which can be seen between the prayers of *Didache* 10 and *Birkat Ha-Mazon*, a link which, he says, "can be explained only by a direct and consciously accepted relation."[19] It is to that relation that we must now direct our attention.

While this similarity of *Didache* 10 to the Jewish grace had been noted already by Kohler in *Jewish Encyclopedia*,[20] the comparison received its first close examination in Louis Finkelstein's magisterial essay on *Birkat Ha-Mazon* in 1929.[21] Presenting the two texts in parallel columns, he did not neglect to take note of the Didachist's inversion of the order of the first two pericopes, although he did not comment on the structural consequence, viz., that it is with the thanksgiving — *Didache*'s equivalent to the *nodeh lekah* of the *Birkat Ha-Aretz* — that the grace begins. "We give thanks to thee, O Holy Father, for thy Holy Name which thou didst make to tabernacle in our hearts, and for the knowledge and faith and immortality which thou didst make known to us through Jesus thy Child. To thee be glory forever."[22] The text then proceeds to the second prayer which, like the opening *berakah* of the Jewish grace, is concerned with God as Creator and with his gift of food. It needs to be noted here, however, that the *baruch* formula has been dropped now that it is no longer the opening *berakah*. Indeed, even the act of pure praise in the last line before the doxology is expressed by *eucharistein*. "Thou, Lord Almighty, didst create all things for thy Name's sake, and didst give food and drink to men for their enjoyment, that they might give thanks to thee, but us hast thou blessed with spiritual food and drink and eternal light through thy Child. Above all we give thanks to thee for that thou art mighty. To thee be glory forever."

[18] W. Rordorf, "Les prières eucharistiques de la Didachè," *Eucharisties d'Orient et d'Occident* I (Lex Orandi 46) 65–82. Cf. Audet, *La Didachè: Instructions des Apôtres* (Paris 1958) 372–433; A. Baumstark, *Comparative Liturgy* (Westminster, Maryland 1958) 46.

[19] Rordorf (n. 18 above) 73

[20] *Jewish Encyclopedia* IV, 587, *s.v.* "Didache."

[21] See n. 8 above.

[22] *Didache* 10.2ff. The translation is that of K. Lake, *The Apostolic Fathers* I (Loeb Classical Library) 323ff.

A view of these first two prayers together gives the effect of two thanksgivings or even of one thanksgiving articulated by doxologies at the middle and at the end. The last of the prayers, however, is still a supplication. In interesting parallel to the supplication for the people Israel and for the building of Jerusalem it prays for the building of the Church, but includes the remembrance theme reminiscent of the embolism for feasts in *Birkat Ha-Yerushalayim*. "Remember, Lord, thy Church, to deliver it from all evil and to make it perfect in thy love, and gather it together in its holiness from the four winds to thy kingdom which thou hast prepared for it. For thine is the power and the glory for ever."

Finkelstein, in commenting on the strong similarities between these texts and the Jewish grace, addressed himself especially to the Christian "spiritualization" of the originals: the substitution of spiritual food and drink for physical, of the Name for the land, and of the Church for Jerusalem and the temple.[23] Beyond these differences, however, two Christian deviations from the structure of the established text should be noted.

First, there is the deliberate inversion of the first two prayers and thus the violation of the rule that the grace must begin with *baruch*. The supposed translation of *berakah* by *eucharistia* cannot even be urged in this case. What is in question here is not a translation of the opening phrase of the *berakah*, but the displacement of the entire pericope in favor of the second, the thanksgiving of the Jewish series. Further, even when the parallel to the first Jewish *berakah* is inserted in second place after the thanksgiving, it is stripped of the language of benediction, and the praise of God as he is in himself is expressed again as thanksgiving.

Second, there is no concluding benediction or *chatimah*. This closing *berakah* is, we have argued, one of the more significant elements in the welter of structural problems encountered in the Jewish liturgy prior to the codification of the rules by the Amoraim. Audet wishes to call this short benediction a doxology, and Finkelstein at times uses the same term (though at other times he more precisely, it seems, calls it the "eulogy"). In any case, the *chatimah* has clearly become a doxology in the strict sense in *Didache* 10: *soi hē doxa eis tous aiōnas*. While this is clearly meant to take the place of the *chatimoth*, the difference is one of structure, not merely a variant translation.

[23] Finkelstein (n. 8 above) 214.

Here, to be sure, we see the pure praise of God without the note of subjective response which characterizes thanksgiving, but there is again the formal deviation of the omission of any motive such as is found in the *chatimah* as in other short *berakoth*. "To thee be glory for ever" is a doxology. It is not a *chatimah* because it is not a *berakah*. Nor, on the other hand, does it have the function of reiterating the original praise word, *eucharistein*; rather, it introduces a new one, *doxa*.

THE PRIORITY OF THANKSGIVING

Such an analysis suggests that while the Jewish tradition is fundamental for primitive Christianity, the practices of the early Church reflect a pattern which is as meticulously different from as it is broadly grounded upon that Jewish tradition. In this respect, *Didache* 10 is not different from *Didache* 8: "Let not your fasts be with the hypocrites, for they fast on Mondays and Thursdays, but do you fast on Wednesdays and Fridays." The Monday and Thursday fasts of pious Jews had the virtue of being as far as possible from one another while taking care to leave a day free from special obligation before the sabbath and following it. Given the centrality of Sunday in the Christian time pattern, if one wished to keep two fast days in the week, it would not be surprising to find an analogous arrangement, fasts on Tuesdays and Fridays. But that is not what we find. The Friday is, of course, easily recognizable as the day of our Lord's passion, but the Wednesday fast seemed for a long time to represent nothing other than a cantankerous Christian insistence on being different from the Jews. While this problem of the choice of Wednesday as one of the primitive stations remains a real one, the problem has at least taken on a different complexion since the recovery of the liturgical calendar of Qumran with its peculiar focus on Sundays, Wednesdays, and Fridays as the only days of liturgical significance.[24] As what seemed in this case to be a senseless difference now presents itself as an intriguing similarity, can we hope to gain from the patterns of difference from the *berakah* tradition insights as helpful as those we have gained from appreciation of the similarities? And are there new similarities to be found in other directions?

While we are, in all likelihood, far from having finished examining the relation of Christian forms to those of the Jewish synagogue and

[24] See A. Jaubert, *La date de la cène* (Paris 1957) Part I, ch. 3.

home rituals, still, as that work continues, we should remind ourselves that thematic similarities to certain groups of *berakoth* have not explained the Christian use of the language of praise, and especially the unmistakable priority that we have seen given here to thanksgiving as over against benediction. As we have argued, this question of the meaning and context of liturgical thanksgiving formulae has been obscured until recent years by the identification of *eulogein* with *eucharistein* and the equation of both with *barak.* Another essay contributed to the liturgical week of the Institut Saint-Serge, however, marked a shift of attention toward thanksgiving forms.

"The Anaphora and the Old Testament," by Henri Cazelles[25] examines the use of *eucharistein* in its several forms together with its Hebrew cognate, *yadah*, in the Old Testament (including both the Septuagint and the version of Aquila), in the Qumran literature, and in Philo. He finds that eucharistic language in a cultic context has a distinct sacrificial value in the first two centuries, evident in Philo, especially, but also in the Old Testament translation made by Aquila in the second century. Aquila undertook his translation after his studies with the rabbis left him dissatisfied with the LXX, a version ill-suited to rabbinic methods of exegesis. In consequence, his version is highly literal and aims at rendering individual Hebrew words and phrases with precision. Thus, where the LXX had rendered *zebach todah* as *thysia tēs aineseōs*, Aquila has rejected *ainesis* for *eucharistia* — not "sacrifice of praise" but "sacrifice of thanksgiving." *Todah* is a noun from the same *yadah* root used in the thanksgiving prayers of the grace after meals and in *Amidah* (where the thanksgiving, *hodaah*, is the penultimate pericope). The *todah* was one of three sacrifices of the *zebach* (communion) type in which a repast was shared with God. Part of the sacrifice was consumed on the altar and part returned to the one who offered to be enjoyed with his friends. It thus combined the notions of meal and sacrifice. The oblations included, in addition to the animal offering, a cake of flour and oil and a libation of wine. Such a sacrificial context for *eucharistia* is encountered strongly again in Philo of Alexandria, and this finding of Cazelles has received broad confirmation in the much more extensive and detailed study of Philo's eucharistic thought published in 1972 by Jean Laporte.[26]

[25] *Eucharisties d'Orient et d'Occident* (n. 18 above) 11–21.

[26] Jean Laporte, *La doctrine eucharistique chez Philon d'Alexandre* (Paris 1972).

This sacrificial use of *eucharistia* is, of course, strongly suggestive for the understanding of *Didache*'s deliberate deviation from the established forms of *Birkat Ha-Mazon*. While it is perhaps too soon still for us to essay an answer to the old question of the relation of the prayers of *Didache* 9 and 10 to the Sunday eucharistic sacrifice spoken of in chapter 14, still — if we consider seriously the precision of the Didachist's revision of the Jewish grace in such wise as to remove all use of the benediction formularies which were critical for the meal *berakoth*, and to give unprecedented priority and prominence to eucharistic forms, and if we further consider this in the light of the sacrificial nuance of such eucharistic language as has been revealed by the studies of Cazelles and Laporte — we should find ourselves much less impressed with what has seemed the wide difference between *Didache*'s two uses of eucharist, as meal and as sacrifice. Indeed, in spite of all the problems of dating, authenticity and the rest, it should not be considered impossible that *Didache* 10 either is (or wishes to seem to be) a careful adaptation of *Birkat Ha-Mazon* to the requirements of the Supper of the Lord become a Christian *zebach todah*, the eucharistic sacrifice.

THANKSGIVING IN EARLY ANAPHORAS

Something of the same alteration of the Jewish grace's pattern of benediction-thanksgiving-supplication to a twofold pattern of thanksgiving and supplication can be seen in the anaphora of the episcopal ordination in the *Apostolic Tradition* ascribed to Hippolytus and in that anaphora published by Garitte[27] which bears the name of Epiphanius (not to be confused with the Ethiopic anaphora of the same name). Père Ligier has singled out these two prayers noting two common characteristics: [1] both devote themselves entirely to thanksgiving down to the institution narrative, giving no place to that pure praise of God as Creator which was the concern of the first pericope of the Jewish grace or of God as he is in himself which Ligier sees leading into the Sanctus in most of the classic oriental anaphoras; and [2] neither of these prayers includes the Sanctus.[28] There are, of course, two major differences between these texts and

[27] Hänggi-Pahl, *Prex Eucharistica*. Spicilegium Friburgense 12 (Fribourg Suisse 1968) 262–263.

[28] L. Ligier, "Célébration divine et anamnèse dans la première partie de l'anaphore ou canon de la messe orientale," *Eucharisties d'Orient et d'Occident* II (Lex Orandi 47) 139–143.

the thanksgiving and supplication of *Didache* 10: [1] the first two doxologies of *Didache* are missing, giving a single continuous prayer instead of the three pericopes of the early Christian text and of the Jewish grace after meals; and [2] there is now the narrative/anamnesis unit to be considered.

Ligier, posing for himself the limited question of the time and manner of the introduction of the narrative/anamnesis group into a structure which seems in so many oriental anaphoras to be derived from *Birkat Ha-Mazon*, calls attention to the embolisms inserted on particular festal occasions into either the second or third pericopes. On the model of these embolisms, Ligier believes that the narrative and anamnesis began to find their way into the anaphoras, either inserted within the thanksgiving or appended to it, but in either case as an addition. This had the effect of bringing a present focus to the past orientation of the thanksgiving which extended to the supplication as well, directing its future orientation toward present action in the development of the epiklesis.[29]

A cardinal example of further influence of *Birkat Ha-Mazon* on the anaphora can be seen in the case of that prayer which has drawn more and more attention over the past decades, the East Syrian (or Nestorian or Chaldean) Anaphora of the Apostles, more popularly known as Addai and Mari. Many of the recent articles which have sought to resolve the problems presented by this prayer have found that in order to engage the issues it was necessary to present once again the history of the discussion and the *status quaestionis*. The complexity of the issues and the limited space at our disposal make such a course impossible here, and we must satisfy ourselves with only the slightest sketch, surrendering any pretense to adequate treatment of the considerable literature.

The structure of the prayer itself is compellingly suggestive of *Birkat Ha-Mazon* and *Didache* 10. It is a tripartite structure consisting of three "prayers of inclination," or *gehanatha*, each preceded by a silent prayer (*kushapa*) and followed by a "canon" (*qanona*) which functions as a doxology. By fairly general agreement, the silent prayers represent later additions to the text, but at that point general agreement has failed and fails still. Part of the reason for the considerable range of opinions was the lack of a critical text of the anaphora.

[29] L. Ligier, "The Origins of the Eucharistic Prayer: From the Last Supper to the Eucharist," *Studia Liturgica* 9 (1973) 176–185.

From the important article of E. C. Ratcliffe[30] in 1929 which drew attention to the importance of Addai and Mari until 1966 scholars were forced to work from late texts. Even the MS materials for a critical text were limited, according to William Macomber, to two MSS of circa 1500 and four others of the 16th century. In 1966, however, Macomber published a critical edition based on the *hudra* (ritual) which he had himself discovered in Mosul, in the church of Mar Eshaya.[31] In this single stroke the MS tradition was pushed back by half a millenium, and Macomber's critical text seems likely to remain the basis of studies in this anaphora for decades to come. It confirmed the late date of the silent prayers (which are lacking in Mar Eshaya), but the basic problems still remain. While not all of them can be dealt with here, three would seem to deserve mention: the relation of Addai and Mari to the third Maronite Anaphora of St. Peter the Apostle (which most, following Baumstark, call *sharar*, from the *incipit* of its first prayer after the creed); second, the problem of the address of the anaphora; and, third, the continuing problem of the evident absence of the institution narrative in Addai and Mari.

The close relation of the anaphora of Addai and Mari to the Maronite *sharar* and the pattern of their similarities and differences suggest that what is, or should be, under consideration today is neither the one nor the other of the two anaphoras but the common source of them both. While Macomber speaks in these terms, others (not always from force of habit) continue to discuss the "original text" of Addai and Mari. Although the close kinship between the two had been pointed out by Rahmani as far back as 1899,[32] the late date of the MS evidence and the lack of a critical edition even of that evidence led most scholars to leave the *sharar* out of consideration. Such was the case, e.g., with the impressive study of Dom Botte which seemed to some to provide a definitive restoration of the original text.[33] One who did not find it finally satisfying was Dom

[30] E. C. Ratcliffe, "The Original Form of the Anaphora of Addai and Mari," *Journal of Theological Studies* 30 (1928–1929) 23–32.

[31] Wm. Macomber, "The Oldest Known Text of the Anaphora of the Apostles Addai and Mari," *Orientalia Christiana Periodica* 32 (1966) 335–371.

[32] Ignatius Ephraem II Rahmani, *Testamentum Domini Nostri Jesu Christi* (Mosul 1899) 192–193.

[33] B. Botte, "L'anaphore chaldéenne des Apôtres," *Orientalia Christiana Periodica* 15 (1949) 259–276.

Hieronymus Engberding. He had already in 1932 taken the position that one could no longer leave the *sharar* to one side when examining Addai and Mari, and found himself in still further disagreement with Botte's reconstruction which depended heavily on the identification as an anamnesis of a prayer which Engberding took to be rather an intercession.[34] Botte's reconstruction fell liable to still further question as a result of Macomber's publication of the earlier text of Addai and Mari since that text lacked a phrase, "in thy name," which seemed critical for Botte's argument for the original presence and position of the institution narrative. With the issues thus reopened, the comparison with *sharar* began to look promising to more and more scholars. Macomber, comparing the two anaphoras with some baptismal consecrations, argued ingeniously that the eucharistic dialogue of Addai and Mari has been conformed to other Nestorian anaphoras and that *sharar* has preserved the original common source for the dialogue and, by implication, for the *incipit* of the first *gehanta* which had been altered in Addai and Mari to provide a connection with the revised dialogue.[35]

This same superiority of *sharar* is suggested in the matter of the address. The present forms of both of the anaphoras address the first *gehanta* to the Trinity. The second, the thanksgiving, on the other hand, is clearly addressed to the Son and the same is true also for the third *gehanta* in *sharar*, even though this includes the narrative of the institution. This third *gehanta* in Addai and Mari, however, vacillates in its address between the Son and the Father. From the evidence, Macomber concludes that the original address was to the Son throughout and that the Trinitarian address of the first *gehanta* is an alteration made in the fourth century. In keeping the address to the Son in the third *gehanta*, however, *sharar* once again shows itself to have maintained the more archaic reading, as Engberding had asserted to be generally the case.

These more primitive readings in *sharar* throw a particularly strong light on the occurrence of the institution narrative there. The lack of this narrative in Addai and Mari has been its most widely

[34] H. Engberding, "Urgestalt, Eigenart u. Entwicklung eines altantiochenischen eucharistischen Hochgebetes," *Oriens Christianus* 7 (Series 3: 1932) 32–48; *idem*, "Zum anaphorischen Fürbittgebet der ostsyrischen Liturgie der Apostel Addaj u. Mar(j)," *Oriens Christianus* 5 (Series 4: 1957) 102–124.

[35] Wm. Macomber, "The Maronite and Chaldean Versions of the Anaphora of the Apostles," *Orientalia Christiana Periodica* 37 (1971) 58–66.

discussed peculiarity, and many (as Botte) have sought its original position in the anaphora or have sought to account for the omission in other ways. Macomber, comparing Addai and Mari to *sharar*, finds that the former manifests its curious vacillation in the address of the third *gehanta* at precisely the point where the *sharar* begins the institution narratives. Macomber can agree with the point made by A. Raes that those passages which are unique to one or another of these two anaphoras lack the stamp of antiquity.[36] "In particular, although the assymetrical form of the narrations of the bread and the wine is a sign of antiquity, the actual wording shows signs of decadence."[37] Macomber rightly notes, however, that decadence is a quality from which it is difficult to divorce subjective judgment.

Although Macomber had reiterated as late as his 1971 article the lament that we still had no critical text of the *sharar*, that lack was happily supplied two years later. In 1973 Josephe-Marie Sauget published in a new fascicle of *Anaphorae Syriacae* a critical text based on the Paris MS used by Macomber.[38] This text does not give such startlingly new evidence as did Macomber's publication of the Mar Eshaya MS, but it does allow sophisticated access to the available evidence. This evidence suggests no significant variety in the readings in the narrative of the institution, especially as to the multiplication of verbs (over the bread: blessed, and marked, and sanctified . . . ; over the cup: gave thanks, and glorified). Such a multiplication (especially given other apparent embellishments and redundancies in the text) might be taken as a symptom of decadence, but it is noteworthy that the first verb of each series, *barekath* and *'oudith*, reproduce that distinction between the short *berakah* over the bread and the thanksgiving of *Birkat Ha-Aretz* over the cup which we noted in the narratives of Mark and Matthew to be consistent with the state of development of the meal blessings in the time of our Lord, according to Finkelstein's reconstruction. Apart from this distinction between blessing and thanksgiving, the *sharar* narrative shows no sign of literary dependency upon either of those synoptic accounts. While I cannot claim that my search has been utterly exhaustive, I have found this distinction in only a very few

[36] *Ibid.*, 74.

[37] *Ibid.* The position quoted is from A. Raes, "Le Récit de l'institution eucharistique dans l'anaphore chaldéenne et malabare des Apôtres," *Orientalia Christiana Periodica* 10 (1944) 222–223.

[38] *Anaphorae Syriacae*, vol. II, fasc. 3. XVII, pp. 275–329.

other anaphoras: the Syrian Anaphora of the Twelve Apostles, and the Nestorian Anaphoras of Theodore of Mopsuestia and of Mar Nestorius.[39] Given the paucity and local definition of this tradition, I would suggest that for more reasons than mere assymetry, the *sharar's* distinction between benediction and thanksgiving is symptomatic of an acute sensitivity to the formal details of Jewish meal prayers and might be a sign of very great antiquity indeed.

This does not, of course, prove the existence of an institution narrative in the common source of *sharar* and Addai and Mari, but it does at least underscore the questions surrounding the eleventh century report by Ibn at-Tayyib that the Anaphora of the Apostles was abbreviated by the seventh century patriarch, Iso-Yabh III, and might reinforce suspicions that the institution narrative in Addai and Mari was a victim of that reform.[40]

In these anaphoras, more than in *Didache* or Hippolytus, there is a distinction between praise for creation in the first *gehanta* and thanksgiving for redemption in the second. The address of the whole prayer to the Son, however, makes such a distinction difficult, and there is slight reference to redemption in the first *gehanta* as well, with Addai and Mari even including there a thanksgiving verb. These references are clearly secondary to the main theme of praise of the Creator, while the second *gehanta*, after the four words added in Addai and Mari to connect with the preceding Sanctus, begins strongly with, "we give thanks to you," and details the work and fruits of redemption. The third *gehanta* with its prayer to Christ to "make a good memorial of all the pious and just fathers," is strongly reminiscent of the festal embolism in the third pericope of *Birkat Ha-Mazon*, to which attention has already been called. The ninth century text of this embolism reads: ". . . may the remembrance of ourselves and of our fathers and the remembrance of Jerusalem, thy city, and the remembrance of the Messiah, the son of David, thy servant, and the remembrance of thy people, the whole house of Israel, arise and come, come to pass, be seen and accepted and

[39] The Anaphora of the Twelve Apostles gives "blessed" over the bread and both "gave thanks" and "blessed" (in that order) over the cup. Theodore, exactly parallel to *sharar*, gives "blessed" over the bread and "gave thanks" over the cup. Nestorius, more rigorously faithful to the actual pattern of *Birkat Ha-Mazon* but less faithful to Mk, Mt and *sharar*, gives "blessed" over the bread and both "blessed" and "gave thanks" (in that order) over the cup.

[40] Macomber (n. 35 above) p. 56 and n. 5.

heard, be remembered and be mentioned before thee for deliverance, for good, for grace, ..."[41] While considerable development seems evident in this rich text, the remembrance theme is so central that it must be taken to be as old as the embolism itself.

THE PATTERN: PRAISE-THANKSGIVING-SUPPLICATION

On the whole, then, it is difficult to take issue with at least the principal thrust of Ligier's analysis, that the *Birkat Ha-Mazon* was the source of inspiration which gave the pattern of the early eucharistic prayer: praise, thanksgiving, supplication. To this, the early prayers suggest, additions were made on the model of the festal embolism in the supplicatory third pericope or on the model of that for Purim and Chanukah in the second, the thanksgiving for redemption. This pattern falls into obscurity, however, when one identifies thanksgiving and *berakah* and thus opens the way for seeking the eucharistic prayer's background in the *berakoth* of the synagogue liturgy. It is quite possible that the Jewish use of *kedushah* (Sanctus) in the synagogue liturgy influenced the Christian adoption of the hymn, and perhaps at an earlier date than has been supposed, but that usage is too clouded by uncertainty from both the Jewish and the Christian sides to justify seeking the roots of the anaphora itself in the *berakoth* and *kedushah* before *shema*.[42] Although further influences may have been at work in the Alexandrian tradition, the basic pattern was already laid down by the grace after meals. We have seen this pattern radically reinterpreted in *Didache* and Hippolytus, and reasserted in the common source of Addai and Mari and the *sharar*, though still giving a prominence to thanksgiving which had characterized the tradition ever since Paul's version of the institution account. While, consistent with this, "let us give thanks to the Lord" would replace the invitation of the Jewish grace, "let us bless Him of Whose bounty we have partaken," still the pattern of the prayers of the Jewish grace can be seen in such classic anaphoras as those of James and Basil where the

[41] Hedegård (n. 11 above) 152.

[42] J. Mann, "Genizah Fragments of the Palestinian Order of Service," *Hebrew Union College Annual* II (1925) 289–290; Elbogen (n. 2 above) 61–62. But, on the contrary, see C. P. Price, "Jewish Morning Prayers and Early Christian Anaphoras," *Anglican Theological Review* 43 (1961) 153–168; L. Bouyer, *Eucharist: Theology and Spirituality of the Eucharistic Prayer* (Notre Dame, Indiana 1968) 88–90 *et passim*; J. Vellian, "The Anaphoral Structure of Addai and Mari Compared to the Berakoth Preceding the Shema in the Synagogue Morning Service," *Le Muséon* 85 (1972) 201–223.

opening praise of the Creator, culminating in the Sanctus, is clearly distinguishable from the thanksgiving for redemption which leads to the institution narrative and anamnesis, and thence to the supplication for the spirit-community, a pattern which could accept with ease and grace the emerging Trinitarian theology. Yet even when this opening praise of the Creator is thus distinguished from the thanksgiving for redemption, it is curious that the Christian eucharistic prayer declines to use the definitive *incipit* of the *berakah*, "blessed art Thou," although noneucharistic prayers in *Apostolic Constitutions* (7.34, e.g.) show that the form was easily translatable. Is it the Christian preoccupation with Christ as redeemer that focused attention on the thanksgiving for redemption in such wise that the original pattern, when recovered, comes back not as benediction-thanksgiving-supplication but as praise-thanksgiving-supplication?

For whatever reason, it would seem that from the beginning similarity of the Christian liturgy to the Jewish has been accompanied by differences which also have claim upon our attention. Yes, as Gregory Dix said, "Jesus was a Jew," and our quest for our origins may never forget that. Still, the relation of Christianity to Judaism is something more complex than the relation of the New Testament to the Old. The Jewish liturgy and the Christian were both under rapid development in the first two centuries of the common era, and to appreciate the influence of one on the other demands a sort of precision of which, I fear, these remarks may only have demonstrated the need once again. Nonetheless, as Ligier has put it, "theological and thematic similarities alone are not sufficient. In order to arrive at firm conclusions, it is necessary to pay attention to the form of the *berakoth* and to the total structure in which they are lodged."[43]

Having at least attempted that, I must conclude: no, *berakah* is not the same as *eucharistia*, and we may hope that further studies will help us to understand better the significance and consequences of that, after all, rather odd fact.

[43] Ligier (n. 29 above) 170.

Aidan Kavanagh

Thoughts on the New Eucharistic Prayers

The proliferation of new eucharistic prayers, both official and unofficial, among Roman Catholic, Anglican and Protestant churches during the past several years has been a phenomenon the dimensions of which have not been matched since the patristic period. For Roman Catholics it has been, moreover, a sudden one. As late as ten years ago, for one to have spoken of an audible canon was avant garde: to have suggested modest reforms of it (such as shortening the lists of saints or eliminating some signs of the cross) was to have approached offending pious ears.[1] But the Council thawed so many glacial assumptions that the situation began to change with increasing rapidity during the sixties. Articles appeared by recognized scholars calling with relative boldness for major alterations in the Roman canon.[2] Studies on eucharistic nomenclature in the New Testament (such as that begun by J. Jeremias as early as 1926 and continually revised by him until 1966),[3] together with fresh examinations of the Judaic character of the eucharistic prayer-form by Audet, Fraigneau-Julien, and Bouyer,[4] opened up dimensions of eucharistic theology formerly not dealt with. Such studies yielded insights that made more radical reform possible by going beyond those questions dealt with in older liturgical works on the Roman canon[5] — not in rendering such works obsolete, but in using the method of biblical

[1] See H. A. Reinhold, *Bringing the Mass to the People* (Baltimore 1960) 63–71.

[2] E.g., H. Küng, "Das Eucharistiegebet: Konzil und Erneuerung der römischen Messliturgie," *Wort und Wahrheit* 18 (1963) 102–107; K. Amon, "Gratias Agere: zur Reform des Messkanons," *Liturgisches Jahrbuch* 15 (1965) 79–98.

[3] The Eucharistic Words of Jesus[3] (New York 1966).

[4] J. P. Audet, "Esquisse historique du genre littéraire de la 'bénédiction' juive et de l' 'eucharistie' chrétienne," *Revue Biblique* 65 (1958) 371–399; B. Fraigneau-Julien, "Eléments de la structure fondamentale de l'eucharistie: bénédiction, anamnèse, et action de grâces," *Revue des Sciences Religieuses* 34 (1960) 35–61; L. Bouyer, *Eucharist*, trans. C. U. Quinn (Notre Dame 1968), the English of which is a second edition of the 1966 French original.

[5] E.g., B. Botte, *Le Canon de la Messe romaine* (Louvain 1935); B. Botte and C. Mohrmann, *L'Ordinaire de la Messe* (Louvain 1953); J. A. Jungmann, *The Mass of the Roman Rite*, trans. F. Brunner (New York 1950) vol. 2, 101–274. For other works see C.

criticism within larger theological perspectives canonized by the Council.

The thrust of all this has been to give us today a degree of technical knowledge about the morphology and content of the eucharistic prayer, and thus of the eucharist itself, far surpassing that of the past. Along with a general renewal in understanding the ecumenical and social dimensions of the eucharist as a sacrament of unity, this has produced a situation with richly creative possibilities for pastoral liturgy and catechesis. Doing something about the Roman eucharistic prayer has become, under such circumstances, not just possible but necessary.

Such is the context of the three new eucharistic prayers finally provided for official use in the Roman Rite. Yet the context should not be romanticized. The intense scholarly work that has been going on has produced, inevitably, tensions of conflicting expert opinions that even Solomon could not have resolved: the committee structure by which the texts were prepared — mainly the Consilium and the International Committee on English in the Liturgy, with their various subcommittees — should not be expected to have done more. Compounding these difficulties is the brittle, even painful, situation of authoritative murmurs and alarums that has grown in the church since the end of the Council. Under these pressures it is astonishing that the work was ever brought to term: that it was is a tribute to the patience and dedication of all concerned. Encomium is surely in order and has already begun to appear in the form of largely positive commentaries on the texts.[6] But other points seem to be in order touching both the structure and content of the prayers in some detail.

GENERAL STRUCTURE

The new prayers have a common structure, noticeably different from the Roman, that may be outlined as follows:

1. *An opening doxology of praise to the Father.*

2. *Statement of motives for praising the Father.* This is begun in the form of changeable prefaces in all but Prayer IV, which remains al-

Vagaggini, *The Canon of the Mass and Liturgical Reform*, trans. P. Coughlan (Staten Island 1967) 20–21.

[6] See P. Coughlan, *The New Eucharistic Prayers* (London 1968); H. Manders, "Tradition and Renewal: The New Roman Anaphoras," *Worship* 42 (1968) 578–586, with bibliography of other recent articles; also Bouyer, 446–461.

ways the same: Prayer II has a set form also that may be used as it stands or may have a changeable preface substituted for it.

3. *The Sanctus hymn.* This is followed by a transitional, or *vere sanctus,* phrase that leads directly into the first epiclesis in Prayers II and III. The phrase in Prayer IV, while not strictly a *vere sanctus,* accomplishes the same effect in order to resume stating motives for praise of the Father.

4. *The first epiclesis.* This prayer asks the Father to make holy or sanctify the gifts of bread and wine by the power of the Holy Spirit: it may thus be termed a "consecratory epiclesis."

5. *The institution narrative.* This is referred to as "The Lord's Supper," and contains what are no longer called *verba consecrationis* but *verba Domini.*[7] After this follows the "Memorial Acclamation of the People" in response to the priest's (deacon's?) exhortation, "Let us proclaim the mystery of faith."

6. *The anamnesis or "Memorial Prayer,"* containing the definitive statement of what is being offered to the Father.

7. *The second epiclesis.* This prayer asks the Father to make all the communicants one by the action of the Spirit.

8. *Intercessions,* in communion with the saints, for the church, clergy, living and dead.

9. *Closing doxology,* in the Roman form for all the prayers.

There is, literally, something for everyone in this hybrid arrangement. It encompasses the Roman element of changeable prefaces as well as unchangeable wholes (Prayer IV and, on choice, Prayer II); consecratory epicleses in the Egyptian place before the institution account; epicleses after the anamnesis in the Egyptian and Byzantine manner; intercessions in the West Syrian position; the Roman final doxology; and a new acclamation after the institution account. It would be querulously unkind to call such a melange a liturgical platypus, and it would be beside the point to object to hybridization of structure, since every anaphora presently in use among Christians is hybrid to some degree. But it does seem to be relevant to ask why so high a degree of syncretism was felt necessary to render the eucharistic prayer more adequate to present needs. This, in turn, raises once again the question of the basic purpose of such a

[7] The secretary of the Consilium, in an official letter dated 6 November 1968, was still speaking of what Manders, 580, terms "the 'transubstantiation' texts" as *formulae consecrationis,* and refers to the Lord's words as *in consecratione panis* and *in consecratione vini.*

prayer in the first place. If eucharistic prayers are to be regarded as the most definitive liturgical expression of the gospel as understood and responded to in the faith-idiom of a given tradition, then the vital signs of that tradition and the physiognomy of its faith-idiom must also be questioned.

SOME QUESTIONS

One has the impression on studying the texts that questions of this nature, unfortunately, did not receive enough attention in the elaboration of the new prayers, or that the attention given them was fairly extrinsic, or that the attention given them has become obscured through the many stages of committee work that went into their development. One suspects that the latter was the case, and that it was perhaps unavoidable. In any case there is strong reason for caution in becoming lyric over their quality and, especially, over their effects. The state of liturgical renewal, it should be evident by now, is ill-served by anything but a tempered realism as regards liturgical reforms — even those of the canon. A certain reserve, therefore, should not be confused with pique when one reads the Consilium's statement that the Roman liturgy is noticeably enriched by these new prayers, since ". . . fresh expression can now be given, among other things, to our theology of the Eucharist, of salvation history, of the people of God and of the Church in particular, as well as to the theology of the Holy Spirit in the Church and, specifically, of the Spirit's role in the Eucharist. The worldwide and ecumenical horizons of the Second Vatican Council and also those of the so-called theology of secular values will find here discreet, biblical and real reflection. All this in no way detracts from the fact that these new texts possess a most definitely traditional character; this is an easily documented fact."[8]

While one hopes the Consilium is correct in its rather generous prognosis of all that these prayers will do, one would be well advised to expect that the results will be somewhat less than massive. There are several reasons why this may be true.

In the first place, the "most definitely traditional character" of the texts is of a selectively syncretistic and extrinsic sort. One looks largely in vain to find some insight that gave rise to a particular

[8] *Guidelines for the Episcopal Conferences for a Catechesis of the Faithful Concerning the Anaphoras of the Mass*, 3 June 1968, p. 6; cited in Coughlan, 7–8.

tradition vigorously recreated, much less prosecuted for the present in a compelling new way. Rather, one finds fairly overt appropriations of forms lifted from other liturgies — such as the six epicleses of the Spirit, three of which come before the institution account (as in some Egyptian texts), and three of which come after the anamnesis, being what Vagaggini misleadingly calls a prayer for a "fruitful communion" (*comunione fruttuosa*).[9] Not only does one wonder what "fresh expressions" of a theology of the Holy Spirit in the church or in the eucharist such extrinsic appropriations will give rise to (expressions not already available to theology and catechesis): one also experiences misgivings that the hallowing and unifying functions of the Spirit have been split, as it were, into two separate moments — the first coming before and the second after the *verba Domini*. More will be said about this later. For emphasis here, however, is that putting an explicitly pneumatic and consecratory epiclesis before the institution account on Egyptian precedent may raise again the tired old controversy between East and West over the agent and moment of consecration.[10] What, moreover, is to be said theologically of the Roman canon's *quam oblationem*, which is neither pneumatic nor unambiguously "consecratory"? Tradition, quite clearly, becomes static repetition without the continuing discrimination of re-creation and re-synthesis on higher levels. Antiquity has nothing to do with insuring against a static outcome, nor does easy documentation have anything to do with tradition as such: were it otherwise, tradition would not have existed prior to the invention of historical method.

In the second place, the basic purpose of a eucharistic prayer, which is to proclaim the gospel in the form of blessing God liturgically, is unevenly represented in the prayers' balance of parts. Only Prayer IV approaches a sort of proclamatory cursus in its blessing content. Prayer II, on the other hand, contains fully as much petitionary as it does proclamatory material: indeed, the largest single section of its text deals explicitly with consecration of the elements (almost 30 percent if one includes the first epiclesis with the institution narrative). This is proportionately more space than was taken by the Roman canon in its corresponding *quam oblationem* and *qui pridie* sections. It is true, as Manders notes,[11] that Prayer II contains only

[9] *Op. cit.*, 91, 92, 100, etc. This understandably gives him problems when it comes to interpreting the Roman *Supra quae* and *Supplices* prayers; 104–105. My own view is in "Thoughts on the Roman Anaphora," *Worship* 39 (1965) 529.

[10] See T. Ware, *The Orthodox Church* (Baltimore 1963) 289–290.

[11] *Art. cit.*, 583.

one statement of offering — it comes in the anamnesis or "Memorial Prayer" where it belongs. In this it differs greatly from the Roman canon, which in its English text makes no fewer than nine references to offering. If, on the basis of such proportionality, Manders can say that the Roman canon ". . . is really a prayer of offering (*anaphora*) rather than a thanksgiving (*eucharistia*),"[12] it would seem just as true to say that Prayer II is a prayer for consecration of the elements more than anything else. This is the more unfortunate since the brevity of Prayer II (the president's part comprises less than 450 words) may recommend it to many.

Much the same might be said of Prayer III, except that 1) variable prefaces may somewhat expand its proclamatory cursus, and 2) its intercessory section is half again the length of that found in Prayer II. One welcomes the relocation of intercessory material after the anamnesis and second epiclesis — not because of its being found in the West Syrian tradition, but because this position seems more clear than having the intercessions strewn throughout the whole canon, thus interrupting the logical sequence modern congregations expect in public declamation. One also welcomes the shortening of the intercessions as compared with the length of those found in the Roman canon. Yet intercessions still take up 30 percent of the president's words, excluding the variable preface, in Prayer III and over 25 percent of his words in Prayer II. The question is not one of whether intercessions should be retained in the eucharistic prayer, especially in view of the reinstituted Prayers of the Faithful:[13] The question is simply one of proportion.

In the third place, the most important point at which one would expect to find basis for giving ". . . fresh expression . . . to our theology of the Eucharist, of salvation history, of the people of God and of the Church in particular," shows marks of compromise. This point is the anamnesis or "Memorial Prayer," together with its statement of the church's faith-response to the gospel as it has been proclaimed throughout the entire anaphora — indeed, throughout

[12] *Ibid.*, 582–583.

[13] Vagaggini is for retaining both — especially those in the anaphora for the curious theological reason that ". . . were [they] completely eliminated, the idea of the Eucharist as a sacrifice that can be offered . . . for someone, and so the propitiatory nature of the sacrifice, would disappear from the canon"? *op. cit.*, 112. For less hyperbolic and thus more compelling reasons that arise from the very nature of the eucharistic prayer-form, see P. J. Leblanc, "A Consideration of Intercessory Prayer Within the Eucharist," *The Dunwoodie Review* 8 (1968) 115–132.

the entire mass — until now. This faith-response of the church is explicitly directed to the Father *not* as coming from some corporate entity alien to him, but as the response that is identical with that of the Son. With the Son the church maintains a communion-identity secured in the Spirit.[14] Such a faith-response is not merely intellectual or emotional: it is total, objectively liturgical, and takes the form of an oblatory self-sacrifice that is eucharistic. Jesus' faithful giving up of himself in response to his Father's will becomes liturgically sacrificial in the eucharistic state of existence the church maintains as a way of life, and in the act this Spirit-filled way of life gives rise to. Jesus continues to give himself only in the first person plural, and this is expressed in the "we offer" of the church's eucharistic anamnesis.

It is clearly for this reason that Christian eucharistic anamnesis invariably have adopted richly ambiguous *sacramental* terms when detailing *what* is being offered at this point. The reality being offered is, in fact, Christ/church. The specifically eucharistic way of saying this is in terms of bread, cup, sacrifice, gifts, "offerings." The Byzantine anaphoras say: "We offer you your own, of what is your own, in all and for the sake of all"; Serapion speaks of offering the bread and cup as "likenesses" of Christ's body and blood; Theodore of Mopsuestia offers "praise, honor, faith and adoration";[15] the Roman canon offers ". . . this holy and perfect sacrifice; the bread of life and the cup of eternal salvation."

Such nomenclature represents the large and vital tradition of the church's cardinal statement of eucharistic offering. "We offer you, Father, this life-giving bread, this saving cup," of Prayer II remains fully in this tradition, as do the words of Prayer III: "we offer you in thanksgiving this holy and living sacrifice." Prayer IV, however, says that "*we offer you his* [Christ's] *body and blood, the acceptable sacrifice which brings salvation to the whole world. Lord, look upon* this *sacrifice which you have given to your Church. . . .*" The meaning is clear: what is offered is understood to be the real presence of Christ's body and

[14] This is the datum of the anaphora's final doxology: "Through him, with him, in him, in the unity of the Holy Spirit, all glory and honor is yours, almighty Father. . . ." That found in Hippolytus seems even more vigorous: "Through your servant Jesus Christ, through whom glory and honor is yours, with the Holy Spirit in the holy church. . . ." This is an element that Prayer II, which uses some texts of Hippolytus, might have effectively employed.

[15] Cited in Vagaggini, 63.

blood, which is the acceptable offering *given to* the church through the extraordinary power of the Spirit and the *verba Domini*. This is quite different from the other Prayers since here we find an offering of the Blessed Sacrament rather than of the church.[16] This is novel, and can hardly be said to retain "a most definitely traditional character." One who has some acquaintance with the medieval and reformation history of eucharistic controversy will recognize the inadequacy of such a position, and may be forgiven his disappointment that its tendentiousness has got into a Catholic formulary precisely at a time when it could have been diagnosed and avoided most easily.

In the fourth place, making the Holy Spirit's role in the eucharist explicit by way of a split epiclesis seems unfortunate. The inclusion of a pneumatic epiclesis just before the institution account not only welds both sections into a unit that is longer and more strongly consecratory than before: it also interrupts the flow of sequence in narrating the divine mercies for which eucharistic prayer is made and sets the institution account off from this cursus. Thus the account of the Lord's Supper structurally becomes not so much the narration of the mercy having the most proximate import for this act of thanksgiving as it does an even more emphatic *formula consecrationis*, whether the rubrics call it this or not. Some may see this as *romanità*,[17] and it may cause them to wonder whether the device is much of an ecumenical step forward since it underlines once again the *vi verborum*. One suspects, however, that this was intended not so much to reinforce typically Roman views on the real presence and moment of consecration as it is the result of a certain liturgiological bias touching the nature and role of the epiclesis in the eucharist.

C. Vagaggini has been an especially forceful advocate of this bias in his book on canon reform: his position on the Consilium makes it plausible that what is found in the new prayers stems from his influence, at least to some extent. His representation of the bias may be seen in his dividing the epiclesis into two parts, a prayer for

[16] The Latin text, by its capitalizations, makes it even clearer that the Blessed Sacrament is meant: *offerimus tibi eius Corpus et Sanguinem, sacrificium tibi acceptabile et toti mundo salutare. Respice, Domine, in Hostiam, quam Ecclesiae tuae ipse parasti. . . .* The English, unfortunately, by using "sacrifice" for both *sacrificium* and *Hostiam*, makes even more adamant the idea that it is the Blessed Sacrament alone being offered. This is the more unaccountable since the proper differentiation *is* made in the English of Prayer III.

[17] See Manders, 585–586.

consecrating the offerings and a prayer for a fruitful communion.[18] This a priori assumption leaves him both puzzled at the apparent absence of such an epiclesis in the primitive Roman canon and unable, therefore, to refrain from prejudicing evidence — e.g., by including in his own reconstruction of the primitive Roman canon explicitly pneumatic epiclesis texts appropriated without further ado from Gallican and Mozarabic sources.[19] Indeed, that the bias survives his own marshalling of evidence is a testament to his faith in his own a priori assumption. Invocatory prayer forms in Jewish liturgical sources, for example, are not discussed, nor is any attention given to the Judaic *proseuche* (petitionary) material found in the eucharistic sections of *Didache* 9 and 10; Hippolytus gives no epiclesis that is consecratory without ambiguity, and none at all except that in the anamnesis;[20] in the text adduced of the "paleo-hispanic anaphora" not only is there no epiclesis but a communion one in the anamnesis, but there is not a single mention of the Spirit, even in the final doxology;[21] the canon of St. Basil has a classic West Syrian invocation of the Spirit on both the church and the gifts in the anamnesis;[22] the canon of Theodore of Mopsuestia prays for the Spirit to hallow the gifts only after the intercessions and just before the final doxology.[23]

It is in Egyptian sources that one finds the epiclesis more often split into two sections by the institution account; but even here one can detect, as in the anaphoras mentioned above, a certain pluralism concerning how the epiclesis functions. In Serapion, whose anaphora Vagaggini dismisses as being a text ". . . not in the least typical,"[24] there is a request before the institution account that the Father fill the sacrifice with "power and participation." After the institution account, which is interspersed with offering statements as well as petitions for church unity similar to those in *Didache* 9, there follows an invocation of the Logos, not the Spirit, to consecrate the bread and cup for communion ". . . for we have invoked you, the uncreated one, through the only-begotten Son in the Holy

[18] *Op. cit.*, 30, 91, etc.
[19] *Ibid.*, 30, 32, 33.
[20] Cited *ibid.*, 27.
[21] *Ibid.*, 44–49.
[22] *Ibid.*, 54.
[23] *Ibid.*, 66.
[24] *Ibid.*, 67. Bouyer, 202, takes it more seriously.

Spirit." The only explicit invocation of the Spirit comes before the Sanctus, asking that the Father "give us the Holy Spirit that we may speak and tell of your unspeakable mysteries" — an epiclesis not for consecration, nor for communion, but for the accomplishment of the church's gospel mission.

In the Alexandrian anaphora of St. Mark (Greek), which is later than Serapion and shows Syrian influence, the split epiclesis is pneumatic. Yet the first invocation is *not* for the transformation of the gifts but for the accomplishment of the sacrifice ("[Father] fill . . . this sacrifice with that blessing that comes from you by the coming of your most Holy Spirit").[25] The second invocation, which follows the anamnesis, is the one that is explicitly consecratory *and* communion orientated.[26] It is only in the manuscript of Dêr Balizeh that preceding the institution account a pneumatic epiclesis that is clearly consecratory can be found: conflating it, however, are the same petitions for church unity, drawn from *Didache* 9, that are found in the institution account of Serapion. It is worthy of note that Vagaggini apparently does not consider these petitions to be of a "communion" nature, yet they are most strongly so: his oversight of this is caused, again, by the bias of looking for "communion" material only after the anamnesis. But it is at this latter point that Dêr Balizeh is incomplete: in one version of the manuscript there is a pneumatic epiclesis here, reminiscent of the pre-Sanctus one in Serapion, which reads, ". . . grant us your servants the power of the Holy Spirit that our faith may grow to the hope of the eternal life to come."[27] In the other version of the manuscript, the Louvain fragment, this text is missing altogether. In view, therefore, of the state of the evidence as well as of the clear words contained in the evidence, it is more speculation than demonstration for Vagaggini to conclude that ". . . Dêr Balizeh and the Louvain fragment separate the two ideas contained in an epiclesis, and put the prayer for consecration before the institution, and the prayer for a fruitful communion after the anamnesis, as is the practice of the Roman canon (*Quam oblationem; Supplices . . . ut quotquot*)."[28]

It is exasperating beyond words to find this conclusion made standard not in one or another of the new eucharistic prayers, but in all.

[25] This is the opinion of Bouyer, 210, as well. The text is cited in Vagaggini, 73.

[26] Cited in Vagaggini, 75–76.

[27] *Ibid.*, 70; Bouyer, 202.

[28] Vagaggini, 69. Compare Bouyer, 209 f.

If it be argued that the split epiclesis is Roman, even granting the argument does not thereby commit one to maintaining it. Other Roman structures have been dropped entirely (such as the position of the intercessions): wholly un-Roman ones have been added. Surely there is as much if not more weight to having a single epiclesis after the anamnesis than there is for having a split epiclesis — quite apart from the difficulties the latter causes in the proclamatory cursus of blessing that embraces the institution account. The former sort of united epiclesis is clearly attested in Hippolytus, and it is in constant use today by the second largest living Rite in Christianity — the Byzantine.

CONCLUSIONS

Other, more minor, questions could be raised. Why, for example, does the English translate in such weakly subjective terms the memorial wording in the anamnesis of Prayer III ("Father, calling to mind . . .") while maintaining greater objective strength in all the others? One wonders, indeed, why Prayer III was included at all, since it really adds nothing to Prayers II and IV except a variable preface (Prayer II permits of this) and a rather lovely commemoration of the deceased in masses for the dead (which could easily be included in either or both of the other two). The new acclamations of the people might just as well have come after the "Memorial Prayer" as before it: the people are at present asked to proclaim something that has not yet been specified by the prayer-leader — the death, resurrection, and second coming of Christ. Finally, the "so-called theology of secular values" the Consilium mentions as being present in the new prayers may be thought by some to be so discreet as to be invisible.

Nevertheless, I expect that the new prayers will be generally well received, and it is appropriate that it should be so. They constitute a real, if modest, step forward so long as they do not come to be regarded as the last word or harbingers of the parousia. It will be excellent if the new prayers, together with the 70 new variable prefaces said to be forthcoming, enlarge and deepen the dimensions of eucharistic experience in the church. Such an effect will far transcend the, hopefully, temporary inadequacies of the present texts: on this one can speculate, and for it one may hope. Perhaps some structure can be given to that hope and speculation in the present. Toward this end I have tried to mount the sort of major criticisms that may aid the future and serve as marks of respect — even in disagreement — for those authors of the prayers who work for the same purpose.

James Dallen

The Congregation's Share In the Eucharistic Prayer

Characteristic of recent liturgical theology is the recognition of the unity of the eucharistic prayer. Less and less, even in popular understanding, is it regarded as merely the setting for the institution narrative. The "words of consecration" are likewise given less emphasis, with the whole prayer from start to finish seen as consecratory. The preface — an unfortunate translation of *praefatio* — is no longer regarded as a preliminary requiring an extra flip of a ribbon but it is seen as making explicit the praise and thanksgiving out of which Eucharist flows.

At the same time there is a deeper realization that because the eucharistic prayer is *the* prayer of the Church, it belongs to the whole community and not exclusively to the priest. Since it gives words to the prayer of Christ's Body, all the members of that Body and all the orders whose union is the Church fulfill their own liturgies in its proclamation. It is a presidential prayer precisely because it is the prayer of the Church; it is therefore led by the one whose liturgy it is to coordinate and to unify the Church, the bishop, or by his delegate.

As president the priest proclaims the eucharistic prayer in the name of the whole community.[1] It is therefore a prayer which by its nature requires congregational participation. The attention which needs to be given to presidential style, particularly here, must not distract us from the ultimate reason for the importance of the style of presidential proclamation: the participation of the congregation. This participation can be expressed in various ways.[2] But apparently

[1] General Instruction on the Roman Missal (1970) 13, 54.

[2] Constitution *Sacrosanctum Concilium* on the Sacred Liturgy (30) lists several means:

there has always been some active congregational involvement in the eucharistic prayer in all rites, and generally this has been expressed in part by verbal participation as well. This verbal participation has ranged from the minimum of the introductory dialogue and the concluding Amen in the early improvised prayers to the extensive involvement of the people in the Ethiopian Prayer of the Apostles.[3]

Until recently the possible involvement of the people in the Roman Canon was limited to the introductory dialogue, the Sanctus and the concluding Amen, the minimal pattern found in all rites since the introduction of the Sanctus in the fourth century. Since the addition of alternative eucharistic prayers in the Roman rite this participation has been extended by the introduction of the "memorial acclamation," and further involvement can be expected in the future — it is, in fact, already taking place in many parishes.

In this paper I wish to examine the present fourfold pattern of congregational involvement in the Roman eucharistic prayers and to point out possibilities for further development on the basis of the present "memorial acclamation" and comparative liturgy.

THE INTRODUCTORY DIALOGUE

The formality of the introduction to the eucharistic prayer highlights its importance. The introduction to other presidential prayers generally consists, at most, of a simple greeting and a rather brief invitation to prayer. Yet as a sign that the eucharistic prayer is *the* prayer in all Christian liturgies the invitation here has become more elaborate.[4] Traditionally the invitation has here taken the form of a dialogue, and while there have been historical variations,[5] since ancient times the pattern has been for the most part invariable. The

acclamations, responses, psalms, antiphons, hymns, actions, gestures, bodily attitudes and reverent silence.

[3] See Anton Hänggi and Irmgard Pahl, *Prex Eucharistica* (Fribourg: Éditions Universitaires 1968) 144ff.

[4] This can become an exhortation or minor homily or even polemical. See, for example, Calvin's exhortation, which echoes the dialogue even though it follows the institution narrative; *Liturgies of the Western Church*, selected and introduced by Bard Thompson (New York: Collins-World Fontana 1961) 207.

[5] For a number of instances see C. A. Bouman, "Variants in the Introduction to the Eucharistic Prayer," *Vigiliae Christianae* 4 (1950) 94–115. The Eastern rites in particular have tended to expand the introduction.

present form of the dialogue in the Roman rite, for example, is still quite close to that found in Hippolytus in the early third century.

Even in "experimental" liturgies there has been little attempt to change this dialogue. The few attempts to develop it have generally been, as in some Eastern rites, the expansion of the simple "The Lord be with you" to a more elaborate greeting, for example, "The grace of our Lord Jesus Christ, the love of the Father, and the fellowship of the Holy Spirit be with you." Some celebrants have also changed "Let us give thanks to the Lord our God" to "Shall we give thanks to the Lord our God?" in order to make explicit the congregation's consent to his speaking in their name.

The Jewish origins of this dialogue make it clear that it functions not only as an invitation to the assembly to join in prayer but also as the assembly's assent to the president's request to pray in their name.[6] This, together with the wording of the prayer, is a clear sign that the eucharistic prayer belongs to the whole assembly. However, only when the prayer was transformed from an improvisation to a fixed form did the verbal involvement of the people in the body of the prayer become possible.

HOLY, HOLY, HOLY LORD

The congregation's participation in the body of the eucharistic prayer has been in connection with its "building blocks": the elements of praise and thanksgiving, remembering and interceding. The Sanctus, with its theme of praise and thanksgiving — at the heart of the notion of *eucharistia* — is the oldest portion of the prayer to be proclaimed by the congregation.[7] Whether or not it was of Jewish origin, it is clear that it was first introduced in the East as a collective song. Although it is not mentioned in the West until about 400, its use belies the later interpretation of the eucharistic prayer as

[6] The General Instruction (54) emphasizes only the invitation to prayer: "In an introductory dialogue the priest invites the people to lift their hearts to God in prayer and thanks; he unites them with himself in the prayer he addresses in their name to the Father through Jesus Christ."

[7] That the Sanctus is actually part of the Prayer and not simply an intervention of the congregation seems incontestable. Some of the evidence will be presented here; for a fuller treatment, see Luis Maldonaldo, *La Plegaria Eucaristica* (Madrid: Biblioteca Autores Cristianos 1967) 485–493. The "General Instruction," 55, states explicitly: "This acclamation forms part of the Eucharistic Prayer, and all the people join with the priest in singing or reciting it."

the holy of holies which the "pontifex" enters alone.[8] In the East the Benedictus has been linked to it since the eighth century.

The Sanctus probably came to Rome from Jerusalem or Syria.[9] In the Roman rite, which has always given little attention to the theme of creation, it has been almost the only cosmic reference in the eucharistic prayer. From its scriptural origin (Is 6) and the manner of its introduction by the closing words of the preface, it is clearly intended as the eucharistic assembly's joining in the song of all creation in praise of God.

While the Sanctus is not found in some of the oldest eucharistic prayers, the fact that the oldest melody which we have for it (Mass XVIII) is simply a continuation of the ferial melody for the preface, again suggests that the Sanctus was regarded as an actual part of the prayer and not a congregational interruption or intervention. This is important for determining the extent to which the congregation may participate in the prayer. Is such participation to be simply a series of short statements of assent or praise — acclamations — or may it be extended to prayers that form part of the eucharistic prayer itself? Although it is generally referred to as an acclamation for convenience's sake, both the length and format of the Sanctus make it more of a hymn or sung prayer than an acclamation.[10]

Finally, one may note that there have been some historical variations in the Sanctus and some contemporary "experimental" prayers have made some minor changes in it, but for the most part the traditional form has been retained.

THE MEMORIAL ACCLAMATION

The second major building block of the eucharistic prayer, that of remembering, has been taken to characterize the "memorial accla-

[8] *Ordo Romanus Primus*, 44; *Les Ordines Romani du Haut Moyen Âge*, ed. M. Andrieu, Spicilegium Sacrum Lovaniense, Études et documents, 23 (Louvain 1948) II:95–96.

[9] See P.-M. Gy, "Le *sanctus* romain et les anaphores orientales" in *Mélanges Liturgiques* (Louvain: Abbaye du Mont César 1972) 167–174.

[10] In their document *Music in Catholic Worship* (Washington, D.C.: United States Catholic Conference 1972), 53, the American Bishops' Committee on the Liturgy describes the acclamations as "shouts of joy which arise from the whole assembly as forceful and meaningful assents to God's Word and Action." Their listing, however, goes beyond what this describes; only the "Amen" strictly fits within it.

The hymnic nature of the Sanctus is undoubtedly what encouraged Luther to expand upon it in the *Deutsche Messe* of 1526; see Thompson, *Liturgies of the Western Church*, 135.

mation." From what will be said, it will be seen that neither the characterization nor the name is completely accurate. Some theological and historical background is necessary before examining the present acclamations of the Roman mass.

The anamnesis of the eucharistic prayer functions as an interpretation of what is being done in fulfilling the Lord's command, "Do this as my memorial." Such a statement parallels the Jewish *berakah's* expression of a motive for praising God. In the Christian eucharistic prayers this anamnesis follows the institution narrative which contains the Lord's command[11] and is generally closely linked with the theme of offering. The pattern of the anamnesis has generally been that of the Lord's death, resurrection and ascension. Frequently the East has expanded the anamnesis on this pattern to include the ministry as well. Both in East and in West an eschatological note has frequently been introduced: the mystery is not simply an historical event.

The anamnesis-memorial is to be realized not only in and by the priest but also in and by the entire assembled congregation, the whole People of God as a prophetic people. As a consequence of this fact it is possible to delineate the proper role of the congregation in the eucharistic prayer. In the Roman Canon, for example, it is "nos servi tui sed et plebs tua sancta" who make the memorial — the priest and the congregation, even though until recently only the priest recited the memorial. In the Eastern rites the priest's prayer generally does not contain an expressed statement that priest and people alike are the subjects or agents of memorializing and petitioning, instead there is usually a congregational prayer. The Egyptian anamnesis, which announces the death, confesses the resurrection and awaits the second coming, is the earliest example. This Eastern practice of a "kerygmatic" acclamation is the source of the present Roman memorial acclamation. It is also important to note that in the Roman rite and in most Eastern rites the memorial is addressed to the Father by the priest, while the congregational acclamations or prayers are generally addressed to Christ.

Until the *Ordo Missae* of 1969 (following the decree of 23 May 1968)

[11] A pastoral suggestion: since it is thus a response to the Lord's words it would seem better in practice to omit "Let us proclaim the mystery of faith" and to have the acclamation simply taken up by the congregation. As will be noted, the memorial acclamation in the strict sense — the first Latin text — is most appropriate here.

the Roman rite did not have such a congregational acclamation.[12] However, the present texts provided in the *Ordo Missae* raise some questions as to whether they are, strictly speaking, *memorial* acclamations. An examination of the texts from the 1970 *Missale Romanum* and the ICEL translation of the Order of Mass will show reasons for these questions.

Mortem tuam annuntiamus, Domine, et tuam resurrectionem confitemur, donec venias.	Christ has died, Christ is risen, Christ will come again.
	Dying you destroyed our death, rising you restored our life, Lord Jesus, come in glory.
Quotiescumque manducamus panem hunc et calicem bibimus, mortem tuam annuntiamus, Domine, donec venias.	When we eat this bread and drink this cup, we proclaim your death, Lord Jesus, until you come in glory.
Salvator mundi, salva nos, qui per crucem et resurrectionem tuam liberasti nos.	Lord, by your cross and resurrection you have set us free; you are the Savior of the world.

The first of the acclamations of the 1969 Roman mass, which is borrowed from the Syrian liturgy of Saint James,[13] is the only one of the three Latin acclamations that, strictly speaking may be called an anamnesis and thus a *memorial* acclamation. Strangely, the ICEL translation provides two variants of it, the first of which is not addressed to Christ — a sharp break with liturgical tradition — and the second of which has assumed a petitionary character. Thus the first of the ICEL variants no longer corresponds to the traditional pattern of an acclamation in that it is no longer a prayer addressed by the congregation to Christ — to whom, in fact, *is* it addressed? — and the second maintains the anamnesis and prayer character but expresses the eschatological expectation in the form of a petition.[14]

[12] It is historically possible that "mysterium fidei" was originally a diaconal or congregational prayer or acclamation. Though various ejaculations and salutations were common in the Middle Ages at the elevation, no prayers corresponding to our present "memorial acclamations" were in general use in the Roman liturgy, even in its Gallicanized form. The "mysterium fidei," from its placement, could refer to the covenant, the blood of the covenant, or the total eucharistic mystery; it certainly does not refer to the real presence. Bernard Botte, "Mysterium Fidei," *Bible et Vie Chrétienne* 80 (1968) 29–34, argues that it is an acclamation of our redemption in Christ.

[13] See Botte, "Mysterium Fidei."

[14] In a commentary, *The New Eucharistic Prayers and Prefaces* (Washington, D.C.: Bishops' Committee on the Liturgy [BCL] 1968) 22–23, the memorial acclamation is

The second acclamation — the third in the ICEL series — echoes 1 Corinthians 11:26. While the memorial character is not altogether absent, the acclamation actually focuses primarily on the eating and drinking; it is thus oriented more toward communion in the meal than verbal memorial, perhaps with a realization that it is the common-unity of the Body of Christ which is the effective proclamation of redemption. A further departure from the usual memorial pattern is the omission of any mention of the resurrection, which is lacking here in the scriptural original. The ICEL text follows the Latin original closely, adding only the words "Jesus" and "in glory."

The third acclamation — the fourth of the ICEL series — is primarily intercessory, although the ICEL translation has suppressed the petitionary character. In the Latin original the prayer is primarily one of petition, invoking Christ as Savior through his death and resurrection.

If we reflect on the Latin texts we see that the traditional pattern has been maintained to the extent that all are addressed to Christ and that all make mention of the passion/death and resurrection.[15] The first two Latin texts express an eschatological orientation; the third does so only by implication in its plea for salvation. It would seem, then, that only the first is a *memorial* acclamation in the strict sense; the second centers on communion in the meal, and the third is a prayer of petition. In effect the Latin texts provide for congregational participation, respectively, in the anamnesis, the communion-epiclesis, and the intercessions.

It is important to examine the Latin texts, since the ICEL translations have distorted the character of the Latin acclamations. Doctrinally, of course, the translations are completely orthodox. But in terms of accuracy and adequacy of translation something is lacking. As Mark Twain once said, the difference between the precise word

discussed, with the emphasis that "this mystery of faith is the Paschal Mystery, the whole mystery of Christ dying, rising, saving men until his second coming; it is Emmanuel, Jesus living in the midst of his people" (p. 23). In notes on the translation the BCL calls attention to this acclamation as the "real creed of the Eucharist" (p. 41). It goes on to offer as rationale for ICEL's first of two variant translations that [1] it is easily understood; [2] the third person format is more closely related to the style of the priest's proclamation of the anamnesis which follows it. It is our opinion that this translation is unnecessarily catechetical in form and reinforces a didactic and exhortatory view of the liturgy.

[15] The second Latin text is an exception, in that, like the scriptural text on which it is based, it makes no mention of the resurrection.

and almost-right word is the difference between lightning and a lightning bug. The distortion introduced by the ICEL texts can have quite an effect on the future development of the eucharistic prayer and of congregational involvement in it because of the possibility of alternative texts. Particularly significant is the fact that the first ICEL text, as a trio of short statements, becomes in effect a profession or proclamation of faith rather than an acclamation as such. Since the first of four optional official texts has been the most widely used, it has set the pattern for alternate forms.[16] What was intended as an acclamation and a prayer thus becomes a form of catechesis and an exhortation to the congregation.

Undoubtedly a reason for the overuse of the first — and poorest — of the ICEL acclamations is the difficulty of "cuing in" the congregation if one of the others is used. It is unfortunate that the French provision of different introductions to each of the acclamations was not copied. This suggestion which was made at the time the three new Latin eucharistic prayers were released has been adopted in Canada.[17]

[16] The alternate text most often used in this country is probably Lucien Deiss's "Keep in Mind." This too is a third-person reminder to the congregation, although it is undoubtedly a more kerygmatic form of catechesis.

[17] Commentators also suggested adaptation of the acclamations to make them more suitable for various cultures; see, for example, C. Braga, "De novis precibus eucharisticis liturgiae latinae," *Ephemerides Liturgicae* 82 (1968) 236. The French acclamations are as follows:

Il est grand, le mystère de la foi:
  Nous proclamons ta mort, Seigneur Jésus,
  nous célébrons ta résurrection,
  nous attendons ta venue dans la gloire.
Quands nous mangeons ce pain et bouvons à cette coupe,
nous célébrons le mystère de la foi:
  nous rappelons ta mort,
  Seigneur ressuscité,
  et nous attendons que tu viennes.
Proclamons le mystère de la foi:
  Gloire à toi qui étais mort,
  gloire à toi qui es vivant,
  notre Sauveur et notre Dieu:
  viens, Seigneur Jésus!

There are other interesting characteristics to the French translations. Only three, all modeled more closely on the Latin texts, are provided. The second adds the proclamation of the resurrection, not found in the original Latin. The third, like the fourth English text, suppresses the petitionary character but, unlike the Latin and the English, adds the eschatological dimension.

We will return to the question of other texts for this acclamation after noting the final form of congregational participation provided for in the present Roman prayers. But, in terms of fundamental building blocks of eucharistic prayer, it is important to note that just as the Sanctus enables the congregation to participate in the element of praise and thanksgiving, the acclamations after the institution narrative make it possible for the congregation to share in memorializing and petitioning.

THE DOXOLOGY AND AMEN

Like the introductory dialogue and the Sanctus, the doxology of the eucharistic prayer has been fairly invariable in the tradition. Following the structure of the *berakah* it is a return to the theme of praise and thanks and sets a seal on this dominant eucharistic theme. Following the pattern of Christian prayer, it is trinitarian in structure. The doxology has generally concluded with a congregational Amen, a genuine acclamation signifying the congregation's agreeing to, and sharing in, what has been proclaimed. This feature was particularly emphasized in the early history of the Roman rite. The ratification of the whole eucharistic prayer by the congregation is the oldest and most basic form of congregational participation in the prayer.

The Amen, however, seems inadequate in our culture to express this. The fact that the Amen, when sung, is almost always multiplied or farced, seems to imply that a single word or even a short phrase is not a satisfactory form of congregational involvement. Thus in many places it is becoming customary for the congregation to join in the doxology itself, whether recited or sung. Objections to this growing practice have been based on the statement that this is part of the eucharistic prayer and thus properly presidential, not congregational. However, as we have seen, the Sanctus is likewise a part of the eucharistic prayer.

OTHER FORMS OF CONGREGATIONAL INVOLVEMENT

From the fact that the congregation has been involved in the praying of the eucharistic prayer, it is obvious that such involvement is possible without destroying the presidential character of the prayer. Theologically such involvement does not eliminate the unique role of the president of the assembly as moderator of its prayer and herald of the *mirabilia Dei.* It would seem that only pastoral and cultural norms can determine the amount and manner of congregational involvement, whether by listening, dialogue, acclamations or other prayers. Likewise, the form such involvement takes should be determined by pastoral and cultural norms: acclamations, prayers, litanies, short hymns, and so on. The purpose of such involvement is to express the role of the people, who they are in the assembly, and to manifest their participation either symbolically (for example, by posture) or verbally. What is important is that any such participation be integrated into the rhythm of the prayer: that it preserve the unity of the prayer and not fragment it and that it be homogeneous with its structure and direction.

As should be clear, such congregational participation is not an interruption of the prayer nor an intrusion, as though somehow really out-of-place or superfluous. Rather, it is the congregation's *participation in* the prayer. With this in mind, it would be well to list the places where the congregation joins the priest in the proclaiming of the eucharistic prayer in other rites.[18]

1. The initial dialogue and final Amen are apparently universal and probably derive from Jewish prayer forms. In improvised prayers no other congregational participation would have been possible.

2. The Sanctus has been in Eastern liturgies since the fourth century and in the Roman since the beginning of the fifth. It has always been placed in the first part of the prayer where the theme of praise and thanksgiving is more clearly expressed. The development of the Roman liturgy stopped here with regard to congregational involvement until the twentieth century, but in other rites there was further development.

3. An acclamation of praise is found in most of the oriental rites as part of the prayer of anamnesis and offering, immediately before the epiclesis.

4. The Egyptian and Palestinian anaphora have a memorial acclamation, properly so-called.

5. The institution narrative is ratified by the congregation's Amen in the oriental rites and in the Western Mozarabic rite. The Greek Anaphora of Saint James provides for distinct roles for priest, deacon and people.

6. The epiclesis is emphasized by an Amen or an intercessory choir chant in some rites, notably the Coptic, Chaldean and Armenian.

7. The congregation frequently takes part in the intercessions, for

[18] For a more detailed study and citation of examples, see J. Gelineau, "Les interventions de l'assemblée dans le canon de la messe," *La Maison-Dieu* no. 87 (1966) 141–149; Maldonaldo, *La Plegaria Eucaristica*, 485–491.

instance, through the Kyrie eleison response; for example, Chaldean, Coptic, Armenian, Saint James.

8. The conclusion of the prayer also provides a place for congregational participation, whether through a simple Amen or a more elaborate acclamation.

Clearly, the conclusion is that there is no part of the eucharistic prayer in which the congregation has absolutely no part to play!

Admittedly, none of these, except for the dialogue, Sanctus, and Amen are part of the Roman tradition. Yet, since the Sanctus itself was borrowed from the East very early and the memorial acclamation was adopted more recently, there is no intrinsic reason why the arrested development of the Roman eucharistic prayers should not be resumed. In fact it has, for the eucharistic prayers for masses with children provide a recurring refrain during the prayer, and this possibility is in practice being extended to adult congregations.

Possibilities, then, for further congregational participation seem possible even under a strict interpretation of the present rubrics. Such participation would follow the pattern of the present "memorial" acclamation as a response to the Lord's words, "Do this in memory of me." The participation could thus be strictly memorial, look toward the completion of the memorial through communion in the meal, or be intercessory — the forms we have seen in our examination of the Latin texts of the official "memorial" acclamations. At this point in the prayer it is, of course, memorial — and thus the first Latin text — which is most appropriate, although the element of communion is obviously not altogether alien since we have just heard the Lord's command to eat and drink. Although the third of the Latin acclamations is itself intercessory in nature, intercession would seem most appropriate *after* the anamnesis and epiclesis.

Several compositions already in use as hymn refrains would appear to be textually suitable for use.[19] Musically, acclamations should be "rhythmically strong, melodically appealing, and affirmative."[20] Beyond this, they should be simple enough to be easily learned and sung from memory. The use of a litany form, making

[19] Deiss's "Keep in mind" is not suitable. Joe Wise's "Anamnesis" and Carey Landry's "Amen, Lord" center around the theme of memorial. Tom Parker's "We Come to join in your banquet of love" expresses a communion theme. Others that would serve as either communion or intercessory prayers include Reilly's "We long for you, O Lord"; Deiss's "You broke the reign of death," "Grant to us," "Glory and praise to you," "Eucharistic acclamation," "Your holy death," and "You alone are holy."

[20] *Music in Catholic Worship*, 53.

use of deacon and cantor in conjunction with the congregation, should not be overlooked.[21]

In terms of the text, then, these compositions should have the following characteristics: [1] They should be addressed to Christ if they immediately follow the Lord's command, "Do this in memory of me." [2] They should be relatively brief. [3] They should speak of memorial or communion or embody an intercession appropriate to this portion of the eucharistic prayer. [4] They should not look to the eucharistic elements themselves in isolation, nor should they be a profession of faith in the real presence; the eschatological element should be clearly expressed. [5] They are intended to be sung.

Two other suggestions might be offered. An epicletic or intercessory acclamation might more appropriately be placed in conjunction with that portion of the prayer rather than follow immediately on the institution narrative. Second, while the present officially provided options are not at all related to the liturgical seasons, it would seem appropriate to have texts which do relate to those seasons.

Acclamations of this type — memorial, communion, or intercessory — are possible even within the present legal restrictions. There should be no doubt of this if they occupy the place of the "memorial" acclamation; it could also be argued that their relocation to a more appropriate part of the prayer is likewise possible, following the precedent of the prayers intended for masses with children. Other developments are taking place which go beyond the present legal bounds. A word of comment on some of these will complete our treatment.

[21] The dialogal character of many of the oriental anaphoras, particularly the Coptic and Ethiopian, offers intriguing possibilities here, as does the recurring refrain in the new eucharistic prayers for masses with children. An example which I composed and which was set to music by Robert Twynham is the "L'Esterel Anamnesis":

Deacon/Cantor:	We proclaim your praise, O Christ our Savior.
Congregation:	You are Alpha, you are Omega, you are the Beginning and the End.
Deacon/Cantor:	The power of your dying bearing fruit in us.
Congregation:	You are Alpha, you are Omega, you are the Beginning and the End.
Deacon/Cantor:	The glory of your rising living now in us.
Congregation:	You are Alpha, you are Omega, you are the Beginning and the End.
Deacon/Cantor:	We proclaim your praise until you come again.
Congregation:	You are Alpha, you are Omega, you are the Beginning and the End.

Ed Gutfreund's "We remember" follows a similar pattern.

James Dallen

Little needs to be said on the practice of having the congregation pray together the whole of the eucharistic prayer: this practice has no basis in the tradition and has little to recommend it on pastoral or cultural grounds. The praying of the anamnesis by the congregation is perhaps more defensible, although it would seem an unnecessary duplication if a memorial acclamation has been sung. Similarly, the joining of the congregation in the element of anamnesis which explicates offering seems intrinsically sound. An even stronger defense of the practice of the congregation's joining in the intercessions of the prayer can be given: these are properly diaconal rather than presidential and in many of the Eastern rites take the form of a litany to which the congregation responds. We have already commented on the congregation's sharing the doxology. Apart from these instances of the congregation's joining in the official text of the prayer, there have been few other developments of which I am aware. Interestingly, although the congregational ratification of the words of the institution narrative with a strong Amen has a sound basis in the Eastern tradition, there seems to have been little use made of the precedent, although Deiss's "Glory and praise to you, Lord Jesus Christ" has on occasion been so used.

In this paper we have stayed close to the pattern presented in the tradition and in official contemporary prayers. We have not examined other literary possibilities and techniques which would be possible in contemporary compositions. While such an examination would be worthwhile, it would not be of practical value in most of our parishes at the present time.

The acclamations in the eucharistic prayer, as we have seen, are not, properly speaking, acclamations at all, with the exception of the Amen; they are rather short hymns or prayers praising the Father (the Sanctus) or acclaiming Christ (the so-called memorial acclamation). The ancient pattern of the Sanctus can be maintained in our culture with little difficulty. The newly introduced memorial acclamation is open to considerable development within existing legislation as congregational participation in anamnesis, communion-epiclesis, and intercession. As is evident from an examination of other rites, there are also other possibilities for congregational involvement in the eucharistic prayer. Some of these are presently being utilized; of these, the sharing of the doxology seems the most likely to receive official approval within the near future.

Philippe Rouillard

From Human Meal to Christian Eucharist

The study which we present here is intended as a contribution to a better understanding of the mystery of the Eucharist and with that to a better celebration of that sacrament. Its basic premise is that the Eucharist, instituted by Christ during the course of a meal, is deeply rooted in a human action indispensable to life and moreover rich in human and sacred symbolism: eating and drinking and having a meal. We cannot understand the full meaning of the eucharistic meal if we do not reflect first on the meaning of the meal as a human reality and then note how in the Old Testament the human symbolism of the meal was enriched with new values by the celebration of the great events of the history of salvation with sacred meals which serve as signs of covenant or memorial. In the gospel Christ, invited to meals and inviting people to his own meal, progressively gives a new meaning and content to the human celebration of the meal. Finally the Church, to which Christ confided his memorial, progressively undertook the ritualization of the Last Supper and the elaboration of its liturgical symbolism; this was largely accomplished in the first few centuries, but periodic adjustment is required — the most recent being achieved with the publication of the Missal of Paul VI.

In the pages which follow we shall attempt to explore, in a somewhat cursory and incomplete way, the abundant riches of the human, biblical and liturgical meaning of the "breaking of the bread" in which the risen Savior reveals himself and gives himself to those who believe in him. This should serve to highlight somewhat neglected aspects of the Eucharist and also to show — at least in our consideration of the liturgical shape of the Eucharist — how the modification of a sign or symbol can alter our perception of the reality signified.

THE MEANING OF NOURISHMENT AND MEAL

Nourishment meets an imperious need of man. But we must also note that in addition to their nutritive function some foods and beverages, such as bread and wine in Mediterranean civilization, possess great symbolic value. Moreover, the meal, which is a specifically human manner of nourishing oneself, is also charged with many meanings.[1]

1. *Hunger, Nourishment and Life.* If man seeks nourishment, it is because he experiences hunger. Hunger — and its corollary, thirst — are fundamental forms of human need. While it is difficult to define hunger, everyone experiences it; it is experienced as an appeal of the body, as a signal that the sources of energy are spent and that they must be recreated or restored. Language reflects this: we give the names "refectory" and "restaurant" to places where we habitually go to seek "recreation" or "restoration."

In speaking of hunger, it is necessary to distinguish between daily, normal hunger, sure of finding nourishment, and extraordinary hunger — famine — where there is no assurance of nourishment. During thousands of years the organization of human groups was dominated by the more or less anxious quest for nourishment, and even today, especially in Africa and Asia, many human beings experience mortal hunger or starvation. Whether chronic or occasional, hunger gives human beings a consciousness of their existence but also an anguished awareness of the cessation of existence. Perhaps it is necessary to have experienced real hunger, if only once, in order to recognize the price of life.

In speaking of thirst, it is necessary to make the same distinction between normal thirst, where one needs to take only a few steps to find some water, wine or whisky, and the anguished thirst of someone lost in the desert and searching in vain for water. Moreover, there is this difference between hunger and thirst: that thirst is a much more urgent need which, if not satisfied, quickly places one in danger of death.

Let us also note that the words "hunger" and "thirst" are often employed in a figurative sense to express all the desires of human beings: one has hunger or thirst for power, for wealth, for happiness, for knowledge. Here, too, thirst expresses a more urgent and ardent desire than hunger. In the religious domain one also speaks of hunger for God and especially of thirst for God: ". . . for you my soul thirsts" (Ps 63:1). The themes of hunger and thirst are also

[1] For this study we have used Mario Bacchiega's remarkable book *Il pasto sacro* (Padua: Cidema 1971).

employed in Christ's discourse on the bread of life: "No one who comes to me shall ever be hungry, no one who believes in me shall ever thirst" (Jn 6:35).

The person who is hungry goes in search of the nourishment, animal or vegetable, which will permit him to escape from the danger of death and still his hunger. Food is for him the assurance of energy, of life, of salvation. Without nourishment man is condemned to die; with nourishment he can struggle against death and continue to live. He places at his own service the energy contained in the food, and this energy becomes human energy.

But we must go further. When I nourish myself, I am always eating a being which I have killed or which I have at least prevented from living. I eat an animal which has been killed for me, my life being preferred to its life. I eat something which would have engendered life or sustained the life of another living being: the egg which contained a life in germ, milk (and its derivatives) which were meant to assure the growth of a young animal, vegetables and fruit, the grain of wheat which was a seed. Thus to insure my life and my survival I must take or threaten the life of another being. I must induce death. I nourish myself with a life sacrificed for me.

In every act of nourishment there is therefore presence of life and death, a struggle for life against the danger of death, theft or gift of a life sacrificed in order to permit another to have life and to have it abundantly. The application of this to the Eucharist is evident: in receiving the consecrated bread and wine I nourish myself with the life of the wheat and the grapes sacrificed for me but also with the body of Christ given for me and with his blood shed for me. The source of energy and strength which nourish my life and preserve me from death is no longer the unconscious sacrifice of the bread and wine but the voluntary sacrifice of Jesus Christ, who gives his life for me.

2. *Symbolism of Bread and Wine.* In the sacrament of the Eucharist Christ communicates himself to us under the double sign of bread and wine. Bread and wine are fundamental elements of the nourishment of people in the Mediterranean basin, and in addition to their nutritive function they are rich in symbolism.

First of all we should note that bread and wine are not natural products that man might find in nature, as he finds water, plants and fruit. Bread and wine require a processing by man, who transforms grain into bread and grapes into wine; they are both artificial products, made by man for man's use. In bread as in wine there is a finality introduced by the intelligence and labor of man; as the prayers of the mass put it, they are "fruit of the earth (or vine), work of human hands."

Every morsel of bread is the product and the result of an entire history. First, in the season for planting the grains of wheat are thrown into the bosom of the earth, which is a fertile mother, and after an apparent death and time of gestation or germination, man, marveling, sees a blade grow. Thus the symbolism of bread implies in the first place the image of death and resurrection in the bosom of the earth, and it is understandable that in several mystery cults the history of the grain of wheat was considered a symbol of human history. Subsequently the grain, carefully harvested, is crushed, ground, almost annihilated; countless grains are pulverized and mingled to make flour, which, thanks to human work and the action of fire, finally becomes bread.

This bread, which has required the work of so many hands and the know-how of so many people, is then received either as the staple food or as that which accompanies all other food. Many expressions of contemporary language express this fundamental value of bread: man must earn his bread and the bread of his family; man must get bread to eat with the sweat of his brow (as it is said in Genesis 3:19 with regard to Adam — at a time when bread obviously did not yet exist); the poor man begs for his bread from door to door, while the rich or generous man shares his bread with the hungry or with his friend. Thus bread is much more than an element of nourishment: it is a symbol of work and a symbol of life and, when shared, it is charged with familial and social values.

Like bread, wine is the product of a long and careful preparation. Before tasting wine man must plant the vine, prune it, harvest the grapes, put them under the press, much as he ground the wheat grain, let the juice ferment, and finally age the wine. Wine is made by man, exclusively for man's use.

Wine gives man vigor and vitality. Because of its red color, and because it springs forth from the cluster of grapes, it is often associated with blood, and this association was adopted by Christ in the Eucharist. Wine is regarded as a beverage of life and immortality. It is not to water, but to alcohol extracted from wine, that the name "eau-de-vie" is given.

Wine stimulates the spirit of man, as language attests with the use of the term "spirituous" to designate wines high in alcoholic content (*spiritueux* in French, *spiritoso* in Italian, *geistiges Getränk* in German). In this vein the entire Christian tradition has seen a special relation between the eucharistic wine and the Holy Spirit.

Absorbed in abundance, wine induces drunkenness, and due to this fact it becomes the means and a symbol of knowledge and initiation. Drinking wine affords access to a new world of vision and intelligence. Thanks to wine the spirit of man is liberated from time and from human misery and enjoys an experience of the marvelous and the inaccessible. In a more religious perspective, drunkenness affords access to the world of the gods, and thus it is understandable how it constituted one of the factors in initiation to the mysteries and to divine life. This initiatory function of wine is to be found in a large number of cultures which have practiced, or still practice, collective ritual drunkenness. "The effect of these drinking bouts," according to G. Durand, "is both to create a mystical bond between the participants and to transform the morose condition of man: the inebriating beverage is employed to abolish the daily condition of existence and to afford an orgiastic and mystical reintegration."[2] Without such excess wine gives rise to joy and merriment, and it is difficult to conceive of a feast where one does not drink wine. Christ himself did not hesitate, at the wedding in Cana, to change water into wine.

Wine is furthermore an efficacious symbol of sharing and communion. Members of a group gathered to celebrate together drink from the same cup, or at least they toast each other, signifying with that gesture their intention of drinking symbolically from one cup. As is known, in the Jewish wedding ritual the two young spouses drink from the same cup, which is then broken as a sign of a union in which no third party can participate.

Finally, because it is costly, and especially because it is regarded as a symbol to blood, wine was often employed in sacrifices. To pour out wine, to make a libation, signifies the shedding of blood and thus the sacrifice of life. Employing the symbolic sign of wine, man offers his own life to the divinity which he wishes to appease or render propitious.

All of this symbolism of wine, particularly in its aspects of sacrifice and communion, underlies the Eucharist. One can therefore only

[2] *Les structures anthropologiques de l'imaginaire* (Paris: Bordas 1969) 299.

rejoice that the Roman Catholic Church of our time, concerned with promoting a better understanding of the symbolic language of Jesus, has restored the possibility of participating in the eucharistic meals under the species of both bread and wine.

At every mass Christ, it should be noted, gives himself to his own not under a single sign: bread *or* wine, but under a double sign: bread *and* wine. Our faith assures us that Christ is really and totally present under each of these signs. However, it is also a fact that Christ wishes to communicate himself to us under this double sign of bread and wine. From this we should conclude that contemplation of the Eucharist should not concentrate exclusively on Christ's presence but also on the meaning of the signs chosen for this and on the complementary character of these two signs.

The use of bread and wine in a sacred meal was not an innovation on the part of Christ. Various peoples, notably the Greeks, had already combined bread and wine in the sacrifices which they presented to the gods. Jewish practice provided an immediate precedent: at the beginning and end of every solemn meal the Jews pronounced a blessing over the bread and a blessing over the wine. In instituting his Eucharist during the course of a Jewish religious meal Christ conformed to this usage already charged with human and sacred values.

The bread and the wine are complementary. The two respond to two essential urges of the human animal, the bread to his hunger, and the wine to his thirst. The bread is the fruit of the earth, a fertile mother, while the wine appears more as the fruit of the sun, without which nothing grows. Bread is a material food which insures existence, while wine is a spiritual beverage which incites to action and to the transcending of the daily limits of existence. The bread is assimilated and transformed in man's body, while the wine has the power to transform man, to cause him to become other. This diversity and this complementarity of signs and meaning must not be neglected in the theology and catechesis of the Eucharist.

These few indications suffice to show that the bread and wine employed in the sacrament are not only food and beverage but that they imply an entire human and religious symbolism. It is thus understandable that the Church intervened during the course of the first few centuries to prohibit the substitution of other elements for the bread and wine used at the Last Supper. Bishops and councils condemned the Aquarians, who from the second to the fourth century presumed to use water instead of wine, and the Artotyrites, shepherds who celebrated the Eucharist in the fourth century with bread and cheese.[3] However, we should note that these episcopal and conciliar condemnations were addressed to communities in the Mediterranean world familiar with bread and wine and their symbolism. They should not be invoked to settle the question for regions of the world not acquainted with wheat and the grape vine. Bread and wine are foreign words for many Christians of Africa and the Far East who do not use them as food and drink. One can very legitimately wonder whether it is in accord with Christ's intention to employ signs which in these regions really do not signify anything and if it would not be better to adopt instead some food and beverage in use in the region in question.[4] A student from Thailand once told me that it would be inconceivable in his country that a religious man should drink wine; it is a fault as grave for a Christian as for a Moslem. There can therefore be no question in such countries of proposing communion from the cup for the faithful. Is it really necessary to conform to Mediterranean usage, or should one seek a local transposition of the elements? At the same time, it cannot be denied that during the course of the past fifty years bread and wine are widely used in regions which previously were unacquainted with them. In modifying the present discipline would we be serving the past or the future. And what future?

3. *The Human Meal.* In instituting the Eucharist Christ took not only the signs of bread and wine but also the sign of the meal. Between nourishment and the meal there is a difference of degree and meaning. The meal consists in eating together and following a certain order. If nourishment responds to a biological necessity, the meal responds to a properly human need. While an animal eats, man has a meal.

For an Occidental at least, a meal implies a succession and a com-

[3] We find references to various groups of Aquarians from the second to the fourth century, notably by Saint Cyprian (Ep. 63; Corpus scriptorum ecclesiasticorum latinorum 3:701–717). The Artotyrites are known to us from the writings of Epiphanius of Salamis (*Panarion*, 49; *Patrologia graeca* 41:880), who associates them with the Montanists; they lived in Galatia in the fourth century. A council of Hippo in 393 rules against all possible deviations: "In the sacrament of the body of Christ nothing must be sacrificed except bread and wine mixed with water" (Canon 23; Sacrorum Conciliorum nova et amplissima Collectio, ed. J. D. Mansi, 3:922).

[4] Cf. R. Luneau, "Une eucharistie sans pain et sans vin?" *Spiritus*, no. 48 (1972) 3–11.

plementarity of foods and drinks, following an order which varies from country to country and from culture to culture. Man seated at table wishes to still his hunger, more or less real, but he also seeks the pleasure of eating and eating well. For him a meal is not only a useful thing but a pleasurable thing.

Moreover, the human meal is normally taken in common: it brings together a family, friends, a community. The meal taken in common seals belonging to a same group. It implies an idea of communion and sharing: those who share a same meal constitute a same body, and the fact of inviting someone to eat with one is perceived as an efficacious sign of integration and communion.

The meal constitutes one of the elements of the human feast. The celebration of an event such as birth or baptism, marriage, funerals, but also some success, an inauguration, an anniversary almost always comprises a festive meal: a feast for the body, thanks to special dishes, and a feast for the familial or social body, thanks to conversation, exchange and sharing. French usage is revealing in this regard: *festin*, a sumptuous meal, derives from *fête*, feast, and the *festin* brings together guests, *convives*, who for at least the time of the banquet are nourished at the same sources of life.

When there is no complete meal, an event may be celebrated by participation in a cocktail or sherry hour with hors d'oeuvres, the purpose of which is not to appease hunger and quench thirst but to provide a snack of tasty food and an agreeable drink and to insure the communion of those who take part. In such cases the nutritive value of the meal is almost entirely superseded by its symbolic value. This is noteworthy, since the Eucharist figures as a meal in which the symbolic and spiritual richness infinitely surpasses its nutritive substance.

4. The Ritual and Sacred Meal. Almost all religions feature a sacred meal or various types of sacred meals, that is, meals in which the god or gods intervene in some way. Four categories or principal orientations can be distinguished: man lets himself be eaten by the god, more or less symbolically, as a sign of homage; man eats the god, in order to receive from him strength and immortality; man and the god share the same meal, for example, to seal a covenant; finally, men celebrate a memorial meal in order to commemorate an event in the history of the relations between the divinity and their people.

Confronted with the divinity, man spontaneously has a reaction of fear and fright, for this power seems to him fearful and often hostile. To obtain the god's favor or to appease his anger man must offer him a sacrifice, that is, consecrate to him something taken from his own goods, preferably a living, eatable being, either vegetable or animal, with which the god can nourish himself. Actually man could and should immolate himself in homage to the divinity, but for reasons easy to understand he prefers to immolate another life, that of a prisoner, an infant or an animal. The victim offered to the god is thus both real and symbolic — real, since a life is really sacrificed, symbolic since this life represents that of man himself.

Thus in New Guinea, during the course of the rites of initiation, boys having reached the age of puberty were symbolically devoured by the spirit of the forest; they crawled into a hut which represented the belly of the spirit and remained there for some days, long enough to be digested, and then left the hut by a small opening, and pigs were immolated in their stead.[5]

From antiquity to our days numerous civilizations have had recourse to human sacrifices: to conciliate the good grace of the god prisoners of war or children were sacrificed to him. The Phoenicians offered their sons to the god Moloch, and we know that more than once the Hebrews practiced human sacrifices — condemned by Deuteronomy 12:31; 18:10. The story of the sacrifice of Isaac is a case of human sacrifice — more precisely that of an only son — replaced by the sacrifice of an animal. As is known, even today, in some regions of Africa, children are offered in sacrifice to bring the blessing of the gods on a new village or to avert an epidemic. The idea underlying these sacrifices is that the divinity has the right to require the life of man for nourishment, just as man sacrifices the life of animals to insure his own subsistence. The life of man has, indeed, more importance than that of animals, but for the equilibrium of the world the life of the gods is still more important than that of man.

Confronted with the divinity, an awesome force, man experiences fear, but he also has the desire to appropriate this force or at least to participate in it. To receive the strength of the god, to participate in his divinity, to achieve divinization in some manner — such is the ideal that almost all religions propose to their adherents. Thus man wishes to nourish himself with the divinity, which will communicate to him its energy, its life, its immortality.

But how does one eat a god? The solution habitually consists in

[5] Cf. Bacchiega (n. 1 above) 92–93.

eating the animal or plant which symbolizes this god. In Ireland there was a great banquet once a year when the king and all the chieftains gathered to eat pork, the pig being the sacred animal which represented the god Lug. Thus the king and the chieftains, and only they, participated in the divine strength and power and governed the people with increased authority. In Greece and elsewhere once a year the faithful of Dionysus, god of the vine and of wine, received the energy of their god by nourishing themselves with a bull, the animal whose appearance Dionysus had assumed to escape from the Titans.

In other religions the faithful were wont to eat a sacred bread; the grain, dead and resurrected, symbolized the god. Thus among the Aztecs, until the Spanish conquest, bread considered the body of the god was eaten. This bread, which had the form of a human person, was broken and distributed to the faithful on the occasion of feasts celebrated twice a year. And the priests brought a morsel of this bread to the sick who had not been able to come to the feast. One cannot but be struck by the parallels with the Eucharist.

These few examples illustrate the desire of man to participate in the divine life, a desire fulfilled thanks to a meal in the course of which he nourishes himself with the god in a symbolic manner. Quite literally, man hungers for God.

A third type of sacred meal is the communion meal. The divinity and the faithful share the same meal, eating the same food, and thus enter into communion. In this case the immolated victim is shared: part is reserved for the god and consumed by fire or eaten by the priests who serve and represent the god, while the other part is eaten by those who have offered the sacrifice. Such a meal has as its purpose to insure communion between the god and men and especially to seal a convenant.

More often the blood and the fatty membrane are reserved for the god, while the faithful nourish themselves with the flesh (cf. Lv 3:1–5; Dt 12:27; Jgs 20:26; 21:4). The same manner of dividing the animal is found in Africa today, where after the sacrifice of a chicken or a goat the blood and the fatty parts, which the fetish is considered to relish, are offered to him, while the flesh of the animals is eaten by the people. In a meal of this type man transposes into his relationship with the divinity what he experiences in his relations with his fellow human beings. In one case as in the other the meal shared is a sign of concord and it is the necessary complement of the conclusion of a pact or a covenant. The accord between two partners, whether equal or unequal, is sealed by the meal which unites them.

The sacred meal can have yet another function and meaning: it can be the means of commemorating, of reviving, so to speak, each year an event in the history of the god or of an intervention of the god in favor of his people. In this case the meal is placed in relation with history, it is "historicized." Thus among the Jews the passover meal was the annual memorial of the liberation of the people by the passage through the Red Sea.

Such a meal is generally accompanied with a recital, an evocation, an instruction, which is an oral commemoration of the event, to which is then added, with the meal, a commemoration in sacrifice and communion. The evocation of the past event is made first at the level of memory, then at the level of the ritual meal. The liturgy of the word elicits the liturgy of the meal, which actualizes here and now the past event, or at least renders present the divine benevolence manifested in the event. The people who celebrate the memorial become conscious of this divine benevolence thanks to the account, and they are nourished with it thanks to the meal which is a complementary form of assimilation.

This brief inquiry should suffice to show how — at least in the Mediterranean world — people have always been attentive to the human value of eating and drinking, how they have recognized and attributed special significance to foodstuffs such as bread and wine, and finally how they have given symbolic value to the meal, locus and means of exchange and communication between the participants, whether these be simple mortals or whether the gods, in some manner or the other, come and are seated at table with men.

To be candid, we must note the limits of these findings. The data we have advanced depends on a particular culture and is not equally valid with regard to all cultures. All those who have lived in Africa know that the traditional meal is not a locus and occasion of exchange and sharing: one eats quickly and in silence, and one does not speak until after having consumed the meal. The African is astonished to see a European remain at table for hours or even for half an hour. Sometimes he considers it improper to eat in the presence of others, particularly in the presence of people he respects.

And in the Western world the symbolic content of eating, drinking and meals which we have analyzed are no longer always experienced. People who have really experienced hunger and thirst are not very numerous, people, that is, who have heard the cries of their bodies. Moreover, bread is no longer that precious food, surrounded with care and respect, which it was for centuries, and the consumption of bread decreases as the standard of living increases: we hunger for richer foods than bread. Nevertheless, in language and certain customs bread still retains great symbolic value. And wine, and especially the practice of drinking together, retain all of their human and social meaning. The same is true, if not of the daily family meal, at least of the festive meal, to which relatives and friends are invited. At the same time the concept of a ritual meal does not in the Western world have any basis in our experience other than the Eucharist. These limits of our human experience can render understanding of the Eucharist more difficult.

SACRED MEALS IN THE OLD TESTAMENT

We shall attempt here to discern the meaning of the meal as a locus and means of encounter between God and his people in the Old Testament. The disciples and the Christians of the first generation could not, after all, abstract from this past in their understanding of the Last Supper. If today we spontaneously interpret the Last Supper in the light of the liturgical Eucharist which the Church has practiced for twenty centuries, it is evident that Christ himself presented it to his disciples in the light of, and as a prolongation of, the meals of the Old Testament. Thus we should at least recall the meals of the Old Testament to which the catechesis of the gospels refers.

As a preliminary comment let us suggest a possible interpretation of chapter 3 of Genesis, where God forbids Adam and Eve to eat of the fruit of the tree which is in the middle of the garden: "You shall not eat of it, even touch it, lest you die" (Gn 3:3). The desire to eat the forbidden fruit is the symbol of all the appetites man must control. Man wishes to seize control of the world, and next he perceives his nakedness. When Adam has eaten the forbidden fruit, he discovers his nudity and hides. Similarly, Noah, at the beginning of the new creation, lets himself become drunk with wine, which gives him access to an unknown world, and he finds himself naked. God forbids man to taste certain fruits which put him in danger of death, and on the other hand Christ declares: "If you do not eat the flesh of the Son of Man and drink his blood, you have no life in you" (Jn 6:53). In one and the same act of eating and drinking life and death intervene, the possibility for man to receive or lose the life of God.

1. *Manna and Living Water.* In the desert the Hebrews, who consider themselves abandoned by God, see manna fall from the heavens: the manna is a food but also a sign of the efficacious presence of God in the midst of his people (Ex 16:1–36). Manna is bread, a gift of God which nourishes the body but which especially restores vigor to weak and discouraged man, to man of little faith. Manna is bread for the route, for the crossing of the desert to the borders of the promised land. This bread serves to test man, since it cannot be kept for the following day; man must live each day with trust. Christ refers to the manna as an incomplete and imperfect figure of the Eucharist.

In the account of Exodus the miracle of the manna is accompanied by the miracle of the water which springs forth from the rock (Ex 17:1–7). In relating these two accounts somewhat artificially the narrator wishes to show that God responds to the hunger and thirst of his people. The gift of water, like the gift of manna, is above all the sign of the sustaining presence of God in the midst of his own. In this rock from which water springs forth Saint Paul sees a figure of the Eucharist (1 Cor 10:4).

The manna and the living water thus appear as God's somewhat delayed response to the hunger and thirst of his people. The manna and the water are genuine nourishment and drink, but at the same time they are "spiritual," as Saint Paul says, and signify the presence of God accompanying and sustaining his people in the long trek across the desert. This nourishment manifests the divine benevolence, but at the same time it provides the occasion for testing the faith of man: as we have already noted, the manna required renewed trust every day, and it is said that Moses himself, at the moment he struck the rock from which water sprung forth, lacked faith (Nm 20:11–12).

2. *The Banquet of the Covenant.* In instituting the Eucharist Christ presents his blood to the Apostles declaring that it is the blood of the new covenant. Thus he refers to the first covenant included or sealed in blood: the covenant of Sinai (Ex 24:1–11). In this admirable text we see that the covenant between God and his people is celebrated by a double rite: the rite of blood (v. 6–8) and the rite of the banquet (v. 11). According to exegetes, we have here two traditions: the Yahwist tradition of the meal before God (v. 1–2 and 9–12) and the Elohist tradition of sprinkling with blood (v. 3–8).

According to the Yahwist tradition — the older — the covenant is concluded by a sacred meal in the presence of God. It is not the entire people but only the chiefs and elders who participate in this meal. The meal is bound to a vision of God, to a contemplation of God: "And they beheld the God of Israel" (Ex 24:10). God, granting his favor to man, lets himself be seen by man and becomes nourishment for man. To eat in God's sight is a theme which recurs in the Old Testament (e.g., Dt 27:7; 14:26) and is found again in the gospel parables of the heavenly banquet. Man fills himself with God by the gaze of contemplation and by the act of nourishment.

According to the Elohist tradition the covenant is celebrated not with a banquet but with the rite of sprinkling blood (v. 3–8). The blood of the sacrificed animals is sprinkled, half on the altar which represents God, half on the people. The same blood covers God and the people, who thus become blood relatives, belong to the same family, have the same life, since blood is life (Lv 17:14). The covenant or marriage concluded at the level of words and contract (v. 3–4) thus receives a ritual, almost a physical, expression.

The biblical account of the covenant of Sinai combines the two traditions, Yahwist and Elohist: the covenant between God and the people is concluded in blood, in a rite of consanguinity, and it is celebrated with a festive banquet, a locus of the manifestation of God. The Eucharist of Jesus will also be a festive banquet, celebrating the new covenant concluded in his blood poured out for the many.

3. *Memorial Meal.* The Eucharist, covenant meal, is also a memorial meal. It responds to the command of Christ: "Do this for my memorial." Moreover, it was instituted during the course of a meal which, even if it was not a passover meal in the strict sense, was situated in the context of the passover feast, the memorial of the liberation of the Hebrew people. The Apostles and the first Christians of a Jewish milieu understood the Last Supper of Jesus in the perspective of the passover memorial. We find in Exodus 12:1–28 the complex theological account of the institution of this feast, which is a meal and a memorial. The memorial (*zakar* in Hebrew) is the rite which recalls each year a past event, asks for its prolongation in the present and anticipates its definitive accomplishment in the future. The rite comprises an oral, explanatory catechesis (v. 26–27) and a meal, all the details of which are significant and pedagogical. This memorial is addressed to God and to men: to God who ought not to

forget his benevolence towards his people and the continuity of his design for salvation, to men who ought to thank God for his intervention, remain faithful to the commitments of their forefathers, and nourish themselves with the salvation of God.

The question which interests us particularly is that of the relationship between memorial and meal, between the act of remembering and the act of nourishing oneself. It is necessary to distinguish between remembering, which is of a psychological order, and the memorial, which is of a ritual, religious order. Remembering is individual: I can remember at any time, alone, and without the stimulation of an exterior element. On the contrary, the memorial is collective, periodic, organized: it involves a meeting, a feast, an action which gathers the participants to commemorate an event they do not wish to forget, which ought to retain an influence on their present life: thanks to the memorial the past penetrates our life to insure continuity between the past and the present. In celebrating the memorial we wish to live today from forces contained in the event (or person) we commemorate.

In this perspective one can understand the necessity of a meeting, a periodic assembly, a gathering around a table. The memorial meal is a way of eating history, of appropriating history to put it at the service of the present.

With this we have certainly not exhausted the theology of the meal in the Old Testament. Almost all the meals mentioned there have a sacred character, for there is always question of immolating an animal life in order to conserve or develop a human life, this life which comes from God and belongs to God.

Throughout the entire Old Testament the meal signifies and provokes exchange, communion, hospitality. Men seal their accord by sharing a meal, and the same is true when they contract a covenant with the almighty God. The sacred meal also becomes the locus of the manifestation of God, the genuine nourishment of the believer. Finally, thanks to the memorial meal, God and men insure together the continuity of the history which unites them and which will find its fulfillment in the coming of Christ.

THE MEALS OF CHRIST IN THE GOSPEL

If meals occupy a large place in the life of human beings, they also have an important place in the life of Jesus and his disciples.

During the course of numerous meals Jesus manifests his mission, his power and his glory. His presence and his intervention provide these meals, already rich with so many human significations, with a new depth of content and meaning.

It is certainly not without advantage, in reflecting on the Eucharist, to recall the principal meals reported in the gospels. There can, indeed, be no doubt that Christ thought long in advance of the sacrament of bread and wine which he wished to leave to his disciples and that the multiplications of loaves and other meals were for him a kind of preparation for, or sketch of, the Eucharist. Moreover, the four evangelists, writing several decades after the death of Jesus, already had a long experience of the Eucharist celebrated every Sunday, and in some cases it is apparent that they proposed a eucharistic interpretation of meals they recorded in the gospels.

1. *Christ Invited to Human Meals.* Often during the course of his public life Christ was invited to share the meal of friends, of officials, or of poor people, and he did not decline these invitations under the pretext of fasting or asceticism. He willingly took his place at table, but he did not — at least in the meals recorded by the evangelists — come with empty hands.[6]

At the wedding in Cana (Jn 2:1–11), to which he was invited together with his mother and his disciples, Jesus appears as one guest among others. When the wine runs out, his intervention is solicited not by the waiter but by his mother, who calls attention to the problem. Providing a hint of the mysterious import of his gesture, Jesus changes water into wine, indeed, into an excellent wine which in an unexpected way rejoices the hearts of the company. In the view of the evangelist John, at least, who rereads the event in the light of his long spiritual and sacramental experience, the sign of wine given to human beings can be wholly understood only in reference to the passion — for which the hour has not yet come — and it manifests the glory of Jesus to his disciples. Thus a wedding banquet was for the Lord an opportunity to provide a glimpse of the mystery of his personality.

The meal which Jesus takes in the home of Matthew (Mt 9:10–13) has another meaning. The new disciple Matthew wishes to celebrate the event of his vocation by inviting Jesus to table with his friends,

[6] For the general treatment of these meals see E. Barbotin, *The Humanity of God*, tr. Matthew J. O'Connell (Maryknoll, New York: Orbis Books 1976) 273–305.

who are like him tax collectors and people of bad reputation. While accepting his invitation, Jesus transforms the meaning of the occasion. Instead of being received, it is he who receives these publicans, sinners and sick people he has come to seek; all of these people more or less excommunicated from society are welcomed and admitted by him to the community, or the communion, of his disciples. Luke (5:29) provides a similar account of this banquet: having come as a guest, Christ reverses the roles and becomes the master of the house who invites and gathers the sick, the poor and the ostracized; the meal in which he takes part is transformed, thanks to him, into a locus of healing and welcome.

When, another day, Jesus is invited to eat at the home of Simon the Pharisee (Lk 7:36–50), a woman reputed a sinner finds her way into the dining room, weeps all the tears of her repentance, and receives the pardon of her sins. Christ's meal thus becomes the moment and place of the forgiveness of sins. However, in a more subtle way it is also the moment and place where the true identity of each of the participants is revealed: Simon, who has not performed his duties as host as well as he imagined he had (7:44–47); the reputed sinner, who in reality has given proof of great love (7:39, 47–48), and Christ himself, concerning whom Simon and his guests were questioning each other (7:39, 49). It is not possible for people to share Christ's meal without their masks falling from their faces.

Invited to the home of Martha and Mary (Lk 10:38–42), Christ proposes another teaching in giving them to understand that he comes rather to give than to receive. If anyone presumes to welcome him, let him not become preoccupied with preparing a great dinner, but rather leave himself time to listen.

The meal taken at the home of a pharisee on a sabbath day (Lk 14:1–6), during the course of which Jesus heals a man suffering from dropsy, provides a new occasion to affirm the relationship between meal and healing. People should not be able to be seated at table and take nourishment without concerning themselves for those who live in difficult conditions. Thus when the occasion presents itself, Christ takes the human meal in hand and makes of it the means of fulfilling all hunger, of restoring life afflicted with whatever infirmity. Is it an exaggeration to see here a parabolic teaching on the signification of the Last Supper?

Finally we should call attention to the mysterious meal to which

Jesus is invited at Bethany a few days before his passion. This meal takes place at the home of Simon the Leper (Mt 26:6–13; Mk 14:3–9), but in John's account (12:1–11) the principal protagonists, designated by name, are Martha, who assures the service, Mary, who anoints Jesus' feet with a perfume of high price, and especially Lazarus, who shortly before had been raised from the dead. The explicit mention of Judas, the allusion by Christ to his coming burial, and the participation in the banquet of such a strange personage as a man come back from the shadows of death are so many signs which lead us to relate this meal to the eucharistic meal and to perceive in the Eucharist thus prefigured and announced a celebration of death and resurrection.

To this list of meals to which Christ is invited we should add the episode of the healing of Peter's mother-in-law, who, hardly back on her feet, begins to "serve" Jesus and his first disciples (Mk 1:29–31); the resurrection of the daughter of Jairus, to whom Jesus recommends something be given to eat (Mk 5:43); and the reception in the home of Zacchaeus, a sinner to whom Jesus brings salvation (Lk 19:1–10). These accounts provide further confirmation that Christ not only recognizes the human value of the meal but that he makes use of it in his mission of salvation. Invited to table by people, he manifests himself as the bringer of comfort, of healing, of life and of joy. What the guests expected of the meal, it is he himself who gives it, but at a deeper level: for people who are hungry he becomes true nourishment, that which restores, renews, gives life; for people who are thirsty he becomes true drink, that which quenches thirst, confers vigor and engenders gladness. It can be said that these meals, purposefully recorded by the evangelists, are sacramental meals, because they are human gestures through which and in which Christ communicates the salvation which comes from God.

2. *The Accounts of Multiplication of Loaves.* We do not propose to give a commentary here on the episode of the multiplication of the loaves narrated by the four evangelists (Mt 14:13–21; Mk 6:30–44; Lk 9:10–17; Jn 6:1–15; with a second version in Mt 15:32–39 and Mk 8:1–10). Let us merely point out that even a somewhat attentive study of the redaction of these text provides incontestable evidence of a progressively eucharistic interpretation of this episode: the authors accentuate the parallelism between the formula of blessing and the distribution of the loaves and that of the Eucharist; they replace the term *eulogein* by the more specific term *eucharistein;* they un-

derscore the function confided to the Apostles of distributing the bread to the crowd, thus making it an apprenticeship for their eucharistic ministry. Finally, John concludes his account with the long discourse on the bread of life, which thus becomes a sort of theological explanation of the miracle.[7]

While the other meals recorded in the gospels orientate us especially toward an understanding of the Eucharist as sacrament of salvation and healing, the multiplication of the loaves — such as it is presented to us by the evangelists decades after the event — invites us rather to see in the Eucharist the sacrament of ecclesial gathering, assured by the ministry of the Apostles.

3. *The Meals of the Risen Christ.* It is striking to note that in the brief lapse of time from the resurrection of Christ to his ascension, or rather in the few pages which the evangelists devote to this period, the meals of the risen Christ with his disciples play an unexpected role. Three or four meals are mentioned, during the course of which Jesus manifests himself to his disciples, still hesitant in faith: Easter evening, after a long walk and a lengthy liturgy of the word, it is in the breaking of the bread that the disciples of Emmaus recognize him (Lk 24:13–35; cf. Mk 16:12–13); that same evening he appears to the Eleven "while they were at table" and reproaches them for their unbelief (Mk 16:14) — probably the same appearance of which Luke writes (24:36–43), adding that in order to overcome the unbelief of the Apostles Jesus eats a morsel of grilled fish in their sight; finally on the shore of the Lake of Tiberias Jesus again makes himself known to some of his Apostles, still hesitant, by inviting them to break fast with bread and grilled fish which he himself has prepared for them (Jn 21:9–14).

The primary purpose of these meals is to convince the disciples of the reality of the Lord's resurrection. In the account of Luke 24:36–43 we find a kind of experimental catechesis of the resurrection: on the one hand, Christ shows the Apostles his hands and feet, that is, the traces of his crucifixion; on the other hand, he eats before them to convince them that he is alive. This double experience of the body of

[7] Recent studies on the multiplication of loaves: A Heising, *La moltiplicazione dei pani* (Brescia: Paideia 1970); J. M. Van Cangh, *La multiplication des pains et l'eucharistie* (Paris: Cerf 1975); S. A. Panimolle, "La dottrina eucaristica nel racconto della moltiplicazione dei pani," in *Segni e Sacramenti nel Vangelo di Giovanni*, Studia Anselmiana 66 (Rome 1977) 73–88; P. R. Tragan, "Le discours sur le pain de vie: Remarques sur sa composition littéraire," *op. cit.* 89–119.

Christ is offered as a response to the unbelief of the Apostles.[8]

But in relating the meals which the risen Christ took with his disciples the evangelists likewise wish to show that the glorious Lord renders himself present among his own in the sign of a meal, which is the efficacious sacrament of his presence. For the first Christians the Eucharist, or rather the breaking of the bread, appears not only as the reiteration of the Last Supper, but also as the memory and continuation of the meals during which the risen Christ manifested himself to those who would be his witnesses. If the Last Supper furnishes the liturgical schema of the blessing, as well as the reference to the saving death, it is the meals with the Lord victorious over death that inspire the joyful and eschatological tonality of the celebration. In assembling for the breaking of the bread, Christians are conscious of assembling around the risen Christ who renders himself present among them with all the spiritual power of his resurrection.

Among the meals that Christ took with his disciples the most important is obviously the one we call the "Last Supper," during which he gave his body and blood under the signs of bread and wine and instituted the sacrament of the Eucharist, confiding to his table companions the mission of doing in his memory what he had just done. Then more than ever Christ took in hand nourishment and human meal — a meal which, as it happened, was already a religious meal and very probably a passover meal — and made bread and wine the body and blood which would nourish Christians with his life and his Spirit, just as he made this festal meal the sacrament which would gather them together in the unity of his Church.

We would greatly exceed the limits of an article in attempting to explain how Jesus inserted his Eucharist in the framework of a human meal, more precisely, a Jewish religious meal, and in any case this is to be found in any more or less complete treatise on the sacraments. Here we have attempted instead to show that the sources of the Christian Eucharist are not to be found exclusively in

[8] The fact that Jesus eats in order to prove the reality of his resurrection is to be compared with his recommendation that something to eat be given to the daughter of Jairus after her resurrection (Mk 5:43). Note also the affirmation of Peter: the Apostles are witnesses to the resurrection of Jesus, for they "ate and drank with him after his resurrection from the dead" (Acts 10:40–41). Their faith and their witness find their nourishment in these meals shared with him.

the Last Supper but also in a certain number of meals in which Christ the Savior took part during his earthly life and in the course of his appearances after his resurrection. The Apostles are not only the ones who received the mission and power to renew the Last Supper but also witnesses who ate and drank with the Lord after his resurrection (Acts 10:41). The Eucharist of the Christian community invokes the memory and symbolism not only of the passover meal but of all the meals in which Jesus revealed himself to human beings and communicated salvation to them, of all the human meals which Jesus transignified in taking part in them.

THE SYMBOLIZATION OF THE EUCHARISTIC MEAL IN THE LITURGY

The sacrament of the Eucharist was instituted by Christ within the framework and under the sign of a meal, specifically under the sign of broken bread and a shared cup of wine. These signs constitute a language, and in the following pages we wish to inquire how Christian communities have spoken this language, how they have more or less modified it, proposing in the process a new interpretation of the Eucharist. It is evident that an evolution in the manner of understanding the Eucharist results in a modification in the manner of celebrating it and that, inversely, an evolution of ritual language leads to a shift of accent in theology.

Throughout the centuries the character of meal, and of communion meal, was gradually obscured, to the benefit of other values of the Eucharist, such as sacrifice or adoration. As a result of a great theological and liturgical effort during the last twenty years the Lord's Supper can once more be understood and experienced as a fraternal sacred meal.

We shall take a few "words" of the ritual language of the Eucharist and show their evolution during the course of the ages, and we shall attempt to ascertain the reasons for this. It was not a matter of no consequence that the celebration of the Lord's Supper passed from a house to a church, from a table to an altar, from evening to morning, from ordinary bread to a sacrificial host, and that Christians passed from communion to adoration. A better understanding of this evolution cannot but aid us in understanding the reasons and the stakes which, in some communities at least, make an inverse movement desirable.

1. From House to Church. Christ celebrated the Last Supper in the "upper room" of a house. In doing so he conformed to Jewish custom in accordance with which a religious meal is not taken in the synagogue (the place for readings and prayer) nor in the temple (the place for sacrifice) but in a family home.

The first Christians likewise "broke bread" in their homes (Acts 2:46; 20:8–9). In the beginning the Lord's Supper was thus not celebrated in a sacred place but where the believers assembled. As long as the community was small in numbers and little structured, the place of assembly could change. When the community increased in size, however, there was need for a more adapted, and therefore more stable, locale. Thus Justin, a priest at Rome around A.D. 150, writes: "On the day called Sunday all those who live in the city and those who live in the country gather together in a same place" (I Apology 67). This place of assembly was not a temple but a *domus ecclesiae*, that is, the house of the assembly. The Apologists of the second and third centuries insist on the fact that Christians, in opposition to pagans, have neither temples nor altars.

Historical studies show that the Eucharist was first celebrated in private houses, then in *domus ecclesiae* belonging to the local community, and then, beginning in the fourth century, that is, after the end of the persecutions, in basilicas or churches which were sacred, consecrated places.[9]

As for the meaning of the Eucharist, we see that in the first centuries the eucharistic celebration was bound to the assembling of a community. The true place of celebration is the assembly of the believers, assembled every Sunday to give thanks to God and to take part in the meal which constituted the memorial of Christ. In view of this one can understand the current desire to return to a type of celebration which attaches less importance to the quality of the place than to the reality of the assembly.

2. *From Table to Altar.* It goes without saying that the Last Supper took place around a table, probably a low table around which the guests reclined on cushions according to antique custom (cf. Lk 22:12). Christians of the first centuries, celebrating the Lord's Supper in private houses or in *domus ecclesiae*, likewise employed a table and not an altar. In the fourth century, however, when Christians began to build churches, stone altars were erected in the center of these

[9] Cf. A. G. Martimort, "Le rituel de la consécration des églises," *La Maison-Dieu* no. 63 (1960) 86–95.

churches; and, whereas the Apologists were at pains to explain that Christians did not have altars, the Fathers would exalt the symbolism of the stone altar as a figure of Christ.

Thus the eucharistic liturgy passes from a table to an altar. This passage, so serious in its consequences, merits some brief reflection. In the Western world, at least, a table is the place, the necessary furniture, for a meal; one is seated at table to nourish oneself but also to seek the company of others, to share with them, to nourish friendship and community. To invite someone to a meal is to invite him to one's table. However, the table can become symbolical when the meal itself tends to be reduced to a symbol — a reception, for instance, with wine and cheese. People are no longer seated around the table but remain standing or are seated at some distance from the table, which then serves only as a support for the drinks and food. For the celebration of the Eucharist, which was almost immediately detached from a genuine meal, it sufficed, and still suffices, to have a small table on which to place the bread and the cup of wine.

An altar has a quite different meaning in that it is not a table for people but a table for the gods. Whether it is made of earth, of wood, or of stone, the altar appears as a place of the divine presence, a symbol of the divinity, and especially as the center of a sacrificial cult. In all religions altars and sacrifice are associated. To install an altar in a church means that one proposes to celebrate a sacrifice there.

To be sure, it would be an exaggeration to say that in celebrating the Eucharist not on a table but on an altar one replaces the meal with a sacrifice. Nevertheless, this change of suggestive "words" of the language of liturgical symbols has obviously contributed to the development of doctrinal reflection on the Eucharist as sacrifice.[10]

The passage from table to altar has, we should note, never been total: the Eucharist is celebrated on an altar which remains a table, for in this mystery there is both an offering of a sacrifice to God and nourishment given to human beings. In the East the altar has always been, and still is, called *hagia trapeza* (holy table), and in the usage of several Western languages Christians approach the "holy table" to receive communion. In contemporary pastoral liturgy there is a

[10] Cf. J. de Watteville, *Le sacrifice dans les textes eucharistiques des premiers siècles* (Neuchâtel: Delachaux et Niestlé 1966). Check "altar" in the Index.

tendency to speak of "the table of the word" in parallelism with the eucharistic table.

Nevertheless, it is a fact that the passage from house to temple and from table to altar emphasized the sacrificial character of the Eucharist at the risk of minimizing the aspect of communal meal. The use of an altar, as well as emphasis on the sacrifice, coincided quite naturally with the progressive elimination of mystery religions and sacrifices in the Graeco-Roman world; Christian worship did not employ sacrificial language unreservedly until a time when all risk of confusion or of syncretism with paganism had disappeared.

Today a rediscovery of the value of the Eucharist as a communion and community meal gives rise to practice of celebrating, on occasion, in homes and on a table. In returning, after sixteen centuries, from church to house and from altar to table, we must, to be sure, be on guard against possible deviations in the celebration of the Lord's Supper, but the practice can be an aid in rediscovering a richness of content and meaning and of imperatives which are an integral part of the human sign of meal which Christ chose for his sacrament.

3. From Evening to Morning. Not less than the place, the time and the hour of the celebration count in the manner in which the Eucharist is experienced. For time, in which human beings live, is rich with a symbolism which we experience daily, and we do not participate in mass in identical fashion whenever it is celebrated — at dawn, at twilight, or at midnight.

Christ instituted the Eucharist in the course of an evening meal. He likewise made himself known to the disciples of Emmaus when the day was "practically over" (Lk 24:29), and he appeared to the eleven Apostles Easter evening "while they were at table" (Mk 16:14). The eucharistic celebration of Paul at Troas, the account of which is so interesting for both historian and theologian, begins Saturday evening and is prolonged — exceptionally — almost all night from Saturday to Sunday (Acts 20:7–11).

However, we find that quite early the Sunday Eucharist began to be celebrated at dawn Sunday — before work, since Sunday was not a free day. The practical reason for this no doubt was that in the Graeco-Roman world day ran from midnight to midnight, while in the Semitic world it ran from sunset to sunset the following day; for an inhabitant of Jerusalem Sunday thus began Saturday evening, while for a citizen of Athens or Rome it began with dawn Sunday. But there was also a theological justification for the practice: since the risen Christ first manifested himself Sunday morning, it is appropriate to perform at that hour the breaking of the bread, thanks to which the risen Savior renders himself present among his own.

From the middle of the third century we have a remarkable text of Saint Cyprian of Carthage: "It was not in the morning but after dinner (*post cenam*) that the Lord offered the cup. Is it not then after dinner that we should celebrate the Lord's Supper? But it was appropriate that Christ made his offering at the decline of day, so that the very hour of the sacrifice might signify the decline and the evening of the world. . . . As for us, it is the resurrection of the Lord that we celebrate in the morning."[11] Thus to the question as to why the Eucharist passed from evening to morning the bishop of Carthage responds that the Sunday liturgy is above all a memorial of the resurrection. Since sunrise is the best symbol of the resurrection, it is appropriate to celebrate at that hour the sacrament of the risen Lord. A celebration which took place at the setting of the sun, at the onset of night, would imply a contrary symbolism. If we reflect on it, it seems surprising and paradoxical that the Church maintained morning celebration of the Eucharist as habitual practice even after the mass came to be regarded less as a memorial of the resurrection than of the passion — a development which logically should have resulted in recourse to nocturnal symbols.

From another point of view, however, the fact of celebrating mass at dawn scarcely favored the conception of the Eucharist as a fraternal meal. People do not gather for a festive meal at seven or eight o'clock in the morning. It is normal that a liturgy intended to foster the values of assembly, of sharing, of communion and of feast take place preferably at the end of the day before the evening meal.

4. From Bread to Host. Christ instituted the Eucharist under the signs of bread and wine. We shall limit our reflection here to the sign of bread and to its liturgical transformation during the course of the centuries, with the conviction that in modifying the appearance and use of the sign one also modifies its signification for those to whom it is addressed. In every celebration of the Eucharist it is assuredly the body of Christ that is given to us, but it is given to us under a sign, and that sign can be very significant or hardly sig-

[11] Letter 63, 16, CSEL III 2, p. 714.

nificant at all. Thus we understand the symbolic language pronounced by Christ and echoed in the Church differently, depending on whether the eucharistic bread is perceived as human food or not and whether the breaking of the bread results in a real sharing or seems to be reduced to a purely ritual gesture.[12]

It is very probable that at the Last Supper Christ employed the unleavened bread prescribed for the passover meal, a bread made of fine wheat flour. However, the evangelists in their institution narratives take account of the liturgical usage of their time and use the simple word *artos* (bread) without further precision. During the first centuries Christians brought to mass little loaves of ordinary bread, a certain number of which were placed on the altar and consecrated, while the rest were distributed to the poor. Here and there it was the custom for the faithful to present loaves shaped in the form of a crown or loaves marked with two grooves in the form of a cross, a feature which facilitated the fraction. Some ancient iron molds for baking bread have been found which bear an inscription or the monogram of Christ. This practice of decorating the bread destined for the liturgy has persisted in both East and West until our own day.[13] It reveals a desire to express the faith, to make explicit what remains hidden to the eyes, but it also entails the risk of overcharging the eucharistic bread with too many secondary symbols to the detriment of its fundamental signification of nourishment.

From the ninth century on, in the West, a more exigent piety with respect to the blessed sacrament led to modifications in the preparation of the eucharistic bread. The custom progressively spread of employing only unleavened bread, very different from the leavened bread used in daily life. At about the same time the preparation of the bread began to be reserved to the clergy, and the bread they prepared began to be called "hosts," a term which evokes a sacrificial context, since in Latin, especially in biblical and liturgical Latin, *hostia* designates the sacrificial victim. A large host was prepared beforehand for the priest, and small hosts for the faithful — to the extent they still communicated. As for the rite of fraction, it lost almost all of its meaning, since the priest broke only his own host and consumed both halves of it himself.

[12] On the vicissitudes of the eucharistic bread see J. A. Jungmann, *The Mass of the Roman Rite* 2 (New York: Benziger 1955) 31–37.

[13] It would be worth the trouble to make a study of the decoration of eucharistic breads, or hosts, and the underlying piety.

From the standpoint of eucharistic symbolism the passage from bread brought by the faithful to hosts prepared by the clergy signified that henceforth the Eucharist was regarded less as food, shared food, than as sacrifice and object of adoration. In this evolution there was interaction between theological reflection occasioned by the first controversies over the real presence and the liturgical and spiritual life of communities.

Until recent times we have remained conditioned by this liturgical practice which, while it had some positive aspects, had the unfortunate effect of obscuring the sign of the meal: when Christians communicated rarely, and preferably outside of mass, and when they were given communion under the species of bread only, and that in the form of a miniscule host, they would have needed great perspicacity to recognize a meal in the mass, to grasp the deeper meaning of the symbolism of the bread, and a fortiori that of the wine, and so discern the true relation between sacrifice and communion. Fortunately the Church has in our time rediscovered, or rather is rediscovering, the symbolism of bread and wine, the meaning of the fraction, the reason for communion under both species, and more fundamentally, the connection between celebration and communion. There can be no doubt that the restoration of this ritual language, which again becomes perceptible and significant for those to whom it is addressed, affords a more profound participation in the sacrament instituted by the Lord.

5. *From Communion to Adoration.* In instituting the Eucharist Christ said to his disciples, at least in the version of Matthew 26:26–27: "Take and eat . . . . Take and drink, all of you." Proffered food is normally destined to be eaten, and can a meal at which the guests abstain from eating and drinking still be considered a meal? Obviously the fact of communicating or not fundamentally modifies the perception and symbolism of the eucharistic meal.

Without resuming here in detail the long history of the practice of communion,[14] let us simply recall that until the beginning of the fourth century Christians could not imagine participating in the eucharistic liturgy without receiving the body and blood of Christ. Only the excommunicated — as the term indicates — found themselves excluded from eucharistic communion, as well as from ecclesial communion. During the course of the fourth century, with the

[14] See Jungmann, *The Mass of the Roman Rite* 2, 359–367.

persecution at an end, the rapidly increasing number of not very fervent Christians led to a rarefaction of communion in many churches. Around 390, in the East, John Chrysostom voiced this complaint: "It is in vain that we ascend to the altar; there is no one to participate."[15] And about the same time, in Milan, the bishop Ambrose alluded to Christians who receive communion only once a year.[16] In 506 the provincial council of Agde imposed a minimum of communion three times a year, at Christmas, Easter and Pentecost.[17] And from the ninth century onwards, at least in the West, the great majority of Christians are content to fulfill the precept of Easter communion — a norm the Fourth Lateran Council would subsequently sanction in 1215.

To be sure, this rarefaction of communion was largely due to ignorance and indifference, but to some extent it was inspired by an excessive, or unenlightened, reverence towards the sacramental body and blood of Christ. Perhaps, as J. A. Jungmann has suggested,[18] the struggle against Arianism, forcefully exalting the divinity of Christ, filled Christians and especially preachers with such a sacred fear, with such a sentiment of reverence before the divine majesty that people no longer dared to receive the body and blood of God incarnate: somewhat paradoxically the bread of human beings became the "bread of angels."

However that may be, it is evident that the Eucharist could with difficulty be considered a meal by Christians who were seated, or rather knelt, at the eucharistic table only once a year. As is known, from the twelfth century on the desire to see the host, to consume it, so to speak, with the eyes, served to compensate, to some extent, for the impossibility of receiving communion: contemplation and adoration, with all the liturgical rites which they inspired, took the place of communion. In that same period, to respond to the same need for compensation, the notion of "spiritual" communion spread: in expressing their desire, their will, to receive the body of Christ, in preparing themselves as best possible for the coming of the Lord into their souls, Christians believed, or hoped, they would receive all the "spiritual" fruits which real communion afforded. The

[15] *In Ephes hom* III, 4; PG 62, 29.

[16] *De Sacramentis* V, 25; ed. B. Botte (Sources chrétiennes, n. 25bis) 132; see his introduction, 16–17.

[17] Canon 8; Mansi, VIII, 327.

[18] *The Mass of the Roman Rite* 2, 362.

idea of "representation" provided another solution: the priest was thought to communicate in the name and on behalf of all the faithful.

It is sufficient, however, to confront these pious justifications with the realism of the gospel to see their fragility. Did not Christ really give his body and blood under the signs of bread and wine? Did he not wish his ecclesial body to be nourished with his eucharistic body? Did he not say, as recorded by Saint John, "If you do not eat the flesh of the Son of Man, and drink his blood, you shall not have life in you" (Jn 6:53)? An excessive spiritualization, however well intentioned it might be, logically results in an abandonment of sacraments which have become superfluous.

We should rejoice in the fact that since the beginning of this century, and particularly since Vatican II, the Eucharist is once again understood and experienced as a sacrificial meal in which the Lord invites us to his table to communicate to us his life, his salvation and his Holy Spirit under the real and symbolical signs which he himself has chosen. Moreover, it is striking — and this could be the object of a separate study — that in spite of all the fluctuations of eucharistic practice the texts of liturgical prayer, and notably the text of the great consecratory prayer, has never ceased to celebrate the Eucharist as the Lord's Supper at which it is expected that all Christians communicate, and indeed, communicate under both species. For sixteen centuries countless priests who celebrated mass using the Roman Canon implored God that the offering they presented be taken by the angel to the altar in heaven so that "as we receive from this altar the sacred body and blood of your Son, we may be filled with every grace and blessing." This petition, which concerns the faithful as well as the celebrant, implies effective communion in the body and blood of Christ, and it could be orchestrated with numerous formularies of postcommunion prayers in the Missal of Paul VI, thanking God for having nourished, or renewed us, thanks to the body and blood of his Son.[19]

Thus the recent liturgical reform, and the entire theological and spiritual movement which accompanied it, has restored readability and vigor to the symbols which Christ himself took in hand in order

[19] For some examples of these postcommunion prayers see the texts for the fifth, the ninth, the twelfth, and the twenty-eighth Sunday in ordinary time; they all speak of our sharing in the same bread *and* drinking from the one cup, or of our being given communion in the body *and* blood of Christ.

to charge them with his life and his salvation. The contemporary Church, pursuing the work that has been hers throughout the centuries, is attentive to the faithful and intelligible transmission of the word and gestures which the Savior addressed to humankind.

Our inquiry into the evolution of some of the symbolic elements of the eucharistic meal remains very limited. Practically, we have taken account of only the Western liturgy; it would have been helpful also to examine the Eastern liturgies, which correspond to a different sensibility and another world of representations. Moreover, there is need to elucidate the difficult and still obscure question of the connection which could have existed in the beginning between the eucharistic celebration and a genuine community meal and to explain why and how the Eucharist was completely separated from, isolated from, such a meal.[20]

At least the facts recalled here suffice to show the importance of the signs and symbols of the liturgy for a theology, a spirituality, and a practice of the Eucharist. If a theology of the Trinity can be elaborated without recourse to liturgical symbols, this is no longer true in the case of christology, which must take account of the various representations of the Pantocrator, the resurrection or the passion. And in the case of the sacraments, and especially the Eucharist, theological reflection is closely bound to the symbolic language which the Church employs in their celebration.

The Eucharist appears as a meal, but a meal of a sacramental and symbolic type. It is not destined to satisfy biological hunger and thirst: one does not give a communicant a pound or two of consecrated bread or a cup full of wine. Through the symbols of human nourishment, transformed into the body and blood of Christ, it is the divine life that is communicated to us. But this divinization or spiritualization should not make us forget that the Christian Eucharist includes all the symbolism of the human meal (hunger, nourishment, sharing, feast), the symbolism of the Jewish religious meal (blessing and thanksgiving), the polyvalent symbolism of the Last Supper, and the different symbolisms of the meals in which Christ participated during his earthly life and after his resurrection. If in other times the signs of the meal became almost unreadable due to the manner of celebrating the Eucharist, and if the Eucharist was

[20] One of the best studies is that of A. Hamman, *Vie liturgique et vie sociale* (Paris: Desclée 1968) 151–227: "L'agape et les repas de charité."

understood too exclusively as a memorial of the passion, in our time there might be the risk of reducing the Eucharist to an evangelical celebration of brotherhood and sharing, forgetting that in this meal it is Christ who takes the initiative, it is Christ the risen Savior who gathers his own, renders himself present among them and makes them participate in his paschal mystery of passion and glory.

We must also note that the perception of the Eucharist as a meal depends on the image and the symbolism of the meal in different cultures. Christ instituted his sacrament in a Jewish world which already had a sacred notion of nourishment and meal: food which nourishes life was understood very directly as a gift of God, and every meal had a certain religious character. In the contemporary West nourishment and meal are rich in symbolisms — as we have shown in the first part of this study — but they have, with some exceptions, lost all religious reference. In traditional African civilizations the act of nourishing oneself is rather a private act, and the mass is spontaneously understood as a sacrifice rather than as a meal — a fortiori as a meal intended to build community. The presentation of the Eucharist thus cannot be identical in all cultures.

As Christ himself did in inserting his sacrament into the real context of the Jewish religious meal, so the Church must transmit that which she has received concerning the Lord's Supper (cf. 1 Cor 11:23), carefully guarding all the mysterious reality of the sacrament, but also taking into account the resources and the experience of each culture, so that the "sign" addressed to human beings may be perceived by them in the best possible conditions.

In concluding this study of the successive stages which led from the human meal to the Christian Eucharist, we are quite aware that we have considered only one aspect of a reality which is also memorial, thanksgiving, sacrifice, real presence and edification of the ecclesial body of the Son of God. Without doubt the width and depth of this mystery, where all the other mysteries of the faith converge, make it very difficult to comprehend it simultaneously in its totality. In different periods, in the light of new perspectives, to respond to hesitations and varying negations, the Church has given greater relief to one or another aspect of that which always surpasses our understanding and our fractured language. We have at least wished to recall here that one cannot sketch a correct reflection on a sacrament without devoting maximum attention to deciphering the signs and symbols drawn from daily human life which Christ, poet of the world and Savior of humanity, wished to take in hand and charge with a new meaning in order to render himself present among his own and communicate to them his life, his strength and his joy.

David Power

Words That Crack: The Uses of 'Sacrifice' in Eucharistic Discourse

Words strain,
Crack and sometimes break, under the burden,
Under the tension, slip, slide, perish
Decay with imprecision, will not stay in place,
Will not stay still.
—T. S. Eliot, *Burnt Norton*, Stanza V

In ecumenical discussion on the Eucharist, the theme of sacrifice seems to be one which still does not fail to cause some embarrassment. The solution has been to relate the theme of sacrifice to that of memorial. This permits all to affirm the once and for all sacrifice of Jesus Christ, while at the same time allowing Catholics to continue to speak of offering sacrifice without excessive offence to Protestant sensitivities. Simultaneously, in the broader field of catechesis, among members of all Christian churches, there may be a tendency to let slip the imagery of sacrifice in favor of other terms. That could indicate a feeling that the ecumenical solution is not wholly satisfactory.

In this essay, I do not want to quarrel with the need to relate sacrificial understanding or words to the pasch of Christ, within the parameters of memorial. It seems to me, however, that many of our difficulties, theological and cultural, spring from what can only be called a reductionist hermeneutic, whereby we blithely take it for granted that performing sacrifice means offering a gift, for whatever purpose that may be. Through this tendency to subject sacrifice to the controlling image of offering, have we in effect lost a fuller appreciation of what is signified in Christian tradition's use of this term? The rationalist tendency to take image and concept to be proportionate may explain the reduction. A fuller awareness of language, of its relation to feeling, of its surplus of meaning, as well as knowledge of the complexity of the conceptual, affords a new examination of the sacrificial within Judaeo-Christian tradition, particularly in reference to its presence in eucharistic practice and doctrine. It will save us from the rather banal explanation of the Eucharist which carries us no further than the harmless observation that the Church now offers herself along with the offering of Christ.

In presenting my viewpoint, I wish to proceed in six stages. First of all, I would like to speak of this as a hermeneutical question. Then I will point to what appear to be striking exegetical factors in the Bible. In the third place, I will discuss the offering of bread and wine in the light of some thoughts gleaned from Irenaeus of Lyons, and fourthly I will have some parallel remarks to make about eating and drinking as eucharistic signs. My fifth paragraph will relate the question under discussion to some anthropological writings, and the final section will draw some conclusions in the form of theses about the Eucharist.

A QUESTION OF HERMENEUTICS

It is correct to state, I believe, that in early Christian literature the words *prosphora* and *thusia* are often (always?) synonymous. Since this seemed to be the current Jewish and pagan practice, Christians were prone also to identify sacrifice with offering. Moreover, the important place which this act had in religious ritual meant that it could not be ignored by Christian communities when they came to speak of their worship, even though their cult was so dissimilar to temple worship of any kind. But what we find in the New Testament and in early writers of the Church, as indeed even before Christ in some sectors of the Jewish community, is a substitution of a metaphorical and spiritual sense of the word for the ritual meaning and practice. It is in this sense that *thusia* is apparently used of [a] the Christian life, [b] the eucharistic celebration, and [c] Christ's death. It is not implied, in any of the three cases, that a gift is offered to God, whether it be person, animal or thing. What is rather suggested is [a] that a life lived in obedience and faith outweighs sacrifice, [b] that because of Christ's death no sacrifices are now necessary, and the praise and thanksgiving of the redeemed people is acceptable worship, and [c] the willing witness to the Father's love which Jesus Christ gave in his death renders absurd and obsolete any further offering of sacrifice.

It is not my intention to present all the exegetical evidence here.[1] I have given the above brief outline so that I may address myself to a question of interpretation method without more ado. This revolves around the understanding of metaphor. It can be too easily assumed that a word like sacrifice is being understood conceptually and applied literally, or that if this be not the case its meaning is rendered void or casual. It seems to me, however, that if we note the metaphorical use of scripture and tradition we are challenged to the exploration of richer meaning. There are those who will readily grant the metaphorical sense of sacrifice when used of Christian life, or even of praise, but who hesitate to allow this usage of Christ's death. Possibly this is due to a feeling that metaphor is empty, or at best colorful appendage, so that Christ's death is left without effect if we say that it is metaphorically a sacrifice. I suggest here that, on the contrary, an awareness that we are hearing a metaphor, pregnant with meaning, allows a fuller understanding and appreciation of the meaning and reality of the redemptive death.

When I write of metaphor, I mean an image whose life has been enriched by stories and ritual practices, now being used as an interpretive key to the significance of Christ's death and to that of the life of the people which has been redeemed in him. Metaphor is the "transposition of an alien name" (Aristotle) or a "deliberate yoking of unlikes" (Owen Barfield). It is a play between identity and difference, and its iconic value lies in the fact that the difference shows in the affirmation of identity. In other words, there is no one-to-one interlacing of images, but a play of imagination which supposes this to be impossible, and so raises the question of resemblance with the supposition of non-likeness. Hence, if the death of Christ is called a sacrifice, in direct or equivalent terms and images, this does not mean that it is being equated, either in genus or in species, with the

[1] I had scarcely finished writing this article when I got a copy of the just published monumental work of Robert Daly, *Christian Sacrifice: the Judaeo-Christian Background before Origen* (Washington 1978). Faced with such massive scholarship I was inclined to allow these words of mine to "fade into silence." However, it seems to me that many of his scholarly conclusions bear out my musings, whatever about particular points of discrepancy, and I still hope that my thoughts on the use of metaphor in the New Testament and early Christian language may shed light from another angle on the main conclusions of Daly's study. It is somewhat surprising to me that he allows

known rituals and purposes of sacrifice, or that some common concept of sacrifice is being employed of all its designates. There is rather a twist given to the image which allows the narrative and ritual tradition to be used as a metaphor, whose revealing character lies in the very supposition of non-likeness. In like manner, if the Eucharist is called *thusia* or the elements *prosphora*, this does not have to mean that *alongside* praise and thanksgiving we have to place offering as a constituent act of the Eucharist. It means rather that praise and thanksgiving, or the eucharistic memorial, are called in an interpretive way by the (alien) name of sacrifice or offering. The force of the metaphor, the revelation which it brings, is to convey that the praise and thanksgiving of Christians, rendered in memorial of Jesus Christ, far surpasses any offering of gift found in pagan or Jewish practice. Furthermore, the cult which is thus yoked with such practice is supposed to be of a far different order of reality.

My hypothesis, therefore, in this essay is that metaphor is the key to the interpretation of Christian sacrificial language, whether it be used of Christian life, of Christian celebration, or of Christ's death. There is no correspondence in reality or concept between the many rites of offering known to religions and the death of Christ, or between these same and the Eucharist. It is common enough to state, and it was often stated in debates during the session of the Council of Trent,[2] that Christ's death is a more perfect offering, a greater sacrifice, and that it fulfills the whole order of sacrifices because of the perfection of the offerer and the gift. If this means that a common definition or genus is applied, the violence done to language in calling Christ's death a sacrifice is ignored, and hence much of the meaning is lost. We are, I think, dealing with an excellent example of what Paul Ricoeur dubs the strategy of metaphor, namely, "to shatter and to increase our sense of reality by shattering and increasing our language."[3]

As a systematic theologian, rather than an exegete or philologist, I am at a disadvantage of sorts when appealing to scriptural texts.

"offering" to dominate nearly his entire discussion of sacrifice, without making much allowance for other interpretations, such as those given by S. Lyonnet, *Sin, Redemption, and Sacrifice* (Rome 1970).

[2] Cf. Societas Goerresiana, *Concilii Tridentini Actorum Nova Collectio* (Freiburg im Br. 1919) Vol. 8, Part 5, 722–788.

[3] "Creativity in Language," in C. Reagan-D. Stewart, *The Philosophy of Paul Ricoeur: An Anthology of his Work* (Boston 1978), 133.

However, I believe that hermeneutics is in some measure liberated from exegesis. It does not dismiss the exegetical detail but it relies more on insight provided by language and on horizon than it does on such detail. The question of sacrifice exemplifies this, and the reductionist hermeneutic to which I have earlier referred is due much more to a conceptual limitation in defining sacrifice and religion than it is to exegetical conclusions.[4]

SOME STRIKING EXEGETICAL FACTORS

At this juncture, I would like to appeal to what is actually contained in the passages of the New Testament often called the Institution Narrative of the Lord's Supper. The few words of Jesus which are reported suggest that in his thanksgiving and proclamation, and in his interpretation of the symbols of the meal, he made use of the Hebrew narratives of the Sinai and paschal sacrifices. Either he or the early Christian tradition included the image of the Suffering Servant of the Deutero-Isaiah's servant songs.

The sacrificial imagery of his reported speech may not, however, have been quite as much to the fore as has often been supposed in later theology. This point is itself pertinent to the interpretation of what actually is meant when this imagery is introduced. Of late, several scriptural scholars have directed our attention to the association between the bread-word and messianic table fellowship in the kingdom which is realized in Christ.[5] This is to say that the primary reference of the bread-word is eschatological or messianic, and that Jesus here promises a share in messianic blessings to those who eat of his body, or, in other words to those who receive the gift of himself which is communicated through the symbol of the bread. If the account of Mark is indeed the oldest, then the words "for you" do not occur in the bread-word, which is to say that it contains no direct image of the sacrificial tradition. What is here promised through Christ's death is a share in the kingdom mediated by the continued giving of himself in the Eucharist, after his death, to his disciples. No further interpretation of how the death achieves this is given.

The appeal to sacrificial imagery occurs then in the wine-word. The words of Jesus reported in the giving of the chalice refer to the

[4] The exegete may also be limited by his conceptions, as happens, I think, when he lets himself be determined by later dogmatic teachings in his reading of texts.

[5] For example, Rudolf Pesch, *Wie Jesus das Abendmahl hielt* (Freiburg im Br. 1977) 70–75.

blood and to the covenant, and seemingly also in the terms "for many" include a reference to the *Ebed Yahweh* of the servant songs. The blood ritual is central to much Old Testament sacrifice, and in a particular way is key to the meaning of the passover and of Sinai, here evoked. The blood ritual of the passover indicated liberation, that of Sinai covenant. Since these rituals do not constitute an offering made by persons to God, but are on the contrary signs of God's giving to the chosen people both his protection and his covenant of love, what Jesus evokes in using the blood image is not something offered to God but God's coming to his chosen. God's revelation of himself to his people, his deliverance of them from captivity, his covenant with them, his promises to them, his expiation of evil from their midst, his life-giving presence: these are the things which Jesus recalls through the images of sacrifice and its ritual, and it is these which are to be used in interpreting his death for his disciples and his continued giving of himself to them in the supper. If some reference to Jeremiah 31: 31 is included in the covenant image, as is highly probable, we see that this serves to project us into a tradition which finds the sealing of covenant in ways other than offerings of any type to God, be it blood or otherwise. It is the obsolescence of such practices which is intended by Jeremiah in the new times of which he prophesies, since they are times marked by the kind of spiritualization of worship desired by the prophetic tradition. This would be a further confirmation of the fact that Jesus intends a metaphor, not a literal indication of a new sacrificial gift.

The *Ebed Yahweh*, also evoked in the wine-word and transferred by a later tradition to the bread-word as well, is a very telling metaphorical indication. This figure occurs on the scene at a moment when the offering of sacrificial gifts was felt necessary, so that the people yearned to be brought back from exile to Jerusalem, where they could continue this cult. The songs do not sanction this desire in any literal fashion, but indicate that eschatological metaphor in Isaiah 53 is metaphor at its most adroit: it breaks down a system in order to reconstruct reality with new meaning. Several characteristics of sacrifice come into play in the metaphor: the offering of gifts in expiation, the legal notion of substitution whereby the offered takes the place of the guilty, the shedding of life which is inevitable in sin-offerings. Likening the suffering and death of the servant to these characteristics infers the dissimilarity which is needed for the iconic value of the predication of similarity. He is an innocent person, sent to the people by Yahweh as his messenger, and though persecuted and reviled by them he is obedient, compassionate, uncomplaining in his death. He achieves all that sacrifice cannot, with its attempts at substitution, its shedding of blood and its making of offerings. Indeed, the advent of such a figure on the scene of history renders sacrifices unnecessary, if not actually obscene. The schema of justice which prevails in the making of sacrificial offering is replaced by the schema of compassion, which witnesses to love and mercy. Expiation is brought about, not by the offerings of the people, but through the witness given in the sufferings and death of the servant, on account of which God manifests him in glory in the eyes of the Gentile nations. It is through this figure, then, this elaborate metaphor, that sacrificial imagery crosses the bridge from the Old to the New Testament in the words of Jesus over the chalice.

I can summarize the preceding by pointing to the fact that there is actually a dual metaphor being employed. In the first place, Jesus' words recall the blood ritual of such sacrifices as the passover and the covenant. In these, the blood ritual has not implications of offering but signifies God's mercy to man. It is this which the eucharistic words use as metaphor, thus indicating a first aspect of the Lord's death. In the second place, an era is also apparently assumed in which the Hebrew people put great store by offering gifts to God. This is necessary to the evocation of Jeremiah 31: 31 and Isaiah 53: 12. It introduces the second metaphor, whereby the death of Jesus is rendered meaningful by way of reference to such usage, so that the similarity of desire or purpose stands out in the evident dissimilarity of means. When this metaphorical usage is placed alongside the promise of the kingdom contained in the bread-word, we are given some indication of the way in which this kingdom is ushered in through the death of Jesus. It is further apparent that in the "sacrifice" of the supper, it is God who gives to man, not man to God.

OFFERING OF BREAD AND WINE IN THE LIGHT OF IRENAEUS

Even further wrestling with words is demanded by what is written of the Eucharist by Irenaeus of Lyons. While earlier texts like the Didache or those of Justin Martyr rely on the metaphorical meaning of sacrifice, so that they can equate it with praise and thanksgiving, Irenaeus of Lyons in the *Adversus Haereses* seems to have a literal offering of bread and wine in mind. Very significantly, he does not speak in his treatise of an offering of the body and blood of Christ at any moment of the celebration, but he does seem to indicate an offering of bread and wine which precedes the eucharistic blessing.[6] In his argument with the gnostics, it is important to him that Christians do indeed offer things of this earth, bread and wine. He explains the significance of this in the context of the Eucharist, wherein by the blessing they become the body and blood and are then given to the faithful for their nourishment, and eventually unto the resurrection of the flesh.

It seems likely that in the time of Irenaeus when the president took the bread and wine from the people he performed some gesture of offering with them. Irenaeus's apologetic is intended to explain the offering of these substances, not as a necessary act so far as God is concerned, but as an expression felt necessary by those who recognize God in the firstfruits of his creation. Free though he or she be in Jesus Christ, the Christian still needs to express acknowledgment of the Creator in this kind of offering. When, however, they are blessed through the prayer of blessing the community does not pass to an offering of the body and blood. The suggestion rather seems to be that the Lord so graciously accepts the gifts of bread and wine, with all their cosmic significance, that he makes of them the body and blood of his Son and returns them to the offerers, thus transformed, as food and drink for body and spirit.

From all of this it would seem that in the early church there was understood to be but one literal offering, namely, that of bread and wine. When the death is commemorated as a sacrifice, this is by way of interpretive metaphor. Cyprian, it is true, talks quite clearly of offering the body and blood of Christ in the Eucharist,[7] but so early on this does not seem to have been a very common thought pattern, however common it became some centuries later. The liturgical evidence of the earlier anaphoras bears out the hypothesis that offering in a literal sense belongs to the bread, in a metaphorical sense to the prayer of praise and thanksgiving. The verbs of offering in the anaphora of Addai and Mari (insofar as we can reconstruct its original form), the prayer of Hippolytus and that of Serapion, refer to the bread and wine offered by the community or to their praise.[8] This

[6] *Adversus Haereses* 17, 5ff.: ed. A. Rousseau, Sources Chrétiennes 100 (Paris 1965) 591–600. Here I do not seem to take the same interpretation as Daly (note 1 above) 339–360.

[7] Ep. 63, CSEL 3, 2, 708–713.

[8] Cf. E. Kilmartin, "*Sacrificium Laudis:* Content and Function of Early Eucharistic Prayers," *Theological Studies* 35 (1974) 268–287.

need not be denied even if they occur after the words of institution, as in the case of Hippolytus, or both before and after, as in Serapion, since these words are not in those contexts given consecratory value. The prayer of the anaphora was a unit of praise and blessing, with one result, not a series of parts to which different effects may be attributed. The symbols of the body and blood would certainly not have been consumed until the thanksgiving prayer had been adequately consummated.

The Protestant tradition has always found the offering of bread and wine somewhat offensive, since in Catholic piety it seemed to take away from the one sacrifice of Jesus Christ. In the most recent liturgical reforms of the mass, the Catholic Church has on its side derogated somewhat from the notion of offering which hitherto accompanied the preparation of the bread and wine. An examination of some very early Christian traditions now seems to indicate exactly the reverse: while the community offered bread and wine, it did not offer the body and blood of Jesus Christ, but praised God for his works of redemption and ate and drank the body and blood as spiritual nourishment, through which it communicated in the blessings of this same redemption. Can we find anything in this sequence of acts to cast light upon the meaning of the Eucharist?[9]

One of the remarkable things about Irenaeus is the way in which he associates the doctrine of creation with that of redemption through the person of the Logos. This is pertinent to the explanation which he gives of the Eucharist. Even before the blessing, the bread and wine are in a manner symbols of the Redeemer Logos, in whom the first creation, spoilt by sin, is recapitulated. Irenaeus seems rather optimistic about the offering of bread and wine and finds it an act so pleasing to God that he graces it by changing the substances into the body and blood of Christ.

At this stage, it can be noted that when Irenaeus closely relates creation and redemption through his image of the Word, his outlook is that of one who attributes historical value to the creation narrative of Genesis. Hence he can find in bread and wine elements which stand not only for earthly life sullied by sin, that is, in its actual state, but also for the glory of the original creation. In parallel fashion, he sees the fruits of redemption as the restoral of an ideal histor-

[9] Aquinas appears to find the realization of sacrifice in the offering of bread and its change into the body: cf. *Summa theologiae* III, q. 83, a. 4: ". . . primo, peragitur oblatio, secundo, consecratio materiae oblatae, tertio, eiusdem perceptio."

ical creation. The act of offering is to take hold of the bread and wine in the moment, as it were, in which they show forth the original creation to which the world is to be restored.

It is difficult today to identify totally with such a perception of the relation between creation and redemption. We know that the Genesis story is not history but myth, and we have some appreciation of the function of myth. Consequently, we may be inclined to understand the logos of the myth differently. The condition of humankind to which the creation story belongs is the despair of sin. The question in mind is whether the chaos which is experienced can be restored to order, whether it is possible to hope. In answer to this bewilderment, the creation narrative affirms a divine creative purpose and a divine benignity, as well as a divine power on which sinners and sufferers can rely. There is nothing historical, however, in the story, which points to a possible future more than it points to a given past. Realizing this relation of the creation narrative to the human story, we may be less inclined than Irenaeus to see the reflection or remnants of pristine glory, either in human persons or in nature and its objects. We are more conscious that we speak out of a condition of ambiguous origins and that we are saved from the fear of an ambiguous destiny only by the belief in a God who is the creator of good and who makes his good prevail over our evil. The prehistory of that good, however, remains clouded to us in obscurity. Myth may reveal, but it also veils. This may in fact save us from naive longing for a lost innocence and lead us to an expectation of God's good gifts, without putting on them the burden of comparison with the idyll of our abandoned inheritance.[10]

Theology has sometimes forced a certain logic upon the thought of Irenaeus which plays it false. Once it is admitted that bread and wine are in fact offered, it seems logical to make the value of this offering depend upon the offering of Christ on the Cross. A further logical step is to say that the rite passes from an offering of the bread to an offering of the body into which it is transformed. In face of such inexorable logic, I appeal once again to the subtle shattering of language and logic which metaphor operates, demanding thereby

[10] In current debates about human rights, some participants define these in terms of an original creation, where they find the ideal of human dignity. Others take their point of departure in an analysis of current situations of distress, and base their grasp of human rights on such analysis. I find that such divergence is keenly pertinent to this reflection on the symbolism of the bread in the celebration of the Lord's Supper.

another interpretation. Irenaeus does not pass from one offering to another, but positing a first offering then abandons the image and speaks instead of what God gives us in the body and blood. The metaphor is to yoke our giving and God's giving. It would be hard to find a more startling pair of unlikes. Irenaeus's own logic, whereby he relates an historical creation to an historical redemption, is in turn shattered by the realization that what are being compared are an historical redemption and a mythical creation.

The destruction of both kinds of logic pertains to what Max Thurian demands when he writes of the meaning of the offertory rite.[11] Since the body and blood of Christ are not offered in any literal sense, the offering of bread and wine is made to stand alone, and since redemption has no known historical past of creation to which to look back, it is made to stand as an act which searches vainly for some meaning and value. No matter how great or how naive and sincere are our attempts at offering, they are vain when seen as the acts of a chaotic human history which has only its present, with no past and no future. If then an offertory rite is included in the Eucharist, what are juxtaposed and violently contrasted are the all too human economy of offering gifts to God and the completely gracious movement of God towards man whereby he expiates sin in the body and blood of the Incarnate Word.[12]

Even if the latest Catholic reforms underplay the offertory ritual, it is not of itself without meaning or challenge. In offering (mere) bread and wine the Christian fellowship is invited to be part of creation and part of humankind striving to attain to God and to build human society. It is with creation in its sufferings and groanings, however, that the Christian fellowship thus identifies, with the weary and ultimately futile attempt of humankind to placate the forces which dominate the world and to build society through the religious and social control systems which human groups initiate of themselves. The effort breaks down and must yield before the prayer which asks for God's own gratuitous intervention and giving.

The place which the offertory rite occupies in the liturgy offers its

[11] M. Thurian, *L'Eucharistie* (Neuchâtel 1963) 2, 297–298.

[12] However much Catholics related their theories to the priestly consecration of Christ through the hypostatic union, perhaps we can begin to glimpse how appalling it must have sounded to the Protestant mind at the time of the Reformation to hear them say that Christianity was the highest among the religions whose cult centered around the offering of gifts to God.

own possibilities of meaning. The fellowship has heard God's word and renewed its part of the covenant by its response to this word. Perhaps it is now tempted to believe that it can renew the earth, find freshness and worth in the work of its hands whereby the things of the earth are perfected. The attempt is abortive, such offering remains inadequate even when done by the justified. The things which the community offers receive their real worth only at the point at which they are turned into epiphanies of God's free grace by the prayer of blessing. At that point they nourish the community and make of it a spiritual sacrifice, that is, a living reality pleasing to God, sanctified by him, but still with nothing in their hands which merits being offered to him in any literal sense.

I have here given two meanings of the offertory rite, the one that of Irenaeus, the other one which seems to relate better to the relation between creation and redemption postulated by the difference between a mythical story and a historical one. Neither meaning need rule out the other, for it is a matter of emphasis, provided the point is clear that *only* in Christ's death is humanity made holy. In fact, other interpretations also seem possible, and we can find them if we look through our liturgical histories. If we follow through history as far as Theodore of Mopsuestia, for example, we can find an interesting variation on the theme of offering and nourishing.[13] Theodore saw the preparation of bread and wine before the anaphora to be already an image of the death of Christ, whereby the Savior offers himself to God. Hence, even at that stage of the ritual they are symbols of the body and blood of Christ, relative to his suffering. Through the blessing in the Spirit they become symbols of his risen and glorified being, so that they now serve as the spiritual nourishment of the community. Theodore here sees the death of Christ as an offering, and he sees the Church to have a share in this offering by her identification with his death. But all of that is anticipatory of God's action in the Spirit, which in the one case glorifies the dead Christ and in the other makes the bread and wine symbols of that glorious being, so that they are now the food and drink of the Christian's life in Christ and in the Spirit. The offering of Christ by his Church, insofar as it can be called such, in no way belongs to the anaphora, but is anticipatory of it. Christ's obedience in death and

[13] Cf. E. Yarnold, *The Awe-Inspiring Rites of Initiation* (Slough 1972) for an English version of the baptismal homilies of Theodore. The relevant text is found on pp. 227–228.

the Church's offering with him, wherever they fit into the scheme of things, are not the constituents of salvation, which comes only from God's intervention in the Spirit.

But enough of such wrestling with words. I have said enough, I think, to indicate that the Eucharist gives preeminence to the metaphorical use of sacrificial language and that where a literal sense of offering does occur it plays a subordinate and dependent role, so that the gratuitous grace of God in Christ and in humankind's salvation remains dominant. The various ways of playing out the role of offering may simply show how nicely "symbol gives rise to thought." Or, perhaps, less nicely, to allegory.

A CRISIS OF MEAL LANGUAGE

If the symbolism of offering of bread and wine eventually plays a critical role in the Eucharist, highlighting the abortiveness of the attempt to gain grace by such action, it seems to me that meal language must play a similar critical role. We know from early church history that agape and Eucharist first went together, so that eating and drinking the body and blood of Christ were related to a full meal. We also know how rapidly the two became dissociated. Many practical reasons for this are, I suppose, quite justly given. Does it not, however, retain some special significance that we continue to use banquet language of what is no more than a morsel of bread and a sip of wine? Nor can it ever be seriously suggested that the act of communion be turned into a satisfying meal, however much we now stress that the forms of bread and wine be more thoroughly respected and hence, of course, the acts of eating and drinking.

The presence of Christ in two kinds is often now supported by the plea that a meal is not complete except in food and drink, and similar argument is used to support that all receive the gifts in the two forms. The argument, however, trembles, when we are handed a mere morsel of bread (and not, for example, a whole dish of lamb), with the promise that we have a place at the eternal banquet. It is likewise in a light sip of wine (and not in a beaker guarding each one's plate) that we are promised the eternal covenant. Eating and drinking are present acts, to be sure, but the meal imagery with all its sense of replenishment belongs more to eschatological hope than to present satisfaction. The present grace, which is certainly given, is not attached to the satisfaction of bodily delights but to the union with him who gives the Spirit, in which he himself has been transformed. There seems to be a prophetic warning here. Humanity may indeed supply the bodily food and drink, and by sharing these express its hope for the world's needs, but it is only through the gift of the Spirit given in the morsel and the sip that true human hopes may be met and the banquet of God's kingdom laid out.

This crisis of meal language can also help us think anew about sacrificial language, and more particularly about the meanings attached to the words about the bread and about the wine respectively. When these two words, or sets of words, are reexamined in the light of the crisis of meal language this bears out my earlier contention that they do not bring sacrificial images to the fore quite as strongly as theology has at times supposed. The primary significance of the words which refer to the bread seems to belong to the image of the messianic kingdom. By sharing with his own at table, and by giving them his own self in the form of bread, Christ promises and to an extent signals the advent of the messianic kingdom and its blessings. He signals its advent inasmuch as he shares a table and bread (his body), he promises its advent inasmuch as the bread yearns for rather than constitutes a meal. As for the words about the wine, the image of covenant is to the fore, that covenant which is to be written on man's heart through the renewal of his spirit. The image of the pouring out of blood, with its references to a sacrificial narrative tradition, suggests, as explained earlier in this essay, the way in which the kingdom is given and the covenant made.

In this context, the action whereby Christ gives his body to eat and his blood to drink takes on its meaning. God gives humankind the kingdom promised in the Messiah and he gives the covenant made new in his death, but he gives them in a form which is still attuned to the conditions of present earthly existence, which is as much hope as it is attainment. Humanity's part in all of this is to take and receive, both the reality and the promise, not however to give or to offer.

A NOTE ON INSIGHTS FROM ANTHROPOLOGY

Anthropologists have as much difficulty getting to the primitive history and to the root-meaning of sacrifice as do biblical scholars. We cannot exactly canonize their work, but their insights into the role which sacrifice plays in human affairs serve in some measure to explain the persistence of the sacrificial metaphor and of the instinct to sacrifice in Christian belief and practice. In other words, they help us to see that if sacrifice remains a category in explaining Christ's death and Christian prayer this represents something more than pure doctrinal exigency. It corresponds to something deeply inseated in human nature. From anthropological studies we learn something of the human and social turmoil which sacrificial practice seeks to bring to order. How this relates to our remembrance of Jesus Christ is a fairly obvious question.

The theories which define the nature of sacrifice are many. The definition given by M. Mauss [14] has attained classical status, and more recent theories relate to it in some way. For Mauss sacrifice is essentially a social rite. It is a mediation, through the victim, and for the good of the social group, between the sacred and the profane.

L. Mumford,[15] keeping the social role to the fore, relates sacrifice to the intertwining of economic, political, and religious forces. There is a necessary urge in human nature, as he sees it, to dominate the earth. Consequently there is a persistent rivalry among humans in their quest to possess it. Ritual sacrifice has to do with the effort to harness the earth's fecundity, to resolve the conflicts over its possession, and to order human society. Sexual fecundity, the life which is in animal blood or human blood, the earth's fertility, the regulation of earth's energy and human power in constructing social order, are all interrelated. An instinctive violence or destructiveness creeps into these efforts and relationships and ritual sacrifice is one of the principal ways whereby it is given an expression which resolves the ensuing conflicts, in the substitution of the victim. Mumford relates the history of sacrifice very closely to the history of war among peoples, for war too channels off the residual violence which could disrupt a society on to an alien object and at the same time reinforces inner cohesion.

Mary Douglas [16] on her part establishes a link between sacrifice on the one hand and the distinction between the pure and the impure on the other. She considers this distinction between the pure and the impure an essential part of social order. The impure is what menaces order, since by definition it does not fit into the scheme of things. From this flow the rites of purification or of sacrifice which

[14] H. Hubert and M. Mauss, *Sacrifice: Its Nature and Function*, tr. W. D. Halls (Chicago 1964).

[15] L. Mumford, *The Myth of the Machine: The Pentagon of Power* (New York 1970).

[16] Mary Douglas, *Purity and Danger* (New York 1966).

seek to do away with the unclean or to integrate it into order. Sacrifice does both. It creates order where dis-order and threat previously existed. An animal which cannot be classified defies the order of things. Hence it is a threat or a menace, an object of fear, the representative of forces out of control. When it is made the object of ritual sacrifice, its extraordinary power is made part of an orderly ritual. It is both honored and put to death, so that death itself which of its nature introduces confusion is made to contribute to order and the wholeness. The threat of the animal as a sign of the unintegrated is removed by death and its extraordinary power at the same time fitted into order by rites of communion.

René Girard[17] also believes that sacrifice is an integral part of society's foundation. For him it is a measure whereby a group can contain its violent instincts by a controlled exercise of violence, directed upon a substitute victim. Aggressivity and violence are essential to human progress and the source of much creativity. They can also be destructive of life and of order, if not given both direction and a release of surplus energies. The victim of sacrifice absorbs, as it were, the destructive element and so allows the creative force to be assumed into the building of society. In the death of Christ, Girard sees the collective transfer of violence to a single victim, and so finds in this an act which makes reconciliation and further renunciation of violence possible.

According to the studies which I have here invoked, sacrificial practice has to do with the resort to violence in the establishment of the human good and with the resolution of this crisis. They serve, I believe, to fill out the polysemy of the sacrificial metaphor since they indicate the polysemy of the sacrificial ritual. Sacrifice points to the fear of the holy which coexists with the desire to commune with it, to the close relation between holy and impure, between beneficence and malevolence, and to the search for the sources of life and power which goes on in social groups, sometimes acquisitively and sometimes for the common good. Hence, when we commemorate the death of Christ through the metaphor of sacrifice we are not only dealing with a rather innocuous demand to be obedient to God even in suffering, to recognize his dominion over us by renunciation, and to follow Christ's example, united with him in love. We resurrect anew by such language all that is ambiguous in the yearning for and

[17] René Girard, *Violence and the Sacred*, tr. Patrick Gregory (Baltimore 1977).

the hatred of the sacred, all that vexes man's quest for order and community, and all that is ambiguous in the death of Christ.

Indeed, violence and blood are so inherent in the images of sacrifice that it has even been suggested that in explaining the death of Christ it might be well to replace the scheme of sacrifice with one of initiation or passage.[18] This is precisely, however, where the power of the metaphor shows itself. The recall of sacrifice keeps in mind the human dilemma and its complexities, and the use of the metaphor in relation to Christ's death shows that redemption affects these realities. At the same time, since it is a metaphor it works the necessary substitution: it is not through his offerings of sacrifice that man is saved, but through the passage of Christ which is his death. Herein lies the Father's response to our needs and the way of peace and reconciliation which he opens out for us. There is no need for a repression or a redirection of urges and instincts and sins, of doubts and ambiguities. On the contrary, we are allowed by the metaphorical language of sacrifice to face these realities consciously, while at the same time consciously choosing to receive the grace which allows us to follow the way of peace proclaimed in Christ's death. If Christian worship is finally and essentially praise and thanksgiving, this is because Christians have received in Christ a way of salvation which breaks the vicious circle of evil, not in the ambiguous way recorded in the history of ritual sacrifice, but by introducing into it an element which can perhaps be no better described than through the word made common to all languages by Gandhi, namely, *ahimsa*.

CONCLUSION: SOME THESES ABOUT THE EUCHARIST

The best way to conclude these thoughts on the use of a word is to enunciate a number of theses about the Eucharist which flow therefrom.

1. In remembering Christ's death and pasch we keep memorial of the Father's initiative in redeeming us. Hence, the primary act of worship for the Christian community is praise and thanksgiving. We do not add an act of offering to this to constitute what is essential to the Eucharist, but this act itself is metaphorically called a sacrifice.

2. In a further metaphorical usage, the Eucharist is called the

[18] Cf. A. Vergote in *Mort Pour Nos Péchés: Recherche pluridisciplinaire sur la signification rédemptrice de la mort du Christ* (Brussels 1976) 35–46.

self-offering of the Church, whereby the faithful unite themselves in mind and heart with the love and obedience of Christ. This aspect of self-offering is not to be emphasized to the extent that it obscures the fact that the first giver in the Eucharist is God and that the gift which is celebrated is his gift to us of his Son's flesh and blood.

3. A literal offering of bread and wine has in the course of time been included in the eucharistic ritual. This is not essential to it, but when added draws out the symbolism of the Eucharist in certain directions. It relates the mystery of redemption to the mystery of creation, it associates the community with humanity's religious and secular strivings, and in the reminder of our own finitude which comes in this abortive gesture there is already a remembering of the grace which is given to us in the gift of the body and blood of Christ.

4. Used in the eucharistic prayer, or elsewhere, as an interpretive key to the meaning of Christ's death, the metaphor of sacrifice has a twofold meaning. If the word is used to signify directly humanity's offerings, then the metaphor used of Christ recalls his willing obedience and the obsolescence of ritual sacrifice which follows on redemption in him. If the word is used to recall that aspect of sacrifice which is to the fore in the blood ritual, and so as a reminder of God's expiation of sin, the metaphor represents the Father's love and the testimony to the Father's love which is found in Jesus Christ. In this latter case, he is presented as the fulfillment of the type of the passover and Sinai sacrifices, as well as of the figure of the *Ebed Yahweh*.

5. When this metaphorical use of sacrifice to speak of Christ's death is amplified through anthropological insight, we are reminded that, ever prone to taking the kingdom of God by violence, we are invited to follow a new path in Jesus Christ, namely, that of pardon, peace and reconciliation, and of the voluntary service of all in need, even to the point of suffering pain and death in the process.

6. To set the two metaphors alongside one another, that is, that of our offering of praise and thanksgiving, and that of God's offering to us in Christ, is to evoke the reality of the Holy Spirit. When the Father gives us the body and blood of his Son Incarnate, in this gift he gives the Spirit who has transformed Christ into a spiritual body and transforms the bread and wine into this same body. Given to us in the eating and drinking of the body and blood, the Spirit makes of us ourselves a spiritual offering, so that we are worthy to render

praise and thanksgiving to the Father as a true and acceptable worship.

7. That this feast is of its very nature an anticipation of the eschaton appears in the use of the language of meal and banquet to speak of the morsel and the sip in which we communicate in the Spirit of Christ, through our eating of his flesh and our drinking of his blood.

Edward Schillebeeckx

Transubstantiation, Transfinalization, Transignification

There have always been controversies over the mode of the real presence.[1] In reaction to the gross interpretation of the high middle ages, which conceived of the eucharistic real presence in a crudely materialistic fashion (in communion I bite the body of the Lord with my teeth), the high scholastics — especially Albert the Great, Bonaventure, and Thomas Aquinas — proposed an altogether new idea. This reaction was somewhat shocking, and it was so progressive that before his death St. Thomas prayed to our Lord with these words: "I refer to the judgment of the holy Roman Church everything that I have taught or written about the sacrament of the body of Christ and the other sacraments."[2]

St. Thomas, like the other great scholastics, emphasized the spiritual presence of our Lord's body in the eucharist (III, q. 76, a. 7). In regard to miracles of bleeding hosts and consecrated white wine turning red, St. Thomas said: "What this miraculous blood might be, I do not know; in any case it is not the real blood of Christ" (III, q. 76, a. 8, c. and ad 2). These new teachers even went so far as to criticize an intervention of the Roman Synod: Bonaventure said that the "profession of faith" which Berengarius had to sign was an ex-

[1] Address delivered in French during the fourth session of Vatican II to fathers of the council at *Domus Mariae* in Rome, and published with permission of the author and Sheed & Ward, holders of the copyright. The translation was made by Rev. David J. Rock. Copyright Sheed & Ward, Inc., 1966.

[2] *Procès de Naples*, ch. 49, 27, 80; Bull of Canonization, Fontes, 523; quoted in A. Walz, *S. Thomas d'Aquin* (Louvain 1962), p. 199.

cessive formulation (*In IV Sent.*, d. 12, p. 1, a. 3, q. 1, ed. Quaracchi, p. 284A); St. Thomas was more tactful and gave a respectful interpretation of the pontifical document, although he appreciably changed its meaning (III, q. 77, a. 7, ad 3).

These teachers proposed opinions which were very disturbing in comparison to the crude representation of the eucharist then current among the common people as well as in traditional theology from the time of Berengarius.

Historia, magistra vitae! In the midst of the feverish modern attempts to re-evaluate the meaning of our faith, a closer look at its history leaves us with a profound calm and prevents premature cries of alarm. Our faith is a faith in historicity. In our times, however, the situational factor is more sensitive, even explosive. In our contemporary history, faith and theology have become subjects of discussion in newspapers, on the radio, and even on television. Because of this fact the theologian finds himself in a new moral situation. He can no longer discuss theology without asking himself: "How will the Catholic world interpret my opinion and my modern evaluation?" The new moral situation forces the theologian to formulate his modern appraisal in such a way that Catholics find in the new formulation their true faith instead of having their faith deeply shaken.

Reflecting on what has happened during the past few years and on what is still happening in the polemics concerning transubstantiation, it appears that there is no question of heterodoxy among the Catholic theologians who have tried to re-evaluate the dogma of transubstantiation. All wish to safeguard the authentic doctrine. They wish, however, to safeguard it in such a way that the people of God, especially the clergy, formed more and more in a non-scholastic mentality, might live it in a more authentic fashion and, so to speak, in a more existential manner.

One might ask whether or not all these theologians have been sensitive enough to the reactions of non-theologians, notably of the majority of Catholics who do not always understand nuances and distinctions and who have, in fact, sometimes received the impression that some theologians wanted to impart to them a Protestant idea of the eucharistic presence. In regard to this Protestant idea, however, there is at present a tendency in Reformation theology to affirm in a more pronounced way the reality of the presence of Christ in the bread and wine at the Lord's supper — that is, the representatives of this theology are minimizing more and more the anti-Catholic tone of the real "Reformation" idea of the Lord's supper. On the other hand, Catholics are toning down the anti-Protestant harshness of their doctrine of transubstantiation. It is quite likely that on occasion this truly ecumenical preoccupation turns into a purely irenic attitude (in a pejorative sense). In every movement toward renewal there are unfortunate elements which can compromise and endanger a worthy cause. In fact, if one examines church history, it becomes clear that such elements have always obstructed worthy causes, at least temporarily.

PRELIMINARY CONSIDERATIONS

Before analyzing the eucharistic controversies, I should like to indicate summarily three factors which have contributed to the renewal of eucharistic theology.

1. Immediately after World War II Catholic theology reappraised the principal idea of the scholastic age: "Sacramentum est in genere signi," as St. Thomas expressed it. In speaking of the church's sacraments, Catholic theologians spoke of *signs*. As a reaction to the Reformation, post-Tridentine theology nearly forgot that in the sacrament of the eucharist there was also a question, not of a physical category, but of a sacramental category, meaning that even the eucharist "est in genere *signi*." Obviously, in saying this nothing has yet been said of the particular mode of the real presence of Christ in the eucharist, but in any case the great scholastics of the thirteenth century did not choose to look for this real presence beside, on the margin of, or beyond the sacramental category or sign: they always spoke of "species sanctissimorum *symbolorum*" (Bonaventure, *In IV Sent.*, d. 9, a. 2, q. 1, ad 5: p. 508B), "non in propria specie, sed sub speciebus huius *sacramenti*" (St. Thomas, III, q. 75, a. 1, ad 2).

After the war the renewal of this theology of sign clearly had an effect upon eucharistic theology. Twenty years ago Father Yves de Montcheuil had consistently emphasized that the "sacramentum-signum" applies also to the eucharist, and he did this in such a way that attention was drawn to the opposition between the sacramental view and the physical-presence view.[3] The physical view as such is not based on sacramentality, but goes beyond the framework of sign and places us in another category, namely, in the realm of the "ex-

[3] "La raison de la permanence du Christ sous les espèces eucharistiques d'après Bonaventure et Thomas," *Mélanges Théologiques*, Sér. Théologie n. 9 (Paris 1946) 71–82.

tra-sacramental." Consequently, in reaction to this stress on the physical aspect, one should seek to appraise the proper mode of the real presence without departing from sacramentality or from the "sacramentum-signum"; the sign itself, this particular eucharistic sign, should be able to account for the proper mode in such a way that there would no longer be an opposition between the "sacramentum-signum" and transubstantiation, yet so that this sacrament would infinitely transcend the more peripheral sacramentality if the six other sacraments. Transubstantiation is profoundly real, but it is so within the framework of the category of "sacramentum-signum."

To all this was added a philosophical renewal of the theory of sign. Theologians are no longer stranded in a purely gnoseological theory of sign as was the case in scholasticism, for which sign was only a cognitive medium. Modern phenomenology had analyzed symbol-making activity from an anthropological point of view. This was the beginning of an "anthropology of sign," to which both philosophers and theologians have contributed.

2. The second factor is more in the philosophical order. For some thirty years there has been heated debate on the notion of "substance" even among the neo-scholastics. As a matter of fact, neo-scholasticism had a clear tendency to reserve the concept of substance to man, that is, to formally spiritual beings; things, especially artificial beings like bread and wine, could not be called substances. At the same time the distinction between a substance and its accidents in the Aristotelian sense of the words was attacked vigorously.

Because of this philosophical discussion on the application of the concept of substance, several theologians undertook a historical analysis of the Council of Trent to determine whether or not the council, in defining the dogma of transubstantiation, had avoided the Aristotelian doctrine. On one side E. Gutwenger affirmed that without a doubt the conciliar fathers of Trent, by reason of their recourse to the Council of Constance, appealed to the natural philosophy of Aristotle,[4] while G. Ghysens was of the opinion that the fathers had explicitly held themselves aloof from Aristotelian philosophy.[5] For his part K. Rahner said that the dogma of transub-

[4] E. Gutwenger, "Substanz und Akzidenz in der Eucharistielehre," *Zeitschrift für Kath. Theologie*, 83 (1961) 257–306.

[5] G. Ghysens, "Présence réelle et transsubstantiation dans les définitions de l'Église Catholique," *Irénikon* 32 (1959) 420–435.

stantiation was not an ontological interpretation of the real presence, but only a logical one. He identifies the dogma of the eucharistic presence with the dogma of transubstantiation; that is to say, the dogma of transubstantiation tells me neither more nor less than the word of Christ saying, "This is my body."[6] In an analysis of the Acts of the Council of Trent, I have tried to demonstrate that the two contradictory positions of Gutwenger and Ghysens both suffer from a lack of well-founded hermeneutics. The conciliar fathers at Trent, while thinking in the Aristotelian categories which were theirs, intended to define dogmatically the reality proper to the eucharistic presence, that is, our Catholic eucharistic faith, and not the categories which they used in discussing and formulating this properly eucharistic presence.[7]

3. The third factor which has contributed to the re-evaluation of eucharistic theology is the renewed appreciation for the several "real presences" of Christ. The restriction of the real presence to the presence of Christ in the eucharistic species only dates from the time of Duns Scotus. But as the Constitution on the Sacred Liturgy (art. 7) and the encyclical *Mysterium Fidei* have recently stated, there is also a real presence of Christ in the ministry of the word, there is a real presence of Christ in the liturgical assembly, there is a real presence of Christ in the priest in liturgical service, there is a real presence of Christ in the souls of the just, there is a real presence of Christ in the sacraments, and finally, there is a real presence of Christ in the eucharist. Each of these multiple forms of "real presence" has its proper mode of reality. The dogma of transubstantiation, then, does not restrict the real presence to the eucharist, but rather evaluates and determines the mode of real presence proper to the eucharist.

Now one of the traits of the modern theological trend concerning the eucharist is to affirm that the real eucharistic presence cannot be isolated from the real presence of Christ in the whole liturgical mystery and in the souls of the faithful. In this manner it reappraises the biblical, patristic, and scholastic thought according to which the eucharistic presence in the consecrated bread and wine is ordered to the ever more intimate presence of Christ in the assembled com-

[6] K. Rahner, "Die Gegenwart Christi im Sakrament des Herrenmahles," *Schriften zur Theologie*, IV, 357–385.

[7] E. Schillebeeckx, "Christus' tegenwoordigheid in de Eucharistie," *Tijdschrift voor Theologie* 5 (1965) 136–172.

munity and in each member of the church. In other words, the real presence is not an end in itself, but the salutary means by which Christ lives more intimately within our hearts. In the eucharist Christ does not come just to sit enthroned in the sacred host, but, as the Council of Trent says, "institutum ut sumatur," or in other words, Christ comes in order that by means of this eucharistic presence he might live in our hearts, in our spirits, in our senses, and in our sanctified bodies.

LOCALE OF THE NEW THEORIES

Where now are these new theories found? And in what respect can they be called "new"?

They are found in Belgium, in France, in England, and in Holland. As far as I know, it was J. de Baciocchi who in 1959 first used the word "transfinalization."[8] Thomas Sartory had previously made suggestions in this direction — that the meaning and the end of the ordinary bread and wine are radically and, in this sense, substantially changed by consecration in the eucharistic mystery: ordinary bread and wine no longer remain, but instead there is the sacramental gift of the living, glorified Christ.

However, the first one who attempted to criticize — at least publicly and explicitly — the Aristotelian and scholastic explanation of the dogma of transubstantiation (not the dogma itself) was the Belgian priest A. Vanneste in 1956,[9] followed by the Dutch priest J. Möller.[10] By taking recourse to modern phenomenology for the first time, Father Möller had subtly reappraised the eucharistic real presence. Although the same periodicals carried severe criticisms of these studies (see footnotes 9 and 10), the polemic remained unknown to the Christian people at large; nothing of these theological debates appeared in the newspapers and the atmosphere remained totally calm.

Meanwhile, two Protestant books on the eucharist were read by

[8] J. de Baciocchi, "Présence réelle et transsubstantiation," *Irénikon* 32 (1959) 139–161 (and in his books).

[9] A. Vanneste, "Bedenkingen tegen de scholastieke transsubstantiatieleer," *Collationes Gandavenses et Brugenses* 2 (1956) 322–335; "Nog steeds bedenkingen tegen de scholastieke transsubstantiatieleer," *loc. cit.* 6 (1960) 321–348. The second article noted here is a reply to criticisms of the first.

[10] J. Möller, "De transsubstantiatie," *Nederlandse Katholieke Stemmen* 56 (1960) 2–14; "Existentiaal en categoriaal denken," *loc. cit.*, pp. 166–177. The second article noted here is in reply to criticisms of the first.

Catholic theologians, one by J. Leenhardt[11] and the other by the subprior of Taizé, Max Thurian.[12] These two books, though obviously stemming from a Reformation background, were both very ecumenical in tone: they even accepted the notion of transubstantiation, but in a non-Aristotelian context. They affirmed the real presence proper to the eucharist in a manner so Catholic in spirit as to disturb certain Protestant circles. While praising L. Leenhardt's book, the exegete Father Benoit of Jerusalem gave it a penetrating criticism from the Catholic point of view. He reproved Leenhardt's book for having made a separation between reality "in itself" and reality seen and constituted by God.[13]

These books stimulated Catholic research. The last phase of the eucharistic debate, immediately preceding the encyclical *Mysterium Fidei*, was more specifically situated in the Netherlands and in England. To begin with the latter, it seems that an article by the great theologian Charles Davis could not be published in England itself; for this reason the author published it in 1964 in the Australian review *Sophia*.[14]

In the Netherlands the new tendency concerning the interpretation of the dogma of transubstantiation was popularized for the general public by Father P. Schoonenberg, first in a catechetical review[15] and then in a well-known Catholic paper.[16] However, the same author had already published these same ideas several years before in the catechetical review *Verbum* without receiving the protests or reactions that his later articles provoked. This indicates that religious sensitivity in the Netherlands had changed since and during the Second Vatican Council.

Moreover, the reactions against Father Schoonenberg cannot be isolated from the nearly parallel publications of Father Luchesius Smits. This theologian had also begun with articles in catechetical journals[17] and later developed his ideas into a book on the eucharis-

[11] J. Leenhardt, *Ceci est mon corps* (Paris and Neuchâtel, 1955).

[12] M. Thurian, *L'Eucharistie* (Paris and Neuchâtel, 1959).

[13] P. Benoit in *Revue Biblique* 63 (1956) 575–583.

[14] April, 1964, pp. 12–24.

[15] P. Schoonenberg, "Tegenwoordigheid," *Verbum* 31 (1964) 395–415; "Eucharistische Tegenwoordigheid," *De Heraut* 95 (1964) 333–336; "Nogmaals: Eucharistische Tegenwoordigheid," *De Heraut* 96 (1965) 48–50.

[16] *Idem*, in *De Volkskrant*, Holy Thursday, 1965; and a small note in the Catholic paper *De Tijd*, December 21, 1964.

[17] L. Smits, "Nieuw zicht op de werkelijke tegenwoordigheid van Christus in de

tic problem: *Vragen rondom de Eucharistie* (Roermond-Maaseik 1965). Several awkward expressions in Father Smits' first articles were corrected in later articles and in his book. According to these expressions, after the consecration the bread remained bread and the wine remained wine, and it was these statements which aroused public opinion among the Catholics of Holland. Certain Catholic circles began to cry out that these two theologians were denying the dogma of transubstantiation, and, as happened during the Christological and Trinitarian controversies in the patristic age, even the man on the street began to "talk theology." Stories developed saying that these innovators and some young priest-disciples were giving consecrated hosts left over from the mass and communion to the chickens. Investigation has already disclosed that some of these legends were the invention of certain conservatives who were circulating them to discredit the more liberal theologians.

Since the quarrels of the Reformation and Counter-Reformation, the Netherlands has been known as a "theologizing country." As a result the eucharistic controversy became very widespread, and several theologians sought to determine the state of the question. Father Trooster chided the "new theologians" because, while refusing the concept of substance, they were introducing it again from another point of view.[18] I myself have attempted to clarify the issue by analyzing in a first article what in fact the Council of Trent wanted to decide dogmatically about transubstantiation.[19] In a second article, not yet published, I intend to ascertain in what measure these new theories correspond to the Tridentine dogma. From my historical analysis of the Council of Trent, it seems necessary to distinguish four points:

1. First, the biblical affirmation of the real presence proper to the eucharist, which is clearly distinguished from a purely symbolical presence and from the real presence proper to the other sacraments.

2. Second, the affirmation of the substantial change of bread and wine as demanded by this eucharistic presence; this is the affirmation of the realistic character or of the ontological dimension of the

Eucharistie," *De Bazuin* 48:9 (November 28, 1964); "Beantwoording van vragen en opmerkingen aan p. Smits," *De Bazuin* 48:23 (March 13, 1965); "Van oude naar nieuwe transsubstantiatieleer," *De Heraut* 95 (1964) 330–344.

[18] S. Trooster, "Transsubstantiatie," *Streven* 18 (1965) 737–744.

[19] "Christus' tegenwoordigheid in de Eucharistie," *Tijdscrift voor Theologie* 5 (1965) 136–172.

presence of Christ in the sign of bread and wine; it is the "*conversio totius entis*," as St. Thomas already expressed it (III, q. 75, a. 4, and q. 75, a. 4, ad 3): the "*transentatio*."

3. Third, the manner of presenting the dogma analyzed under 1 and 2, that is to say, the presentation of this "conversio totius entis" on the level of philosophy of nature: the "*transsubstantiatio*."

4. Fourth, the question of terminology or lexicography, the question of the word "transsubstantiatio," which was used for the first time between the years 1100 and 1130, even before being interpreted in an Aristotelian sense. Of the word itself the canon of Trent says only that it is *apt* for formulating the dogma of the "conversio substantialis." (On the very eve of the solemn session in which the dogma was defined, many conciliar fathers wished to omit — as they expressed it — this rather technical and at the same time "barbarous" word.)

From this analysis, compared with the interpretation of the Greek fathers, who spoke of "*transelementatio*" (*metastoicheíosis*) or of a "conversio substantialis" in an ontological sense that was, however, completely foreign to the Aristotelian philosophy of nature, it appears that, even though the conciliar fathers of Trent were all *thinking* in Aristotelian categories (each in his own manner), the dogma itself is foreign to the Aristotelian categories of "substance" and "accidents." The dogma obliges the Catholic to admit the profound realism, or the ontological dimension, of the eucharistic presence in such a way that after the consecration the *reality* present is no longer ordinary or natural bread and wine, but our Lord himself in the presence of bread and wine which has become sacramental. This leaves the door open to a conceptual presentation of the dogma different from the medieval and Thomistic conception.

The dogma insists that there be an ontological change. This means that the terrestrial reality, bread and wine, is affected not just by an extrinsic declaration which would not intrinsically touch it. Rather, the consecratory anaphora makes of this bread the real and realistic gift of the body of our Lord as spiritual nourishment for the soul. The bread has become sacramental. And as one reality cannot be at the same time two realities, what is *really* present after the consecration is no longer bread, but the body of the Lord, our Lord himself, under the sign of *sacramental* bread.

It is also this dogma which the bishops of Holland defended in their pastoral letter;[20] or, rather, there was no need for them to defend it because everyone accepted it. The bishops were simply reassuring their people by saying that if a theologian accepts the eucharist in the biblical sense, explained by the Tridentine dogma, he has the freedom to advance the understanding of this mystery. Uncertainty remained in some circles, however, especially because a number of so-called conservative theologians identified — and continue to identify — the Tridentine dogma with the Aristotelian and Thomistic theory of substance and its accidents. Obviously these new theories deviate from the scholastic interpretation of the dogma, but they do not deviate from the dogma itself. Rather, they try to present that dogma in existential categories that are at once ontologically profound and more intelligible to the people of our day.

In my opinion, all the theologians mentioned admit this Tridentine dogma, although here and there it might have been expressed in such a way that some uninformed persons feared they were being deprived of the faith for which their ancestors had given their lives at the stake. It is against this real danger of misunderstanding these new theories that Pope Paul solemnly protested in his encyclical *Mysterium Fidei.* To Catholics the eucharistic mystery is too precious to permit even the *danger* of placing the faith of uninformed Christian people in jeopardy. Some of the new formulations of this "fides maiorum" might be reproached for not having more satisfactorily taken into account the "fides minorum." There are some preachers who seem never to have closely observed how a gardener treats older plants which have to be transplanted. After having first examined the sky and the weather, he begins to move them cautiously and carefully. He knows that it is urgent to transplant them, but he also knows that this demands special care. It is only in this regard that certain of the contemporary theological writings are somewhat lacking. On the other hand, the uncertainty raised in the minds of some of our Catholic people has been fostered not only by a few unfortunate expressions formulated without sufficient care; it comes just as much from the clumsy reaction of certain conservative theologians who identify the dogma of transubstantiation with an almost chemical theology, denying in fact the category of "sacramentum-signum" and interpreting the dogma by having recourse to chemical theories of atoms and molecules.

[20] May 9, 1965; see *Katholiek Archief* 20 (1965) 598–600; also in *Ephemerides Theologicae Lovanienses* 41 (1965) 690–693.

In this sense the eucharistic debate was first begun, not in the Netherlands, but in Italy. During the years 1949–1960, although the average Christian heard nothing about it, the same debate took place between two Italian theologians, Professor (now Bishop) Carlo Colombo of the Milan Major Seminary and Professor F. Selvaggi from the Gregorian University.[21] Professor Colombo argued rightly that transubstantiation is not a physical change but an ontological change, while Selvaggi continued to identify the Tridentine dogma with a physical and even chemical change. It is against this same background of a physical change theory that the reaction of the so-called new theology should be considered.

However, there is a perceptible difference between the reactions of Professor C. Colombo and the theologians of the Netherlands against this theory.[22] In the Colombo-Selvaggi debate ontology alone was pitted against cosmology. In the present debate, however, the theologians, while siding with Professor Colombo, concentrate upon the relationship between the ontological element and the "sacramentum-signum" (which was left aside in the Italian polemic). In this sense, the eucharistic controversy has entered into a truly new phase. Certain of these theologians have perhaps forgotten to put the emphasis explicitly on the ontological dimension of the "conversio substantialis" (which they admit). Nonetheless, they have a keen sensitivity to the fact that this ontological dimension is such only within the framework of a sacramentalization. In other words, they insist that the ontological dimension is a *dimension of* "sacramentum-signum." They no longer look for realities outside of eucharistic sacramentality. To do so would be to leave the eucharistic framework

[21] F. Selvaggi, "Il concetto di sostanza nel dogma eucaristico in relazione alla fisica moderna," *Gregorianum* 30 (1949) 7–45. C. Colombo, "Teologia, filosofia e fisica nella dottrina della transsustanziazione," *Scuola Cattolica* 83 (1955) 89–124. F. Selvaggi, "Ancora intorno ai concetti di 'sostanza sensibile' e 'realtà fisica,'" *Gregorianum* 38 (1957) 503–514. C. Colombo, "Ancora sulla dottrina della transsustanziazione e la fisica moderna," *Scuola Cattolica* 84 (1956) 263–288. C. Colombo, "Bilancio provvisorio di una discussione eucaristica," *Scuola Cattolica* 88 (1960) 23–55.

[22] The eucharistic controversies in the Netherlands which were carried on in Dutch, not a "world-wide" language, were reported throughout the whole world by *Time* magazine (July 2, 1965, pp. 68, 70), which gave a completely inadequate resumé, and in more accurate and understandable accounts in *Informations Catholiques Internationales* (no. 248, September 15, 1965) and in *Herder Korrespondenz* (August 1965, pp. 517–520), while an alarming article by Father Schoenmaeckers was published in *Orientierung* (January 31, 1964) and *The Month* (June 1965). See also the resumé of the different positions in *Katholiek Archief* 20 (1965) 626–645.

and consider the bread and wine as a physicist or a botanist would, who is forced to say that after the consecration he cannot experimentally prove any change in the physical composition of bread and wine! The conversion is *sacramental*, and, within this framework, it is ontological. The ontology of physical reality, however, is not situated at the same level as the ontology of eucharistic sacramentality. It is this aspect of the present controversy which makes it different from the debate between Selvaggi and Colombo (who incidentally was already nearly suspected of heresy by Selvaggi).

SOME MODERN PERSPECTIVES OF THE EUCHARIST

In my concluding section I now intend to examine, within this sacramental framework, the core of the theories called "transfinalization" and "transignification" as interpretations of transubstantiation.[23] I will clarify the position of these theologians by referring to the well-known classic distinction: sacramentum, res et sacramentum, and res sacramenti. Applied to the sacrament of the eucharist, sacramentum is the consecrated bread and wine: these are sacramenta-signa. Sacramentum et res is the real presence of Christ in these sacramenta-signa. The res sacramenti, as the leading scholastics say, is the communio ecclesiastica, that is, the unity of the mystical body: the life of the community in Christ and, for the individual, the life of Christ in his soul, manifesting itself by an intimate sweetness, the "dulcedo eucharistica."

Holy scripture, the writings of the patristic age, and medieval scholasticism, in contrast to the theology of the post-Tridentine era, always emphasized the *res* sacramenti. Obviously, this presence of Christ in our hearts (res sacramenti) is brought about through the medium of the sacred host, and this implies the real presence of

[23] R. Masi ("Transsustanziazione, transsignificazione, transfinalizzazione," *Osservatore Romano*, November 4, 1965, p. 5) affirms that according to these modern theologians the eucharistic change is only a psychological phenomenon, in such a way that the eucharistic presence is merely a symbolic presence. This is an implicit admission that he has not read the authors in question, and, even more, that he seems to identify the ontological with the physical. In *Osservatore Romano*, September 13, 1965, the Pope was reported as saying that these new theories were not "vere e proprie eresie," but only that the encyclical "avverte del grave pericolo cui le nuove opinioni espongono la retta fede." But R. Masi concluded that they were true heresies because he himself interprets the anthropological approach of these theologians in the gnoseological perspective of the scholastic theory of sign, which is quite different from the modern "anthropology of sign."

Christ in the host. Yet, the emphasis is placed not on the eucharistic presence but upon the *purpose* of this presence, the presence of Christ *in us.* It is for this purpose ultimately that the sacrament of the eucharist was instituted by Christ: "Institutum ut sumatur" (Council of Trent). Forced by circumstances and already preceded in this by medieval piety, post-Tridentine theology shifted the emphasis. The res sacramenti was pushed into the background, while the res et sacramentum, that is, the real presence in the sacred host, was emphasized so much that it seemed to be an end in itself and not a res et sacramentum, that is, totally oriented toward the res ultima: the growth of Christ in the heart of the community.

The consequence of this transfer of emphasis was that in popular piety devotion to the blessed sacrament was almost isolated from the context of the eucharistic celebration or of the holy mass. The blessed sacrament was adored; it was no longer eaten. Modern theologians, while accepting the real presence in the eucharist as well as the legitimacy of the adoration of Christ in the blessed sacrament, want only to replace the emphasis where the New Testament, the fathers, and the great scholastic theologians placed it, that is, on the res sacramenti, the end for which Christ instituted it. In my opinion, that is the central point of this whole new theology regarding the eucharist; and to a certain degree it is acknowledged by the Constitution on the Sacred Liturgy. What preoccupies these theologians is the eucharistic celebration and the active participation of the faithful, culminating in holy communion.

But this shift of emphasis has its repercussions on the concept of the eucharistic presence. Because the "new" emphasis is concerned with the intimate presence of Christ in the hearts both of the individual believer and of the community of Christians, the eucharist must remain on the level of interpersonal relationship: of the presence of one person to another person. For man, each interpersonal presence is communicated by means of a spatial, visible, tangible, and even tasted presence. But in this case the spatial presence is integrated into the personal presence, that is, the body and the corporeal elements receive a new dimension: they become *signs* of a person who is present, signs which effect this presence, and signs which are real because they "realize" this presence.

This is what is effected, in an infinitely, ontologically deeper way, in the intimate presence of Christ in our hearts by means of his real presence offered to us in bread and wine become sacramental food and drink. The "real presence" must be viewed against the background of the saving act of Christ, who in this sacramental bread gives himself to us. Christ remains truly present in the sacred host before being received in communion, but always as an offer; it is a "praesentia oblata." The presence becomes reciprocal — that is to say, presence in the full and completive human sense — only in the acceptance of this offered presence, and in that way it becomes the presence of Christ in our hearts, which is the very purpose of the eucharist. Only a eucharistic presence that is personally *offered and accepted* becomes an altogether complete presence. The presence of Christ in the tabernacle is therefore real, but as such it is only offered, and in this sense it is secondary in relation to the complete, reciprocal presence to which it is directed as to its end and perfection.

From this it follows that these theologians accept the real presence proper to the eucharist, but they do not want to place it outside of the context of an interpersonal relationship, even though this relationship is in fact accomplished by means of earthly things transformed in such a way that these things become a sign effecting the offer of this real presence. Here these theologians invoke an analogy or a comparison. When a housewife gives a party and serves her guests food and drink, the nourishment and beverages are assumed into an interpersonal relationship. They become a sign of the love and hospitality of the hostess. And she would take pains to see that the coffee or tea, for example, would be delicious so that in the excellence of the drink one might, so to speak, savor the love and the hospitality of the hostess. Recall how, especially in the Arab countries on the occasion of a visit, the preparation of tea or coffee becomes a ceremony in which honor and hospitality are at stake.

As a matter of fact, it was particularly these analogies and comparisons which raised many questions in Holland. Without any doubt analogies always limp. Still they express something of the symbol-making activity of man; in a practical way they give us an "anthropology of sign." But in the eucharist this anthropology is assumed into the dynamism of the Holy Spirit, the Spiritus Creator who effects the ontological depth of Christ's gift of self in the sacramental sign of bread. This gift of himself in and through the bread and wine transubstantializes the bread and wine in their proper being.

Some persons ridiculed these theologians, saying that the eucharist means no more to them than the loving gesture of someone who gives his friend a piece of chocolate! However, these theologians have only reacted against a eucharistic materialism, whereas in the eucharist we ought to be concerned with an interpersonal relationship between Christ and us, an interpersonal relationship in which Christ gives himself to man by means of bread and wine which, by this very gift, have undergone a transfinalization and an ontological and therefore radical transignification. The bread and wine have become this real presence offered by Christ, who gave his life for us on the cross; offered by Christ in order that we might participate in this sacrifice and in the new covenant which is life for us all. The chemical, physical, or botanical reality of bread and wine is not changed; otherwise, Christ would not be present under the sign of eatable bread and drinkable wine. Eucharistic sacramentality demands precisely that the physical reality does not change, otherwise there would no longer be a eucharistic sign. But in its ontological reality, to the question "What *is* this bread ultimately, what *is* this wine ultimately?" one can no longer answer, "Bread and wine," but instead, "The real presence of Christ offered under the sacramental sign of bread and wine." Therefore, the *reality* (that is, the *substance*, because that is the meaning of "substance") which is before me, is no longer bread and wine, but the real presence of Christ offered to me under the sign of food and drink. This is precisely what the Holy Father said in his encyclical *Mysterium Fidei*: "After transubstantiation has taken place, the species of bread and wine undoubtedly take on a new meaning and a new finality, for they no longer remain ordinary bread and ordinary drink, but become the sign of something sacred, and the sign of a spiritual food. However, the reason they take on the new significance and this new finality is simply because they contain a new 'reality' which we may justly term ontological."[24] In other words, the encyclical admits transfinalization and transignification on condition that they are not considered as an extrinsic designation or as a peripheral change, but rather as having a profound and ontological content. That is the very meaning of the dogma of transubstantiation. "Vanum videtur contendere de *nominibus* ubi constat de *rebus*" (S. Thomas, Responsum 9 ad Lectorem Venetum).

[24] Peracta transsubstantiatione, species panis et vini novam proculdubio induunt significationem, novumque finem, cum amplius non sint communis panis et communis potus, sed *signum rei sacrae* signumque spiritualis alimoniae; sed *ideo* novam induunt significationem et novum finem *quia* novam continent *realitatem*, quam merito ontologicam dicimus." (Encyclical Letter *Mysterium Fidei* [September 3, 1965]. English translation published by the National Catholic Welfare Conference, Washington, D.C.)

Donald Gray

The Real Absence: A Note on the Eucharist

The mode of presence of the risen Jesus in the eucharist has always been recognized as being of an odd, indeed *sui generis*, character. The broad Christian tradition has generally rejected the notion that this presence is to be understood as simply a presence in the memory of the faithful. On the contrary, the presence is a real one. All the problems on the mode of the presence stem fundamentally from this affirmation. What after all does it mean to be *really* present?

As soon as one affirms that the real eucharistic presence of Jesus is irreducibly mysterious, then one has already admitted that this particular mode of real presence can only be approached analogically (or, as we might say today, through the use of models) and hence never exhaustively. We really do not know in any definitive sense what the mode of Jesus' eucharistic presence is. The appropriateness of such initial agnosticism is perhaps self-evident enough, but its importance warrants its being underlined.

Granted the mysteriousness and hence *sui generis* character of the eucharistic mode of the risen Jesus' presence with his people, what analogies or models derived from experience become appropriate for gaining some insight into this presence? We might begin by asking if Jesus is present eucharistically in the *modus* of an object. We do not mean by this: is there any sense in which the risen Jesus might be designated an object of the believer's faith. Obviously, there is some sense in which he is such an object. What we mean to ask is: is Jesus present in the eucharist as a stone or a tree or a plant is present in human experience? Is Jesus' presence object-like, is his presence physical?

We feel divided at this point, I think, because the word physical might be taken to point to the bodily dimension of the risen life of Jesus and hence we should like to say that he is physically present. On the other hand, we do not wish to say that Jesus' presence is like that of an object in the world. However, there is a danger that this presence will be understood on analogy with that of an object because material objects, viz. bread and wine, are employed as the symbols of this presence. Jesus is not present to the community as bread and wine are present in the world but rather he is present in the mode of bread-and-wine symbol. These are quite different modes of presence.

There is a point, and a crucial one I believe, at which the mode of presence of an object does tend to become operative as the determinative model in our understanding of the eucharistic presence of Jesus. Our experience of an object is that it is either present or absent, either there or not there, and that such presence or absence is empirically determinable. The traditional and perfectly legitimate stress on the real presence tends to militate against any corresponding insistence on a real absence. This is so because the presence of the risen Jesus is implicitly understood in an object-like way as a presence which is to be either affirmed or denied. To some extent this difficulty is overcome in the awareness that the risen Jesus is not present here in such a way that he cannot also be present simultaneously elsewhere. This type of presence could of course never be affirmed of any ordinary object in experience. Nonetheless it does not normally occur to us to affirm a real absence of the risen Jesus in conjunction with our affirmation of a real presence. The term presence itself, particularly when understood on the model of object-like presence, prevents the notion of such an absence from ever offering itself for possible reflection and affirmation. The question is: why would anyone care to consider, let alone affirm, such an absence?

If we press our analysis of appropriate eucharistic models further, we will at the same time move closer to an answer to this question. Granted that the mode of presence of an object does not provide an appropriate model for eucharistic presence, surely personal modes of presence in our experience do offer a rich source for such models. The risen Jesus is interpersonally present as a subject of encounter. Christ acts personally through sacraments, as we have frequently been told in recent years.

While personal or interpersonal models clearly represent a considerable advance over non-personal or object models, they are themselves by no means exhaustive of the eucharistic mystery, although this has probably not been sufficiently stressed in our enthusiasm to go personalistic. The mode of presence of a person is a limited one in that it is restricted to a being here or there with the other, at least "objectively" speaking. The presence of a person may be indefinitively multipled in the subjectivity of other persons either through present awareness or memory. However, if we were to understand the eucharistic presence of Jesus in this way, we would seem to run into trouble with the word "real" as traditionally interpreted. The personal presence of the risen Jesus in the eucharist is indeed of an odd sort which cannot be adequately captured in interpersonal models even if these are illuminating in a suggestive way.

May it be said of personal modes of presence that they do not require a simple and unqualified affirmation or negation of presence or absence? Is it possible to say of the other as personal that it is simultaneously present and absent without contradiction? Whether the other as personal is physically present or not allows of only a straightforward affirmation or negation. Whether the other as personal is also personally present, i.e., *really* present as a free personal subject, is a much more complicated matter. It would seem that sheer physical presence without authentically personal presence is possible. We say of the other, for example, that he is a million miles away even though he is clearly standing right here. We speak of failure to communicate, lack of attention, unconcern, indifference, carelessness, superficiality in interpersonal relations, thus pointing to a real absence in the midst of a real presence of a physical, object-like kind.

Even in the most intimate of relationships there is a holding back, an inadequacy of giving, a falling short of response to the other. In short our personal self-communication to the other is always fragmentary and partial. We may be physically present and personally absent; indeed we may be personally present and absent at the same time in contradiction to our own deepest intentions but without any necessary contradiction in experience or thought.

This inevitable element of absence in all interpersonal relations seems inappropriate, however, as a model for understanding the eucharistic presence of the risen Jesus. We feel compelled to speak of ourselves as both personally present and absent in the eucharistic encounter, but we could hardly justify speaking of Jesus' presence as marked by superficiality or distraction, inadequacy of giving or egoism of any sort. The risen Jesus is really present and really is not absent. So it would seem at least at the level of interpersonal models.

And yet we confront at this point a liturgical practice in earliest Christianity which seems curious in the light of the above affirmation of full, "real" presence. The liturgical prayer *Maranatha,* which is most probably to be translated "Come, Lord," suggests not simply a petition requesting the immediate coming into the midst of the eucharistic assembly on the part of the risen Jesus, but also and what is more important, points ahead in time to the definitive coming into the midst which is termed the parousia, or presence. The eucharist represents a celebration of Jesus' death until he comes and no matter how many times he comes into the midst of the community assembly, he still has not come.

This situation is surely not overcome by the reservation of the sacrament as if a transient coming into the midst were thereby transformed into a permanent being there. Even when the risen Jesus is really there with his people, he is also not yet there with them in that definitive mode of presence which is termed parousia and which is even more mysterious than the eucharistic mode of presence.

It would seem then that the risen Jesus' eucharistic presence is of an anticipatory or proleptic character. It is a presence which not only does not exclude absence but which actually contains absence as an essential dimension of its mode of presence. Not only is the risen Jesus with his people in the interpersonal mode of presence, he is also and equiprimordially with his people in the mode of futurity. Because of the essentially eschatological nature of both Christian faith and Christian cult, the presence of the future suggests itself as an appropriate model for the interpretation of the mysterious eucharistic presence of the risen Jesus with the community of disciples.

Before exploring this possibility further we might simply suggest that because of the essentially historical nature of both Christian faith and Christian cult, the presence of the past also suggests itself as an appropriate model of interpretation. In point of fact the interaction between models of presence in terms of both past and future would seem to render up the most satisfactory understanding of the eucharistic presence in terms of a tension between an historical already and an eschatological not yet. Jesus is already present with his people but he is at the same time not yet with them. This formulation safeguards both a necessary presence and a necessary absence. However, since we wish to underline here the dimension of absence in the eucharistic presence we shall limit ourselves to a few brief observations on the model of futurity by way of conclusion.

We noted previously that neither the model of object-like presence nor the model of subject-like presence were able to account satisfactorily for the virtual omnipresence of the risen Jesus in the eucharist.

The limitations of presence that apply to both non-personal objects and personal subjects do not apply to the eucharistic presence. This is precisely one of the difficulties with all essentially spatial models — they allow for a being here but exclude a simultaneous being there. This is surely one of the reasons why the notion of the God up there has fallen on hard days. And what often appears as a kind of pantheism (e.g. in a Robinson or a Tillich) may just as well be accounted as an attempt to safeguard and give meaning to the divine omnipresence. The model of depth perhaps does not achieve this purpose adequately because of its spatial connotations, but it involves an effort which is moving in the correct direction.

At any rate, time models fortunately do not partake of this particular disadvantage. The future is omnipresent, i.e. it is an integral and indispensable dimension of every present, just as the past is omnipresent. The future (or the past) cannot be limited to being here or there. Every present here or there is inescapably penetrated by the future. The presence of the risen Jesus in the eucharist is the presence of the future; it is the anticipatory presence of the parousia as both the ultimate future and the ultimate presence. The parousia as the definitive presence of the risen Jesus comes out of the future and into the present without however ceasing to be future. The eucharist is not then simply the re-presentation of the death and resurrection (however that is to be understood), but it is also and preeminently the pre-presentation of the parousia. It is the future of the risen Jesus which comes into the midst of the present. And because the future of Jesus is the future of every and all presents it is omnipresent everywhere and at all times.

The future is present in every present but it is also clearly distinguishable from every present because of its not yet character which allows it to be spoken of as absent. Jesus' coming into the midst of the community is a coming in the mode of futurity which establishes a real presence but one which does not rule out a real absence at the same time.

If the risen Jesus is really present in some sense as the future is present, we might ask further if this presence in the mode of futurity is in any way related to the meal-symbolism of the eucharist. In the eucharist the future becomes present in the shape of a community meal. We are accustomed to thinking of the community meal as a remembrance of the final supper of Jesus with his disciples. In this way each eucharist becomes repetitive of a past meal; it serves to make the past present again in some way.

This emphasis is perfectly legitimate and intelligible but it needs to be complemented by the awareness that the eucharistic celebration is anticipatory as well as repetitive in character, that it summons into the present the eschatological banquet and hence the eschatological community of the end-time. This future assembly is really present in but also really absent from the historical assembly. The future might well in this context be said to be more genuinely creative of the eucharistic assembly than the past. The eschatological takes priority over the historical without thereby destroying the essential importance of history.

The eucharistic assembly not only tells us something about the shape of the future, but actually represents a real anticipation of that future. In fact it is not too much to say that it is precisely by anticipating the future that the eucharistic assembly tells us something about the shape of the future. The fact that the future comes into our midst in the form of bread and wine is of immense significance for our understanding of the future. The bread-and-wine symbol indicates that the Christian finds in the future as made present eucharistically nourishment and sustenance for his life in the present.

In general the future reaches man in an ambiguous form — it may suggest hope and expectation on the one hand or meaninglessness and despair on the other. The future may nourish and build up or it may deprive and tear down. The Christian is not rescued from the ambiguity of the immediate future through the eucharist, but he is rescued from the terror of ultimate meaninglessness by the coming into the present of the ultimate future in the eucharist. This coming into the midst of the ultimate future is achieved through the real presence of the risen Jesus, the herald and harbinger of the eschatological kingdom of God. And through the provisional and anticipatory presence of the ultimate future the Christian is enabled to go out into every immediate future without terror. The eucharistic presence of the ultimate future sustains our presence in every immediate future.

The purpose of these reflections has been to underline a fact which is receiving increased attention in recent theological work: that the Christian lives from the future. This is not quite the same as saying that he lives for the future, which is true in a certain sense but which might be taken to mean that his interests are exclusively otherworldly. The Christian lives from the future in the sense that the eschatological future of God's kingdom, which has already been announced in and through the resurrection of Jesus, is the ground of his present piety and politics, his suffering and his activity.

This living from the future is dramatically focused in the cultic assembly by the coming into the midst of the community by the risen Jesus in the mode of futurity. This means that the risen Jesus becomes really but not exhaustively or definitively present with his people in the eucharist. The real presence is accompanied by a real absence which summons the people of God into the future promised by the resurrection. The purpose of this real absence is to call the people of God to greater intimacy of presence in the immediate future and to definitive presence in the ultimate future.

In employing a model of futurity to explore the meaning of the real presence we do not wish thereby to displace the model of interpersonal presence. Both models are needed, and undoubtedly others in addition. No one model can exhaust the mysterious presence of the risen Jesus. Even taken conjointly all models together fail to achieve full clarity. Each model separately and all together in reciprocal interaction illumine the mystery. That is all we can ask of theological reflection and theological language.

Hervé-Marie Legrand

The Presidency of the Eucharist According To the Ancient Tradition

"In the primitive Church priests presided at the Eucharist because they presided over the Christian community." Impressed with finding this idea expressed twice, parenthetically, in the *relatio* of the Central Theological Commission of Vatican II on number 28 of *Lumen Gentium,*[1] we thought it would be interesting to verify it at a

[1] *Schema Constitutionis De Ecclesia (1964), relatio* on number 28, pp. 101–102: "Cum jam in Novo Testamento et in aevo post apostolico Eucharistia ut 'sacrificium' intelligatur, et presbyteri ut rectores communitatis sint rectores eucharistiae, sacerdotium ministeriale Novi Testamenti suam propriam dignitatem a Christo institutam ostendit.

Hervé-Marie Legrand

time when the need for a more serious reflection on the conjunction between the Eucharist, the Church and the ordained ministry is widely recognized. To contribute to this reflection we propose in this present study to establish: [1] who in actual fact presided at the Eucharist in the pre-Nicene Church and with what title; [2] how this presidency, when it results from an ordination, appears as the liturgical dimension of a pastoral charge; [3] how the entire assembly celebrates the Eucharist; and [4] the meaning of the presidency of the Eucharist by ordained ministers.

1. WHO PRESIDED AT THE EUCHARIST IN THE PRE-NICENE PERIOD? WITH WHAT TITLE?

The New Testament is not concerned with explicitly specifying whose lot it is to preside at eucharistic assemblies. We have only allusions to their celebration. Thus at Troas (Acts 20:7–12), while nothing is said of the Eucharist itself, we see the assembly gathered to break bread as well as to listen to the word. If Acts 13:1–2 in fact describes a eucharistic celebration, it is prophets and teachers who preside.[2] There is never any mention that a cultic, sacerdotal qualification is required to preside at the Eucharist; in fact, none of the numerous ministries to be found in the New Testament is qualified as sacerdotal.[3] As a matter of fact there is question of priesthood in the New Testament only apropos of Christ (a theological construction of the Letter to the Hebrews) and apropos of the ecclesial community (1 Peter and Revelations). Is this to say that the presidency of the Eucharist could devolve on any Christian?

This seems very unlikely for three reasons. The first is of an exegetical order: recent research on 1 Peter and Revelations has shown that their sacerdotal affirmations do not apply to individual believers (we should translate "priestly people," not "people of priests"); the theme is not one of cult, but of election.[4] A second

Functio rectorum communitatis cum functione cultica coniuncta apparet."

[2] This is what the *Traduction Oecuménique de la Bible* (Paris 1972) suggests in loco, p. 396, note u. The presidency of the Eucharist by the prophets in the Didache strengthens this probability.

[3] See the different opinion of A. Feuillet, *Le sacerdoce du Christ et de ses ministres d'après la prière sacerdotale du quatrième évangile et plusieurs données parallèles du Nouveau Testament* (Paris 1972). This thesis runs into difficulties of methodology noted by J. Delorme, "Sacerdoce du Christ et ministère (à propos de Jean 17). Sémantique et theologie biblique," *Recherches Sc. Rel.* 62 (1974) 199–219.

[4] Cf. J. H. Elliott, *The Elect and the Holy. An Exegetical Examination of I Peter 2, 4–10* (Leiden 1966).

reason is related to the history of the liturgy: the Christian Eucharist developed in critical symbiosis with the Jewish liturgy, the presidency of which is strictly regulated.[5] Beyond these reasons, the earliest witness to the Eucharist we have (around 52) leads us to exclude the possibility that anyone could preside. Paul introduces his witness with the solemn formula: "What I have received, I have handed on to you" (1 Cor 11:23), a formula he does not otherwise employ except to introduce the kerygma (1 Cor 15:3). What does he develop with such a solemn guarantee? Essentially the relationship of the eucharistic celebration to the Church: it is the supreme manifestation of the Church as actualization of the Covenant, and it is thus that the body of Christ is built up.[6] Given the importance of what is at stake, it is highly unlikely that the presidency of such an act was left to hazard; on the contrary it is probable that the structure of the gathered assembly was based on the very structure of the community which gathers in "Church," to employ an expression of Père Grelot.[7]

The parenetic passage of Paul on the charisms in the Church of Corinth precludes speculation on a would-be charismatic structure of that church in opposition to a ministerial structure.[8] Moreover, we know from Acts (13:1) that the prophets and teachers are anterior to Paul and independent of him. Does he himself not cite them in 1 Corinthians 12:28 in the first place after the apostles?[9]

Considering only these texts, it seems possible that the presidency of the Eucharist was committed to this group, just as it seems to be

[5] On the Jewish origins of the Christian Eucharist, henceforth consult the important article of T. Talley, "From Berakah to Eucharistia: A Reopening Question," *Worship* 50 (1976) 115–137.

[6] Note the vocabulary of assembling ("synerkomai," 1 Cor 11:17, 18, 20, 33, 34), the convocation of the "Church of God" opposed to the *schismata* (v. 18), to the *haireseis* (v. 19), to private meals (v. 21). There is question of actualizing the New Covenant (v. 25). Demonstration in P. Neuenzeit, *Das Herrenmahl* (Munich 1960) 188–235. Concordant indications in P. Grelot, "Réflexions générales autour du thème du Symposium: le ministre de l'Eucharistie" in *Ministère et célébration de l'Eucharistie* (Studia Anselmiana 61, Rome 1973) 22–25.

[7] P. Grelot, "Réflexions générales . . ." *ibid*. 22–23.

[8] Cf. H.-M. Legrand, "Recherches sur le presbytérat et l'épiscopat," *Rev. des Sc. Phil. Théol*. 59 (1975) 670–671.

[9] H.-M. Legrand, *ibid*. 672–673, and especially H. Merklein, *Das kirchliche Amt nach dem Epheserbrief* (Munich 1973) 235–331.

committed to them in Acts 13:1–2 and will continue to be committed to them with priority in the Didache.

We can therefore conclude that Scripture observes a total silence concerning a sacerdotal office to which the presidency of the Eucharist is committed and that it prescribes nothing in this regard. On the other hand, we can suppose (we have noted three indications of probability in this sense) that those who presided over the Church (apostles, prophets and teachers) probably presided at the Eucharist, although we cannot generalize this hypothesis as valid for the Church as a whole in New Testament times.

We propose to analyze here all the evidence anterior to Nicaea which provides information relative to the presidency of the Eucharist. Paradoxically, Clement of Alexandria and Origen, both of them very much concerned with the Eucharist, make no significant allusions to our question, at least as far as we have been able to ascertain.[10]

The Didache: Prophets, apostles (messengers), bishops (without apostolic succession) preside at the Eucharist. There is general agreement with J. P. Audet today to date this document before the year 100. Chapters 9 and 10, which are increasingly regarded as eucharistic,[11] concludes with the injunction: "let the prophets pronounce the blessing as

[10] On the eucharistic doctrine of Clement see the detailed study of A. Mehat, "Clement of Alexandria" in *The Eucharist of the Early Christians* (New York: Pueblo Publishing Company 1978) 99–131. P. Jacquemont treats the doctrine of Origen, *ibid.* 183–193. For a more topical treatment, J. Lécuyer, "Sacerdoce des fidèles et sacerdoce ministériel chez Origène," *Vetera Christianorum* 7 (1970) 253–264 (however, Origen does not employ the expression "ministerial priesthood").

[11] The following deny its eucharistic character: R. H. Connolly, J. Jeremias, A. Baumstark, J. P. Audet and W. Rordorf. However, study of the Jewish substratum of the Christian Eucharist is leading to a serious reassessment of the question. As T. Talley notes (note 5 above) 129: ". . . if we consider seriously the precision of the Didachist's revision of the Jewish grace in such wise as to remove all use of the benediction formularies which were critical for the meal *berakoth* and to give unprecedented priority and prominence to eucharistic forms, and if we further consider this in the light of the sacrificial nuance of such eucharistic language as has been revealed by the studies of Cazelles and Laporte . . . it should not be considered impossible that Didache 10 either is (or wishes to seem to be) a careful adaptation of *Birkat Ha-Mazon* to the requirements of the Supper of the Lord become a Christian *zebach todah*, the eucharistic sacrifice." Similar views have been expressed by P. Prigent, G. Bornkamm, J. Quasten, J. Daniélou and J. de Watteville.

they like."[12] These prophets seem to be interchangeable with the apostles of Didache 11, 5–6. Is it inconceivable that they presided at the Eucharist? Not at all, according to what we have already seen (Acts 13:1–2 and 1 Cor 12:28), for they preside over the Church and over her construction (cf. Eph 2:20 and 4:11). These prophets are not sacerdotal figures, Didache 13, 3 notwithstanding: "You shall take the firstfruits of all the produce and give them to the prophets: for they are your high priests." "High priest" is employed here in a purely allegorical sense to justify economic support of the prophets. Furthermore, high priests did not teach.

If any doubts remain concerning the eucharistic nature of chapters 9 and 10 and the presidency of the prophets and apostles, they are dissipated by Didache 14, 1 and 15, 2: "The day of the Lord assemble for the breaking of the bread and the eucharist. . . . Choose bishops and deacons worthy of the Lord . . . for they, too, fulfill among you the office (*leitourgia*) of the prophets and teachers. Do not hold them in contempt: for they count as honorable men among you, along with the prophets and teachers." Note that the bishops are chosen here by the community directly in function of the Sunday Eucharist: they are entrusted with the "liturgy" of the community, that is to say, its direction, liturgical included. However, the bishops and deacons do not replace the prophets and teachers. As J. P. Audet notes: ". . . they share with the prophets and teachers a liturgy which has become too heavy in its demands. . . . Still less could they assume the 'succession' of the apostles."[13] As a matter of fact, it is considered opportune to recommend the bishops and deacons to the "consideration of the Churches" (Didache 15, 2). It is the prophets and teachers who serve, psychologically, as the point of reference: bishops and deacons come after them.

In short, as Odo Casel demonstrated nearly fifty years ago,[14] in the Didache the presidency of the Eucharist is committed to prophets, apostles (messengers) and bishops (who are not successors of the apostles). Their denominations are quite other than sacerdotal.

The Letter of Clement to the Corinthians: Bishops-presbyters, established in succession to the apostles, preside over the Church and at the Eucharist.

[12] We follow the version of J. P. Audet, *La Didache, Instructions des Apôtres* (Etudes bibliques, Paris 1958).

[13] *Ibid*. 466.

[14] O. Casel, "Prophetie und Eucharistie," *Jahrbuch für Liturgiewissenschaft* 9 (1929) 1–19.

Contemporary, like the Didache, with the last writings of the New Testament (around 95), this letter is a letter from the Church of Rome to that of Corinth. It was attributed very early (around 170) to Clement, no doubt the spokesman of the presbyteral college of Rome. It contains this admonition: "It would not be a slight fault for us to expel from the office of bishop those who have presented the gifts (*prosenegkontas ta dôra*) in a holy and blameless fashion. . . .

Fortunate are the presbyters who have run their course and have completed a fruitful and perfect life. . . . We see some whom, in spite of their good conduct, you have discharged from their functions, which they exercised with honor and in a blameless fashion" (44, 4–6).[15] What do these gifts represent? Probably, A. Jaubert responds with most commentators, the material gifts which accompanied eucharistic sacrifices and the eucharistic elements themselves.[16] Thus here the presidents of the Eucharist are the presidents of the local community: its bishops or presbyters (the vocabulary is still fluid), established by the apostles "or afterward by other eminent men with the consent of the whole Church" (44, 3). These chiefs, however, do not derive their office simply from a linear succession to the apostles; they have not assumed their office without the consent of the community.

Are these bishops-presbyters sacerdotal personages? No. Clement contents himself with a comparison which by the deliberate choice of certain nonritual terms precludes the assimilation of the ministers of the New Testament to those of the Old Covenant.[17]

[15] *Clément de Rome, Epître aux Corinthiens*, ed. A. Jaubert (Sources Chrétiennes 167, Paris 1971) 173.

[16] *Ibid.*

[17] Cf. M. Jourjon, "Remarques sur le vocabulaire sacerdotal dans la *Ia Clementis*" in *Epektasis (Mélanges Card. Daniélou*, Paris 1972) 109: "Jamais le ch. 40 ni aucun autre passage de la lettre ne qualifient de prêtres les chefs de l'Eglise, mais la *Ia Clementis* estime que ces chefs sont à l'Église ce que les prêtres et les lévites étaient au peuple de Dieu. . . . En 44, 4 [présenter les dons] il corrige la portée ritualiste du texte par deux adverbes qui n'appartiennent nullement au vocabulaire sacrificiel: *amentôs* et hosiôs. . . . Ce n'est pas pour les ritualiser ou judaïser ou pour faire d'eux des sacrificateurs que la *Ia Clementis* compare épiscope et diacres aux prêtres et lévites. C'est que la rectitude et l'intégrité conviennent à l'unique dessein de Dieu, à travers le peuple prophétique de l'Eglise." G. Blond, who comments on the same passage, "Clement of Rome," in *The Eucharist of the Early Christians* (note 10 above) 29–30, does not seem familiar with Jourjon's work.

In short, for Clement of Rome those who preside over the Church preside at the Eucharist, for "we ought to do in order all those things the Master has ordered us to perform" (40, 1). These bishops-presbyters, established in the succession of the apostles, are not sacerdotal figures in the sense of the Old Testament.

Ignatius of Antioch: The bishop, principle of the unity of the Church, presides at the Eucharist or otherwise someone he delegates. The correspondence of Ignatius of Antioch dates from around the year 110. In his Letter to the Smyrneans he explicitly reserves the presidency of the Eucharist to the bishop in the following terms: "Apart from the bishop no one is to do anything pertaining to the Church. Only that Eucharist is to be considered legitimate (*bebaia*) which is celebrated under the presidency of the bishop (*hē hypo episkopou ousa*) or under that of the one he appoints *(epitrepsi)*. There where the bishop appears let the community be, just as where Jesus Christ is, there is the whole Church. It is not permissible, apart from the bishop, either to baptize or to hold an agape. But whatever he approves is also pleasing to God — so that everything you do may be secure and legitimate" (8:1–2).[18] Let us note that for Ignatius all the churches are presided over by a bishop assisted by a presbytery and deacons. He is silent on this point only in the case of the Church of Rome: is this due to the fact that at that date the Church of Rome was still governed by a presbyteral college?[19] The key to his insistence on the role of the bishop in his letters to the other churches is a mystique of unity of which the Eucharist is for him the sacrament, as Camelot has well shown.[20] Such for Ignatius is the manifest basis of the presidency of the Eucharist by the bishop. It is not to be sought in a sacerdotal qualification of the ministers, for he never applies sacerdotal vocabulary to the heads of the Church. Likewise he never traces the heads of the Church back to the apostles, nor does he employ the terminology of succession.[21]

[18] Version of P. Camelot (Sources Chrétiennes 10, 4th ed. Paris 1969) 139–141.

[19] This fact would explain why the letter to the Corinthians, studied above, does not allude to a Roman bishop.

[20] He summarizes the doctrine of Ignatius under the title: "le docteur de l'unité" (note 18 above) 19–47.

[21] Three comparisons of the presbytery and the bishop with the Apostles and Christ (Magnesians 6, 1; Trallians 2, 2 and 12, 2) do not suffice to attribute to him the idea of apostolic succession; moreover, in Magnesians 6, 1 the bishop represents God. For a similar opinion, cf. M. Jourjon, "La présidence de l'eucharistie chez Ignace d'An-

To summarize the explicit thought of Ignatius of Antioch: the bishop, guarantor of the unity of the Church, presides over the sacrament of its unity. Apart from him the Eucharist is illegitimate, not secure. Is the one he delegates to preside a member of the presbytery? Is he another Christian? We do not know. It is astonishing that the presbytery is not mentioned in this context when we recall how pleased he is to speak of it elsewhere. Is the delegation permanent or for a given celebration? Again let us confess our ignorance. And let us retain the basic perspective that the one who presides over the Church presides over the sacrament of the unity of the Church.

Saint Justin: Those who preside over the Church preside at the Eucharist. Justin wrote his Apology around 150. In it he describes two Eucharists, one baptismal (1 Apol 65), the other a Sunday Eucharist (1 Apol 67), in both of which the role of the president is clearly distinguished from that of the assembly.[22] Thus we read in chapter 65: "Bread and a cup containing water and wine mixed with water are brought to him who presides *(proestôs)* over the brethren. He takes them and offers prayer, glorifying the Father of all things through the name of the Son and the Holy Spirit; and he then utters a lengthy eucharist. . . . When he has finished, all the people present give their assent: Amen."

The same thing is repeated in chapter 67, 5. The presidency in both cases is the act of a single individual to whom a specific role is attributed, clearly distinguished from that of the people. How are we to interpret it?

It would be a mistake to see in this single president the successor of the apostles, alone qualified to offer the Eucharist, because in chapter 66, 3 Justin concludes the institution narrative with the remark: "And he gave them [the bread and the cup] to them [the Twelve] alone." For with this remark Justin means to emphasize that Jesus confided the Eucharist only to Christians, to their assembly; his concern is to disqualify the cult of Mithra, for he adds immediately: "And the evil demons have imitated this and ordered it to be done also in the mysteries of Mithra" (66, 4).

Nor does anything in the text permit us to see a sacerdotal figure

tioche," *Lumière et Vie* 16 (1967) 26–32. For a more technical treatment, cf. G. Dix, *The Shape of the Liturgy* (London 1970, c 1945) 28–33.

[22] Cf. M. Jourjon, "Justin" in *The Eucharist of the Early Christians* (note 10 above) 71–85.

in the one who presides: there is no question of a *hiereus*, even if Justin, in his Dialogue with Trypho (116, 3–117) conceives the Christian people as being corporately "an archpriestly race" in the offering of the eucharistic sacrifice.[23] This represents a development of the literal sense of the affirmations of 1 Peter and Revelations which was very early adopted by the ancient Church as a whole: God's people is priestly not only through its election but in and through its cultic life.[24]

Finally, should we think that Justin, addressing himself to pagans, deliberately chose a neuter word, accessible to them, and that this is why he speaks of the *proestôs*? Quite the contrary, this term is not neuter in Christian language. In Scripture it designates those who preside over the life of the community, expending themselves, without, however, any special reference to the liturgy (cf. especially Rom 12:6–8; 1 Thes 5:12–13; 1 Tm 5:17). Half a century later Tertullian will also employ this vocabulary of presidency. In a word, Justin lets it be clearly understood that those who preside over the entire life of the ecclesial community preside at the Eucharist.

Saint Irenaeus and Saint Anicetus: The bishop presides at the Eucharist. Towards 190 Irenaeus intervened in the controversy concerning the date of Easter which had led to a conflict between the bishops of Asia Minor and the Roman See. Eusebius of Caesarea has recorded for us his letter of mediation in which he appeals to a precedent dating back to the year 154: "[Polycarp and Anicetus having been reconciled] entered into communion with each other, and Anicetus ceded the Eucharist to Polycarp, obviously out of deference, and they parted in peace" (*Eccl. Hist*. V, 24, 17).

Thus it is clear that in Rome around 150 the presidency of the Eucharist is an episcopal office: Anicetus' gesture indicates that the presidency is his by right, and if he cedes it to his guest, it is in

[23] We disagree here with J. de Watteville, *Le sacrifice dans les textes eucharistiques des premiers siècles* (Paris 1966) 72–73. He concludes from the expression "archpriestly race" that the president is specifically a *hiereus*. Such an interpretation is excluded, since for Justin the term applies to all Christians. Cf. A. Quacquarelli, "L'epiteto sacerdote (*hiereus*) ai cristiani in Giustino martire (Dial. 116, 3)," *Vetera Christianorum* 7 (1971) 5–19.

[24] This exegesis of 1 Peter is very primitive. Cf. G. Otranto, "Il sacerdozio commune dei fedeli nei riflessi della I Petr. 2, 9 (I e II secolo)," *Vetera Christianorum* 7 (1970) 225–246, a good article in spite of the anachronistic vocabulary of the title.

order to honor him. Forty years later Irenaeus evidently is of the same opinion.

Hippolytus: The bishop, who presides over the Church by virtue of an ordination conferring an apostolic charism, presides at the Eucharist as high priest. We cannot date with precision the Apostolic Tradition of Hippolytus, bishop (antipope?) of Rome between 217 and 235. However, since the document does not conceal its conservative tendencies, it must provide information concerning usages dating back at least to the youth of its author, that is, around 180.[25] From it we learn that the one to be ordained bishop "has been chosen by all the people" and that to ordain him other bishops "lay hands on him" while the presbytery is to "stand by and be still" (T.A. 2). According to the prayer of ordination, the bishop is, to begin with, one who receives the apostolic charism, and it is his role first of all "to feed the holy flock and to exercise the high priesthood . . . and to offer to you the gifts of your holy Church" (T.A. 3). The ordination is situated within the setting of a Eucharist, and we see the new bishop recite the anaphora over the oblation which is that of the entire Church (T.A. 4). He certainly recites the anaphora alone, for in the period it was still improvised.

Hippolytus witnesses to the continuity which we have constantly noted so far: the one who presides over the Church presides at the Eucharist. However, he is more explicit than all of his precursors with regard to the titles of the president of the Church: elected by all, ordained, he receives an apostolic charism and a pastoral charge which includes the exercise of the high priesthood — an attribute which will appear more and more in subsequent documents. When Hippolytus credits the bishop with the high priesthood, the ministry of the presidency is sacerdotally qualified for the first time. Note, nevertheless, that the bishop serves *as* high priest (T.A. 3, twice; T.A. 34) and not his priest (*hiereus*) and that the presbyters are not sacerdotally qualified, at least not directly; their task is the collegial government of the Church. According to this equilibrium there is scarcely any danger that priesthood become the specific attribute of the president. On the other hand, this danger will be potentially

[25] We shall use the edition of B. Botte, *Hippolyte de Rome, La Tradition apostolique* (Sources Chrétiennes 11 bis, 2nd ed. Paris 1968). For further citations: T. A., followed by the number of the paragraph.

there, as G. Dix has noted, when there is a passage from the distribution: bishop *(archiereus)*/assembly *(hiereus)* to the new distribution: bishop *(archiereus)*/priests *(hiereis)*/assembly.[26]

Thus with Hippolytus we find ourselves confronted with a capital testimony concerning the presidency of the assembly to which it will be indispensable to return for a more detailed consideration.

Tertullian: As president of the Church, the bishop presides at the Eucharist with a sacerdotal ministry; in case of necessity a layman can celebrate with the title of his priesthood. According to Tertullian, "we receive the Eucharist from no one other than our presidents" (*De Corona* 3, 5). Only proven elders receive this office of presidency (*Apol.* 39, 5; *Pud.* 14, 16). Presidents exercise "sacerdotal charges" (*De Praesc.* 41, 8; *De Exhort. Cast.* 11, 1–2). They are high priests (*De Bapt.* 17, 1; *Pud.* 21, 17). On the other hand, the presbyter is never called priest (*sacerdos*).

However, it would be well to adopt the reservation of a specialist of the period, M. Bévenot, who writes: "One cannot be certain that the *sacerdos* is so named because he celebrated the Eucharist, nor that, granted that he did, that that was the primary reason for so naming him. . . . Tertullian never says that it is because of this function that a bishop is named *sacerdos*."[27]

If Bévenot is right, as we think he is, Tertullian does not base the presidency of the Eucharist on a specific, sacerdotal qualification. He is basically in accord with the testimonies studied so far and full weight should be given to the text from *De Corona* cited above emphasizing the bond between the Eucharist and presidents. For as G. Pelloquin has shown in his very careful philological study of the term "preside," presidents, in the vocabulary of Tertullian, are those who, at the head of the community, have the care of its life as a whole.[28] For Tertullian the presidency of the Eucharist is thus based essentially on the presidency of the Christian community and not,

[26] Dix, *The Shape of the Liturgy* 33–35. For the expression of this equilibrium in the ordination liturgies in East and West see the technical study of P.-M. Gy, "La théologie des prières anciennes pour l'ordination des évêques et des prêtres," *Rev. Sc. Phil. Théol.* 58 (1974) 599–617.

[27] M. Bévenot, "Tertullian's Thoughts about the Christian 'Priesthood'" in *Corona Gratiarum (Miscel. E. Dekkers)* vol. 1 (Bruges 1975) 126.

[28] G. Pelloquin, *Le sacerdoce de l'évêque chez Tertullien* (dactylographed thesis, Toulouse 1959) 173–190.

we might add, on a priesthood pertaining exclusively to the ministers.

This seems all the more probable when we consider the following declaration of Tertullian: "Where there is no body of ordained ministers in residence, you celebrate the Eucharist, layman, you baptize, and you are yourself your own priest, for where two or three are gathered, there is the Church, even if these three are laymen" (*De Exhort. Cast*. 7, 3).[29] Such a declaration is not incoherent even if it is clear for Tertullian that there is a difference between bishops and the faithful, *ordo et plebs*, and even if "sacerdotal charges" pertain to the ordo. He is simply asserting that when ordained ministers are lacking, the faithful can exercise their cultic functions: baptize and celebrate the Eucharist. With this assertion he does not contradict himself in the face of the Montanists, whom he reproached for confiding "sacerdotal functions to laymen" (*De Praesc*. 41, 5–8), for they did so without any necessity.[30] Moreover, this text cannot easily be attributed on a presumed Montanist influence on Tertullian, for it has been shown that his conception of the priesthood did not vary during the course of his career.[31]

We should, however, point out the isolated character of this position of Tertullian in the tradition of the Church. When Saint Augustine asked himself the same question in the case of a group of captives without a priest, he replied that they could not have the Eucharist; and the reason was probably not solely the fact that the captives were women.[32] In the ancient Church perhaps the only historically attested case of the Eucharist celebrated by baptized Christians without a priest is that of the first lay evangelizers of Ethiopia, in the beginning of the fourth century.[33]

[29] "Ubi ecclesiastici ordinis non est consessus, et offers et tinguis, et sacerdos es tibi solus: scilicet ubi tres, ecclesia est licet laici."

[30] Cf. C. Vogel, "Le ministre charismatique de l'eucharistie: approche rituelle," in *Ministères et célébration de l'Eucharistie* (note 6 above) 198–204, for a rigorous interpretation of all of the texts of Tertullian relative to this subject.

[31] For a demonstration of this cf. G. Otranto, "Nonne et laici sacerdotes sumus? (Exhort. Cast. 7, 3)," *Vetera Christianorum* 8 (1971) 27–47.

[32] Letter 111, 8 (CSEL 34, 655): "In their captivity . . . they can neither place the offering on the altar of God nor find a priest through whom they might offer to God."

[33] Theodoret, *Hist. Eccles*. I, 23, 5 (GSC I, 73): "Aedesius and Frumentius . . . recommended to the merchants who arrived in this region that they assemble after the manner of the Romans and celebrate the divine mysteries (*epitelein tas theias leitourgias*)."

Cyprian: The bishop, the bond of unity, presides at the Eucharist; in presiding he is sacerdos *and symbolizes Christ; exceptionally presbyters delegated by the bishop preside.* For Cyprian it is the bishop who presides at the Eucharist. But with him we find the first written testimony concerning the celebration of a Eucharist by presbyters without the bishop; in his Letter 5 to the priests and deacons of Carthage he advises them to celebrate in prison for the confessors.

With him we note a marked progression of sacerdotal vocabulary applied to the ordained ministry, for if the presbyters are never sacerdotally qualified independently of the bishop,[34] they are so qualified together with him.[35] This evolution is related to Cyprian's predilection for the sacrificial vocabulary of the Old Testament, applied by him, as was already traditional, to the oblation of the eucharistic sacrifice in the tradition of the *Testimonia*, evoking the caducity of the sacrificial rites of the Old Law and their abrogation by the sacrifice of Christ.[36] He would not be followed in this regard by Augustine, who would remain quite reserved with respect to the sacerdotal designation of the episcopal and presbyteral ministry.[37]

It is likewise with Cyprian that we note, for the first time, that the bishop presides at the Eucharist *vice Christi*,[38] a theme which would have an interesting medieval destiny[39] and a modern fortune under the form of the priest as an "other Christ," so disputable that Vatican II completely ignored it.

But without doubt the principal emphasis of Cyprian is on the fact

[34] Cf. V. Saxer, *Vie liturgique et quotidienne à Carthage vers le milieu du IIIe siècle* (Studi di Antichità cristiana 29, Rome 1969) 85, note 59, *in fine*.

[35] Cf. H. Janssen, *Kultur und Sprache. Zur Geschichte der alten Kirche im Spiegel der Sprachentwicklung von Tertullian bis Cyprian* (Nijmegen 1938) 84–88.

[36] Cf. V. Saxer (note 34 above) 194–202, especially 198–199.

[37] Augustine's reserve as regards vocabulary is accompanied with a marked accent on the oneness of the sacrifice of Christ and with a refusal to consider the Christian priest a mediator (*Contra Ep. Parm.* 2, 8, 15; PL 43, 59–60). This has been studied by D. Zaehringer, *Das kirchliche Priestertum nach dem hl. Augustinus* (Paderborn 1931) 115–118; he relates Augustine's position in this regard to his rejection of Donatist deviations with respect to the priesthood.

[38] Letter 63, 14 (CSEL 3, 713): "For if Jesus Christ our Lord is himself the high priest of God the Father and has first offered himself in sacrifice . . . certainly the priest fulfills the role of Christ (*vice Christi*) when he imitates what Christ did, and he offers a true and perfect sacrifice in the Church to God the Father when he offers it in accordance to what he sees Christ himself to have offered."

[39] B.-D. Marliangeas, "In persona Christi, in persona Ecclesiae," *Spiritus* 70 (1978) 19–33.

that there can be no Eucharist *against* the bishop. He is obsessed with this question, while he does not pose Tertullian's question of a Eucharist *without* the bishop. In his eyes the union between bishop, Church and Eucharist is so close that to separate oneself from the bishop, to oppose him, is to become an enemy of the altar, a rebel in relation to the sacrifice of Christ. To attempt a Eucharist in rivalry with the bishop is a profanation of the divine victim, a sacrilege. Outside of the Church there can be no Eucharist.[40] It would be wrong to characterize this position of Cyprian as pre-Donatist: as a matter of fact, we find it expressed through the entire first millennium, and even beyond, as late as Peter Lombard.[41]

Why does the presidency of the Eucharist, according to Saint Cyprian, pertain to the bishop? First of all, because the Eucharist is "the sacrament of unity" (Ep. 45) and because the bishop is the guarantor of the unity of the Church: "You should know that the bishop is in the Church and the Church is in the bishop and that if someone is not with the bishop, he is not in the Church" (Ep. 66, 8). In his presidency of the Eucharist the bishop is *sacerdos.*

A Canonical Tradition Deriving from Hippolytus: A confessor can take his rank, without ordination, among the presbyters and, by virtue of this fact, preside at the Eucharist. As is known, the Apostolic Tradition of Hippolytus provides that "a confessor, if he was in chains for the name of the Lord, shall not have hands laid on him for the diaconate or the priesthood, for he has the honor of the priesthood by his

[40] The texts are multiple and very explicit; for example, Letter 69, 9, 3; Letter 72, 2, 1: Priests who offer "outside . . . over against the one divine altar" . . . offer "false and sacrilegious sacrifices" ("false" because "offered outside"); *On the Unity of the Catholic Church* 17: "Such a one is to be avoided, whoever he may be, that is separated from the Church. He is an enemy of the altar, a rebel against the sacrifice of Christ. . . . Despising the bishops and deserting God's priests, he presumes to erect another altar, compose another prayer with illicit words, and profane the true offering of our Lord with false sacrifices."

[41] In the East, Cyril of Alexandria, *Resp. ad Tiberium Diac.* C. 11 (PG 76, 1097); Aphraates, *Dem.* 12, *De Paschate*); 9 (Patr. Syr. 1, 525–528). In the West, Jerome, Ep. 15, 2 to Damasus (Hilberg, pp. 63–64); Innocent I, Ep. 24, 3 (PL 20, 549); Leo the Great, Ep. 80, 2 (PL 54, 914); Pelagius I, Ep. 24, 14; 35, 3 (edition Gasso-Battle). The text of Leo the Great declaring that in schism: *nec rata sint sacerdotia, nec vera sacrificia* would be included in the Decretum of Gratian (II, c. 1. q. 1 c. 73 and 78; Friedberg 1, 384). Thus for early scholasticism the consecration of heretics and schismatics is not valid; cf. Peter Lombard, Sent. IV, d. 13.

confession; but if he is appointed bishop, hands shall be laid on him" (T.A. 9). Among the canonical texts which derive from the Apostolic Tradition the most important are to be found in the so-called Canons of Hippolytus and the *Testamentum Domini*. In a Canon of Hippolytus we find the following prescription: "If someone's slave has endured punishment for the sake of Christ, he is presbyter for the flock; although he has not received the form of the priesthood, he has nevertheless received its Spirit. The bishop shall therefore omit the part of the prayer concerning the Holy Spirit."[42]

The implications of this text seem clear, for [1] in antiquity a slave was never ordained; [2] it is not a matter of bestowing on him an honorary position in the assembly, for it is expressly stated that he is "presbyter for the flock"; [3] he could thus be led to preside at the Eucharist without having received the imposition of hands (parallel canons), for in certain regions (Africa, Asia, Rome) a presbyter could be led to preside at the Eucharist apart from the bishop. Although we have little proof of the effective force of these canonical dispositions, their spirit is not at all surprising, for confessors and martyrs are, very precisely, the successors of the prophets and teachers,[43] whom we have already seen preside at the Eucharist (Acts 13:1–2; Didache). Note, finally, that this Christian is not an ordinary Christian: his presbyteral ministry is accepted as such, even if he has not acceded to it through ordination.

This last testimony strengthens the hypothesis according to which one presided at the Eucharist in the pre-Nicene Church because one presided over the Church. For in this precise case the power to preside at the Eucharist must be ascribed to the pastoral charge one has assumed by virtue of a charism received without ecclesial mediation and not by virtue of an "uninterrupted chain" of impositions of hands.

If we summarize the testimonies of the pre-Nicene Church, a general perspective emerges. The bond between the apostles and presidents of the Eucharist is to be found only with Clement and secondarily with Hippolytus. The perception of the president of the Eucharist as an explicitly sacerdotal figure is not attested before the

[42] C. Vogel (note 30 above) reproduces these texts and comments on them, 191–198.

[43] For the correspondence between these figures, see M. Lods, *Confesseurs et Martyrs, successeurs des prophètes dans l'Eglise des trois premiers siècles* (Cahiers théologiques 41, Paris: Neuchâtel 1958).

beginning of the third century (Hippolytus, Tertullian and Cyprian).[44] On the other hand, with all of the witnesses we note that it is a fact, and most often it is axiomatic (Clement, Ignatius, Justin, Tertullian, Hippolytus, Cyprian and the canonical tradition deriving from Hippolytus), that those who preside over the life of the Church preside at the Eucharist. The formula of the Central Theological Commission does not, to be sure, reveal all the complexity of the figure of the Christian *leitourgos*, but it does, for the period indicated, represent a fundamental axis of intelligibility. Yes, "priests presided at the Eucharist because they presided over the Christian community."

2. THE PRESIDENCY OF THE EUCHARISTIC ASSEMBLY: A LITURGICAL DIMENSION OF THE PASTORAL CHARGE.

A note concerning methodology. For any attempt to clarify the relationship between ministry and the Eucharist, the testimony of Scripture is, as we have seen, very insufficient. Confronted with this difficulty, theologians seek their data in the positive statements of the conciliar (or extraconciliar) magisterium relative to the presidency of the Eucharist. The relevant councils, for the past, are essentially Lateran IV,[45] Florence and Trent. But these statements, marked by particular circumstances, manifestly do not provide a sufficient basis to discern the whole ecclesial tradition in regard to the relationship between the ordained ministry and the Eucharist. Thus, for example, Pius XII did not hesitate to determine the matter and form of the sacrament of orders otherwise than Florence.[46] Trent, more prudent, wished only to defend the tradition in particular points, so much so that the fundamental theological datum concerning our problem is not to be found in the particular statements of this council, but in the tradition which it is concerned with protecting. Thus for our question it would be good methodology to attempt to inte-

[44] For a comprehensive study of the sacerdotalization of ministerial vocabulary, see P.-M. Gy, "Remarques sur le vocabulaire antique du sacerdoce chrétien, in *Etudes sur le sacrement de l'ordre* (Lex Orandi 22; Paris 1957) especially 133–145. English translation in *The Sacrament of Holy Orders* (London 1962) 98–115.

[45] Lateran IV was the first council to declare the belief of the Latin Church on this point; it did so in a conceptuality which would remain dominant until our day: "Et hoc utique sacramentum nemo potest conficere, nisi sacerdos qui rite fuerit ordinatus, secundum claves ecclesiae (c. 1)."

[46] Pius XII: *Sacramentum Ordinis*, AAS 40, 1948 (Denz.-Schönm. 3857–3861).

grate the successive magisterial interventions in a systematic construction which would synthesize them, but the point of departure must be a comprehensive historical vision of the tradition itself. For prior to any statement of the councils (or of the papacy) there exists a perennial, global tradition, the primary expression of which is not of the order of *definition*, but of a liturgical, institutional, and secondarily, homiletic order.[47]

The decisive testimony of the Apostolic Tradition of Hippolytus. If the preceding remarks concerning methodology are well founded, the Apostolic Tradition of Hippolytus acquires a decisive importance. On the one hand, the prayer for the ordination of a bishop which we have from Hippolytus has been literally reproduced in the new Roman Pontifical, with the result that the theology of the episcopate expressed in it has become the ecclesial teaching of today. On the other hand, the Eucharist in which the ordination is inserted is the most ancient source of known eucharistic liturgies, even if contemporary liturgists would no longer accept the affirmation of Lietzmann: "What we have there, apart from some changes in the christological preface, could have been pronounced in the time of the Apostle Paul at Corinth or Ephesus."[48] Since this is the case, we can surely consider this testimony particularly important for an understanding of the tradition as a whole. We shall therefore analyze the prayer of ordination (T.A. 3) and the structure of the Eucharist (T.A. 4) which follows.

The charism implored in favor of the bishop is that of *pneuma hēgemonikon*, of *spiritus principalis*, an expression which signifies both the gift which the Apostles received to guide and rule the Church and the prophetic spirit which they received at Pentecost.[49] The originality of the episcopal ministry is thus described first and

[47] In this regard let us refer to the stimulating remarks concerning methodology of H.-J. Schulz, "Die Grundstruktur des kirchlichen Amtes im Spiegel der Eucharistiefeier und der Ordinationsliturgie des römischen und des byzantinischen Ritus," *Catholica* 29 (1975) 325–340. Another work of this same author likewise merits attention: "Das Liturgisch-sakramental übertragene Hirtenamt in seiner eucharistischen Selbstverwicklichung nach dem Zeugnis der liturgischen Ueberlieferung," in *Amt und Eucharistie* (Paderborn 1973) 208–255.

[48] H. Lietzmann, *Messe und Herrenmahl* (3rd ed. Berlin 1955) 181.

[49] This could settle the debate between J. Lécuyer, "Episcopat et presbytérat dans les écrits d'Hippolyte de Rome," *Rech. Sc. Rel.* 41 (1953) especially 30–31, and B. Botte, "Spiritus principalis," *Notitiae* no. 100 (1974) 410–411.

foremost as the participation in the power of the Spirit who rules and as the task of "feeding the holy flock." Then follows an enumeration of the specific attributions of the ministry: the offering of the gifts of the Church, the remission of sins and the distribution of functions. This enumeration of tasks appears not so much as the collation of powers as the indication of the roles pertaining to the pastoral ministry. In the Eucharist there is question of building up the Church: here we see the episcopal function assume the roles that pertained to the apostles, prophets and teachers in Ephesians as well as in the Didache.

When we examine the structure of the Eucharist which immediately follows the ordination, we note that the acts of the bishop do not appear as manifestations of a special and isolated power of offering and consecrating but as the liturgical dimension of his presidency over the body of Christ in the act of worship; the bishop is the high priest of a sacerdotal assembly.

As a matter of fact, it is the ecclesia which offers (the gifts are hers) and gives thanks. She is the subject of the *offerimus panem et calicem* in the anamnesis. When the bishop imposes his hands on the offerings and recites the anaphora, anyone familiar with the Jewish liturgy will clearly identify him as president of the assembly, as high priest of a sacerdotal assembly. The Eucharist cannot be understood as his sacrifice, his personal contribution: his role cannot be understood on the basis of late ritual additions such as *accipe potestatem offerre sacrificium, sacerdos oportet offerre* anymore than the anaphora can be considered the *formula consecrationis*.[50] In the anaphora, it is as pastor and prophet that he proclaims the history of salvation, announcing in the mode of praise the presence of this salvation and evoking in response the offering of all who become the body of Christ by their communion in the offerings transformed by the Spirit. Thus is the Church built up.

Thus presidency of the eucharistic assembly is seen as the liturgical, prophetic and mysteric dimension of the pastoral charge of building up the Church which is conferred in ordination.

The ancient prayers of ordination witness to the primary character of the pastoral charge. Since we cannot enter here into the details of a dos-

[50] Such an interpretation is excluded, for example, in the anaphora of St. John Chrysostom, which puts the institution narrative in the past tense.

sier, the pieces of which are very complex,[51] let us appeal to the eminent liturgist B. Botte for a characterization of the figure of Christian ministers according to the testimony of the prayers of ordination: "The bishop and the priest have nothing in common with the Roman *sacerdos* . . . nor do they have much in common with the priest of the Old Testament. . . . In spite of the typology, the Christian priesthood is of another order: it is charismatic and spiritual. That it is endowed with juridical and liturgical prerogatives is evident. . . . But to see only this aspect is to risk impoverishing the notion of Christian priesthood. The episcopate, the priesthood and the diaconate appear less as ritual functions in the ancient documents than as charisms aimed at *the upbuilding of the Church*."[52]

Two canonical indications of the priority of presidency over the upbuilding of the Church in relation to the presidency of the Eucharist. The first is the nullity of absolute ordinations. The terms of canon 6 of the Council of Chalcedon are well known: "No one should be ordained in an absolute manner, neither a priest nor a deacon . . . unless an urban church, a rural church, a martyrion or a monastery has been specifically assigned to him. As for those who have been ordained in an absolute manner, this synod has decided that such an ordination is null and void, and they cannot exercise their ministry anywhere." Noting that this canon has remained in vigor in the East until our day (at least in written law, we would say), C. Vogel has well shown that it was also unanimously received in the Western Church until the late twelfth, early thirteenth century.[53] It is only from that time on that theology, abstracting ordination from its ecclesial context, has considered it efficacious in itself *ex opere operato*, provided the matter and form are respected. This development contributed to a modification of the practice of the Latin Church.

As the same author remarks: "From the thirteenth century on a bishop and a priest, even when they are ordained without a 'title,' nevertheless acquire the episcopal or presbyteral character." And he

[51] This has been very well established by P.-M. Gy, "La theologie des prieres anciennes pour l'ordination des évêques et des prêtres," *Rev Sc. Phil. Théol.* 58 (1974) 599–617, here p. 608.

[52] B. Botte, "L'ordre d'après les prières d'ordination," in *Etudes sur le sacrement de l'ordre* 33–34 (emphasis added); *The Sacrament of Holy Orders* (note 44 above) 22.

[53] C. Vogel, "Vacua manus impositio. L'inconsistance de la chirotonie absolue en Occident," in *Mélanges Liturgiques offerts au Dom Botte* (Louvain 1972) 511–524.

adds: "And they keep it even after abandoning the ministry or after their deposition, even if they have become apostates, heretics, schismatics or unworthy."[54] Note, for our purposes, that during the first dozen centuries those who were ordained absolutely could not exercise their functions anywhere, in accordance with the terms of the Council of Chalcedon. Such a disposition is clear: if one does not preside over the Church, one cannot preside over the sacraments of the Church, and of course one cannot preside at the Eucharist.

The second indication is that deposition formerly entailed a real return to the lay state. In contemporary Catholic theology a priest can validly preside at a celebration of the Eucharist even if he has been returned to the lay state, provided he has the intention of doing what the Church does. But in the tradition anterior to the thirteenth century this was not so. Until that time, as C. Vogel has shown in a convincing fashion,[55] deposition returned a priest to the rank of layman in the full sense of that term, that is to say, to the situation that was his before his ordination. Here we have yet another indication that we must begin with the charge, with presidency over the Church in understanding the presidency of the Eucharist.

Let us summarize: for the ancient tradition, whether we refer to the liturgical texts having the most authority or to canonical texts, the presidency of the eucharistic assembly appears as the liturgical dimension of the pastoral charge. It remains to be seen how the roles of the ordained ministers and the faithful are articulated within the assembly before we can conclude on the meaning of the presidency of bishops and priests.

3. THE ASSEMBLY AS A WHOLE CELEBRATES THE EUCHARIST

The schema in accordance with which priests celebrate the mass and the faithful attend, which infiltrated even into the language of the encyclicals,[56] is a modern schema, without foundation in tradition.

[54] *Ibid.* 511.

[55] C. Vogel, "Laica Communione contentus. Le retour du presbytre au rang des laïcs," *Rev. Sc. Rel.* 47 (1973) 56–122.

[56] Thus we read in *Mediator Dei*, the important encyclical of Pius XII on liturgical renewal: ". . . as often as a priest repeats what the divine Redeemer did at the Last Supper, the sacrifice is really completed. . . . This is undoubtedly true whether the faithful are present . . . or are not present, since it is in no wise required that the people ratify what the sacred minister does" (AAS 38 [1947] 557).

For the Fathers the perspective was quite different, as Congar has demonstrated in a study of an abundant richness, the title of which well expresses the equilibrium of the ancient tradition: "The Ecclesia or Christian Community, Integral Subject of the Liturgical Action."[57] Even the formula of the Constitution on the Liturgy of Vatican II concerning the need for "the active participation of the faithful" is ambiguous.[58] Are the faithful called to participate with faith and devotion in an action of which the minister alone is the subject? Or are all, whatever their place or their ministry (and there are several ministries in an assembly apart from the priest) called to constitute, whatever the diversity of their functions, a single celebrating assembly? An analysis of the liturgical vocabulary of the first millennium shows that all celebrate and that all offer the sacrifice. Liturgical commentaries and homilies allow us to determine that these are actions accomplished as a body.

Philology can be a precious aid for rediscovering the ancient liturgical equilibriums. A systematic study of the verb "celebrate" in the Roman liturgy has shown that it always had as its subject the "we" of Christians and never the "I" of the priest. Not a single prayer of the sacramentaries of the Latin liturgy has the priest as subject; the priest is found as subject only in the rubrics of the Gelasian sacramentary, and even there it is clear that the priest celebrates *with* the community.[59] Naturally, this is also true of the Eastern liturgies. The East Syrian liturgical practice provides a striking example of this perception that all celebrate as a body: during the course of the Eucharist the bishop never goes up to the altar, and he does not recite the anaphora, this ministry falling to the lot of a simple priest.[60]

The assembly as a whole offers the sacrifice. The question of the subject of the offering of the sacrifice has been systematically studied in

[57] In *La Liturgie après Vatican II* (Unam Sanctam 66; Paris 1967) 241–282. The rich bibliography facilitates further analysis.

[58] Constitution on the Liturgy 19. However, article 14 provides a more balanced formulation: "full, conscious and active participation."

[59] Cf. B. Droste, *"Celebrare" in der römischen Liturgiesprache* (Munich 1963) especially 73–80. For examples from the Gelasian, 80.

[60] Cf. A. Raes, "La concélébration eucharistique dans les rites orientaux," *La Maison-Dieu* no. 35 (1953) 25–27. If one applied our modern categories to the ancient practice of the East Syrians, one would have to say that from the day of his ordination the bishop never celebrated mass!

the theological commentaries of the early Middle Ages by R. Schultze,[61] as well as in the texts of the Roman liturgy by R. Berger.[62] Schultze concludes his monograph in this way: "From Isidore (d. 636) to Remy of Auxerre (d. 908), in the domain of the Visigothic liturgy as well as in that of the Roman liturgy, there is full accord to see in the offering of the eucharistic sacrifice an act of the Church. . . . This point is above all controversy: no one felt any special need to insist on it or to defend it."

As for Berger, he shows that *offerre pro* is not to be translated in general as if the priest offered in place of the people. The expression has a triple sense: it signifies first of all the indication of the feast, then the object of the intercession proposed to all and only as a third sense to offer in the name of those absent. The addition in the tenth century of the formula *pro quibus tibi offerimus vel* (*qui tibi offerunt*) to complete the initial formula *qui tibi offerunt* signifies that the priest renders present absent donors at a time when the practice of mass stipends was being introduced.[63] One should therefore refrain from interpreting *pro quibus* in a strong sense (for example, "in place of lay people, who would be incompetent"). After all, the ancient formula, "who offer," was nowhere suppressed. Moreover, the addition must not have had much theological weight, since the Cistercians adopted it only in the seventeenth century.[64] However, according to Berger, this addition was subsequently employed to emphasize the "consecratory power of priests" and to distinguish it from the offering of the sacrifice by the faithful.[65]

Even in his own action as head of the assembly the president of the Eucharist also acts as a member of the assembly. Here, as summarized by Schultze, is how the first millennium sees the unity of the celebrating

[61] R. Schultze, *Die Messe als Opfer der Kirche. Die Lehre frühmittelaltlicher Autoren über das eucharistische Opfer* (LQF 35; Münster 1959). Schultze is acquainted with the work of A. Kolping, "Das aktive Anteil der Gläubigen an der Darbringung des eucharistischen Opfers," *Divus Thomas* 27 (1949) 369–380; 29 (1950) 79–110, 147–170.

[62] R. Berger, *Die Wendung "offerre pro" in der römischen Liturgie* (LQF 41; Münster 1965).

[63] Cf. J. Jungmann, *The Mass of the Roman Rite: Missarum Sollemnia* (New York 1955) 2, 167.

[64] *Ibid.* note 44.

[65] Berger (note 62 above) 246. Note that Vatican II would refuse to say that priests join the sacrifices of the faithful to that of Christ. That is done by the faithful themselves. Cf. *Presbyterorum Ordinis, Expensio modorum*, pp. 22–23.

assembly: "The qualification and the capacity to offer the sacrifice pertains to each member, priest or lay person, *because* he is a member of the body. The perspective of our authors is thus not that the Church offers the sacrifice because such and such an individual [physical person] offers the eucharistic sacrifice. Their perspective is inverse: because Christ offers, the Church also offers, she who is the body of Christ, the spouse of Christ. And because the body offers, each individual member offers."[66]

For lack of space we cannot multiply citations here.[67] As a witness from the East, here is Saint John Chrysostom: "The eucharistic prayer is common; the priest does not give thanks alone, but the people with him, for he begins it only after having received the accord of the faithful. . . . If I say that, it is so that we learn that we are all a single body. Therefore let us not rely on the priests for everything, but let us, too, care for the Church."[68] In the West, until the end of the twelfth century, the ancient equilibrium can still be heard, preached, for example, by Guerric d'Igny: "The priest does not consecrate alone, does not sacrifice alone, but the entire assembly of the faithful consecrate and sacrifice with him."[69]

Obviously every celebration is grounded in the communion of the Holy Spirit and in dependence on his power (epiclesis).[70] This point alone would merit a study.

4. CONCLUSION: THE LEGACY OF THE ANCIENT TRADITION

It pertains to those who preside over the upbuilding of the Church to preside over the sacraments which for their part build up the Church. If we refer to the current opinion of Christians, the perception in accordance with which priests preside at the Eucharist because they preside over the Church appears very obscured. According to the most

[66] Schultze (note 61 above) 188.

[67] One might read: Basil of Caesarea, *Reg. brev. tract. Interr.* 265 (*PG* 31, 1261); Theodoret of Cyr, *Interpret. Ep. 1 ad Tim. 2, 8* (PG82, 800); John Chrysostom, *In 2 Thess. hom.* 4, 4 (PG 62, 491–492).

[68] *In 2 Cor. hom.* 18, 3 (PG 61, 527).

[69] Serm. 5 (PL 185, 57).

[70] Note, for example, John Chrysostom, *De sancta Pentec. hom.* 1, 4 (*PG* 50, 458–459): "The priest never touches the offerings until he has invoked the grace of God on you and until you have responded: 'and with your spirit.' With this response you remind yourselves that it is not the one who is present who effects anything . . . but that it is the grace of the Spirit, coming upon the offerings, which accomplishes the mystical sacrifice."

widely held opinion the faithful attend, or actively participate in, a mass celebrated by a priest by virtue of a priesthood which affords him a special participation in the priesthood of Christ. This priesthood is a personally possessed power. It cannot be lost, even when the Church prohibits its exercise, for it is based on an indelible character.

How did such an evolution occur? It did not happen abruptly.[71] For Congar it is to be explained by a passage from an ecclesiology of communion to an ecclesiology of powers[72] which was effected in the beginning of the thirteenth century. "While for the ancients," Congar writes in the study cited above, "it is existence in the body of the Church which makes it possible to perform the sacraments, after the twelfth century there emerged a theology of self-contained powers: if one personally possesses them, one can posit the sacraments."[73] To confront this theological development with the liturgical tradition as a whole in its equilibrium is surely a task to be accomplished by a study of the complete dossier on the question.

For our part, we have retained but one thread of the dossier of the ancient tradition we have tentatively examined: there are many others. It is for the reader to see if his understanding of the Eucharist and the ordained ministry is enriched by this thread of the tradition; to see if the closeness of the bonds between the Eucharist and ministry, thus emphasized, does not make more clear how the Eucharist is, among other things, very concretely the Eucharist of both the assembly and the Church as a whole, the meal of Christians and the meal of Christ, who is the principal host, the locus of the manifestation of the Spirit in the body of Christ.

Can the preceding rapid evocation of the ancient tradition be an aid in current debates on the presidency of the Eucharist? It is our profound conviction that the role of tradition is adequate in itself, without serving as a legitimator for our practices. There is certainly

[71] Already before the twelfth century there was more than one axis of understanding the presidency of the Eucharist. The sacerdotal axis is ancient: as early as the Carolingian period specific actions such as *conficere, consecrare* and *immolare* began to be attributed to priests. Consult Schultze's *indices*, even if the point of view is that of Florus of Lyons (c. 840), adopted word for word by Innocent III in the beginning of the thirteenth century: "That which is accomplished by the ministry of the priests is also done in common by the prayer (*votum*) of the faithful" (*De sacr. alt. myst.* III, 6: PL 217, 845).

[72] Ch. Duquoc, Ministère et pouvoir," *Spiritus* 70 (1978) 8–18.

[73] *Op. cit.* (note 57 above) 261–267.

one thing it would not legitimate: a Eucharist celebrated in the refusal of communion with the Church and her ministers! Note also that it never conceives that the "common priesthood of the faithful" can be the legitimate basis of an *ordinary* ministry (not even Tertullian). To be sure, in the pre-Nicene period we find cases of presidency more diversified than ours (they cannot be reduced without exception to presidency based on presbyteral-episcopal ordination); but the rule is constant that it pertains to those who preside over the upbuilding of the Church to preside over the sacrament of her unity, over the sacrament which causes her to exist more profoundly in act. It is not possible to say more. It is only by beginning with the theological interlocking of the meaning of the Eucharist and the meaning of ordained ministry taken together that the understanding of the presidency can be deepened. That is why we have endeavored in this contribution to enlarge our memory as regards this meaning and this coherence.

Interrogations of our modern practices. Nevertheless, beyond this general conclusion, and although they have not been the object of explicit analysis in the preceding pages, it seems that there are three particular points which merit the attention of us modern Christians relative to the presidency of the Eucharist, for they represent ways in which we separate ourselves from the best founded and best assured tradition.

1. In that period the bond between church (Christian existence) and Eucharist is so strong that the local community is not conceived without the Sunday Eucharist. The bond between the Eucharist and Christian life is sometimes perceived in such vital fashion that Christians prefer to die rather than renounce it, as the martyrs of Abitena declared to the Roman procurator.[74] How is it that we modern Christians accommodate ourselves to pastoral structures which, in some churches, render possible only a few masses a year?

2. If the Eucharist has become so rare in some churches in our day, it is because of the lack of someone to preside. This was not the case in the ancient Church, for, following in this the custom of the Jews, Christians of the pre-Nicene period probably gave an ordained president to a Church as soon as she had assembled a dozen heads

[74] They reply: "sine dominico esse non possumus." Cf. T. Ruinart, *Acta primorum martyrum sincera* (Paris 1689) 414.

of family.[75] In any case, the essential is this: a local church always provides herself for her presidency, with the indispensable assistance of the heads of neighboring churches.[76]

Would this not mean for today that once Christians are competent to preside over the upbuilding of their local church they are likewise competent to receive the ordination which entitles them to preside at the Eucharist? On the other hand, the medieval practice of ordaining priests only for the celebration of mass has no claim to inspire us, for it breaks the real bond between Church and Eucharist, between pastoral charge, prophecy (word) and sacrament.

3. While today there is a lack of presidents of the Church, and consequently of presidents of the Eucharist, because there is a lack of "vocations" (that is to say, candidates), that was not the case in the ancient Church, where, however, no one sought the priesthood. On the contrary, according to a literary commonplace which often corresponded to the institutional reality, one was ordained "unwilling and constrained."[77] A vocation is, objectively, the appeal which the community addresses to one or several of its members which it considers suited to the ministry, even if they have never wanted it. It is true that to accept it did not then entail celibacy. Is our modern conception of vocation truly balanced theologically? Is it not too subjective, too individual, too little ecclesial?

Fundamentally, even in these three somewhat marginal interrogations of our modern practices by tradition, we are confronted with our essential question: do we take the relationship between the Eucharist and the Church seriously enough? Once again we find revealed the implications of the quotation which introduced our article: "because they preside over the Church, they preside at the Eucharist." What consequences ought we to draw from this?

[75] Thus St. Gregory Thaumaturgos was ordained bishop of Neocaesarea, where only seventeen Christians lived. Cf. Gregory of Nyssa, *De Vita S. Gregorii Thaumaturgii* (PG 46, 909). Even if after Sardica such small communities no longer receive bishops, they did have priests.

[76] See 421–422 above, and H.-M. Legrand, "Theology and the Election of Bishops in the Early Church," *Concilium* (September 1972) 31–42.

[77] Cf. Y. Congar, "Ordinations 'invitus, coactus' de l'Eglise antique au canon 214," *Rev. Sc. Phil. Théol.* 50 (1966) 169–197.

Jean Leclercq

Eucharistic Celebrations Without Priests In the Middle Ages

The problem to which the title of this article refers is a real one: it is already a fact for some communities of nuns, and it is not impossible that in the future it will be the case of a greater number of communities. In 1978 the Conference of American Benedictine Prioresses declared: "Particularly where ordained ministers are lacking, daily Eucharist may not always be possible."[1] Nor is the solution suggested by the title a matter of imagination: it had precedents in the Middle Ages which are often forgotten. While there is no question of returning to the practices of the past, these can provide ideas about what could be done today and tomorrow, differently to be sure, but in continuity with the same tradition.

It is well known that St. Basil allowed communion without a priest for lay people in case of necessity and for monks as normal practice. He wrote to a patrician lady named Caesaria about the practice of "communicating daily, thus partaking of the holy Body and Blood of Christ." He added: "As to the question of a person being compelled to receive communion by his own hand in times of persecution, when there is no priest or minister present, it is superfluous to show that the act is in no way offensive, since long-continued custom has confirmed this practice because of the circumstances themselves. In fact, all the monks in the desert, where there is no priest, keep communion in their house and receive it from their own hands. In Alexandria and in Egypt, everyone, even among the lay people, almost always keeps communion at home and communicates himself when he wishes."[2]

However, St. Basil was not content with approving the practice.

[1] *Of Time Made Holy.* A Statement on the Liturgy of the Hours in the Lives of American Benedictine Sisters (Conference of American Benedictine Prioresses, Madison, Wisconsin, 5 March 1978) 1; Erie, Penn.: Benet Arts 1978.

[2] St. Basil, *Letter 93.* Cf. œA¼The Fathers of the Church, vol. 13, trans. Agnes Clare Way (New York 1951) 208–209.

He also very firmly indicated a theological interpretation of the practice by insisting on the bond between communion and the celebration of the Eucharist by a priest: "When the priest has once completed the sacrifice and given communion, he who has once received it as a whole, when he partakes of it daily, ought reasonably to believe that he is partaking and receiving from him who has given it. Even in the church the priest gives the particle, and the recipient holds it in his power and so brings it into his mouth with his own hand. Accordingly, it is virtually the same whether he receives one particle from the priest or many particles at one time."[3]

Later, in the East, Theodore the Studite was to allow this practice only in case of necessity. But according to him, even then one should communicate himself only after "the recitation of hymns."[4] Communion was still part of a complete celebration.

In the West, already in the time of St. Gregory the Great, according to the interpretation that Martène was to give to some of his letters, there were monasteries and parishes without a priest.[5] And this must have been the case still later. Thus it is understandable that early medieval manuscripts not only attest the practice of communion without a priest but conserve the texts of the more or less developed celebration which accompanied it.

Here we will consider two examples of such celebrations. Before indicating their doctrinal content we need to present these texts and emphasize their distinctive character compared with other manifestations of the piety of Christians, and in these two cases, of monks and nuns. For these manuscripts are monastic books.

The first of these rituals is conserved in a group of manuscripts the most important of which was copied at Monte Cassino in the time, and very probably for the use, of Abbot Odesius, who from 1097 to 1105 governed this abbey the role of which was so important in the preparation of the Gregorian Reform.[6] Other manuscripts which depend on this one will be indicated later, as well as another

[3] *Ibid.*

[4] *Letter 219*, PG 99, 1661.

[5] E. Martène, *Regula commentata, PL* 66, 867. Concerning the more or less great frequency in monasteries of the Middle Ages, see J. Dubois, "Office des heures et messe dans la tradition monastique," *La Maison-Dieu* no. 135 (1978) 61–82.

[6] Paris Mazarine ms. 364, 26–34. Text edited by A. Wilmart, "Prières pour la communion dans deux Psautiers du Mont Cassin," *Ephemerides liturgicae* 43 (1929) 320–323.

manuscript which is witness to another text of the same genre. In treating of these texts, historians of the liturgy have spoken of "private devotion,"[7] thus distinguishing them clearly from properly liturgical documents. To express oneself thus is to assume that there exists, in a given period, a clear distinction, admitted by everyone, between what is "liturgical" and what is not. But are not these historians, who have themselves established this distinction, or received it from a recent tradition, projecting it on ancient periods during which it did not exist?

If one examines the manuscript of Monte Cassino, one notes that it is, in major part, a psalter — the basic book for the divine office. It was very carefully copied and adorned with artistic decoration, as was done especially in the case of volumes employed in the solemn liturgy. Furthermore, it also includes a calendar — a liturgical text if any is — an ordo for the anointing of the sick, prayers for the dying, an office of the dead and, finally, prayers for the adoration of the cross. Thus the context is constituted by texts which are liturgical in the sense that they are destined to serve in the offices and sacramental rites of the Church.

The rite for communion is presented, in its title, as an *ordo*, a term employed to designate liturgical services. It is therefore not a matter of texts left to the initiative of individuals; on the contrary, these texts have been put in "order" with a view to the needs of an entire community and even, as we shall see, of several communities, and they consequently have a public, not a private character.

As a matter of fact, this ordo for communion, as well as the other texts of the same manuscript, is structured as a liturgical service: it includes an introduction with opening invocations, then the *Pater*, psalms, and prayers preparing for, accompanying and following the rite of communion.

This ordo enjoyed a certain diffusion, as other manuscripts attest. One is of special interest because it was copied in the eleventh or twelfth century at the Abbey of Saint Sophia of Benevento, founded in 780 as a monastery of nuns, which it remained until the fourteenth century when the nuns were replaced by monks; it is reported that towards the end of the eighth century the monastery

[7] Wilmart, *art. cit.* 320 and *Auteurs spirituels et textes dévôts du moyen âge latin* (Paris 1932) 140, note 1; J. Jungmann, *The Mass of the Roman Rite* 2 (New York: Benziger 1955) 369.

counted as many as two hundred nuns.[8] From what we know of the relations of Monte Cassino with Saint Sophia, we may assume that the text of the first of these monasteries passed to the second. Two other witnesses to the same text are provided by a second psalter of Monte Cassino,[9] dating from the same period and carrying the title of "Psalter of the Dean John"[10] and by a manuscript, likewise of the same period, which comes from the Benedictine Abbey of Nonantola in Italy.[11] Thus we have four books with this in common: they are all monastic and situated within the sphere of influence of Monte Cassino, symbol par excellence of what one can call "Benedictine" in the Middle Ages. One did not incur the expense of copying manuscripts which would not be used; thus we have every reason to suppose that they were used, and in more than one place.

A second example of an ordo for communion without a priest is provided by a manuscript of the tenth or eleventh century, now conserved in the library of Auxerre, in France.[12] It is noteworthy that in this manuscript the formulas are in the feminine: in this case not only the provenance of the manuscript, as in the case of the manuscript of Saint Sophia, but the text itself leads us to assume that it was used by nuns. It is time to examine the content of these texts.

Let us begin with the ordo of Monte Cassino, which is the most developed. First we have three psalms: Psalm 51 (*Miserere*) and Psalms 16 and 39; according to the rubrics these are to be "chanted," not merely recited — another confirmation of the character of solemnity, and normally of conventuality, which we have already noted. Then follow the litany (*Kyrie, Christe, Kyrie eleison*), the *Pater*

[8] Concerning this manuscript (Vat. Lat. 4928, pp. 89–100) and St. Sophia of Benevento, see Wilmart, *Auteurs spirituels* 140–145; P. Salmon, *Les manuscrits liturgiques latins de la Bibliothèque Vaticane* I (Studi e testi 251, Vatican City 1968) 85–86, ms. 160.

[9] Ms. Urbin. lat. 585, ed. Wilmart, "Prières pour la communion," 321; P. Salmon, *op. cit.* 82.

[10] Wilmart, "Prières pour la communion," 325–327 has edited the ritual which concerns us.

[11] Ms. Sessorianus 71, Rome, National Library. Salmon is preparing a study concerning the relationship between the four manuscripts we have cited and the Beneventan liturgy. I am indebted to him for some precious information, for which I thank him. Wilmart had already made much use of this manuscript; references in *Auteurs spirituels*, Tables p. 598.

[12] Ms. Auxerre 25, ed. J. Leclercq, "Prières médiévales pour recevoir l'Eucharistie, pour saluer et pour bénir la Croix," *Ephemerides liturgicae* 79 (1965) 327–332.

and the *Credo*; these are under the same rubric and therefore are likewise chanted. The following rubric announces a "confession," and is in fact followed by one of the formulas of general confession that were in use throughout the Middle Ages.[13] It is followed by a "prayer" to obtain the pardon of sins: a sort of absolution in deprecatory form. A series of ten verses from the psalms provides a transition from supplication for pardon to thanksgiving for having received it. Note that this ensemble corresponds more or less to the series of texts which serve as an introduction to the Mass: entrance psalm, litany, penitential rite, collect and profession of faith.

Then begins a series of "prayers," the first of which are addressed to the Father. "Participation in communion and in the chalice of Jesus Christ" is given as the means of having a share in the resurrection and the Holy Spirit. Let it make of each of us an abundant sacrifice, acceptable to God (*pingue et acceptabile*)! What God announced and prefigured in the Old Covenant, he has now realized; through Jesus, the eternal pontiff, one renders him thanks for this. May the Father grant to each person who communicates the grace to accomplish his will. After this the Son is addressed, he who loved to pardon: "May the fact of receiving his Body and Blood be the cause, not of condemnation, but of healing and eternal salvation." Here we recognize expressions which formed part of one of the prayers accompanying communion in the rite of the Mass prior to the ordo of Paul VI. Finally, "another prayer" is addressed to the Holy Spirit: he is praised for his intervention in the mystery of the incarnation of the Word in Mary, in that of the transformation of bread and wine into the Body and Blood of Christ, and in that of the remission of sins. May he communicate love to each one, may he make of each one the body of Christ. Here we have ideas which formed part of the traditional epicleses and which found a place in the Roman rite.[14] Let us admire the theological correctness of all of these formulas and their Trinitarian character. A perfect equilibrium is maintained between the Christian attitudes and the operations attributed to each of the Three Persons.

Two rubrics now indicate that the moment has come to receive, or more exactly to "take" (*sumere*), communion. "Before taking, say

[13] Concerning these formulas of confession, see J. Leclercq, "Fragmenta Reginensia II. Formules de confession et d'absolution," *Ephemerides liturgicae* 61 (1947) 290–295.

[14] Concerning the significance of the epiclesis see L. Bouyer, *The Eucharist* (University of Notre Dame Press 1968) 263–267.

three times: 'Lord, I am not worthy.'" "After having taken, say three times: 'The Word became flesh and dwelt among us. To you be praise, to you be glory, to you be thanksgiving forever and ever, O Blessed Trinity.'"

Next we have the concluding part of the ritual. It includes several prayers "after communion." Thanks is given for having received communion, and there is petition for the remission of faults, the strength of the faith, perseverance in the will to serve God, and admission to the heavenly banquet, all of this through the Lord Jesus, "who, through the Holy Spirit, offered himself on the altar of the cross as a victim (*hostia*) for our salvation and redeemed us with his precious and holy blood." Then, just as in the part of the ritual which precedes communion, Christ is addressed, here with one of the two formulas which still form part of the Roman Mass, and in which allusion is made to the "cooperation of the Holy Spirit" in the work of salvation. Then follows the prayer which was found in the Roman Mass prior to the ordo of Paul VI and in which one asks "that the Body which I have taken and the Blood which I have drunk may cleave to every fiber of my being so that no stain of sin may be left in me." The object of this petition is no longer pardon, which has been obtained, but the disappearance of the consequences of sin which remain even when sin is remitted. This effect of communion is also the object of the final prayer, together with that other related effect: the possibility of being always "devoted to Christ wholeheartedly (*toto corde devotum*)."

All of these formulas are redacted in the first person singular; here they are in the masculine gender, but in the manuscript of Saint Sophia of Benevento they are in the feminine. It is never said or supposed that the one who recites them is a priest. Nevertheless, in their ensemble they really constitute a long eucharistic prayer. Mass has previously been celebrated by a priest, and the rite, with which one now participates in its effects, is at one and the same time a means of communion and a means of remission of sins.

In the Psalter of the Dean John the "ordo for taking the Body of the Lord" contains pretty much the same formulas; however the order in which they are given is different, and there are some other formulas. For example, the general confession at the beginning is much more developed. It comprises, as in the case of other formularies, a long enumeration of sins, not that everyone is supposed to have committed all of them; rather, it serves as a kind of universal examination of conscience valid for all, in which everyone can recognize what applies to him.[15] One notes other modifications of the same kind, as well as some additions. This is evidence of the liberty enjoyed in this domain: the theological inspiration remained the same, while its expression could vary, within the same monastery and in the course of a few years.[16]

In the manuscript of Auxerre, which is independent of the tradition of Monte Cassino, the "prayer for receiving the Eucharist" likewise begins with formulas of introduction: the prayer of the publican, "God have pity on me, a sinner," an invocation of the Trinity, another to the "good angel," the *Pater*. Then follow the prayers of preparation for communion, which include a profession of faith in the real presence, in the veracity of the sacrifice through which redemption is obtained, in eternal life, and as of now, the remission of sins. The same ideas, together with a mention of the role of the Holy Spirit, recur in the prayers which follow communion. Some of these prayers are redacted in the plural, and some in the singular; these latter, as we have noted, are in the feminine. Communion under both kinds is always mentioned or supposed.

Neither the ordo of Cassino, in its different forms, nor that of Auxerre gives any indication of the frequency with which this eucharistic rite was celebrated — daily or only on Sundays and feast days. Nor do they relate it to any special circumstance or to the anointing of the sick. Was the ordo of Cassino more fully developed because of a doctrinal controversy such as that associated with the name of Berengarius of Tours, the object of which was the real presence? Nothing leads us to think so. The fact that the text of Auxerre is more brief could be sufficiently explained by the fact that it is older.

In any case, these two texts, or groups of texts, separated in time and space, have two traits in common. On the one hand they include explicit mention of the eucharistic sacrifice, and thus the relation to the Mass, which St. Basil already considered essential, is maintained. On the other hand, there is no attempt to copy the Mass, merely omitting the institution narrative. There is no prayer of a sacerdotal type, such as the preface, reserved to a bishop or priest. Nor is there any liturgy of the Word, and that is understandable: all of the liturgical services of the monks and nuns include

[15] This text is similar to the one I published in *Fragmenta Reginensia, art. cit.* 294.

[16] This freedom, within a general structure, had already been pointed out by Wilmart, "Prières pour la communion," 322, note 2.

readings; a liturgy of the Word would have been still another way of copying the Mass. The aim here was to have something other than the Mass but still related to it. What we have here is incorporation of communion in the Body and Blood of the Lord into a celebration during the course of which the eucharistic mystery, such as it was conceived by the piety of the tenth and eleventh centuries, is evoked in all of its fullness.

From this examination of some witnesses of the past can we draw some conclusions or suggestions for our time? While eucharistic piety has not been transformed, it has evolved in the course of time. With regard to sin and pardon, we would no doubt emphasize less today the keen sense of culpability we find expressed in these ancient texts. A eucharistic rite could be structured otherwise than it was in those times and include biblical readings which would also evoke the eucharistic mystery. Throughout the formulary the manner of expression could be less individual, more communitarian, more ecclesial. In short, the possibilities are many, and in some places some of them have already become reality.

It will suffice, in conclusion, to underscore, without according it the developments to which it could lead, the traditional datum strongly emphasized in these ordos for communion: the fact of receiving, or as our texts say, taking the Body and Blood of Christ is one of the means by which sins are remitted and their aftereffects healed in the measure of which God is judge.[17] The rituals which we have analyzed in this article are at once eucharistic celebrations and penitential celebrations. During the centuries when our manuscripts were used confession was practiced between members of monastic communities; there is no need to prove this once again, with supporting documents.[18] At least we understand better the importance

[17] Let us select only a few examples from the vast bibliography relating to this subject: D. A. Tanghe, "L'eucharistie pour la rémission des péchés," *Irénikon* 24 (1961) 165–181; M. R. Tillard, "L'eucharistie, purification de l'Église périgrinante," *Nouvelle Revue Théologique* 84 (1962) 449–475; for the East: L. Ligier, "Pénitence et eucharistie en Orient," *Orientalia christiana periodica* 29 (1963) 5–74. As for "healing" through communion, traditional witnesses have recently been gathered by Daniel-Ange, "Le Coeur de Jésus," *Nova et vetera* 55 (1980) 67–73.

[18] Texts have been cited, for example, in A. Teetaert, *La confession aux laïques dans l'Église latine depuis le VIII jusqu'au XIV siècle* (Paris 1926); K. M. Koeniger, *Die Beichte nach Caesarius von Heisterbach* (Munich 1906) 77–91, 125. Other witnesses from monastic milieux could be added. I hope elsewhere to treat in detail of an eminent witness of monastic confession made between monks — St. Bernard.

which the pardon of sins obtained through communion could assume.

Similarly the anointing of the sick, which was sometimes administered by women in antiquity,[19] was and remains a means of remission of sins:[20] "in case of necessity," says the new Ritual. The same necessity which in the time of St. Basil, of St. Gregory, today and tomorrow provides occasion for eucharistic celebrations without priests can invite attention to that aspect of a sacrament the reception of which is for some, even in our day, the normal sequel of a preparation for death, which has sometimes included, even in the absence of a priest, a review of the past that is the equivalent of confession. In a period of the long history of the Church, at a moment in its evolution when the practice of the sacrament of penance raises problems, much as does the possibility of participating in Mass or of placing a priest at the disposition of the sick and dying, it is not without interest to recall such facts.

[19] Mary Lawrence McKenna, *Women of the Church*, with a foreword by J. Daniélou, 152. J. Daniélou, "Le ministère des femmes dans l'Eglise ancienne," *La Maison-Dieu* no. 61 (1960) 83 and 94 is affirmative concerning the subject of the imposition of hands by women on sick women, and he adds: "the sacrament of last anointing in this regard."

[20] B. Poschmann, *Penance and the Anointing of the Sick* (New York: Herder & Herder 1964) 245–246. In the eleventh century Jonas of Orléans, citing Innocent I, Ep. 1, 8, cited in turn by Bede, wrote that "in case of necessity it is licit, not only for priests, but for all Christians to give this anointing," provided that it be with oil consecrated by the bishop. *De institutione laicali*, c. 14, PL 106, 261.

John Quinn

The Lord's Supper and Forgiveness of Sin

At present, baptism and penance have an exclusive role as the sacraments of pardon. Baptism removes original sin and with confirmation and the eucharist initiates one into the Christian life; it is also the basis for receiving the sacrament of penance. But penance is considered the sacrament of pardon *par excellence* because it purifies the Christian for the reception of communion. Yet baptism has a continuing effect of pardon and the eucharist is the perfection of the remission of sins because the cross, the mystery of reconciliation, is present in it alone. For centuries the church lived on these truths, allowing the sacrament of penance its extraordinary role. Since the Middle Ages the remission of sins conferred by the eucharist has suffered almost complete neglect. This article will try to present the views of writers who have given attention to this effect of the eucharist, especially as it appears in liturgical texts, in an effort to achieve a balanced approach to the relationship between the sacraments.

The Instruction on Eucharistic Worship of 25 May 1967, proposed that the faithful be instructed about the purifying effects of the eucharist. The Council of Trent was quoted to the effect that the eucharist is an "antidote by which we are freed from our daily faults and preserved from mortal sin" (Denz. 875).

The Council of Trent also "teaches that this sacrifice is truly propitiatory, and that through it, if we come to God with a true heart and right faith, with fear and reverence, in contrition and penitence, we obtain mercy and find grace to help us in time of need (cf. Heb 4:16). For appeased by the offering of this sacrifice, the Lord grants grace and the gift of repentance, and forgives sins and even the greatest of crimes" (Denz. 940).

This forgiveness is the effect of the sacrifice alone; communion is forbidden the pardoned sinner, but as J. Tillard[1] points out, his "gift of repentance" is a desire for the sacrament of penance. All mortal

[1] "Pénitence et Eucharistie," *Maison-Dieu* 90 (1967) 103–131.

sins are to be confessed and, in accordance with the church's custom, this is required before the reception of communion unless a confessor is lacking. The sinner's certainty of contrition is not enough. While people who are obliged to be present at the Lord's supper and who otherwise participate in the eucharistic blessing over the bread and wine are not permitted to receive communion without confession of mortal sins (even if they are well disposed and have repented of their sins), they may make a "spiritual communion."

In the past, public penitents may have been required to assist at mass while avoiding communion. But "spiritual communicants" are not normally public penitents or public sinners. The period of public penance for public sins led to the private penance for private sins and for a long time now we have had private penance for both public and private sins. When, long after Trent, on most Sundays only a few people fasting from midnight went to communion, no one else at mass was in effect a public penitent except those who had committed public sins. Now, when materially speaking it is easy to receive communion every Sunday and it is the practice to do so, the requirement of the sacrament of penance for all mortal sins before receiving communion tends to produce a new penitential discipline: public penance for private sins.

When the church had three sins which required public penance, it was still understood there could be other grave sins which were not scandalous but which repented of did not prevent access to the eucharist. In today's circumstances of frequent communion and numerous "mortal" sins instead of the early church's three, the law of automatic exclusion from the community meal on Sunday can appear unrealistic and penal without achieving any real pastoral or evangelical end. Together with any renewed understanding of the distinction of sins and with any renewal of church discipline in terms of personal and communal values, the purifying effect of the eucharist, as sacrifice and meal in their inseparable unity, should be taken into account.

D. Tanghe[2] and J. Tillard[3] have examined liturgical texts used in the East and in the West which indicate that the Lord's supper gives the forgiveness of sins to the properly disposed. But it is especially

[2] "L'Eucharistie pour la rémission des péchés," *Irénikon* 34 (1961) 165–181.

[3] *L'Eucharistie, Pâque de l'Église* (Paris 1964).

the work of L. Ligier[4] on the liturgical texts of the eastern churches which has shown that the eucharist in its integrity as sacrifice and communion has for centuries been considered to have as one of its effects the forgiveness of grave sins, without requiring of itself or in the church's practice recourse before or after to the sacrament of penance.

PENANCE AND JEWISH TRADITION

For an understanding of these texts, it is necessary first to see their background in Jewish practices at the time of Jesus. Our interpretation of the relationship between penance and the eucharist in the apostolic times will depend on the writings of J. Murphy-O'Connor[5] and J. Audet.[6]

For certain moral faults, a general confession of sins integrated with a prayer of repentance such as a penitential psalm and a sacrifice of expiation was in Judaism a condition for forgiveness. "When a man is guilty in any of these, he shall confess the sin he has committed, and he shall bring his guilt offering to the Lord for the sin which he has committed . . . ; and the priest shall make atonement for him for his sin" (Lev 5:5f). Where there was a consciousness of moral wrong done and the required confession of the offense sprung from a sense of penitence, the sacrifice was considered efficacious.

The public, collective confession of the sins of the people spoken by the high priest on the Day of Atonement over the head of the goat that was to be sent away was also general in form: "O Lord, thy people Israel have sinned, done iniquity, transgressed before thee. O Lord, forgive the sins, iniquities, and the transgressions which thy people Israel have sinned, done, and transgressed before thee, as it is written in the law of Moses, thy servant, 'On this day shall atonement be made to purify you; from all your sins before the Lord shall ye be purified (Lev 16:20).'" The people responded: "Blessed be his name whose glorious kingdom is forever and ever" (Mishnah, Danby 169).

In the time of Christ, Philo wrote of the synagogue service on the Day of Atonement that this "greatest of feasts" is "entirely conse-

[4] "Pénitence et Eucharistie en Orient," *Orientalia Christiana Periodica* 29 (1963) 5–78.

[5] "Péché et Communauté dans le Nouveau Testament," *Révue Biblique* 74 (1967) 161–193.

[6] "La penitenza cristiana primitiva," *Sacra Doctrina* 46 (1967) 153–177.

crated to prayers and supplications. For from dawn to sunset the people have no other occupation than to make invocations full of prayers by which they try to render God favorable, asking pardon for sins voluntary and involuntary, hoping for benefits, not out of consideration for themselves, but by reason of the benevolent nature of him who prefers pardon rather than punishment."[7]

Philo's reference to "sins voluntary and involuntary" raises the question, what kind of sins could be forgiven on the Day of Atonement? While any type of sacrifice sufficed for the forgiveness of "inadvertent" faults, "the man who sins deliberately [literally, 'with a high hand'] outrages Yahweh himself. Such a man must be outlawed from his people; he has despised the word of Yahweh and broken his command" (Num 15:30–31). According to this unique biblical source for a clear indication of the distinction of sins, deliberate, premeditated, "high-handed" sin cannot be cleared by any sacrifice. But this means acts, not just knowingly committed, but committed defiantly and of set purpose, as distinct from sins committed in moments of weakness. The Pentateuch provided no sacrificial atonement for such "deliberate" or "voluntary" sins.

In the Judaism of Jesus' time, nevertheless, it is clear from the Mishnah, the Talmudic commentaries on the Mishnah, and the Sifra on Leviticus that even these grave sins committed with a "high hand" could, if they were repented of and confessed, be forgiven on the Day of Atonement. In the Mishnah (*Shebuoth* 1:6, Danby 410) we read: "For uncleanness that befalls the temple and its hallowed things through wantonness, atonement is made by the goat whose blood is sprinkled within [the holy of holies] and by the Day of Atonement; for all other transgressions spoken of in the law, venial or grave, wanton or unwitting, conscious or unconscious, sins of omission or of commission, sins punishable by extirpation or by death at the hands of the court, the scapegoat makes atonement." In Sifra on Leviticus 16:16[8] the words used in the high priest's confession to describe the sins of the people are interpreted in this way: "'Iniquities' are the 'insolent' misdeeds; 'transgressions' are the 'rebellious' acts; 'sins' are the 'unwitting' offenses."

This change was due to the developing concern shown in the biblical writers and in the Jewish tradition with the importance of re-

[7] *De Specialibus Legibus*, Bk. II, 196, 23, ed. Cohn, pp. 134–135.

[8] J. Bonsirven, *Textes Rabbiniques des Deux Premiers Siècles Chrétiens* (Rome 1955) p. 140.

pentance and above all with the boundless character of God's mercy. The problem was how to advance these religious and ethical insights without scandalously contradicting the ancient cultic provisions of the Law which allowed no expiation for thirty-six voluntary sins punishable by extirpation. The solution which prevailed was to recognize the changed attitude of the repentant sinner evident in his confession of these voluntary and grave sins and to give them the preferential treatment provided in the Law for involuntary and inadvertent sins. In effect, only those who continued impenitent after the original rebellious act were incapable of receiving pardon on the Day of Atonement.

A similar interpretation was applied to the three cardinal sins, murder, apostasy, and adultery. Tradition distinguished these from the other voluntary sins as involving the deliberate and willful rejection of the authority of God. Upon repentance they also could be forgiven on the Day of Atonement, like the sins of ignorance and weakness. However, these extreme sins, called "uncleanness" in Leviticus 18:3, 20:3, and Numbers 35:34, were included among the "uncleanness of the children of Israel" for which expiation was to be made by sprinkling the blood of the goat in the holy of holies (cf. Lev 16:16). As we have seen in the last quotation from the Mishnah, the other voluntary sins were pardoned by the rite of the scapegoat. Sins of ignorance and of weakness, unconscious and involuntary sins, could be remitted by any kind of sacrificial expiation in the Law and of course by the Day of Atonement.

PENANCE AND THE NEW TESTAMENT

For Christ, the synoptics, and St. Paul, the sins of Israel and mankind are not sins of weakness or of ignorance, but deliberate and voluntary sins, rebellious acts which reach their extremity in encompassing the death of Christ. But Christ as the Servant of God and as the high priest accomplishes once and for all a sacrificial atonement which is efficacious for all who bring to it their repentance. Dying, he prayed that through his sacrifice of expiation, repentance might come to rebellious sinners, and that their deliberate and voluntary sins should, as on the Day of Atonement, be considered as sins of ignorance and forgiven (cf. Lk 23:34).

In the context of the celebration of the eucharist, the death of Christ continually assumed in greater degree the aspect of a ritual act, and also a sacrificial and priestly character. The addition of the phrase "for the remission of sins" to the words said over the cup in Matthew 26:28 (which Bultmann calls a "correct exegesis" of Christ's death as an expiatory sacrifice for sin[9]), is evidence for the belief that through the cross present in the eucharist, including of course communion, forgiveness of sins is extended to the community. Baptism as the means of access to the cross is finally the means of access to the eucharistic celebration, where the permanence of the mystery of the cross as mystery of reconciliation is given to the church. The remission of sins is first acquired through baptism and the eucharist, for reconciliation has no meaning unless it is fulfilled through the eucharist itself.

Because of its regular use in the eucharistic celebration, the phrase "for the remission of sins" must represent the understanding the primitive church had of the eucharistic sacrifice as the summit of the redemptive ministry which Christ continued to exercise in the assembly. Of course it is required that a man "prove himself," examine himself to see that he has dispositions approved by God for partaking in the eucharist, above all fraternal charity (1 Cor 11:28). But the New Testament offers us no evidence of the ritual of the sacrament of penance. There is a reference to a laying on of hands (1 Tim 5:22) which is possibly a reference to a rite of reconciliation, but there is no case of anyone being reconciled after exclusion from the community. Christians can be and are excluded from the community after refusing fraternal correction for scandalous sins, but it is not the initial sin itself which is punished by exclusion — as with us today in the case of every mortal sin — but only the sin of obdurate refusal to repent of his initial sin after several brotherly admonitions. This marks the exceptional intervention of the heads of the community. The sins given as reasons for separation from the community are incest (1 Cor 5:2), apostasy (Heb 10:29) and possibly murder (1 Jn 5:16); these are radical breaches with the Christian way of life.

There is evidence in the New Testament of one tendency towards pessimism and severity for lapsed Christians as well as of another tendency towards mercy and forgiveness for them. But there is no suggestion that all that we call grave sin excluded from the eucharist and required the use of the sacrament of penance. A great deal is made of what we would call the virtue of penance, but nothing of the sacrament. A great deal is made of confession integrated with prayer and of mutual reconciliation. James 5:16 seems to counsel

[9] R. Bultmann, *Theology of the New Testament*, vol. 1 (New York 1951) p. 146.

confession of sins which are not public and therefore are not the concern of the community. The confession is made in a general way so as to motivate the intercession of the brethren; there is assurance that, if the intercession of the elders for the sick is efficacious, prayers for one another are also efficacious for the forgiveness of sins. Reconciliation seems to remain something between the sinner and God alone.

Jesus gives an example of the community confession of sins in the Our Father, to which, together with other New Testament texts on mutual reconciliation, the community gave a liturgical context. The original words of Jesus concerning reconciliation before offering a gift at the altar (Mt 5:23–24) receive a specifically Christian formulation for the community's liturgical assemblies: "When you are standing at prayer, forgive whatever you have against anybody, so that your Father who is in heaven may pardon you also your offenses" (Mk 11:25). Mark's "your Father who is in heaven" appears to be the liturgical language of the Our Father. In Judaism, as we have seen, the confession of sins with prayer always accompanied the sacrifice of expiation. Without a confession of sins the sacrifice would not be pure, because the heart of the offerer would not be in his offering and the divine forgiveness would not be forthcoming. The Our Father is surely the oldest penitential rite used in the Christian liturgical assembly. The examination of eastern and western liturgies would lead us to conclude that it is the fundamental and most ancient rite preceding communion.

LITURGICAL EVIDENCE

L. Ligier[10] has shown that in the fourth and fifth centuries in the East there is striking evidence that while in the New Testament the theme of the Day of Atonement has been applied to the passion of Christ and the eucharist is implicitly a sacrifice for sin, the eucharist at this time is treated explicitly as the fulfillment of the sacrifice of the Day of Atonement and all the consequences for the various types of sin are plainly spelled out in the prayers now added to the rites. We have quoted above some of the texts from which the composers will borrow the terms they will use. In addition, they found models and sources in the prayers used by the congregations in the synagogues on that greatest of feasts. Not only do the eastern litur-

[10] L. Ligier, *Péché d'Adam et Péché du Monde*, vol. 2 (Paris 1961).

gies borrow key words from the synagogue service; they also borrow the very order of the words.

In the light of the scanty liturgical documentation we have from the previous period, this sudden absorption with the Day of Atonement could appear as a bolt from the blue. We have mentioned the Matthean addition to the words over the cup. There was also in the epiclesis of the anaphora of Addai and Mari in the third century, the idea of the eucharist as a sacrifice for sin: "May your Holy Spirit come O Lord and rest upon this offering of your servants and bless and sanctify it, that it may be to us O Lord for the remission of trespasses and the forgiveness of sins. . . ." But also in the third century Origen, whose influence was to be enormous in the east, frequently applied the themes of the Day of Atonement to penance and the eucharist. Echoing the texts cited previously from Leviticus and Numbers, Origen wrote: "The priests of the Law are prohibited from offering sacrifice for certain sins, so that the faults of those for whom sacrifice would be offered might be remitted. And the priest, who has the power of making the offering for *certain involuntary faults*, does not offer for adultery, for deliberate murder, or for other very grave sins, the holocaust and the sacrifice for sin."[11] Having made the same distinction of sins as the Law and the Jewish tradition, he applies this to the sacrifices offered by the apostles and bishops: "Therefore the apostles also and the successors of the apostles, priests according to the high priest, having received the knowledge of divine healing, know through the teaching of the spirit for what sins it is right to offer sacrifice, when and in what manner, and they know the sins for which it is not right to do so."[12] Origen becomes more explicit: "I do not know how certain people, arrogating to themselves a more than priestly power, although they lack perhaps priestly knowledge, pride themselves on being able to remit the sins of idolatry, adultery and fornication, as if the prayer they pronounce over those who dared commit these crimes would efface even mortal [literally, 'unto death'] sins. They do not read the scripture: 'There is a sin which leads to death; it is not for this that I say to pray.'"[13]

In these remarks made while commenting on the plea for forgiveness in the Lord's Prayer, Origen, while insisting on public penance

[11] *De Oratione*, 28, P.G. 11, 528D–529A.

[12] *Ibid.*, 529A.

[13] *Ibid.*, 529B.

for the three capital sins, indicates that at that time the eucharistic prayer understood as a sacrifice of intercession had penitential value. Evidently there are some like the Copts who in their liturgy prayed every Sunday for the forgiveness of even the three great sins, but even Origen allows the forgiveness of other sins through the eucharistic sacrifice.

At the end of the fourth century, the West Syrians placed within the eucharistic prayer, at the end of the intercessions for the living and the dead and before the doxology, a penitential prayer. It reads (Congregation:) "Remit, acquit, pardon us and them [the living and the dead just commemorated] the sins which we have committed before you voluntarily and involuntarily, knowingly and in ignorance." (Celebrant:) "Remit, acquit, pardon our sins which we have committed voluntarily, involuntarily, knowingly, in ignorance, in deed, in word, in thought, in secret, openly, by design, by error, those which your holy name knows."[14] Through the anaphora of St. James this passed into the Syrian, Byzantine, Armenian and Ethiopian rites. It repeats almost exactly the eight terms of the ancient prayer *Al Chet*, recited in the synagogue on the Day of the Atonement and found in *Seder Amram Gaon*: ". . . the sin that we have committed before you voluntarily, involuntarily, in secret, in public, through constraint, with full consent, unconsciously, inadvertently, the sins which are manifest to us and those which are not manifest to us."[15] Many other examples of similar borrowing could be given. Many examples could also be given of penitential prayer found at other places in almost all eastern liturgies, whose original purpose is unobserved.

It is clear that our distinction between mortal and venial sin was unknown in the East throughout Christian antiquity. The great sins "which reject the law forever," idolatry and apostasy, murder, adultery and fornication, were submitted to a canonical penitential discipline which was very flexible for pastoral reasons. Sins of "ignorance and of weakness, unconscious and involuntary," did not prevent the reception of communion. Except for the three capital sins already mentioned (and the Copts did not except even them) all "voluntary and conscious" sins, venial and even grave, were included simply in the general confession of sins made in the course of the eucharist, as in the Our Father with its prologue and embo-

[14] F. E. Brightman, *Liturgies Eastern and Western* (Oxford 1896) p. 58.
[15] Cf. L. Ligier, "Pénitence . . . en Orient" (n. 4 above), 21.

lism; the sacrifice and the communion forgave these sins without specific confession. Sometimes these penitential rites appear to Ligier to include a sacramental absolution because they appeal to Matthew 16:19, Matthew 18:18, or John 20:23. From the age when public penance flourished until individual confession became general, that is from the fourth to the ninth century, the eastern churches made use of a general confession of venial and even mortal sins not requiring public penance joined to the eucharistic sacrifice and communion for the pardon of these sins.

In the West too very little use was made of the sacrament of penance. Vogel[16] thinks that repentant sinners went to communion without the reconciliation of the sacrament of penance while they hoped and prepared to receive it when they would come to die. In the first centuries only a small number would have participated in the celebration of the eucharist while many others remained simple catechumens. With the decline of the catechumenate after the peace of Constantine, people went to communion who should have been ranked among the penitents. The bishops excommunicated the most unworthy but advised others to abstain temporarily from communion. Vogel thinks it "infinitely probable" that the faithful who repented and performed works of penance and tried to be worthy of receiving penance on their death-bed were admitted without the reconciliation of sacramental penance to the eucharist. Browe[17] thinks that except for sins which required public penance, confession was not demanded before the eighth century. At the beginning of the tenth century it was imposed universally, but the rule was sanctioned only at the Council of the Lateran in 1215. This requirement, Browe believes, was slow in coming because of the lack of a strong distinction between mortal and venial sin and because of the quite widespread conviction during the high Middle Ages that communion itself remits sin. He finds in the texts of the liturgy strong indications of this last belief. The prayers cannot all be asking for the pardon of venial sins through communion, especially when such terms as *crimina* are used. There are still traces of such prayers in our present Roman liturgy. Browe was led to conclude from the evidence that the desire to prevent the unworthy reception of communion

[16] C. Vogel, *Le Pécheur et la pénitence dans l'Église ancienne* (Paris 1966).

[17] P. Browe, "Die Kommunionvorbereitung in Mittelalter," *Zeitschrift für Katholische Theologie* 56 (1932) 375–415.

contributed to the encouragement and use of private penance. The piety of the faithful and especially of the monks extended the use of private penance, required only for grave faults, to even light faults.

The doctrine of the remission of sins conferred by the eucharist has had a long and varied history of use and neglect in the church. Granted that the forgiveness of sins is not the chief object of the eucharist and that no one wants a return to the days when the mass was over-emphasized as a sacrifice of propitiation for sin, Christ made the forgiveness of sins an essential dimension of it. The eucharist must of course be approached with purity of intention. A penitential act which is part of the eucharist can help to achieve it. But we should not want a penitential preparation at the beginning which would convey the idea of achieving forgiveness of sins as something separate from the eucharist itself, which would be simply joy and praise, admiration and thanksgiving. All Christians come as sinners seeking forgiveness in the eucharist. We are beginning to understand that in the service of the word there is "the power of God unto salvation to those who believe." Forgiveness is the concern of the Kyrie, Gloria, Per evangelica dicta, the "words of consecration," Nobis quoque, Agnus Dei, and prayers at communion. The penitential act *par excellence* in preparation for communion is the Our Father. St. Augustine emphasized the reason for its place: "Before communion these words remove our sins of weakness." In every liturgy it has this role. Perhaps its prologue and embolism could be improved by comparison with similar prayers in other liturgies which develop the theme of forgiveness of sins and preparation for communion. Of course a sacramental absolution at mass, at whatever point it would come, would unnecessarily obscure and duplicate the effect of the sacrifice-meal. The structures of the two sacraments are different. Perhaps penance might be likened to the shepherd seeking the lost sheep and to the prodigal son returning home. But the eucharist is the father celebrating with his son the meal of reconciliation.

Robert Taft

Ex Oriente Lux?
Some Reflections on Eucharistic Concelebration

The following notes on concelebration do not pretend to offer a complete study of the Eastern tradition, nor definitive solutions to the growing dissatisfaction with the restored Roman rite of eucharistic concelebration. But they may help to clarify the *status quaestionis*, rectify misinterpretations of early eucharistic discipline, and dispel misconceptions concerning the antiquity and normative value of Eastern usage. I'll begin with the latter and work backwards.

It has long been a theological device to turn eastwards in search of supporting liturgical evidence for what one has already decided to do anyway. Something like this was at work in certain pre-Vatican II discussions on the possibility of restoring concelebration in the Roman rite. The underlying presupposition seems to be that Eastern practice will reflect a more ancient — indeed *the* ancient — tradition of the undivided Church. Let's review the evidence.

CONCELEBRATION IN THE CHRISTIAN EAST TODAY

The information on contemporary Eastern forms of eucharistic concelebration given by McGowan and King[1] is generally accurate, with a few exceptions that will be corrected here.

The *Armenians* practice eucharistic concelebration only at episcopal and presbyteral ordinations, a custom they may have borrowed from the Latins.[2]

The *Maronites*, also influenced by the Latins, probably owe their practice of verbal co-consecration to scholastic theology of the

[1] J. McGowan, *Concelebration: Sign of the Unity of the Church* (New York 1964) 39–53; A. King, *Concelebration in the Christian Church* (London 1966) 102–132. The basic general study is A. Raes, "La concélébration eucharistique dans les rites orientaux," *La Maison-Dieu* no. 35 (1953) 24–47.

[2] On Latin influence in Armenia, see G. Winkler, "Armenia and the Gradual Decline of its Traditional Liturgical Practices as a Result of the Expanding Influence of the Holy See from the 11th to the 14th Century," in *Liturgie de l'église particulière et liturgie de l'église universelle* (Conférences Saint-Serge 1975. Bibliotheca "Ephemerides Liturgicae," Subsidia 4, Rome: Edizioni Liturgiche 1976) 329–368.

Eucharist. Before the seventeenth century, concelebration without co-consecration was in use.[3]

In the *Coptic Orthodox* Church several presbyters participate in the common Eucharist vested, in the sanctuary. Only the main celebrant (who is not the *presiding* celebrant if a bishop is present) stands at the altar, but the prayers are shared among the several priests. Some prayers, but not necessarily the "consecratory" part of the anaphora, are the preserve of the main celebrant at the altar.[4] *Catholic Copts*, like the Maronites, have adopted a type of verbal co-consecration. This could represent the revival of an older usage. In several ancient Alexandrine manuscripts, diaconal admonitions at the words of institution exhort the concelebrants to join with the main celebrant at this solemn moment of the anaphora.[5] Though not necessarily a proof of *verbal* co-consecration, this certainly implies "concelebration" even in the narrow modern sense of the term.

Among the *Syrian Orthodox* it is customary for several presbyters to join with the bishop in the celebration of the liturgy. Only the bishop is fully vested. The assisting presbyters wear just the stole over their clerical gown, a garment similar to the Byzantine *rason*, but at the beginning of the anaphora one of them puts on the *phaino* (Greek *phainolion*, the principal outer vestment) and joins the bishop at the altar for the anaphora. Though the bishop shares the various prayers of the anaphora with the presbyters, he alone recites the words of institution and the epiclesis up to and including the blessing of the gifts,[6] at which point he retires to his throne while the presbyter in the *phaino* takes over at the altar to complete the epicletic prayer and share the rest of the anaphora with the other presbyters. At the end of the anaphora the bishop again takes his place at

[3] Cf. P. Daou, "Notes sur les origines de la concélébration eucharistique dans le rite maronite," *Orientalia Christiana Periodica* 6 (1940) 233–239. Daou (236–239) denies that the Maronite practice arose in imitation of Latin liturgical usage, but it is certainly the result of Latin eucharistic theology, of which his very article is the perfect example.

[4] Information from my colleague Samir Khalil, professor at the Pontifical Oriental Institute and priest of the Coptic rite.

[5] See R.-C. Coquin, "Vestiges de concélébration eucharistique chez les melkites égyptiens, les coptes et les éthiopiens, *Le Muséon* 80 (1967) 37–46; also J.-M. Hanssens, "Un rito di concelebrazione della messa propria della liturgia alessandrina," *Studia orientalia christiana* (Collectanea 13, Cairo 1968–1969) 3–34.

[6] That is, up to the "Amen" in F. E. Brightman, *Liturgies Eastern and Western* (Oxford 1896) 89 line 11.

the altar, and the assisting priest retires to remove the *phaino*. It is necessary only for the bishop to communicate, but of course the concelebrants may if properly disposed. Though this form of concelebration is not mentioned in descriptions of the West-Syrian rite, I have assisted at such a celebration and, on inquiring, was assured that it is common usage. In addition, both Orthodox and Catholic Syrians practice a rite of "synchronized masses," each celebrant having his own bread and cup.[7]

The *Ethiopians* have a similar rite of "synchronized masses," as well as a form of eucharistic celebration in which several presbyters — ideally, thirteen — take active part with various functions and prayers distributed among them, that is, not done simultaneously by all as in verbal co-consecration.[8] Indeed, this is the normal form of Eucharist among the Ethiopian Orthodox, and at least five presbyters, and preferably seven, are considered essential if the Eucharist is to be celebrated at all. These presbyters must all communicate at the celebration.

In the traditional *East-Syrian* Eucharist, the bishop surrounded by his presbyters presides over the liturgy of the word from the bema in the middle of the nave.[9] When the time for the anaphora approaches, one of the presbyters is selected to read it. He alone "consecrates." In this tradition *all* services and sacraments are "concelebrations" in which all the various orders of ministers participate according to their rank: singers singing, lectors reading, deacons proclaiming, presbyters sharing the prayers. But they do not *all* say the *same* prayers. Distribution is the principle.

In the *Byzantine* tradition we see, as in the West, the inexorable growth in the verbalization of eucharistic concelebration, with the same prayers being said by all concelebrating ministers.[10] In this as

[7] Cf. King, *Concelebration* 121–122. Personal inquiry among the Syrian Orthodox clergy has confirmed that this rite is still in use.

[8] My information on Ethiopian usage is from Abba Tekle-Mariam Semharay Selim, *Règles speciales de la messe éthiopienne* (Rome 1936) 10–13.

[9] See W. F. Macomber, "Concelebration in the East Syrian Rite," in J. Vellian (ed.), *The Malabar Church* (Orientalia Christiana Analecta 186, Rome 1970) 17–22; S. Y. H. Jammo, *La structure de la messe chaldéenne du début jusqu'à l'anaphore. Étude historique* (Orientalia Christiana Analecta 207, Rome 1979) *passim*; R. Taft, "On the use of the Bema in the East-Syrian Liturgy," *Eastern Churches Review* 3 (1970) 30–39.

[10] The best study on Byzantine concelebration is H. Brakmann, "*Kai anaginôskousi pantes hoi hiereis tén eucharistérion euchén.* Zum gemeinschaftlichen Eucharistiegebet byzantinischer Konzelebranten," *Orientalia Christiana Periodica* 42 (1976) 319–367. Note

in other traditions one must distinguish Orthodox from Eastern-Catholic practice. Many Eastern-Catholic priests, under Western influence, say mass daily out of devotion, even when there is no pastoral need for them to officiate, so for them concelebration is much the same as for their post-Vatican II Latin confrères: a means of satisfying their private devotion, their desire to "say mass" every day, while avoiding the dissolution of eucharistic *koinonia* represented by that curious counter-symbol of ecclesial communion, the so-called "private mass."[11]

Among the *Byzantine Orthodox*, concelebration is normally practiced only when a bishop is celebrating solemnly, or to solemnize a festive presbyteral liturgy. Thus in a monastery on an ordinary day, one priest would celebrate and the others assist *modo laico*, unvested, in the nave or in the sanctuary. On feasts a few concelebrating presbyters would join the principal celebrant. A bishop is usually joined by numerous concelebrating presbyters, and even by other bishops.

Byzantine Catholics and those Orthodox that follow the *Russian* usage in this matter practice verbal co-consecration. This was once thought to be the result of Western influence in the sixteenth cen-

that each concelebrant says the prayers to himself. There is no common choral recitation as in Latin usage, except among some latinized Eastern Catholics at the same parts of the liturgy.

[11] This discomfort with the private mass is based not on the Reformation critique of medieval eucharistic theology, but on ancient elements within the Catholic tradition of East and West. The point is not whether only two or three can constitute a Christian community to celebrate the Lord's Supper, but rather the multiplication of individual, "private masses" ("divisive mass" would be a more accurate term) *within the same community at the same time and place*. Hence the evidence sometimes advanced to demonstrate the existence of "private mass" in antiquity is beside the point. Such celebrations were what we would call "small-group masses," which are another matter entirely. The issue is not the "head count," but the weakening of *koinonia* by placing it second to the devotional desires of individual presbyters to say "their" mass. This would have been inconceivable in antiquity. Even anchorites wishing to participate in a eucharistic liturgy had to leave their solitude and come to the common synaxis. It was either that or go without mass. Relics of this traditional approach were retained by the Latin Church until recently. The absolute prohibition of private masses on Holy Thursday, at papal conclaves, at the opening of a synod (cf. McGowan, *Concelebration* 55ff) shows that when the Church wished to manifest in its fullness the eucharistic sign of ecclesial communion, eucharistic dispersion into individual masses was forbidden. If the multiplication of masses or the devotional desires of the individual celebrant to say "his" mass was truly of more spiritual value, a source of more grace and glory to God, then what possible right could the Church have had to limit God's grace and glory in this way?

tury, but recently scholars have challenged successfully this theory.[12] Besides, A. Jacob has shown that verbal concelebration was in use in Constantinople by at least the tenth century,[13] and it is hardly possible to postulate the adoption of Latin usage there during that period of growing estrangement and ritual dispute between the Byzantine and Latin Churches.[14]

Among the *Greek Orthodox*, however, there appear to be conflicting usages coexisting in peaceful competition. One priest whom I questioned assured me that all concelebrants should say all the priestly prayers, including the words of institution and epiclesis; another informed me that only the main celebrant consecrates. The 1951 Athens *Hieratikon* contains a rubric for the beginning of the anaphora that "all the priests read the eucharistic prayer,"[15] but the same edition gives the impression later in the text that only the main celebrant says the institution narrative and epiclesis.[16] H. Brakmann, however, has shown that these rubrics refer to the main celebrant's role, and cannot be interpreted restrictively as excluding the recitation of the consecratory prayers by the concelebrating presbyters.[17] Nevertheless, the 1962 *Apostoliké Diakonia* edition of the *Hieratikon* makes it quite clear that only the first priest consecrates.[18] Here we seem to have a case where verbal concelebration is in use *except for* the consecration! But we must not immediately conclude that this practice is in direct continuity with ancient tradition. It may be the result of the teaching of Nicodemus the Hagiorite (1749–1809), who held that in order to preserve the unity of the offering, only one

[12] Cf. Brakmann, "Zum gemeinschaftlichen Eucharistiegebet" 321 ff, 337–367, and A. Jacob, "La concélébration de l'anaphore à Byzance d'après le témoignage de Léon Toscan," *Orientalia Christiana Periodica* 35 (1969) 249–256.

[13] Cf. the previous note.

[14] Cf. O. Rousseau, "La question des rites entre Grecs et Latins des premiers siècles au concile de Florence," *Irénikon* 22 (1949) 248 ff.

[15] In the appendix "*Hieratikon sylleitourgon*" 170.

[16] *Ibid.* 170–171.

[17] "Zum gemeinschaftlichen Eucharistiegebet" 324–334.

[18] Appendix "*Hieratikon sylleitourgon*" 248–249, rubrics 15–16. The final rubric (no. 25, p. 250) could not be more explicit: if the first celebrant concedes to the concelebrants the parts that are proper to him, especially the blessings (the consecratory blessings of the epiclesis, undoubtedly), this would not be a sign of courtesy and humility on his part, but a high-handed violation of ecclesiastical discipline regardless of the pretext! Such admonitions are of course usually meant to counteract existing practice.

priest should say the prayers.[19] But it is obvious from Nicodemus's polemic against "certain concelebrants . . . each of whom has his separate book of the Divine Liturgy and recites the prayers privately" that he was arguing against an existing practice.[20]

It is worth noting that in the Byzantine, as in other traditions, concelebration is not limited to the Eucharist. The same norms apply to other services. When a bishop celebrates vespers, a vigil, a requiem, he always has concelebrants, and the same is true of more solemn services even when there is no bishop celebrating. In such concelebrations, various parts are reserved to the main celebrant, others parceled out. The anointing of the sick is done (ideally) by seven presbyters. But except for the blessing of the oil in this rite, and the prayers of the eucharistic liturgy, the concelebrants do not all recite the *same* prayers in these services. Rather, *distribution* is the norm. But the anointing of the sick is a real "sacramental" concelebration, since even the anointings are shared. A similar rite is found among the Copts and Armenians.[21]

We do not yet have the studies at our disposal to evaluate the reasons for the appearance and spread of verbal concelebration in the East. But it does not represent the practice of the primitive Church.

EUCHARISTIC CELEBRATION IN THE ANCIENT CHURCH: CELEBRATION OR CONCELEBRATION?

In 1 Corinthians, our earliest witness to the Eucharist, Saint Paul presents the ideal form of this service as one fraternal banquet which the whole community "celebrates" together (11:17–34; cf. 10:16–17). I presume that one community leader presided over the celebration and said the prayer of table blessing, after the manner of Jewish repasts.[22] Paul seems to imply this in 1 Corinthians 14:16–17: ". . . if you bless with the spirit, how can any one in the position of an outsider say the "Amen" to your thanksgiving when he does not

[19] On Nicodemus, see Brakmann, "Zum gemeinschaftlichen Eucharistiegebet" 334ff. Cf. the similar objection in Thomas Aquinas, *ST* III, 82, 2.

[20] *Heortodromion étoi herméneia eis tous asmatikous kanonas tôn despotikôn kai theométorikôn heortôn* (Venice 1836) 576 note 1.

[21] Cf. H. Denzinger, *Ritus orientalium coptorum, syrorum et armenorum, in administrandis sacramentis* . . . vol. 2 (Würzburg 1864) 483ff, 519ff.

[22] Cf. L. Bouyer, *Eucharist. Theology and Spirituality of the Eucharistic Prayer* (Notre Dame 1968) 80 ff.

know what you are saying? For you may give thanks well enough, but the other man is not edified." And his insistence on unity in 1 Corinthians 11 would seem to demand one blessing of the shared food.

To speak of "concelebration" in this context would of course be tautological, implying a clergy-laity division that had not hardened so early. Paul does speak of a variety of roles and ministries at the common services (1 Cor 12 and 14), and of the need for order in the community (1 Cor 12:27–30) and in its assemblies (1 Cor 14, esp. 26–40). But one certainly does not get the impression of a community divided into "celebrants" and "congregation." Rather, the whole problem in 1 Corinthians 12 and 14 is that everyone got into the act without due regard for one another, thereby provoking disorder and disunity in the (ideally) one celebration.

This same concern with unity runs through the Last Supper discourse in John (13:4–16, 34–35; 15:1–12; 17:11, 20–23) and descriptions of the primitive ecclesial assembly in Acts (1:14; 2:1, 42–47; 4:32–35; 20:7). And it is uppermost in the mind of the Apostolic Fathers. Ignatius of Antioch at the beginning of the second century is the classic witness:[23] "Take care, then, to use one eucharist, for there is one flesh of our Lord Jesus Christ, and one cup of union in His blood, one altar just as there is one bishop together with the presbytery, and the deacons, my fellow servants . . ." (*Philadelphians* 4; cf. 6.2). ". . . All of you to a man . . . come together in one faith and in Jesus Christ . . . to show obedience to the bishop and presbytery with undivided mind, breaking one bread . . ." (*Ephesians* 20.2; cf. 5.1–3). ". . . Strive to do all things in harmony with God, with the bishop presiding in the place of God, the presbyters in the place of the council of the apostles, and the deacons . . . entrusted with the ministry of Jesus Christ. . . . Love one another at all times in Jesus Christ, let there be nothing among you that could divide you, but be united with the bishop and those presiding. . . . Just as the Lord did nothing without the Father, being one with Him . . . so neither should you undertake anything without the bishop or

[23] Having found the versions available to me inadequate, I give my own rendering from J. A. Fischer (ed.), *Die apostolischen Väter* (Munich 1956). For the most recent discussions of the Ignatian question, see J. Rius-Camps, *The Four Authentic Letters of Ignatius, the Martyr. A Critical Study based on Anomalies contained in the Textus Receptus* (XPICTIANICMOC 2, Rome 1979); R. Joly, *Le dossier d'Ignace d'Antioche* (Travaux de la Faculté de philosophie et lettres de l'Université de Bruxelles 69, Brussels 1979).

presbyters. Do not try to make anything private appear reasonable to you, but at your meetings [let there be] one prayer, one supplication, one mind, one hope in love, in the blameless joy that is Jesus Christ, above whom there is nothing. Come together all of you as to one temple of God and to one altar, to one Jesus Christ . . . (*Magn.* 6–7; cf. *Smyr.* 8).

Barnabus (*Ep.* 4.10) and Clement of Rome (*Ep.* 34.7) reflect the same concern.[24] But in this literature we see more than a continuation of the Pauline preoccupation with unity at Corinth. By the end of the first century a more articulate ministerial structure has emerged to serve this unity, and is reflected in the order of services. The presiding minister or "high priest" is joined in the celebration by other ministers. They are distinguished from the "layman" — the term first appears at this time[25] — by role and seating in the assembly. If such a system cannot yet be considered general, the *Letter of Clement* testifies to it at least for Rome and Corinth by around A.D. 96: "40.1. . . . We should do with order (*taxis*) all that the Master has prescribed to be accomplished at set times. 2. Now He ordered that the offerings (*prosphorai*) and public services (*leitourgiai*) be done not haphazardly or irregularly, but at fixed times and hours. 3. And He has himself determined by his supreme will where and by whom He desires this to be done. . . . 4. Thus those who make their offerings (*prosphorai*) at the appointed times are accepted and blessed. . . . 5. For the High Priest (*archiereus*) are assigned the services (*leitourgiai*) proper to him, and to the priests (*hiereis*) has been designated their proper place (*topos*), and on the levites [i.e., deacons] have been imposed their proper ministries (*diakoniai*). The lay person (*laikos anthropos*) is bound by the regulations for the laity. 41.1. Let each of us, brothers, be pleasing to God in his own order (*tagma*) . . . without infringing the prescribed rule of his service (*leitourgia*). . . ."[26]

Here we see at least an adumbration of the system that emerges in documents of the third century: presbyters other than the assembly president cannot be said to have participated in the services simply

[24] Barnabus, *Ep.* 4.10 *PG* 2, 733–734; Clément de Rome, *Epître aux corinthiens*, ed. A Jaubert (Sources chrétiennes 167, Paris 1971) 156.

[25] Our first witness is the text of Clement (40.5) cited below. Cf. I. de la Potterie, "L'origine et le sens primitif du mot 'laic'," *Nouvelle Revue Théologique* 80 (1958) 840–853.

[26] My translation from the edition of Jaubert, 166.

"as laity." They were not just "in attendance" at the service, albeit with "reserved seats"; they also performed liturgical actions.[27] But any attempt to interpret this participation as "concelebration" in the sense of consciously exercising in common some sort of sacramental "power" proper to their order, seems to go beyond the evidence. Rather, one gets the impression of a single common assembly at which each category of laity as well as clergy had its special place and role. Indeed, most sources say far more about the role of the deacons and people in the eucharistic celebration than they do about the role of the presbyters, yet no one would think of calling them "concelebrants" in the narrow, contemporary sense of the term!

Since the fourth century, Eastern evidence generally concurs that the full-blown Eucharist involved the bishop surrounded by his presbyters, who were not merely "in attendance" in the presbyterium but actively particpated in the ritual in a manner reserved to their order.[28] This is clear from canonical literature such as canon 1 of the Council of Ancyra (c. 314) or the *Second Canonical Letter* of Saint Basil (d. 379), which envisage the case of a presbyter under ecclesiastical sanction preserving his seat in the presbyterium while suspended from all ministerial functions, including the right to "offer" the

[27] Cf. *Apostolic Tradition* 4, ed. B. Botte, *La tradition apostolique de s. Hippolyte. Essai de reconstitution* (Liturgiewissenschaftliche Quellen und Forschungen 39, Münster 1963) 11; *Didascalia* II, 57, R. H. Connolly, *Didascalia apostolorum* (Oxford 1929) 119–120 = F. X. Funk, *Didascalia et Constitutiones apostolorum* (Paderborn 1905) I, 158–166.

[28] Cf. *Apostolic Constitutions* (late 4th c.) II, 57 and VIII, 11.12; 12.3-4, ed. Funk I, 159–165, II, 494, 496, and later related literature: *Didascalia arabica* 35, *ibid.* II, 124–125; *Ex constitutionibus capitula* 14, *ibid.* II, 139; *Constitutiones ecclesiae aegyptiacae* I (XXXI), 10, 31, *ibid.* II, 99, 102; Theodore of Mopsuestia (ca. 388–392), *Homily 15*, 42; *Hom. 16*, 24, ed. R. Tonneau and R. Devreesse, *Les homélies catéchétiques de Théodore de Mopsueste* (Studi e testi 145, Vatican 1949) 527, 569; the Synod of Mar Isaac (A.D. 410), J. Chabot, *Syndicon orientale* (Paris 1902) 268; *Testamentum domini nostri Iesu Christi* (5th c.) I, 23, ed. I. E. Rahmani (Mainz 1899) 34–36; Ps.-Denys (end 5th c.) *Ecclesiastical Hierarchy* 3, 2 *PG* 3, 425; Narsai (d. 502) *Homily 17, The Liturgical Homilies of Narsai*, trans. R. H. Connolly (Texts and Studies 8.1, Cambridge 1909) 4–5, 9, 27; the 6th c. *Ordo quo episcopus urbem inire debet*, ed. I. E. Rahmani (Studia Syriaca, fasc. 3, Charfeh 1908) 3–4 [22], trans. G. Khouri-Sarkis, "Réception d'un évêque syrien au VIe siècle, *L'Orient syrien* 2 (1957) 160–162, R. Taft, *The Great Entrance. A History of the Transfer of Gifts and other Preanaphoral Rites of the Liturgy of St. John Chrysostom* (Orientalia Christiana Analecta 200, Rome 1975) 40–41; Canon 11 of the Letter of Išo'yahb I to the Bishop of Darai (A.D. 585), Chabot, *Syndicon* 430; Gabriel Qatraya bar Lipah (ca. 615), ed. Jammo, *La messe chaldéene* 33ff; and the later sources adduced in Jammo, *passim*, and Taft, *Great Entrance* 166–168, 197–198, 201–206, 210–213, 264ff, 291–310.

Eucharist.[29] Here a clear line is drawn between presbyters in attendance at the Eucharist and those who "offer." But one cannot press the theological significance of this for concelebration. A similar situation was envisaged for laity in the final stages of penance: they were *sustantes*, allowed to "attend" the whole liturgy without, however, participating in the "offering."[30]

So it is not easy to know what theological meaning should be attached to such evidence without seeming to read history backwards. Where the evidence is clear, as in the Syrian traditions, it favors the conclusion that only the main celebrant "consecrated" the gifts.[31] But by then sacrificial theology is in bloom, and we find texts which say that concelebrating ministers of at least presbyteral rank "offer" (*prospherein, offerre*), even "as priests" (*hierourgein*) the common Eucharist.[32] Now though we must be wary of reading our later theological presuppositions into texts that seem to affirm what we hope to find, we must also avoid giving a minimalist interpretation to texts just because they do not meet modern Roman requirements for "true, sacramental" concelebration. The homilies of Theodore of Mopsuestia, for example, make it quite clear [1] that the concelebrants "offer" the Eucharist, [2] that this involves the exercise of a ministry proper to their order not shared with the laity, [3] that only the bishop says the eucharistic prayer.[33]

Two conclusions seem obvious: [1] From the fourth century we see a growing consciousness that presbyters celebrating the Eucharist together with the bishop are doing something that the

[29] Basil, *Ep. 199*, 27 *PG* 32, 724; Ancyra, canon 1, Mansi 2, 514 (cf. Neo-Caesarea, canon 9, *ibid.* 542).

[30] Basil, *Third Canonical Letter* (= *Ep. 217*, 56, 75, 77 *PG* 32, 797, 804–805).

[31] Theodore of Mopsuestia, see below, note 32; Narsai, *Homily 17*, in Connolly 4, 7ff, 12ff, 18ff, but esp. 27; Ps.-Denys, *Eccles. Hier.* 3 *PG* 3, 425; *Test. domini* I, 23, ed. Rahmani, 38ff.

[32] Council of Neocaesarea (ca. 315) canons 13–14, Mansi 2, 542–543; Theodore of Mopsuestia, *Hom. 15*, 42, ed. Tonneau-Devreesse, 527; the letter of Presbyter Uranius describing the Eucharist celebrated on his deathbed by Paulinus of Nola (d. 431) together with two visiting bishops Symmachus and Acindynus: ". . . una cum sanctis episcopis oblato sacrificio" (*Ep.* 2, *PL* 53, 860); Evagrius Scholasticus' account of the visit of Bishop Damnus of Antioch to Simon Stylites (d. 459) and the Eucharist they celebrated together: . . . *To achranton hierourgésantes sôma* . . ." (*Hist. eccl.* I, 13 *PG* 86², 2453).

[33] *Hom. 15 passim*, esp. 36, 41, 44, *Hom. 16*, preface and 2, 5–16, 20; ed. Tonneau-Devreesse, 517–519, 525, 529, 531–535, 537–559, 563.

laity cannot do, something only they have the mandate to perform. [2] This cannot be interpreted, without further evidence, to mean that they were "co-consecrating" verbally, that they recited in common the prayer of blessing of the gifts. Such a presumption would be anachronistic, based on the later identification in scholastic theology of the "essence" of the eucharistic sacrifice with the "consecration" of the gifts. This theory is coherent and may even be true. But it is not primitive, and that is the point at issue here.

G. Dix thought this growing consciousness that "concelebrating" presbyters "co-offer" the sacrifice with the bishop reflects the extension to presbyters of what had once been the preserve of bishops.[34] When the episcopal system of church order described by Ignatius of Antioch first appears on the scene, it seems that only the bishop presided over the eucharistic assembly, except when he would depute a presbyter to preside in his name over the assembly of some outlying community. But I would suggest that the origins of our "concelebration" are to be sought elsewhere, not in this expression of the *koinonia* of the local church, celebrated by the bishop together with the presbyters, deacons, deaconesses, widows, virgins, and so on, but rather in the "eucharistic hospitality" accorded visiting bishops as a sign of communion among sister churches. There are several clear historical instances of this in the case of visiting bishops or bishops in synod.[35] On the local level the same privilege was allowed "chorbishops" (i.e., suffragan, country bishops) by their superior, the town bishop.[36] It is precisely in the latter instance that we first see the term "concelebrants" (*sylleitourgoi*), and it is this that canon 13 of the Council of Neocaesarea (ca. 315) explicitly forbids to country presbyters.[37] But as it became more and more common for presbyters to be assigned the eucharistic presidency, perhaps a consciousness grew that even at the bishop's liturgy they too could

[34] *The Shape of the Liturgy* (London 1945) 34.

[35] Several examples in McGowan, *Concelebration*, 24ff, 40ff. But even in the earliest of such cases there is no evidence of "co-consecration," though the *episcopé* of the assembly was shared and this was called a "concelebration." Those texts that are clear on the matter seem to indicate that in such cases the guest bishop was "conceded" the blessing of the gifts. Cf. Eusebius, *Hist. eccles.* V, 24, 17, *Eusebius Werke* II, 1, ed. E. Schwartz (GCS, Leipzig 1903) 496 = *PG* 20, 508; *Didascalia* II, 58, ed. Funk I, 168 = Connolly 122.

[36] Neocaesarea, canon 14, Mansi 2, 542–543. "Chorbishop" is from the Greek *chôra* meaning "country" as opposed to town.

[37] *Loc. cit.*

"co-offer," just as visiting bishops were wont to do.

What is certain is that however it happened, this consciousness did indeed grow, to the extent that a few centuries later the Eastern "*sylleitourgein*" had become, for the Latins at least, "co-consecrate,"[38] and we are on the threshold of "concelebration" identified as the verbal co-consecration of the same eucharistic elements by more than one minister of at least presbyteral rank. In the West we find it in a seventh-century passage of *Ordo romanus III.*[39] Our earliest Eastern evidence is a rubric from a tenth-century Byzantine diataxis or rubric book incorporated into Leo Tuscan's version of the Chrysostom Liturgy.[40]

Interestingly enough, this latter text witnesses to another innovation previously unheard of: a eucharistic concelebration of *presbyters alone*, without the presidency of the bishop. Just what ecclesiology such a service is meant to represent has been questioned by the late Russian-Orthodox ecclesiologist N. Afanas'ev in his slender but valuable study, *The Lord's Table.*[41]

REFLECTIONS

The above evidence reveals at least this much: that there is no one "Eastern" tradition to turn to for support, nor, as both Jungmann and Dix showed a generation ago, can one simply presume that "Eastern" equals "ancient."[42] The presbyteral, co-consecratory concelebration practiced in most Eastern-Catholic traditions has nothing to do with ancient usage, but is derived from more recent developments and is colored by later scholastic sacramental theory of individual priestly sacrifice and the "special grace" (plus stipend) accru-

[38] Cf. the letter of Pope John VIII to Photius (A.D. 879), *Ep. 248 PL* 126, 871: "tecum . . . consecrare" = "*sylleitourgesai soi*" in the Greek version in Mansi 17¹, 413 B.

[39] III, 1, *Les "Ordines romani" du haut moyen-âge*, ed. M. Andrieu, vol. 2 (Spicilegium sacrum lovaniense. Études et documents, fasc. 23, Louvain 1960) 131. On the question of dating and on the inclusion of this text in *Ordo I*, cf. *ibid.* 127.

[40] Jacob, "Concélébration;" cf. Taft, *Great Entrance* 124ff.

[41] *Trapeza Gospodnja* (Paris 1952) 64ff. A. calls such a concelebration a "liturgical paradox," for the *raison d'être* of concelebration was to represent the unity of the local church: bishop, presbyters, deacons, people. Presbyters celebrated the Eucharist when sent to a part of the local community as representative of the bishop, but did not "concelebrate" with one another in the bishop's absence.

[42] J. A. Jungmann, "The Defeat of Teutonic Arianism and the Revolution in Religious Culture in the Early Middle Ages," in *Pastoral Liturgy* (New York 1962) 9–15; *The Place of Christ in Liturgical Prayer* (New York 1965) part 2 *passim*, Dix, *Shape* 264ff. In fact the Roman rite has preserved important primitive elements long obscured in the East.

ing therefrom. And this is what was instituted for the Roman rite at Vatican II. What *is* ancient about Eastern eucharistic practice is not its various modes of concelebration, some quite admirable, others less so, but its preservation, by and large, of the ancient ideal of eucharistic unity: one community, one altar, one Eucharist. This is the crux of the matter as I see it today: the Eucharist as sacrament of the *koinonia* that is the Church. This is the real issue and it is an ecclesiological one.

The Council Fathers, in restoring concelebration at Vatican II, were aware of this issue (*Orient. eccl.* 15; *Presbyt. ordinis* 7). But they were more concerned with the (for me) secondary question of concelebration as a manifestation of the unity of the ministerial priesthood (*Sacrosanctum concilium* 57). From that standpoint the restored rite must be declared a marked success. Catholic priests have learned once more to pray together. No longer are religious communities of priests faced with the supreme irony of a community prayer-life in which everything is done in common except the one thing Christ left them as *the* sacrament of their unity in him.

It was to such largely clerical concerns that much of the pre-Vatican II preparatory literature on concelebration was dedicated. Re-reading some of this material, I was struck by how totally foreign the concerns of these authors are from those of the present. Much of their discussion is focused on whether a presbyter who does not verbally co-consecrate can be said to "offer the sacrifice" by intending to "exercise his priestly power" in gesture and intention, through the voice of the main celebrant. Even Rahner's articles, among the most sane interventions in the whole pre-Vatican II debate, are overly concerned with the celebrant and what he gets out of it.[43]

I see the present crisis as a healthy sign that, having benefited immensely from the priestly unity in prayer fostered by the restored rite of concelebration, we are now ready for a broader perspective. Excessively narrow clerical concerns are now rejected as irrelevant, and the actual rite is more and more perceived as a celebration of division — no longer the eucharistic division among priests caused by the private mass, but the division of the community into those "celebrating" and those who "attend." I do not think that concelebration necessarily manifests *division* rather than the *hierarchic struc-*

[43] K. Rahner and A. Häussling, *The Celebration of the Eucharist* (New York 1968).

ture of the ecclesial community. But when one thinks of those top-heavy mob concelebrations that have become common coin; of the confusion of roles created by having the laity join the concelebrants around the altar for the anaphora and even recite it with them; or worse, when one suddenly sees a hand shoot out from the pews, and a priest attending mass with the faithful begins to mumble the words of institution — when one has been subjected to such aberrations, it is difficult not to share the growing malaise.

What we are dealing with here (in addition to plain ignorance and bad taste) is a conflict of two theologies. It is my own conviction that only a balanced theology of Church can be the guiding norm for the shape of our celebration, and not the "devotion" or desire or supposed "right" to "exercise one's priesthood" or to "offer sacrifice" or whatever of anyone, priest or otherwise. I think the basic problem in Roman Catholic liturgical theology has been the classic distinction between Eucharist *ut sacramentum* and Eucharist *ut sacrificium*, with the reduction of the former to a discussion of the "real presence," and the overwhelmingly predominant role until recently of the latter in the theology of the eucharistic celebration. As sacrifice, the Eucharist is effected by the priest in the consecration. Even if done privately, it is still said to be "public," offered, like the offering of Christ on the cross, for the salvation of the whole world. The mass is the sign of this offering, and as such shares its impetratory and satisfactory value. Further, the priest offers acting *in persona Christi*, and every priestly offering involves a "separate act" of Christ the High Priest (Pius XII).[44] Since this is true of five private masses, or of one verbal co-consecration by five priests, but *not* true (again, Piux XII[45]) of mass said by one priest with four others attending or only "ceremonially concelebrating," not "sacramentally," then the conclusion for Catholic priests formed in this theory is ineluctable: everybody should "co-consecrate." Helping to sustain this is the notion that somehow "more sacrifice," "more glory," is thus offered to God, and "more grace" acquired for the co-consecrator and those for whom he offers. For someone who believes that this is what the Eucharist is all about, I see no way around the problem.

We need to return to a saner theology, such as that of Saint Thomas Aquinas, who said that the fruit of the Eucharist is the unity

[44] *Magnificate dominum*, 2 November 1954, *AAS* 46 (1954) 668ff.
[45] *Loc. cit.*

of the Mystical Body of Christ (*ST* III, 82, 9, ad 2), and that "the Eucharist is the sacrament of the unity of the Church, which results from the fact that many are one in Christ" (*ST* III, 82, 2, ad 3). It was this *koinonia*, and it alone, that determined the shape of the Eucharist in the early Church.[46] One community, one table, one Eucharist was the universal rule. And it remains so still in much of the Christian East. A recovery of this vision is the only way out of the devotional narcissism prevalent in Latin priestly spirituality. What is important is that the gifts *be* blessed so that all may share them. Whether or not *I* am the presbyter that says the prayer of blessing is irrelevant: to do so is a ministry, not a prerogative.

It is this sacramental manifestation of ecclesial communion, more than the choreography of who stands where and says what, that is the substance of the matter as I see it, in function of which all the other issues are to be decided. In this, history can be instructive, but not determinative, for each generation manifests its own shifts in ecclesial consciousness with corresponding adjustments in the liturgical models by which this is expressed.

What history shows us is that the external shape of the eucharistic celebration changed according to what people thought the Church and its service were all about. When the Church was a somewhat amorphous society, the Eucharist had a less structured shape. As orders and structures emerge and harden, these quite naturally find expression in the assembly: elders and deacons have special places and ceremonial roles at the worship presided over by the bishop, and visiting ministers are invited to take the place befitting their rank. Those who today are distressed by the presence of numerous vested presbyters in the sanctuary will find little comfort in history!

But somewhere along the line a turn in the road is taken, and the service begins to appear less the common celebration of all, each according to his or her rank and role, and more and more that which is done *by* the ministers *for* the rest. From high priest (bishop) presiding over a whole priestly people as the model, we have shifted to high priest/priests (presbyters)/laity.[47] I suspect that the breakup of effective eucharistic unity through the fourth-century decline in communion and division of the community into several non-communicating categories (catechumens, *energoumenoi, illuminandi*,

[46] See L. Hertling, *Communio. Church and Papacy in Early Christianity* (Chicago 1972).

[47] Dix, *Shape*, 33ff; H.-M. Legrand, "The Presidency of the Eucharist according to the Ancient Tradition," *Worship* 53 (1979) 422.

penitents) were at the origins of this process. The Eucharist was no longer able to sustain an ideology of *koinonia* which the service in fact no longer expressed, so the ideology collapsed and the rite (ritual always outlasts theory) was forced to find ideological support elsewhere.[48]

This occurred in both East and West. The West alone, with that inexorable logical consistency with which it drives everything into the ground, took the next step of concluding (implicitly, at least) that the *laos* could be dispensed with, and private mass was off and running. But even before that, we see a growing consciousness that "concelebrating" ordained ministers "co-offer" the Eucharist in a way different from that in which the whole Church can be said to offer, a consciousness that eventually finds its liturgical expression in co-consecratory concelebration.

I doubt very much whether an *in persona Christi* theology of the eucharistic minister had anything to do with the origins of this practice in the East. But that is surely what keeps it alive in the Catholic Church today. What priest wants to give up the right to exercise this privileged role, especially when it is the basis for his whole priestly spirituality and devotion?

Let me stress that the above remarks are not to be construed as an attack on the theology of Eucharist as sacrifice. My concern is liturgical: whose sacrifice of what, offered by whom, for what purpose, and how expressed? Some years ago Aelred Tegels expressed where the answer to what should be the form of concelebration lies: "God is worshiped in the liturgy to the extent that the worshiping people are sanctified, and they are sanctified to the extent that 'conscious, active and full participiption' is procured. Liturgy is essentially pastoral. The ideal form of celebration is that which will most effectively associate this congregation, at this time and in this place, with Christ's own act of worship."[49] Before this norm all discussion of how this or that priest gets more or less devotion, how many "acts of Christ" or "sacrifices" are offered, who does or does not "exercise his priesthood," whether one or more "masses are said," becomes totally secondary.

But even if one were to prescind from all ecclesial and pastoral

[48] I discuss this in my forthcoming article, "The Liturgy of the Great Church: an Initial Synthesis of Structure and Interpretation on the Eve of Iconoclasm," to appear in *Dumbarton Oaks Papers* 34 (1980).

[49] "Chronicle," *Worship* 44 (1970) 183.

questions and simply accept the fact that Roman Catholic priests must "exercise their priesthood," one can hardly consider the present Roman rite of concelebration ideal from a liturgical point of view. According to the present discipline of the Roman Catholic Church, no presbyter can be said to "validly" concelebrate the Eucharist unless he recites the prayer of consecration, regardless of what else he might do in gesture or symbol to show that he clearly intends to participate in — that is, concelebrate — the eucharistic liturgy according to his presbyteral rank.

Even if one rejects the presuppositions of medieval Latin eucharistic and sacramental theology that have led to such a conclusion, one can hardly question the right of the Roman Church to determine the concrete praxis of her ministers in the discipline of concelebration. But to raise such particular disciplinary exigencies to the level of a universal dogmatic principle, and then apply it in judging the practice of other churches or other epochs, is an unjustifiable procedure. If we approach our early and Eastern sources with such presuppositions, we are forced either to conclude that no "real" concelebration ever existed in ancient christendom, or else to invent for the ancient period a new form of concelebration, never heard of then: "ceremonial" as opposed to "sacramental" concelebration, which is the only one held to be "real." To maintain that "verbal" concelebration is the only "real" one is also to question much of Eastern tradition.

In fact this whole problematic is foreign to a sane liturgical mentality, in which the whole body of presbyters is the moral subject of the common ministry performed by them *in solidum*. To demand that they all recite certain words together manifests an ignorance of the hierarchical and symbolic nature of sacrament expressed in presence and gesture and witness, as well as in word.[50] Concelebration even in the narrow clerical sense is the common act of a *collegium*, not the synchronization of the sum of the acts of several individuals. Hence even for one with purely "clerical" concerns, the present Roman rite of verbal co-consecration seems more a denial than a manifestation even of the collegial unity of the presbyterium.[51]

[50] Thus for centuries the three bishops that imposed hands at episcopal ordination were rightly considered true "co-consecrators." It would be a distortion of the whole tradition to consider them anything else, though only one said the formula of consecration. But since Pius XII all three co-consecrators have to recite the formula (*Episcopalis Consecrationis*, *AAS* 37 [1945] 131–132). Cf. McGowan, *Concelebration* 66–67.

[51] See the concluding remarks of B. Schultze, "Das theologische Problem der Konzelebration," *Gregorianum* 36 (1955) 268–271.

And for one with broader pastoral concerns for the liturgical expression of the unity of the whole Church-*koinonia* in the eucharistic rite, presbyteral concelebration in some of the forms presently in use leaves much to be desired as a symbol of our unity, and not of what separates us.

R. Kevin Seasoltz

Monastery and Eucharist: Some American Observations

In the past four centuries there has been a gradual change in the cultural context of Western theology from what has been called a classical culture to what is known as a scientific or contemporary culture. The former culture was preoccupied with the abstract, the ideal, the universal and the essential. Concerned with sameness and permanence, it did not attend to differences, process or development. In contrast, contemporary culture, influenced above all by the development of modern science, is preoccupied with probability, process and the particular. This shift has resulted in the dissolution of a common world of suppositions, principles and methods.[1]

Certainly this shift is reflected in the documents of the Second Vatican Council. The Constitution on the Church in the Modern World affirmed the principle of cultural pluralism as a fundamental ideal of the Church.[2] Other documents sanctioned a political shift in the structures of the Roman Catholic Church and the relationships among church members at every level.[3]

Although we are especially conscious of theological and structural pluralism in the Church today, the history of the Church shows that there have been various conceptual and organizational frameworks

[1] See Bernard Lonergan, "The Transition from a Classicist World-View to Historical-Mindedness," *Second Collection*, ed. William F. Ryan and Bernard J. Tyrell (Philadelphia: The Westminster Press 1974) 1–9; Edward Braxton, *The Wisdom Community* (New York: Paulist Press 1980) 28–39.

[2] Nos. 53–62: *AAS* 58 (1966) 1075–1084.

[3] See Aidan Kavanagh, "The Politics of Symbol and Art in Liturgical Expression," in *Symbol and Art in Worship*, ed. Luis Maldonado and David N. Power, *Concilium* 132 (2/1980) (New York: The Seabury Press 1980) 29.

used to articulate, interpret and implement the Christian faith.[4] Certainly in the New Testament itself there is a plurality of theologies proclaiming the one Christian faith. In our own day, theological pluralism results from various efforts to articulate the faith by drawing on the diverse contemporary self-understandings of human persons in order to help men and women grasp the gift of faith and appreciate it on deeper levels. Obviously the theological expression of one period is not always appropriate or helpful to another age or culture; consequently there is a continual need for critical reflection and reinterpretation. Each theological expression is apt to strike a certain emphasis not found in the others; this sometimes leads to misunderstanding, even to judgments that some theological positions are inappropriate or even unorthodox. Nevertheless, at root sound theological pluralism leads to an enrichment rather than to an impoverishment of Christian faith. However, it should be noted that there are within the Roman Church those who still espouse a classical culture. Although their lives are influenced in many ways by scientific culture, in the realm of religion they are adamantly opposed to changes in both technology and church practice. It is possible then that within the same Catholic community people operate out of starkly contrasting world views. Although they may be in geographic proximity to one another, it surely may not be said that they live in a world of common meanings.

These general observations are especially important in any discussion of the Eucharist, since eucharistic theology is an area where historically diverse explanations of the one faith have been prominent and where different aspects have received contrasting emphases.[5] The real presence, the relation of sacrifice to meal, the roles of the ordained ministers and of the community in eucharistic celebrations are all topics about which widely differing theological views have been proposed. Furthermore the same reality of the Eucharist has been expressed in theory and practice in different ways because of divergent human assumptions and expectations de-

[4] See Karl Rahner, "Pluralism in Theology and the Unity of the Creed in the Church," *Theological Investigations* 11, trans. David Bourke (New York: The Seabury Press 1974) 19–26; David Tracy, *Blessed Rage for Order: The New Pluralism in Theology* (New York: The Seabury Press 1975); Avery Dulles, *The Survival of Dogma* (Garden City, New York: Doubleday and Company 1971); Bernard Lonergan, *Method in Theology* (New York: Herder and Herder 1972).

[5] See Joseph M. Powers, *Eucharistic Theology* (New York: Herder and Herder 1967) 11–47; Edward Schillebeeckx, *The Eucharist* (New York: Sheed and Ward 1968).

pendent on the age, cultural background, education, or emotional needs and responses of the participants. Obviously these differences, whether the theological or cultural, create problems of understanding, communication and mutual acceptance.

It should be noted too that those who follow the Rule of Benedict in this country have roots in a variety of monastic traditions. Many are heir to the traditions of Abbot Boniface Wimmer[6] and Mother Benedicta Riepp,[7] but many others are heir to vastly different traditions. As a result there have been and there still are diverse eucharistic theologies and practices in American monasteries.

Against that background, the object of this article is to set out briefly the history of the Eucharist in monastic life lived according to the Rule of Benedict and then to highlight some of the strengths and weaknesses of eucharistic theology and practice in American monastic communities today.

MONASTIC HISTORY AND THE EUCHARIST

At the start it should be stressed that there is no one monastic tradition, no one Benedictine tradition concerning the Eucharist. Hence history in this regard can be instructive but it is not necessarily determinative or normative, since each generation of Benedictines has manifested its own shifts in ecclesial and monastic consciousness with corresponding adjustments in the liturgical, and specifically eucharistic forms by which this consciousness is expressed. Benedict himself was undoubtedly heir to a variety of eucharistic traditions. Certainly there were various monastic movements in the fourth century, some of which were cenobitic, others eremitical; some were centered in urban areas, others in the country; some were what we would call ecclesial, others were more marginal. In short, monasticism was a highly diversified institution manifesting itself in a plurality of doctrines, organizational structures, and liturgical practices. Just as there was no single liturgical orientation common to all fourth-century monastic movements, so there was no uniform eucharistic practice.[8]

[6] See Jerome Oetgen, *An American Abbot: Boniface Wimmer* (Latrobe, Pa.: Archabbey Press 1976).

[7] See Grace McDonald, *With Lamps Burning* (St. Joseph, Minn.: St. Benedict's Priory Press 1957).

[8] See Rudolf Lorenz, "Die Anfänge des abendländischen Mönchtums im 4. Jahrhundert," *Zeitschrift Für Kirchengschichte* 77 (1966) 1–61; Armand Vellieux, *La Liturgie dans le Cénobitisme Pachômien au Quatrième Siècle:* Studia Anselmiana 57 *(Rome: Herder 1968).*

Adalbert de Vogüé has suggested that in the early period of Christian monasticism ascetics, both men and women, probably related to the Eucharist in one of three ways: [1] They could have taken part in the weekly celebration of the Eucharist by the local Christian community. This practice was probably the one adopted by the early Pachomian monastic communities and also by the nuns gathered around Paula at Bethlehem. [2] The monastic communities could have brought in ordained ministers to celebrate the Eucharist within the confines of the monastery. [3] The monastic communities could have taken part in a Eucharist celebrated by one of their own members who had been ordained a priest.[9]

The three possibilities set forth by de Vogüé provide a convenient context for analyzing the material on both the Eucharist and the ordained ministry found in the Rule of the Master and the Rule of Benedict. In chapter 62, the Rule of Benedict states that "If any abbot wish to have a priest or deacon ordained for his monastery, let him select one of his subjects who is worthy to exercise the priestly office." In chapter 60, however, there seems to be a reluctance to admit those who have already been ordained to the monastic community: "If anyone of the priestly order ask to be received into the monastery, permission shall not be granted too readily." In spite of Benedict's different approaches to ordaining one of the monks and receiving as a monk one who has already been ordained, his teaching stands in marked contrast to what is contained in the Rule of the Master. There in chapter 83 we read: "Priests are to be considered outsiders in the monastery, especially those who retain and exercise their presidency and preferment in churches. If their choice is to live in monasteries for the love of God and for the sake of discipline and the pattern of a holy life, even so it is only in name that they are called fathers of the monastery, and nothing is to be permitted them in the monasteries other than praying the collects, saying the conclusion, and giving the blessing."[10] In the Rule of the Master, the abbot himself is identified as a layman;[11] nothing is said

[9] *La Communauté et l'Abbé dans la Règle de saint Benoît* (Paris: Descleé de Brouwer 1961) 327–347; *La Règle de saint Benoît*, t. I (Paris: Cerf 1972) 104–113. This material is summarized in "Le Prêtre et la Communauté monastique dans l'Antiquité," *La Maison-Dieu* no. 115 (1973) 62–65. Some additional information is provided in "Scholies sur la Règle du Maître," *Revue d'Ascétique et de Mystique* 44 (1968) 122–127.

[10] *The Rule of the Master*, trans. Luke Eberle; introduction by Adalbert de Vogüé, trans. Charles Philippi (Kalamazoo, Mich.: Cistercian Publications 1977) 248–249.

[11] *Ibid.*

about the decision to have one of his monks ordained a priest.

Although the Master seems to be opposed to the presence of priests in the monastery, he did make provision for his monks to receive communion under both kinds every day.[12] This communion service was not the celebration of the Eucharist; it was presided over by the abbot, a layman not a priest, and it took place in the oratory before the daily meal. De Vogüé maintains that the Master's monks probably went to the parish church for the Sunday celebration of the Eucharist presided over by the diocesan clergy.[13] There are only two specific occasions noted in the Master's Rule when the Eucharist was celebrated in the monastic oratory: on the occasion of the blessing of a new abbot,[14] and on the patronal feast of the saint to whom the oratory was dedicated.[15]

In short, the Master indicates three occasions when the community either receives or celebrates the Eucharist: [1] There is a daily communion rite held in the oratory. The abbot, a layman, presides. The monks receive communion under both kinds. [2] The Eucharist is celebrated on the occasion of the abbot's election.[3] The Eucharist is celebrated on the occasion of the patronal feast of the oratory. A priest from outside the community would have presided whenever the Eucharist was celebrated. The monks may have taken part in the weekly celebration of the Eucharist held on Sunday in the parish church, but there is no explicit mention of this practice in the Rule of the Master.

In the so-called "liturgical code" of the Rule of Benedict (chapters 8–20), there is no explicit mention of the celebration of the Eucharist. The term *missa* appears a number of times in the code — and elsewhere in the Rule — but it generally means the concluding part of the rite or the dismissal. These texts have been carefully analyzed by contemporary scholars; their general conclusion is that we have little certain knowledge of eucharistic practice in the Rule of Benedict.[16] De Vogüé, for example, concludes that "At most it is possible that a conventual Mass in St. Benedict's monastery was celebrated on Sun-

[12] Ch. 21, *ibid.* 171–172.

[13] *Ibid.* 33.

[14] Ch. 93, *ibid.* 276.

[15] Ch. 45, *ibid.* 204.

[16] See Angelus Häussling, *Mönchskonvent und Eucharistiefeier* (Münster: Aschendorffsche Verlagsbuchhandlung 1973) 19–21; B. Steidle, "'Missae' in der Regel St. Benedikts," *Benediktinische Monatsschrift* 28 (1952) 456–461.

days and feast days. But perhaps Mass was celebrated less often, even without fixed regularity."[17]

There may have been a daily communion service in Benedict's monastery, but unlike the Master, Benedict provides us with no description of the rite. Although Benedict was most probably familiar with the practice of monks attending the Sunday Eucharist, there is no clear evidence that it was celebrated in the monastery nor that the monks went to the local parish. In chapter 35, Benedict does mention the solemn days when the server at table should fast *usque ad missas*; likewise in chapter 38, he notes that the weekly table reader should ask for prayers *post missas et communionem*. It is most likely that both of these texts refer to the celebration of the Eucharist, but they do not yield any clear evidence of eucharistic practice. Possibly Benedict was not very specific in his comments about the Eucharist because he did in fact make provision for the ordination of one of his monks as a priest; hence his community would not have been so dependent on priests from outside the monastery for the celebration of the Eucharist. It is quite probable, then, that given the abbot's freedom to have or not to have one of his monks ordained, there was diversity of practice in early Benedictine communities concerning the reception and celebration of the Eucharist. Our information concerning early monastic communities of women and their relation to the Eucharist is also scant. The *Lausiac History of Palladius* notes that in some Pachomian monasteries of women, priests and deacons came to the monastery on Sundays for the celebration of the Eucharist.[18] In sixth-century Gaul, communities of women living according to Caesarius of Arles' Rule for Nuns must have observed a similar practice. The rule stresses that no man may enter any part of the enclosure "except the bishop, the provisor and priest, the deacon and the subdeacon, and one or two lectors whose age and life commend them, and who are needed to offer Mass sometimes."[19] In place of the celebration of the Eucharist on Sundays, some communities of women may have just received communion on Sundays. One might come to that conclusion in light of

[17] "Problems of the Monastic Conventual Mass," *Downside Review* 87 (1969) 328.

[18] *Palladius: The Lausiac History*, trans. and annotated by Robert T. Meyer (Westminster, Md.: The Newman Press 1965) 95.

[19] *The Rule for Nuns of St. Caesarius of Arles: A Translation with Critical Introduction* by Mother Maria Caritas McCarthy (Washington: The Catholic University of America Press 1960) 182–183.

the Rule of Aurelian of Arles. According to that document, generally thought to be contemporary with the Rule of Benedict, Mass was celebrated when the abbess thought it appropriate.[20]

This brief survey indicates that in monasteries of both men and women before and during the time of Benedict, there was most probably no daily celebration of the Eucharist. Daily communion was the practice in some monasteries, but not necessarily all. A Sunday celebration of the Eucharist either in the monastery or at the parish church seems to have been quite common, but it was not necessarily the practice in all monasteries of the West. A daily communion rite would not have required the ministry of a priest or deacon, even in communities of women. Certainly the *Apostolic Tradition* of Hippolytus indicates that it was customary for Christians to take the Eucharist home with them after Sunday Mass in order that they might communicate themselves in the course of the week.[21] That Roman document would have set forth a precedent for the daily communion rite described in the Rule of the Master. It is possible that such a daily rite prevailed in the monasteries that followed Benedict's Rule. What is clear is that daily celebration of the Eucharist was not the norm.

It should be noted here that sacramental theology in the West is something that has undergone extensive development since the time of both the Master and Benedict. This theological development has in turn influenced sacramental practice; shifts in practice have also influenced the theology. Although the monks of the first seven centuries generally did not distinguish themselves in their eucharistic piety and practice from other Christians in their neighborhood, the situation changed remarkably in the next few centuries. By the eleventh century, many monks were ordained priests, and daily Mass was considered normal in the monasteries. In fact many Masses were usually celebrated each day. In addition to the Masses celebrated by individual priests in what we would probably denote a "private" fashion, there was the *missa matutinalis*, the *missa maior*, and sometimes a *missa in suffragio*. Gregory III, Alcuin, Benedict of Aniane, Adalhard of Corbie and Angilbert of Centula would have all been familiar with the multiplication of daily Masses in the monas-

[20] *Regula ad Virgines*, *PL* 68:406B: "Missae vero quando sanctae abbatissae visum fuerit tunc fient."

[21] *La Tradition Apostolique: Texte Latin, Introduction, Traduction et Notes* by Dom B. Botte (Paris: Cerf 1946) 66–67.

teries of the eighth and ninth centuries. Certainly by the time of the Carolingian and Cluniac reforms, the Eucharist played a key note in the spiritual orientation of Benedictine communities.[22] The *Regularis Concordia*, a tenth-century English document formulated under Dunstan, speaks of two community Masses celebrated daily, one after terce and the other after sext.[23]

The practice of celebrating several conventual Masses and allowing all priest-monks to celebrate Mass daily was not due only to subjective eucharistic piety but was also the result of an effort to replicate in the monasteries the solemn liturgy as it was celebrated in Rome. The local church gathered in an abbey was thought to parallel the local church of the diocese, especially the diocese of Rome. Just as there were various daily celebrations in Rome at the numerous titular churches and sanctuaries, so it was thought desirable to have many daily eucharistic celebrations in each monastery in order that the liturgy might be as solemn as possible. Such a liturgy obviously called for a great number of priests; therefore many monks were in fact ordained.[24] It should be observed also that the practice of daily communion by the whole community seems to have declined by the tenth century, since the *Regularis Concordia* makes a point of encouraging the monks to receive communion daily.[25]

We see then that within four centuries after the composition of the Rule of Benedict the eucharistic orientation of various Western monastic communities had undergone extensive modifications. In place of daily communion rites and the Sunday celebration of the

[22] Häussling (n. 16 above) 32–72.

[23] *Regularis Concordia: The Monastic Agreement of the Monks and Nuns of the English Nation*, translated with introduction and notes by Thomas Symons (New York: Oxford University Press 1953) 16, 21. In summer the morning Mass was celebrated after prime and the principal Mass was celebrated after terce: *ibid.* 54. See also *Tenth-Century Studies: Essays in Commemoration of the Millennium of the Council of Winchester and Regularis Concordia*, edited with an introduction by David Parsons (London: Phillimore and Co. 1975), esp. the essays by D. H. Farmer, "The Progress of Monastic Revival," 10–19; and Thomas Symons, "'Regularis Concordia': History and Derivation," 37–59.

[24] Häussling, 298–347. This position is different from that held by Otto Nussbaum and others who maintain that subjective piety was the primary reason for multiplying Masses in monasteries: *Kloster, Priestermönch und Privatmesse* (Bonn: Hanstein Verlag 1961).

[25] *Op. cit.* 19.

Eucharist, there were daily Masses celebrated by the priest-monks and communion received occasionally by the other monks. This shift in eucharistic practice was accompanied by major modifications in the celebration of the Opus Dei.[26]

The abstention from holy communion and the multiplication of Masses certainly occasioned the development of eucharistic devotions that were wholly unknown in the early centuries of both the Church and Benedictine communities in the Church.[27] As a reaction to the eleventh-century Berengarian teaching with regard to the mode of Christ's presence in the Eucharist, there tended to be an upsurge of eucharistic devotion which gathered impetus through the centuries and which has declined only in recent decades.[28]

The increasingly widespread abstention from communion on grounds of unworthiness and reverence prompted people to seek devotional compensation by adoration of the divinity of Christ present in the eucharistic species. This was reinforced during the twelfth and thirteenth centuries by the practice of elevating the host immediately after the consecration.[29] Popular devotion tended to focus on that moment; in general special importance was placed on seeing the host.

The eucharistic rites of Holy Thursday were enhanced throughout the late Middle Ages.[30] In 1264 the feast of Corpus Christi, originally established as a local feast at Liège in 1246, was approved for the universal Church.[31] A procession with the blessed sacrament soon became a feature of the new feast, and the blessing with which the procession concluded was subsequently attached to other exercises of piety, such as the *Salve Regina* in honor of Our Lady.[32] Exposition

[26] See Josef A. Jungmann, *Christian Prayer through the Centuries* (New York: Paulist Press 1978) 58–95

[27] Jean Leclercq, François Vandenbroucke and Louis Bouyer, *The Spirituality of the Middle Ages* (London: Burns and Oates 1968) 243–248.

[28] See J. de Montclos, *Lanfranc et Bérenger: La controverse eucharistique du xiᵉ siècle* (Louvain: Spicilegium Sacrum Lovaniense 1971), esp. 3–245; Burkhard Neunheuser, *Eucharistie in Mittelalter und Neuzeit* (Freiburg: Herder 1963) 11–24.

[29] J. Jungmann, *The Mass of the Roman Rite* 2 (New York: Benziger Brothers 1955) 205–212.

[30] J. Kettel, "Zur Liturgie des Gründonnerstags," *Liturgisches Jahrbuch* 3 (1953) 60–74. Jungmann, "Die Andacht der vierzig Stunden und das heilige Grab," *Liturgisches Jahrbuch* 2 (1952) 184–198.

[31] P. Browne, "Die Ausbreitung des Fronleichnamsfestes," *Jahrbuch für Liturgiewissenschaft* 8 (1928) 107–144.

[32] J. B. O'Connell, "Benediction," *Clergy Review* 57 (1972) 452.

of the host for some time outside Mass was introduced in the fourteenth century.[33] In 1527 at Milan the forty hours devotion was introduced.[34]

Efforts to communicate a balanced sacramental theology in general and eucharistic theology in particular were made in the thirteenth, fourteenth and fifteenth centuries,[35] but as often happens, imbalances were corrected by other imbalances. The end result was the Protestant Reformation and the Council of Trent.[36] Instead of presenting the Tridentine teaching as a response to very specific issues raised by the Reformers and as an assertion of that minimum required for the validity of the sacraments, traditional Roman Catholic manuals of theology, developed after the Council of Trent and used regularly in the education of seminarians including monastic clerics, reproduced the Tridentine teaching as though it constituted an all-embracing treatment of sacramental theology.[37] In rejecting the inadequacy of the theology of the Reformers, Roman Catholic teachers of theology often espoused inadequate theologies, especially in their treatment of the sacraments, including the Eucharist.[38]

Some examples might clarify these assertions. The Reformers began by attacking abuses. They objected to the use of the Eucharist as a means to ward off evil, but then they went to the extreme of describing adoration of the Eucharist as idolatry of a piece of bread. They sought to restore the early Christian character of the Mass as a meal but they went to the extreme of maintaining that there was no eucharistic presence outside of the meal. Likewise, they insisted so strongly on the uniqueness of Christ's sacrifice in the order of history that they ended up denying the presence of Christ's sacrifice in the order of symbol. They wanted to affirm that an act that took

[33] Herbert Thurston, "Benediction of the Blessed Sacrament: Part 2, Exposition," *The Month* 98 (1901) 58–69; "Exposition of the Blessed Sacrament," *The Month* 99 (1902) 537–540.

[34] J. Jungmann, "Forty Hours Devotion and the Holy Sepulchre," *Pastoral Liturgy* (New York: Herder and Herder 1962) 223–238.

[35] See Neunheuser (n. 28 above) 24–51.

[36] See Reinold Theisen, *Mass Liturgy and the Council of Trent* (Collegeville, Minn.: St. John's University Press 1965).

[37] Powers (n. 5 above) 31–43.

[38] Louis Bouyer, *Liturgical Piety* (Notre Dame: University of Notre Dame Press 1954) 1–9, 38–56. For an understanding of Church and priestly ministry during this period see J. D. Crichton, "Church and Ministry from the Council of Trent to the First Vatican Council," in *The Christian Priesthood*, ed. Nicholas Lash and Joseph Rhymer (London: Darton, Longman and Todd 1970) 117–139.

place once in history could not be repeated as the same historical act, but they went on to deny the symbolic representation of the sacrifice in the Mass. In other words, the truth of the ultimate reality of Christ's presence was retained by the Reformers at the price of denying his proximate presence in and through symbol.[39]

The Fathers of Trent rejected the Reformers' belief in Christ's presence "in sign and figure only" but unfortunately the result of their reaction to the Protestant teaching was an inadequate understanding of the real nature of sacramentality on the part of post-Tridentine Catholics.[40] Furthermore the failure of the Council of Trent to implement positive liturgical reforms such as use of the vernacular and communion under both kinds — reforms which were in fact supported by some of the council fathers — was most unfortunate. The Tridentine settlement left Catholics with a concise statement concerning the real presence of Christ under the species of bread and wine, but the Council said nothing about the further real presences of Christ with which the Reformers were so preoccupied, namely, his presence in the word, in individual persons, and in communities. It was left to the Second Vatican Council to reaffirm those modes of presence.[41] It should be noted here that the latter modes of divine presence were in fact the very modes that Benedict stressed in his Rule. They are also the modes of divine presence that post-Reformation monastic communities following Benedict's Rule tended to forget in favor of his presence in the eucharistic species.

It is interesting to observe in the light of this history that when Benedictine monasteries of men were revived throughout Europe in the nineteenth century, the leaders and the recruits were often diocesan priests. Prosper Guéranger, the founder of Solesmes, had been a priest-secretary to an aged archbishop; Maurus and Placid Wolter, the founders of the Beuronese Congregation, were also diocesan priests.[42] In Bavaria where there was a superfluity to diocesan priests, the bishop of Regensburg encouraged them to join the new monastic houses.[43] This naturally gave a strong clerical charac-

[39] Gerard Sloyan, "Debate on the Eucharist," *Commonweal* 84 (17 June 1966) 359. See also Theisen (n. 36 above) 29–113; Schillebeeckx (n. 5 above) 25–86.

[40] Sloyan, *op. cit.* 360.

[41] Constitution *Sacrosanctum Concilium* on the Sacred Liturgy 7: *AAS* 56 (1964) 100–101.

[42] Daniel Rees, "Benedictine Revival in the Nineteenth Century," in *Benedict's Disciples*, ed. D. H. Farmer (Leominster: Fowler Wright Books 1980) 290–293.

[43] *Ibid.* 287.

ter to Benedictine houses of men. Many of the monasteries were deeply involved in pastoral work, providing the Mass and sacraments for the faithful. The French and Beuronese Congregations, however, deliberately sought to differentiate themselves from the Swiss, Bavarian, and Austrian Congregations by maintaining a more rigorous monastic observance and stricter adherence to enclosure. Nevertheless, both of these congregations took on special pastoral work such as giving retreats and parish missions.[44] At the time both of these ministries required ordination to the priesthood.

One of the primary goals of the seventeenth-century monks who refounded the English Congregation was the conversion of England.[45] To achieve this end monk-priests were sent to England as individuals in order to celebrate Mass and to instruct the people. All of the monks took an oath acknowledging their willingness to serve on the English missions. Those who died as martyrs were honored because of their priestly work.[46] In this they were looked upon as descendants of St. Augustine of Canterbury and his missionary monks who first brought the Christian faith to the Anglo-Saxon countries.[47]

When the Benedictine communities moved back to England in the last century, they opened schools which were generally conducted by the very young monks who were also preparing for ordination to the priesthood. When these monks were called to serve on the missions they were withdrawn from the jurisdiction of their local superiors and subjected to the congregational authorities responsible for administering the missions. The strong clerical character of the Congregation, which has prevailed to the present time, resulted in deep involvement of the monks in the life of the Catholic Church in England. From its ranks in the last hundred years have come many distinguished priests and bishops.[48]

The German and Swiss monks who came to the United States in the last century were also keen missionaries. Boniface Wimmer sought to minister to German Catholic immigrants by founding rural Benedictine monasteries which could set up extensive mission sta-

[44] *Ibid.* 295.

[45] *Consider Your Call: A Theology of Monastic Life Today*, ed. Daniel Rees (London: SPCK 1978; Kalamazoo, Mich.: Cistercian Publications 1980) 339–341.

[46] Geoffrey Scott, "Three Seventeenth-Century Benedictine Martyrs: John Roberts, Alban Roe and Ambrose Barlow," in *Benedict's Disciples* 246–262.

[47] *Consider Your Call* 340.

[48] Rees (n. 42 above) 302–304.

tions and also schools for the training of future priests. Wimmer himself had to struggle for an activist missionary interpretation of Benedictine monasticism against the frequent objections of his confreres who sought a stricter observance and greater fidelity to enclosure. Frontier bishops petitioned him to open houses in their dioceses with the result that a chain of monasteries spread across the States. There is no doubt that Wimmer left his mark on American Benedictinism. His foundations were established on a large scale; they were outward-looking and quite diversified in their operations. Nevertheless much of the work presupposed that many of the monks were ordained to the priesthood.[49]

The Swiss foundations in Indiana and Missouri were less flamboyant. Although their observance was stricter than that in Wimmer's houses, they too got deeply involved in parochial work and also in the training of diocesan priests.[50]

The Benedictine houses of women which were restored in Europe in the last century were enclosed communities under solemn vows. Their observance was both deeply monastic and rigorous.[51] When foundations were made in the United States, however, strict enclosure was rendered impossible both because of the nature of the buildings in which the women lived and also because of the work which was imposed on them by American bishops. As a result these women were not allowed to take solemn vows; consequently they became sisters rather than nuns.[52] It should be noted that their lifestyle was really no different from that of the monks who were nevertheless allowed to take solemn monastic vows. In many ways, the monasteries of women were basic training centers from which numerous Sisters went forth to work in schools, hospitals and parishes. Their monastic formation was often minimal and was presumed to take place automatically by reason of their subjection to the demands of observance placed on them by their vows and the demands of hard work placed on them by priests and bishops, some of whom were Benedictines.[53]

[49] *Ibid.* 287–289. See also Oetgen (n. 6 above).

[50] Rees, *art. cit.* 289.

[51] *Ibid.* 295 See also Benedictines of Stanbrook, *In a Great Tradition* (London: John Murray 1956).

[52] See Mary Collins, "I Fail to See the Logic of This Approach," in *Climb along the Cutting Edge* by Joan Chittister and others (New York: Paulist Press 1977) 73–75, 290–291.

[53] See McDonald (n. 7 above) 1–55; also Regina Baska, *The Benedictine Congregation of*

Certainly there are a number of important Benedictine monasteries in this country which have roots different from those described above; nevertheless it is accurate to say that those Benedictines, both men and women, who came to the United States in the nineteenth century and the decades of the twentieth century preceding the Second Vatican Council generally brought with them a eucharistic theology and eucharistic practices that were decidedly different from what would have prevailed at the time of Benedict. They also had a very different understanding of the role of priests both within the monastery and in the Church at large. Although certain theologians in the early decades of this century, including the Benedictines Lambert Beauduin,[54] Odo Casel,[55] Virgil Michel,[56] Anscar Vonier,[57] and Columba Marmion,[58] tried to restore a balanced eucharistic theology, their work had limited effect in counteracting the eucharistic piety that was instilled in the minds and hearts of most Benedictines. That critical transformation was left to the Second Vatican Council.

The pre-Vatican II eucharistic piety which prevailed in houses of both monastic men and women expressed itself in a number of practices and attitudes. First of all, daily Mass was considered normal; in fact it was generally obligatory for all. However, in the nineteenth century daily communion was considered unusual for all those who were not priests. That attitude prevailed into the twentieth century and only gradually disappeared with the implementation of St. Pius X's decrees on frequent communion and the admission of children to the sacrament.[59]

Secondly, in many American Benedictine houses, especially those of monks, during the nineteenth century and even up to the time of the Second Vatican Council, communion was not regularly received

St. Scholastica: Its Foundation and Development: 1880–1930 (Washington: The Catholic University of America 1935).

[54] *Mélanges Liturgiques* (Louvain: Abbaye du Mont César 1954), esp. "La liturgie eucharistique au Concile de Trente," 201–227.

[55] *Das christliche Kultmysterium* (Regensburg: Verlag Friedrich Pustet 1932).

[56] *The Liturgy of the Church according to the Roman Rite* (New York: The Macmillan Co. 1937); *My Sacrifice and Yours* (Collegeville, Minn.: The Liturgical Press 1927).

[57] *A Key to the Doctrine of the Eucharist* (London: Burns Oates and Washbourne 1925).

[58] *Christ the Life of the Soul,* trans. Mother M. St. Thomas (St. Louis: B. Herder 1922), esp. 238–282; *Christ the Life of the Priest*, trans. Matthew Dillon (St. Louis: B. Herder 1952), esp. 209–223.

[59] *Sacra Tridentina Synodus*: *ASS* 38 (1905) 400–406; *Quam singulari*: *ASS* 2 (1910) 577–583.

at the conventual Mass but rather at an earlier Mass celebrated specifically as a communion Mass or at the individual Masses celebrated by the monk-priests in the monastery. This was partly due to fasting regulations and the monastic horarium which set the time for breakfast before the time for conventual Mass, but it also reflected the general practice in this country and other parts of the world whereby the faithful regularly did not communicate at special Masses such as the Sunday High Mass in parish churches or at funerals and weddings.

Thirdly, most American Benedictines have had a strong commitment to devotional practices associated with adoration of the Eucharist apart from Mass. Since the Second Vatican Council, however, some communities have set aside practices such as benediction, exposition, forty hours devotion, and eucharistic processions. This recent shift in eucharistic orientation has often occasioned pain and division in monastic houses.

STRENGTHS AND WEAKNESSES OF THE TRADITIONS

In assessing the strengths and weaknesses of our Benedictine traditions, one must keep in mind that St. Benedict's general spiritual teaching delineates a distinctive way of responding to the word of God, but just as organic development has occurred in the understanding and articulation of Christian revelation throughout the centuries, so also organic development has taken place in both Benedictine spiritual teaching and practice.[60] Nevertheless, Benedictines today are quite conscious that the author of their rule was quite reticent about a number of issues which are of special importance in the life of the Church today. These issues include the positive value of virginity and human sexuality and the place of pleasure and leisure in the equilibrium of Christian life. As already noted, Benedict was especially reticent about the Eucharist, which is now acknowledged to be of key importance in the life of all Christians, and consequently of all Benedictines.[61]

Benedictines, however, make their profession not only under the Rule but also under an abbot. In a sense the Rule and the abbot are

[60] The author wishes to acknowledge his dependence in the last part of the article on various discussions of the monastic theology commission of the English Benedictine Congregation.

[61] See *Sacrosanctum Concilium* 2, 41, 47: *AAS* 56 (1964) 97–98, 111, 113; *Eucharisticum mysterium* 59 (1967) 539.

meant to complement one another; what the first lacks the other should provide, although the abbot himself is always subject to the Rule.[62] Because it is not developed in the Rule, the area of eucharistic theology and practice is one where the superiors of contemporary monasteries should exercise strong, creative leadership. They have the responsibility to provide initiative, illumination, education and direction in the area of eucharistic theology, either through their own conferences and homilies or through lectures and courses given by others.[63] But illumination and education are not enough. They must strive to bring their communities to a consensus concerning the dominant eucharistic orientation and the various practices that flow from that orientation. In this regard there is room for a plurality of theologies and practices; what prevails in one congregation or community need not prevail in another. However, without consensus, what is meant to be a source of unity and peace in a community is apt to be a cause of deep division and pain.

The theological and cultural differences which shape the eucharistic orientations of monastic communities do not only have a theological or speculative significance; they manifest themselves in the actual celebrations of the Eucharist in such matters as the style and frequency of celebration and in various eucharistic devotions; hence the actual liturgical celebrations can create very real tensions in a community. The recent liturgical reforms have occasioned such diversity of practice and understanding of the Eucharist within many communities that the concrete celebration of this mystery actually frustrates and contradicts its sacramental or symbolic power to create unity. At the present time, then, it might well happen that the members of a community operate out of such different world views and espouse such different theologies that consensus about eucharistic practice is not possible. Most likely this will happen in other areas of community life too. In that case the abbot's responsibility in justice is for all the members of the community, not simply for those who happen to espouse his particular theological outlook or for those who constitute a majority in the community.[64] This is where his creative leadership should intervene, possibly in establishing small communities or making foundations so that the Eucharist will

[62] RB ch. 2.

[63] *Consider Your Call* 91–92.

[64] RB ch. 2.

be a source of life and peace not only for some of his monks but for all.

As we have already seen, a number of complicated factors have shaped the eucharistic orientations of Benedictine communities in this country. Many, but certainly not all, of the communities here have been since their foundation deeply involved in the broader pastoral work of the Church in America. They have been conscious of their pastoral responsibility because of their missionary, educational and parochial work. Their eucharistic orientation and practices then have regularly been situated within the broader context of pastoral ministry. It has sometimes been lamented that such involvement has prevented many American Benedictines from being faithful to their primary vocation to live according to the Rule which prescribes life in common, solitude, holy reading, asceticism, and the celebration of the liturgy of the hours. At times this has undoubtedly been the case; however, it should be noted that the pastoral work of many Benedictines has in fact helped them remember that the Eucharist is not the possession of a clerical or religious elite but is meant to be the celebration of all of God's people in Christ. Certainly all Benedictine communities should establish monastic priorities and see that in practice those priorities are primary and central. But there will always be tensions between monastic and professional or pastoral responsibilities, between work and prayer. The challenge is to keep those tensions poised and to see that they are conducive to monastic growth rather than decline.[65] The statements issued in the last few years by the Conference of American Benedictine Prioresses, especially those on prayer and stewardship, reflect sound and realistic efforts to remain faithful Benedictines and to be responsible to the contemporary Church and world.[66] Experience often teaches us that what seems ideal in theory is not always ideal in practice because of our histories, our past formation, our resources, and our long-term commitments. Communities are not always free to leave behind commitments in the Church that their predecessors have made on their behalf.[67]

As we have seen, the eucharistic orientation of communities of

[65] *Consider Your Call* 310–312.

[66] *Of Time Made Holy* (Erie: Benet Arts 1978); *Of All Good Gifts* (Erie: Benet Arts 1980).

[67] This is especially evident in contemporary efforts to close schools or give up parishes.

monks in this country has often been determined by the clerical character of the houses. However, there are many priest-monks today whose primary work does not appear to require ordination to the priesthood. Their ordination to the service of the word and the sacraments often does not find adequate expression in what is traditionally called priestly ministry. Certainly this anomalous situation should not be perpetuated in the future.

In communities of monks the Second Vatican Council's emphasis on the communal nature of the eucharistic celebration sometimes clashes with the traditional and often unanalyzed assumption that a priest should celebrate Mass every day. For a variety of reasons, both theoretical and practical, some monk-priests still prefer private celebrations, a preference which is protected juridically by the Church's legislation.[68] It should be acknowledged here, however, that one of the strong motivating factors for each priest celebrating daily Mass is not only priestly piety but also the custom of receiving a stipend for celebrating. In many monasteries stipends constitute a rather sizeable source of income. Although both theologians and canonists have raised serious questions concerning the practices surrounding stipends,[69] the issue is usually never discussed in communities lest the monastic economy be jeopardized.

In most houses of monks, concelebration prevails as a compromise solution enabling all priests to celebrate personally and yet to celebrate together. There is at the present time, however, a widespread dissatisfaction with the rite of concelebration. Although the primary value to be expressed and constituted in concelebration is eucharistic unity (one community, one altar, one Eucharist), the Fathers at the Second Vatican Council seemed more concerned with what many consider to be a secondary value, namely, the unity of the ministerial priesthood. From that point of view, the experience of concelebration over the past fifteen years has been successful, since many Roman Catholic priests have learned to pray and worship together. But in many circles, including monastic circles, such clerical concerns are looked upon as narrow, elitist and in-

[68] *Eucharisticum mysterium* 47: *AAS* 59 (1967) 565–566; *In celebratione Missae*: *AAS* 60 (1972) 563.

[69] See Karl Rahner and Angelus Häussling, *The Celebration of the Eucharist* (New York: Herder and Herder 1968) 88–125; Harmon D. Skillin, *Concelebration: A Historical Synopsis and Canonical Commentary*, The Catholic University of American Canon Law Studies, n. 450, 116–118.

appropriate. Hence the actual rite of concelebration is more and more perceived as a celebration of distinctions, dividing the community into those who celebrate and those who attend.[70]

While the Second Vatican Council called monastic communities to abolish class distinctions and to integrate all into the life and activities of the community, the daily concelebration of the Eucharist often symbolizes distinctions and causes divisions. Those who feel they should concelebrate are sometimes judged harshly by those who do not; likewise, those priests who communicate at Mass without concelebrating are sometimes judged harshly for not following the directives of the Holy See which regularly insist that priests should take part in the Eucharist as priests, that is, "by celebrating or concelebrating the Mass, and not by limiting themselves to communicating like the laity."[71] On certain occasions, concelebration in a monastic community seems quite appropriate, as when priestly and diaconal ordinations take place. The general rite, however, was one of the first new rites formulated after the promulgation of the Constitution on the Sacred Liturgy. It is clearly in need of reevaluation and reform.

In most houses of monks, an effort has been made to keep the vesture of the concelebrants as simple as possible — a stole is worn over a well-designed alb. Many feel, however, that it would be more appropriate for the concelebrants just to wear a stole over the monastic habit or cowl so as to play down the difference between the concelebrants and the other monks in choir. Most communities of monks have retained the monastic habit at least for choir. It seems appropriate that monastic communities which almost always have a highly ritualized liturgy should also have ritual vesture. Monastic communities of women in this country have in many instances not retained a monastic habit, but they usually do have a highly ritualized liturgy. It would seem then that they should try to confront this issue on both liturgical and aesthetic grounds. The comment from the Rule of Taizé is apposite here: "The liturgical vestment worn for the office is to remind us that our whole being has been clothed by Christ. It is also a

[70] For a balanced and informed treatment of these issues see Robert Taft, "Ex Oriente Lux? Some reflections on Eucharistic Concelebration," *Worship* 54 (July 1980) 308–324.

[71] See *Eucharisticum mysterium* 43: *AAS* 59 (1967) 564; *In celebratione Missae*: *AAS* 60 (1972) 561.

way of expressing the praise of the Lord by means other than words."[72]

On a deeper level monastic communities of men need to take a serious look at the clericalization of monasticism and the problems it has caused and continues to cause monastic life, and the way in which it affects the eucharistic orientation of the various houses. First of all, it should be pointed out that the clericalization of monasticism did in fact assure some theological education of monks after the novitiate. However, their theological formation was almost identical with that given to seminarians destined to be diocesan priests. As a result there was little or nothing distinctively monastic about their training; consequently, there has often been little or nothing distinctive about the ministry of monastic priests and monastic parishes.[73] However, monk-priests were certainly more fortunate than lay brothers and most Benedictine women whose theological formation after the novitiate was dependent on their own spiritual reading and the conferences of the annual retreat and was often presumed to take place simply by living in a monastic environment.

The clericalization of monasticism, nevertheless, has regularly identified monastic life with the hierarchical rather than the charismatic dimension of the Church.[74] The revised constitutions of Benedictine congregations of men have officially de-clericalized the communities by affirming that all finally professed monks may be admitted to solemn vows with equal rights and responsibilities. The proposed schema of canons on institutes of life consecrated by profession of the evangelical counsels says specifically that monastic institutes of themselves are neither clerical nor lay.[75] In the years following the Second Vatican Council there was a serious effort to declericalize the character of various monasteries, but more recently in many American communities there seems to be an unreflective return to the earlier policy of ordaining all the monks who have satisfactorily completed a prescribed course in theological studies and

[72] (Taizé: Les Presses de Taizé 1968) 27.

[73] See Ernest Skublics, "A Contemplative Ministry?" *Worship* 45 (October 1971) 480–487.

[74] I have discussed this issue in an earlier article: "The Blessing of an Abbot," *Worship* 54 (May 1980) 197.

[75] Canon 100, *Schema of Canons on Institutes of Life Consecrated by Profession of the Evangelical Counsels: Draft* (Washington: United States Catholic Conference 1977) 61.

who request ordination, regardless of whether or not the community in fact needs more priests. Such an indiscriminate policy is surely not in accord with the Rule of Benedict.[76] The incongruity of multiplying priests in the monastery is highlighted by the recent document of the Sacred Congregation for the Clergy, calling for efforts to re-distribute the world's clergy.[77] It is also curious that at the present time many Benedictine novices and juniors wear clerical collars when they are outside the monastery and so look very much like priests. Certainly the way to eliminate distinctions in the monastery is not to clericalize everyone. One of the traditional difficulties in a monastic community is that stress on priestly ministry tends to overshadow and downplay the importance of the witness and ministry of a monastic community as such. Hopefully the various problems caused by the clericalization of religious life in general and monasticism in particular will be understood and taken to heart by Benedictine women and other religious sisters who want to be ordained priests.

Along with the need for the de-clericalization of monasticism is the need to de-episcopalize the abbatial office.[78] There is little doubt that when an abbot pontificates wearing the mitre as the principal celebrant of a Eucharist while concelebrating with his priest-monks the image that is communicated is that of a bishop celebrating with his presbyterium. The confusion between abbatial role and episcopal role is sometimes further reinforced in monasteries by naming the abbot along with the local bishop in the eucharistic prayer. The close alignment of monasticism as a whole and the abbatial office in particular with the hierarchical dimension of the Church results in a less than full expression of the charismatic dimension of the Church which is just as divinely instituted as the hierarchy.[79] This has significant ecclesiological implications and operates to the detriment not only of religious life in particular but of the Church as a whole. Both clericalization and episcopalization within monasticism deeply affect the eucharistic orientation of a monastic community.

[76] RB ch. 62.

[77] "Norms for the Cooperation of the Local Churches among Themselves and Especially for a Better Distribution of the Clergy in the World," 25 March 1980: *Origins* 10 (4 September 1980) 185–192.

[78] See "The Blessing of an Abbot," 197.

[79] See Dogmatic Constitution *Lumen gentium* on the Church 43: *AAS* 57 (1965) 50.

By their monastic profession, Benedictines are committed to serve the community in their liturgical celebrations under the direction of their superior. This service would include exercising the role of reader and minister at the altar. The apostolic letter reforming the discipline of minor orders prescribed that all candidates for ordination as deacons and priests should receive the ministries of reader and acolyte.[80] It also noted that the ministries may be committed to other lay Christian men; hence they are no longer reserved to candidates for the sacrament of orders.[81] However, it seems inappropriate to institutionalize these or similar ministries in monasteries by formally installing monks according to the revised Roman rites. The procedure seems to imply an inadequate understanding of the full implications of monastic profession and the responsibilities that are assumed at that time. One might even question the appropriateness of installing as lectors and acolytes those monks who are candidates for orders. Those professed in clerical religious institutes are not bound to the rite admitting men to candidacy for ordination.[82] By analogy, one might argue that monastic profession already seems to include a commitment to minister as lector and acolyte in the monastic liturgy. Excessive institutionalization of ministries in the Church builds up the impression that one may not minister unless one has been duly installed. Monastic profession in itself is an installation into a state in which one has both the right and the responsibility to exercise ministerial gifts under the direction of the superior.

The eucharistic orientation of Benedictine women in this country is conditioned and shaped by a number of factors. The membership in most priories is quite large; work then tends to divide the larger communities into smaller missions with the result that many Benedictine women belong to a primary community and one or even several local communities such as the mission, the school, the parish, or the hospital. Certainly there are occasions when the whole priory should celebrate the Eucharist together, such as profession days, jubilee days, election days, special chapter days, and patronal days. Such celebrations enrich the common heritage and traditions of the group, affirm the shared faith of the community, and express

[80] *Ministeria quaedam* XI: *AAS* 64 (1972) 532.

[81] *Ibid.* III: *AAS* 64 (1972) 531.

[82] *Ad pascendum* Ia: AAS 64 (1972) 538.

the unity of all in the Body of Christ. One sometimes hears complaints, however, that such celebrations are often unduly clericalized by the presence of many priests who concelebrate without regard for the character of the community and the spatial limitations of the chapel. Such liturgies are primarily the celebrations of the communities of monastic women, not primarily the celebrations of visiting priests. Careful attention should be given then to the symbolic structure of such liturgies.

The effectiveness of eucharistic celebrations in communities of women will to a great extent be conditioned by the abilities of the principal celebrant and homilist who is usually the chaplain at the priory. It is widely acknowledged that religious women in general, including Benedictine women, have often been ill-served by chaplains who have been assigned to convents because they could do nothing worthwhile in their own communities or simply because they needed a place to stay while teaching in schools or working in other institutions. Surely every effort should be made to secure and to appoint competent chaplains; it is especially helpful if they come out of and understand the general monastic tradition as well as the distinctive traditions of a particular community. But while unfortunate experiences in this regard are certainly regrettable, it should be pointed out that some Benedictine communities of women have been greatly blessed by the generous services of holy, learned and wise monks. Not only have the experiences enriched the life of the communities but the communities have enriched the lives of the monks. These are the traditions on which the future should be built.

There are, however, some occasions when a community of Benedictine women does not have a regular chaplain. It would seem both legitimate and helpful for such communities to celebrate at least at times a communion service within the context of a liturgy of the word and prayer. Such celebrations should of course be based on genuine need in which there is no opportunity for the celebration of a Eucharist or in which the Sisters should be celebrating as a distinct monastic community and not simply as members of other ecclesial bodies.

Some priories of Benedictine women in this country and elsewhere in the world are specifically committed to adoration, even perpetual adoration of the Eucharist. The celebration of the divine office in such communities has helped to situate the eucharistic devotion of the community in the broader context of God's word; however, such communities do seem to be facing an identity problem. Older members of the community often think of themselves primarily as adorers of the Eucharist, whereas the others think of themselves primarily as Benedictines. Although the challenge is complex, perhaps above all from emotional points of view, it seems imperative that such communities establish clear monastic priorities in their constitutions and directories so as to transmit a sure sense of monastic identity in the future.

Unlike various late medieval groups such as the Dominicans, the Carthusians, and the Premonstratensians, Benedictines have basically observed the Roman rite in the celebration of the Eucharist, though a monastic calendar has generally been followed. They have, however, regularly maintained what might be called a monastic choreography in both the divine office and the Eucharist. The rightful autonomy of Benedictine monasteries and their long-standing traditions entitle them to continue their proper postures and even to develop them as they see fit. In other words local bishops should not interfere in the sound ritual practices of monastic communities.

In concluding it should be stressed that the Eucharist, like the other sacraments, is always a guaranteed gift of God, no matter how it is celebrated. As such it possesses an inherent power to transform people and to create unity. Certainly, the quality of the celebration regularly affects the faith response of individuals, but their personal transformation is conditioned by their own willingness to allow the Lord to convert them away from their own self-willfulness. On an aesthetic level, it may often happen that the actual celebration of the Eucharist conflicts with personal desires and tastes. If this situation is not to degenerate into indifference and frustration, a genuine interior spirit of generosity must be built up so that the Eucharist may be a bond of faith and peace in the community. In this regard it must be remembered that Benedictines are cenobites living according to a Rule and an abbot; they are not sarabaites living according to their own whims. The Eucharist is meant to be a community celebration.

The monastery is a community bound together by the Spirit of Christ; it is therefore in a sense one of the symbols of the Church. But one must be careful in speaking of the monastery as an *ecclesiola*, a little Church. The institutional unity of a monastery has a variety of sources, including a sharing of life and goods, a common submission to the Rule and an abbot, a common prayer life, and often a common apostolate. It may not be said therefore that a monastery is constituted as a monastery by the power of the Eucharist in the same way that such a statement may be rightly made of a diocese or a parish. The Eucharist does express and realize the identity of the monastic community with the Christ-event, but the unity of the monastery has other realizing factors which are distinctively monastic.

It follows therefore that monastic unity does not imply the uniformity of eucharistic practice in one conventual Mass, nor does it follow that the centrality of the Eucharist in the life of a monastic community necessarily implies daily celebration. If possible, a common daily celebration will usually be the regular practice. But if small groups within the community should occasionally celebrate the Eucharist themselves, this may in fact lead to a building up of the community rather than division. Plurality and flexibility of practice are not necessarily incompatible with unity.

Tolerance, acceptance and patience, based on an internal peace of heart, form a very real part of contemporary monastic asceticism, and like the best forms of asceticism it flows from a realistic and positive acceptance of people and situations as they truly are. It is part of the accepting obedience to the members of the community in their strengths and weaknesses that Benedict asks of his disciples.[83] A generous spirit of give-and-take is just as much required in the contemporary age of flexibility as it was required in the post-tridentine era of uniform liturgical practice. Benedict calls the nineteenth chapter of his Rule *De disciplina psallendi*. What he says of the divine office may in a sense be transposed to the Eucharist, for those who have worshiped in choir for any length of time know from painful experience that much discipline is needed to make the venture a success.[84]

The celebration of the Eucharist provides Benedictines with many opportunities for the humble use of their talents and for the exercise of obedience and self-forgetfulness. But in the last analysis, growth in God's life is never the result of human ascetical endeavor; it is always the work of Christ living in human hearts and communities

[83] RB ch. 71.
[84] *Consider Your Call* 259.

through the power of his Holy Spirit. The primary responsibility of Benedictines in making Eucharist together then is to embrace the gift which is given through the various modes of Christ's presence. They are called to structure the rites and place the symbols as effectively as possible so as to facilitate receptivity, but they must remember that ultimately God alone gives. It is he who through the celebration of the Eucharist brings Benedictines into communities that are one in mind and heart.

Kenneth Smits

A Congregational Order of Worship

A significant shift in Roman Catholic approach to worship was reflected in a short sentence of the Constitution on the Sacred Liturgy: "When the liturgical books are being revised, *the people's parts must be carefully indicated* by the rubrics."[1] This directive for reform has resulted in revised rites, particularly for the celebration of Eucharist in which much more account is taken of the people's role. This represents healthy progress beyond the Missal of Pius V, in which the private mass of the priest was the normative model.

The question can be raised whether the direction of reform has been pursued far enough in current revision and implementation of Roman Catholic rites. Admittedly some further progress has taken place since the Constitution. In that document limited use of vernacular was envisioned "in those parts which pertain to the people" (no. 54). Accordingly early stages of the reform retained the use of Latin for the orations and the eucharistic prayer, since these were regarded as more strictly the priest's part. A few years of limited vernacular clearly showed that all parts of the mass belong to the congregation, but in different ways.

[1] No. 31, emphasis mine. *Vatican Council II: The Conciliar and Post Conciliar Documents*, ed. Austin Flannery (Collegeville 1975) 11. This shift in thinking is indicated in many parts of the Constitution, but no. 31 is, so to speak, the bottom line in legislative force and authority. The Flannery translation is used throughout this study for documents of Vatican II.

This essay proposes to go further. What are the possibilities of studying the order of eucharistic worship viewing *the general role of the congregation as the principal one*, with all the special ministries, including that of the one presiding, as serving this principal role of the congregation?[2] The root questions then become: What is the congregation doing? How well are they responding in their role? How well are they being assisted by all the special ministers? The quality of special ministries remains important, not in themselves but rather as the vehicle for enhancing the quality of the general role of the congregation's worship.

The contention underlying these questions is that in liturgical reform to date there is still too much preoccupation, both in theory and in practice, with the role of the one presiding. The traditional sacramental categories of minister and recipient are still too influential. There has not been enough of a shift to thinking and acting primarily in terms of a celebrating community. Accordingly, the first part of this study will seek to develop a theological justification for the position that the general role of the congregation is the most important role in the liturgy. The second part will develop a method for studying the present order of the mass and will apply this method extensively to actual and possible structures of the mass. A concluding part will study the related issues of major adaptation and cultural legitimation.

The People of God and the Manifold Presence of Christ. In seeking to establish the affirmation that the role of the congregation is the most important in worship, an appeal to the Constitution on the Church may be convincing. Chapter 2 spells out the general nature of the People of God, what all have in common; subsequent chapters treat specific offices and ministries. Giving priority to what all have in common may be conducive to approaching worship primarily in terms of what all do in common, such as joining in song, hearing the word of God and engaging in vocal or silent prayer together. It is also significant that the concept "People of God" tends to emphasize the historical character of the Church, its unfinished state and its

[2] This has already been done in a popular way by Eugene A. Walsh in *The Ministry of the Celebrating Community* (Glendale, Arizona: Pastoral Arts Associates of North America 1977). The author deals with the current order of eucharistic worship. This study will attempt to go further in critiquing and in suggesting alternatives to the present order.

openness to the eschaton.[3] This is in contrast to an exclusive use of the "Body of Christ" approach, which tends to be ahistorical and somewhat perfectionist. The two contrasting concepts are inextricably mingled in the Constitution, but the emphasis upon the People of God tends to tone down the heavy manner in which Pius XII used the "Body of Christ" concept in the encyclical *Mystici Corporis* to justify the hierarchical structure of the Church.

Keeping in mind the pilgrim state of the Church, appeal can also be made to the doctrine of the manifold presence of Christ, not only as presented in the Constitution on the Liturgy of 1963 (no. 7) but more so as developed in the later encyclical on the Eucharist: *Mysterium fidei* of 1965 (nos. 35–38), and the Instruction on Eucharistic Worship of 1967. In the Constitution the order of presenting modes of Christ's presence is from his presence in the eucharistic species to a presence in the believing community, "where two or three are gathered together in my name" (Mt 18:20). This order is reversed in the later Encyclical and Instruction. The starting point is Christ's presence in the community, after which are spelled out the other ways in which this presence in the community is enriched through the presence of Christ in ministry, in word and in sacrament. Such a change is more conducive to viewing an order of worship such as the mass as the ritual unfolding of the presence of Christ in manifold ways. But this could also suggest that *the* fundamental and abiding presence of Christ is his presence in the believing community, and that the other manifestations in ministry, word and sacrament are more in service of the community. Even the eucharistic presence is of a less enduring nature, destined as it always is "to be eaten," as the Council of Trent taught.[4] Thus with the conclusion of worship the cycle is completed in the enduring presence of Christ in the community.[5]

[3] Developed extensively in Chapter 7, "The Pilgrim Church," Flannery, 407–413.

[4] The words of Trent are: *ut sumatur, institutum*. Denzinger-Schönmetzer, *Enchiridion Symbolorum* 1643. The eucharistic presence can be spoken of as relatively "permanent" in the sense that it can be ceaselessly renewed, or reserved for a time for communion to the sick and for veneration. It partakes of the perishable nature of food, while the abiding presence by grace is meant to endure, even into eternity.

[5] The General Instruction on the Roman Missal (hereafter GIRM, followed by the corresponding number) recapitulates the doctrine of the manifold presence of Christ in no. 7, its most succinct liturgical exposition of the nature of the mass. The Flannery edition fails to note that it is the *revised* version of the General Instruction, published in English in 1974, not the original version published in 1969. The original version did

A Method for Exploring an Order of Worship. A theological construct such as the doctrine of the manifold presence of Christ admits of only quite general application in the formulation and examination of an order of worship. More refined tools, particularly those developed by the behavioral sciences, would be necessary for an adequate study.[6] This present attempt proposes a more modest goal, a method largely restricted to the field of liturgy and to easily observable behavior, with some reference to general cultural context. It is a simple method available to all engaged in preparing and celebrating liturgy, and has been used by the author for years to help people understand and develop effective orders of worship. Obviously the advantages of simplicity go hand in hand with the dangers of superficiality and facile solutions to complex issues.

The method is simply to examine an order of worship in terms of liturgical function and lines of communication among the various participants. Furthermore the method arises from the kind of thinking that went into the reformed rites in present use. For instance, the functioning of the introductory rites of the mass is described in these words: "Their *purpose* is to help the faithful who have come together in one place to make themselves into a worshiping community and to engender the dispositions they should have when listening to God's word and celebrating the Eucharist" (GIRM 24). The description of the entrance antiphon, or opening song, is as follows: "Its *purpose* is to open up the celebration, to foster union among the people, to direct their minds to the sacred mystery being celebrated, and to accompany the incoming procession" (no. 25).

In other words, some thinking in terms of liturgical function entered into the construction of the order of worship for the mass. There was some precise positioning and ordering of parts with overall worship goals in mind. Moreover the major parts of the mass were clearly marked off from one another, establishing in place of the former run-on character of the Latin mass a clear distinction be-

not have the summary of the doctrine of the manifold presence of Christ. The Flannery translation also omits an important mode of Christ's presence in no. 7: his presence in the word (*verbo suo*).

[6] Among many such approaches, consideration could be given to Victor Turner's anthropological theory, in which ritual is viewed as sociocultural drama, involving key metaphors. See *Dramas, Fields, and Metaphors: Symbolic Action in Human Society* (Ithaca: Cornell University Press 1974) 23–59. The reform of the Mass of the Roman Rite has undoubtedly brought about some shift or modification in the complexity of key metaphors at work.

tween introductory rites and liturgy of the word, and between liturgy of the word and presentation rites. If this kind of thinking went into the construction of an order of worship, with all the limitations it may involve, it is legitimate to examine the effectiveness of an order of worship from the same point of view, as a contribution toward understanding it.[7]

The recent reform of the mass also substantially altered the lines of communication. The previous Latin mass was from the viewpoint of the congregation largely directed Godward in a vague and rather undifferentiated way. The reformed mass in the vernacular introduced more differentiated lines of communication in which the congregation speaks variously to God, to Christ or to itself, and engages in ritualized conversation with various ministers. It is legitimate, then, to examine how this communication works.

In working out this twofold method in detail, each item in the order of worship is first examined in itself. It is assigned a liturgical classification (such as greeting, invitation, song, or prayer of various types); then its function is investigated, and finally the lines of communication are determined (who is speaking to whom). In a further step, function is examined in terms of successive items in the order of worship, to see whether or not there is a strong functional link in the order of parts — for instance, between the "Lord have mercy" and "Glory to God." Finally, the overriding function and lines of communication are looked at in terms of a whole section of the order of worship, such as the introductory rites. This is the method of analysis which underlies the following discussion, taking the typical Sunday celebration as model.

Critique of the Introductory Rites.[8] It is immediately evident how complex the introductory rites are, both in kinds of address or prayer and in directions of address. These rites are characterized by high differentiation of parts, in contrast to the relatively low differentiation of, for example, an order of worship which would begin with

[7] This is admittedly a quite behavioristic approach, and is done with full knowledge of the critique of such a method by V. Turner, in "Passages, Margins, and Poverty: Religious Symbols of Communitas," *Worship* 46 (1972) 392. But his critique would seem to limit the contribution of this approach, not to rule it out completely.

[8] This section rejoins much of the critique of Ralph Keifer, but provides a more elaborate analysis as well as other concerns. Cf. "Our Cluttered Vestibule: The Unreformed Entrance Rite," *Worship* 48 (1974) 270–277.

ten or fifteen minutes of singing of hymns until the congregation was sufficiently unified and ready to hear the word of God. It can be asked whether a typical congregation is normally capable of adequately mastering this complex series of religious acts. It would demand skilled and careful leadership, giving separate and adequate time to each part, and a preference for prolongation in sung rather than in spoken form. One would have to ask whether all this time and effort are needed to accomplish the general purposes of the introductory rites. Experience indicates what happens all too often with such a highly differentiated ritual. Perception is selective. Congregations tend to simplify their participation to a relatively undifferentiated series of prayers, said mostly by the presider.[9] And those presiding tend to pray them as so many prayers to get through before the liturgy of the word begins. The old syndrome of the presider "saying mass" rears its head, and the primary role of congregational activity is reduced to rather passive participation in the role of the presider.

Questions can also be raised about the inner workings of this series of religious acts. The opening song, sign of the cross,[10] mutual greeting and call to worship[11] flow nicely from more general activity to that which gives particular focus to the celebration. But the ensuing penitential rite, a complex series in itself with many variables, calls for an abrupt shift in religious stance and mood. The "Glory to God" calls for another abrupt shift, with no apparent close functional relationship to what precedes and follows, and may well duplicate the function of the opening song in a less successful manner. Finally, the opening prayer is so separated from the beginning of the

[9] The term "presider" is drawn from GIRM 7, *"sacerdote praeside"* in the original Latin. The effort is made to seek a precise term for describing his function without getting into distinctions between baptized priesthood and ministerial priesthood, and in preference to such a vague term as "leader" or an overly political word like "president." The writer would prefer "presider's prayers" for the eucharistic prayer and orations, rather than "presidential prayers" in GIRM 10. The cultural ramifications of the term "presider" are discussed in the final part of this study.

[10] It is rather curious that the formula for the sign of the cross is done in responsorial form, since, to the writer's knowledge, it had been the custom in Catholic piety, until the revised mass came along, for everyone to recite this invocation together, as well as to join in the gesture.

[11] This term is borrowed from Protestant worship, but might better serve to indicate and specify function than the vague term "introduction."

celebration that it appears more as the concluding prayer to a demanding set of religious exercises.

One might also ask questions about how well these introductory rites serve the theological construct of invoking and celebrating the presence of Christ in the community of believers. Of particular concern here is the standard entrance procession. Functionally it serves as a way of getting the presider and other special ministers to the sanctuary area. But it probably does more to highlight the importance of the presider than to establish the self-identity of the congregation, as indicated by commentators who say: "Let's rise and greet Father with a song." That remark may be considered a liturgical abuse, but it may also be a true reflection of how many congregations perceive the entrance procession and its accompanying song. Moreover, the opening song is too often subordinated to the length of the procession, although it is meant to have its own independent value. This independent value could be emphasized by an order of worship in which the special ministers, after informal mixing with the congregation, simply take their places in the sanctuary when the celebration is ready to begin. The entrance procession is probably much overused, and is not the only way to begin a celebration.

Some questions can also be raised about the practice of having a music rehearsal preceding the liturgy. Such rehearsals are usually approached quite functionally as something to take care of before the real worship begins. Given the fact that the community has already begun to gather as the manifestation of the presence of Christ, and some have started to pray and orient themselves to worship, it is questionable whether mere rehearsal is a sufficient justification. Such a preparation is already worship; it involves the purpose of the introductory rites and should be approached in that manner. The goal is to help a congregation pray and experience a text and song. When this has been realized to a sufficient degree, much of the purpose of introductory rites has been achieved.

The ritual greeting between presider and congregation also touches on a number of issues. This ritualized conversation has the latent function of marking off the presider from the congregation, something which needs to be done but can be achieved much better in a mutual greeting than in the overblown entrance procession. While it may be well to have the congregation greet the one who presides, this says nothing to the question of how the people in the congregation meet and greet one another. In line with the theological construct in use here the latter is probably far more important than greeting the presider. This can be accomplished informally in the very manner in which people come together, either in an area adjoining the worship space or within the worship space itself, if people are not too inhibited by past training on silence in churches. This training was inculcated as a way of showing reverence for Christ present in the tabernacle. This is all the more reason for situating the tabernacle in an area adjoining the main worship space suitable for private devotion; its presence in the main worship space can inhibit the development of the sense of Christ in the worshiping assembly.

In addition, the role of ushers (or better greeters) might well profit from a deeper and more theological focus in their ministry. If they were to understand and accept an ultimate goal of promoting the sense of the presence of Christ in the community at this gathering time, they could contribute significantly by their manner and behavior. Moreover, the presider and other ministers could also be circulating in the assembly, promoting a warm and confortable presence of believers to one another.

Besides completely informal procedures, is there sometimes need for a more general ritualized expression of greeting one another in the introductory rites? This raises the question of the function and purpose of the sign of peace, and the relative value of its position within the liturgy. While there may be a good theological fit between the expressed purpose of the sign of peace and its close proximity to the action of sharing Eucharist (GIRM 56b), it is somewhat incongruous that people should be together for more than half an hour before exchanging a more personalized greeting. Normally people exchange a handshake at the beginning and/or end, but not in the middle.[12] Placed toward the beginning, the sign of peace might not have all the profundity of the orientation to communion, but it could, suitably introduced, foster the experience of the presence of Christ in the community.

There are other possibilities of ritual expression. An available option is the blessing and sprinkling with holy water. When used, it replaces the penitential rite, although it is not a full functional

[12] This raises the issue of liturgical legitimation of cultural practices, which will be discussed in the final part.

equivalent. The penitential rite concentrates on personal sinfulness and even more on God's mercy. The rite of sprinkling is a renewal of baptism; suitably carried out with appropriate texts, it could highlight the dignity and identity of the congregation as baptized people, and so further recognition of the congregation as image of Christ. Since it is a procession of sorts, it obviates the need for an entrance procession. It could even take place at the very beginning with the ritual sprinkling accompanying the opening song. At any rate two processions within the introductory rites would seem a heavy and cumbersome procedure.

Perhaps even more to the point but more sophisticated in ritual expression, would be a ritual incensation of the whole congregation. Ritual incensation of the table is already an available option at the beginning of the liturgy (GIRM 27), but one can question whether the ritual reverencing or incensation of the altar is appropriate at this point when the concentration should be upon the assembly. The rich symbolism could speak not only of reverencing the congregation as the presence of Christ but also allow for overtones of purification, thus becoming functionally equivalent to the penitential rite. Suitably introduced with invocation of the mystery of Christ's presence in the congregation, the incensation could be accompanied by an appropriate opening song.

Introductory rites are the most arbitrary part of any ritual. Accordingly they should be approached as functionally as possible, and should allow for as much flexibility as possible. There is an incongruity between constantly changing Scripture readings and relatively unvarying introductory rites. Ultimately it becomes a pragmatic question of what will work. On a given Sunday what does this congregation need to do to become ready to worship — to realize they are the presence of Christ, to become sufficiently united and ready to hear the word of God? Beyond that, verbal simplification is needed, more options must be made available and more stress given to ritual activity involving the whole congregation.

The Liturgy of the Word. The liturgy of the word requires only brief attention since analysis shows that it is quite admirably constructed in functional outline and in lines of communication. The general pattern is biblically one of call and response. Ritually it is a very developed and codified form of conversation between God and his people. Theologically the assembled congregation, already the presence of Christ, is further enriched by his presence in the word. Good principles of theater are at work, in which the ritual builds to a high point in the gospel and homily, then moderates into forms of response such as the expression of faith and prayers of petition. The homily serves as the crucial bridge in this pattern of call and response, developing the call and making it more concrete, and already suggesting elements of a response. So while there are pressing problems of good execution, the general structural arrangement is very commendable.

The weakest area has been the responsorial praying of the psalms after the first reading. This is not to fault the General Instruction, for it clearly shows a preference for sung form and makes provision for seasonal psalms in the face of difficulties of using a new psalm every Sunday (GIRM 36). But what has in fact happened is that in most cases the psalm is approached as just another reading, with the added complication of a new and constantly changing response by the congregation. This "lowest common denominator" form of handling the psalms is probably the least desirable of all. If congregations are ever to get to know and love the psalms, good solo praying or singing of the psalm is probably much more effective. The association with song has probably been the chief feature in their continued use and popularity throughout the centuries. However, since the beautiful singing of the psalms in divine office has for centuries been reduced by church leaders to the private or choral recitation of series of psalms, one can perhaps see why these same church leaders would be satisfied with the same kind of recitation in the mass. There may well be a connection between restoration of the singing of psalms in common prayer and their treatment in the mass.

It may also be questioned to what degree a particular congregation is served by the flood of commercially prepared and canned general intercessions for the Sundays and feasts of the year. Such publications tend to usurp the role of the congregation. It is not enough to have these intentions proclaimed by a member of the congregation. They should also be formulated and phrased so as to ring true as the prayer of this particular congregation.

A Question of Transitions. In a typical Sunday celebration the transition from the liturgy of the word to the presentation and preparation of gifts is clearly indicated. The congregation changes its posture and moves from the more specific activity of participation in the general intercessions to the more diffuse activity of participating in the collection. But in liturgical history this has more traditionally been the place for the exchange of the sign of peace, with an obvious reference to Matthew 5:23–24.[13] This suggests other possibilities within the rich symbolism that the sign of peace can have. Here it evokes a strong focus on reconciliation, perhaps sorely needed in the alienating context of American society and family life. It can be functionally equivalent to some dimensions of the penitential rite, thus eliminating the need for that rite earlier in the liturgy. It can also follow as a particular way of responding to the word of God proclaimed and preached. Moreover, it can have strong links to the subsequent collecting and presenting of gifts, suggesting that this must be done with a pure heart and a clear conscience. In a functional approach to worship, one looks for how strongly a rite can function in relation to what comes before and after.

Another consideration enters here: the tendency among many congregations to depart from ritual and to make the sign of peace a more spontaneous and prolonged expression of fellowship. From a purist point of view one could hope for congregations which easily perceived that the ritual exchange of the sign of peace with a few surrounding people is symbolically an exchange of the sign of peace with all. But pastorally and culturally that level of sophistication may never be reached. The sign of peace may be a time to let the congregation be the congregation in as full and natural a way as possible. Prolonged displays of warmth and affection are obviously meeting some needs, and one could argue that the context of Christian worship is not alien to such display. Finally, if there is the tendency to "fall out" of ritual, it is better to place this congregational activity at the point of a natural break in the service rather than to have it interrupt the flow of the communion rites.

The Presentation of Gifts.[14] The basic ritual pattern of the Eucharist originates from a reduction of the seven acts of Jesus as presented in

[13] "So, then, if you are bringing your offering to the altar, and there remember that your brother has something against you, leave your offering there before the altar, go and be reconciled with your brother first, and then come back and present your offering" (Jerusalem Bible). For details, see Josef A. Jungmann, *The Mass of the Roman Rite*, Vol. 2 (New York: Benziger 1955) 321–332.

[14] This also rejoins much of the critique of Ralph Keifer, but with some independent

the institution narratives to the four acts of taking, blessing, breaking, and giving. But following the contention that the principal role is that of the congregation, it might be better to rephrase these activities in terms of the congregation rather than the presider: presenting gifts, blessing them, breaking the bread, and partaking of the gifts. To what extent can these activities be performed and perceived as those of the congregation, and what is there in the reformed rites of the mass which helps or hinders such a realization?

The first is the presentation of gifts of bread and wine, to which has been joined the collection on Sundays. Even here language betrays us, for "taking up the collection" speaks mainly of what the ushers do, rather than the presentation of monetary offerings which is what the congregation is doing. The most important point would seem to be to allow full time and scope for this action as an integral part of the presentation of gifts so that the monetary offerings can be brought up by representatives of the congregation along with the gifts of bread and wine. For the presider to proceed with his role is to ignore and downgrade a significant congregational activity, and is to say the least bad manners in presiding.

In turn, what is the significant role of the presider? It would seem to be to accept the gifts of the people, and to place the bread and wine upon the table, with the option of incensing both table and gifts. Spending a lot of time on arranging bread, pouring wine, adding water and washing hands would seem to be a lot of inconsequential busywork and rather marginal to the role of the congregation. These actions may well contribute to a sense of ritual, but that should be accomplished in more central and significant ways. Gifts can be prepared ahead of time so that the presentation and their being placed upon the altar can be done in noble simplicity.

The same concerns must be brought to the series of private, semiprivate and public prayers which the missal provides for the presider. First of all, what is the purpose of having and even prescribing forms of silent prayer for the one presiding, above all in the Eucharist, the most public activity of all? Judicious development of the proper times for silent prayer with the congregation would seem to be sufficient. Secondly, many presiders, perhaps perceiving the incongruity of prescribed silent prayers, have turned them into public prayers. If one considers this a liturgical abuse and wishes to

points of view. Cf. "Preparation of the Altar and the Gifts or Offertory?" 48 (1974) 595–600.

correct it, there is really only one satisfactory solution: excise them from the order of worship. This would be minor surgery at most, and it would work.

Semipublic prayer appears in the two blessing prayers over the bread and wine. It can be noted that these prayers echo the primary Jewish sense of blessing which is to acknowledge that the gifts presented are first of all God's gift to us, for which we bless him. This could have significance particularly if these prayers were proclaimed in the actual reception of the gifts, rather than after being placed upon the table. But the use of these prayers is marred by the addition of the phrase "to offer." If, as recent writers suggest, the word "sacrifice" is first of all a descriptive interpretation of Christ's death rather than a literal historical account, and if the notion of "offering" is only a further interpretive way into the mystery of the union between Christ's death and our present celebration of Eucharist, then one runs the risk of a terribly misplaced concreteness in using such a strong term in the presentation of gifts.[15] These are gifts "to present" rather than "to offer."

The ritual of adding water to the wine with accompanying *silent* prayer appears ambiguous. On the one hand, those responsible for this order of worship must have judged the ritual gesture to be too significant historically and liturgically to drop it from the mass. On the other hand, they did not consider it significant enough to merit public evocation of its meaning in prayer. It would seem to be a compromise which needs to go one way or the other. But it would be difficult to perceive this ritual activity as in any way significant for the congregation, and it largely passes unperceived.

The only fully public prayers are the invitation to prayer and the response (again a very heavy sacrificial language), and the presidential prayer over the gifts, with its response: Amen. Both texts seem to have the same function, but they operate along different lines of communication. The first is a ritualized conversation between presider and congregation, the second is addressed directly to God in the name of all. Both texts anticipate to some extent the epicletic function of the eucharistic prayer. One marvels at the effort that

[15] Cf. David N. Power, "Words That Crack: The Uses of 'Sacrifice' in Eucharistic Discourse," *Worship* 53 (1979) 386–404; Robert Daly, *The Origins of the Christian Doctrine of Sacrifice* (Philadelphia: Fortress 1978). The latter is a more popular summary of his *Christian Sacrifice: The Judaeo-Christian Background Before Origen* (Washington, D.C.: The Catholic University of America Press 1978).

must have gone into finding or creating so many texts of the prayer over the gifts, all trying to say much the same thing: accept our gifts. It is no wonder many of them are quite banal, for there are only a limited number of creative ways to say the same thing. If such a prayer is desirable, it might have been better to propose a selection along the lines of prefaces for Sundays, weekdays, and special seasons and feasts, rather than to duplicate the pattern of the opening prayer.

In all these presentation and preparation rites, what best serves the needs of the congregation? The main emphasis should be upon the congregation's making individual contributions and then representative members presenting the gifts to the presider, who places them upon the table. If words are desirable (and none are where music, preferably choral or instrumental, accompanies these activities), it might be well to reformulate blessing prayers to be prayed over the gifts as they are presented to the one presiding. Reservations about any other public prayer arise first from the fact that they seem to anticipate the eucharistic prayer, and second, from the desire to have the eucharistic prayer stand out as clearly as possible. It is a rather lengthy prayer calling for sustained attention to verbal proclamation. It would seem to be ritually unwise to precede the eucharistic prayer with a series of prayers calling for the same kind of attention, as well as a throwback to the syndrome of "saying mass." Let the congregation be silent, so that it can begin anew with the eucharistic prayer.

The Eucharistic Prayer.[16] What are the possibilities of the congregation's role in the rites of blessing, of praising and thanking God in reference to gifts of bread and wine? This clearly presents a challenge because aside from the introductory dialogue the creation acclamation, the memorial acclamation and the Amen, the rest is assigned to the presider. But it is that type of prayer called a presidential prayer, one to be prayed in the name of all and in such a way that the congregation is able to experience it as its prayer. This makes great demands on quality performance by the presider and places principal responsibility on him to learn and develop the art of proclamation to the best of his ability. But the presider could be aided in his role by more generous provision for congregational acclama-

[16] Worth consulting here is James Dallen, "The Congregation's Share in the Eucharistic Prayer," *Worship* 52 (1978) 329–341.

tions throughout the prayer, as found in the Eucharistic Prayers for Masses with Children.[17] This means revised or newly composed eucharistic prayers which make more generous and specific provision for acclamations, as well as suitable musical development of these acclamations.

A final comment: one notes the fairly widespread tendency for congregations to join in the final doxology, rather than restrict their participation to the Amen. From a purist point of view, only the Amen is the congregational response. However, there is difficulty trying to express either in spoken form or in song all that this most important response of the mass means, when one has only a single two syllable word. This has led naturally to endless repetition of the word or to adding other texts. Here again, perhaps we should let the congregation be the congregation. Limited to the doxology, such a custom of congregational participation might be of more benefit than harm.

The Communion Rites. This part of the ritual is meant to be governed by the activities of breaking bread (and pouring wine) and partaking of the bread and cup. However, ritual analysis using the method described above reveals an amazingly complex series of ritual activities and directions of communication before arriving at communion. It is no wonder that the breaking of bread gets lost. There is just too much to do. Again the specter of the presider "saying mass" is raised, which is especially disconcerting since he has just concluded a lengthy prayer. What can be proposed to bring out more clearly the principal role of the congregation?

The Our Father has long been associated with preparation for communion.[18] While the request for bread makes it an apt preparation for communion, the Lord's Prayer also has penitential overtones ("forgive us our trespasses" — a functional equivalent to some dimensions of the penitential rite) and an opening to reconciliation ("as we forgive those" — a functional equivalent to some of the possible meaning of the sign of peace). The many functions of this prayer allow one to imagine other ritual positions in view of a more

[17] Published in 1975 in English translation by the NCCB. In addition to the introductory dialogue, the first and third prayers contain five acclamations, the second, eleven. If such brief prayers can contain so many acclamations, there may be all the more need for them in longer prayers.

[18] Details in Jungmann, *The Mass of the Roman Rite* (n. 13 above) 277–293.

transparent passage from the blessing to the breaking. The Our Father could conclude the general intercessions, substituting a community prayer for the improvised presidential prayer. Its petition for daily bread could be seen as preceding the whole eucharistic action, rather than just the communion, and so provide a transition from the liturgy of the word to the liturgy of the Eucharist. An even more functional arrangement would occur if the Our Father flowed immediately into the sign of peace as a gesture of reconciliation, an acting out of the words "as we forgive others."

Even if it remains in its traditional place, the Lord's Prayer needs to be rejoined to its doxology. The current situation is one of compromise. The doxology found its way into the order of worship but did not succeed in completely displacing the presider's embolism of the last petition of the Our Father. Given the fact that the joined text dates back to the *Didache* and is so widely used in other churches, it would be a significant contribution to ecumenism and to the shared texts of prayers if it were used in the mass. Adoption of a uniform English text, however, presents its own difficulties in such a favorite and traditional prayer.

Next, one encounters a series of texts and rituals on the theme of peace, beginning with a presidential prayer addressed to Jesus! Only a severe lapse in liturgical sensitivity could allow for such a departure, after the strong direction to the Father in the preceding prayers. This may pass unperceived in many congregations and even among presiders. However, some presiders have been perceptive to the change of address and have directed the prayer to the bread, certainly a rather curious development.[19]

The sign of peace is described as expressing the close connection between Christian love and the sharing of Eucharist. This is only one of many meanings it could express; it is doubtful whether this close connection with communion is always adequately perceived. Conversely this link with communion could be maintained even if the sign of peace were placed elsewhere, either in the introductory rites after the general intercessions, or at the close of the liturgy.

[19] This is no more curious than the missal's directive to "bow slightly" while proclaiming the dominical texts over the bread and the wine. The directions of communication here are complex. The institution narrative takes place in the context of a prayer to the Father. Yet the dominical words lend themselves to direct address to the congregation in reference to the bread and wine. However, one is not solely addressing words to the bread and wine, as the rubric might suggest.

There are several drawbacks to its present position. Unless carefully restricted in expression and time, it tends to stop the flow of ritual and create a break in the preparation for communion. It also overburdens the preparation for communion, to the point where the breaking of bread becomes an insignificant gesture. Finally, the current position lacks due sensitivity to popular Catholic belief in reverence for the eucharistic presence. After the gifts of bread and wine are prayed over, they are the body and blood of Christ destined for the nourishment of the congregation. Sensitivity to popular Catholic piety would suggest that this is not the best time for so exclusively mutual a gesture as the sign of peace, particularly when this departs from ritual and becomes a general break in the service.

Next comes the breaking of bread and pouring out of wine. How can the congregation share these actions? It can do so representatively through members of the congregation who come forward to engage in this rite, and who follow through as assisting ministers of communion. But the whole congregation can participate in its meaning through appropriate song. Apparently the problem is that the ritual activity, if properly carried out, outlasts the accompanying music. There is merit in developing the Lamb of God in litany form, but this should not be seen as the only choice. A more fitting solution would be to transfer some, if not all, of the verses of a communion song to this part, as a splendid opportunity for community song leading into sharing Eucharist. This singing could pause for the invitation to communion, and then begin again. Or, alternately, the communion procession could be accompanied by choral or instrumental music, given the difficulty of congregational song during a procession. One could also question whether a general invitation to communion (calling for faith response) is strictly needed, since each person is addressed individually in the act of sharing Eucharist. In this perspective the breaking of bread could flow without interruption into the partaking. And if all or most of the prayers and gestures between the eucharistic prayer and the breaking of bread were removed, the dynamic interrelationship of the central actions of blessing, breaking, and partaking would really become apparent. One could afford to spend time on central acts like breaking bread and pouring wine, instead of on long series of prayers.

There is a minor gesture, the commingling, which accompanies the breaking of bread. Its retention seems ambivalent, too important to drop and not significant enough for public prayer or congregational participation. While it may have had some strong meaning in the past,[20] it presently functions primarily to ensure a minimal breaking of the bread. In a restored breaking of the bread it could pass away with no significant loss to the congregation.

The rites of communion conclude with the prayer after communion, which suffers from the same overdevelopment as the prayer over the gifts. This is often followed by brief announcements while the people remain standing. *Provided* there is suitable time for personal prayer and quiet after communion, it would seem more natural to make the announcements at the conclusion of the period of personal prayer while all remain seated. Then the service could come quickly to a close with concluding prayer, blessing and dismissal, and closing song or instrumental music. If a formal procession from the church is desired, this would serve no more than the pragmatic purpose of getting the special ministers to places where they could greet parishioners as they leave the assembly.

Ritual Activity as a Form of Prayer. The main features of these proposals are the elimination of many prayer texts and the development of ritual activity as a form of prayer. This may pose some difficulty for congregations, and even more difficulty for presiders. It may seem much more like "saying mass" to go through a series of prayers than to engage in ritual activity. But if the congregation is truly to participate in the celebration of the entire mass, and if there is to be enough time for the significant rituals of presenting, breaking, and partaking, something will have to give. And it will have to be the many prayer texts and minor rituals which presently clutter up the order of worship.

Many of these proposals could find adequate expression only in a fully developed Sunday celebration, with all the ministries this involves. What is to be done in smaller celebrations or where music ministry is lacking? Perhaps it is time to return to the notion of several orders of worship for the mass, as originally envisioned by the Consilium for the Implementation of the Constitution on the Liturgy.[21] In small celebrations or where music ministry is lacking,

[20] See Jungmann, 311–321.

[21] *Notitiae* no. 35 (November 1967) 371–380.

texts could be provided, for instance for the breaking of bread, to be proclaimed by someone other than the presider.[22] For private celebration of mass devotional texts could be supplied in any number, if this did not lead to the abuse of using them in other circumstances. The norm of a single order of worship for the mass that is relatively the same in all circumstances may need to be reevaluated.

Major Adaptation and Cultural Legitimation. The Constitution on the Liturgy specifically provided for the possibility of major adaptation of the new rites where elements of a given culture could harmonize with its true and authentic spirit (nos. 37–40). The Bishops' Committee on the Liturgy has recently announced a study of possible adaptation.[23] One of the questions to be faced is whether there are cultural expressions or patterns which can find a legitimate place as liturgical expression. This is a major step beyond dealing with the niceties of liturgical form or moving beyond some of the compromises of the present reformed rites. If a culture is worthy of the name, it surely must have something more to contribute to the liturgy than its language and music. An example would be the occasional use of applause within the Christian assembly. Can it find a natural place within the liturgy? Does it harmonize with its true and authentic spirit? When it is used in worship, does it take on some of the richness of faith and become a truly Christian expression? This last point is important because the faith context is meant to inform and enrich expressions taken from surrounding culture.

Several instances of possible liturgical legitimation of cultural expression have surfaced in this study. A first concerns the place and meaning of the sign of peace. It would be important here to study the ways in which people meet and greet one another in ordinary human discourse, as well as to note regional, ethnic or racial variations. What are the form and depth of such expressions, what is their meaning, and what needs are being met? In the liturgical assembly, what are the possibilities of enriching and deepening this gesture by faith? What is the best placing and setting to accomplish this purpose, or are there a number of possibilities?

A second instance would be the use of the term "presider" to specify the one leading the worship of the assembly. The term is

[22] As provided by J. Mossi in *Bread Blessed and Broken* (New York: Paulist 1974) 108–152.

[23] *Newsletter* of Bishops' Committee on the Liturgy, Vol. 15 (June 1979).

used to specify liturgical function and is not meant in any way to derogate from the norm that the office of ministerial priesthood is required to preside at Eucharist. The term seeks rather to link this ministerial function to a significantly widespread phenomenon of presiding at meetings and other activities, cultural practice within the social, political and religious fields. This is to say that the function of presiding at gatherings enjoys a wide cultural acceptance and has accordingly found a place in many religious gatherings. Just as a pastor presides over many of the activities of the congregation, so he presides in the liturgical assembly. But in the liturgical assembly the role of presider attains its own specific richness and content, exercised in prayer leadership, in preaching and above all in the proclamation of the eucharistic prayer in the name of all. This last point is particularly important. Whatever the merits of theological discussion on priesthood and "powers of consecration," it is at least liturgically clear that whatever the presider does in the eucharistic prayer, and granting that the function is reserved to him, he does in the name of all.

A third and final instance would be the whole notion of starting from the role of the congregation as the primary role. The cultural correlative to this is a participative model of American society and increasingly of the general conduct of affairs within the Catholic community of the United States. It is based upon the presumption that people do not build or maintain deep loyalties to institutions in American society unless they feel they have something to say or something to contribute to the overall direction of the institution. These participative models are already quite widespread in the Catholic community, from nomination of candidates for the episcopacy to the local parish council. They find expression also in the many ministries and services developing within the local parish. And they find liturgical expression in the many special ministries developing in worship. The basic question raised by this study is whether and how the general role of the congregation can become a more participative model — indeed, the prevailing participative model in the liturgy. Can the liturgical assembly be principally acted out and perceived as gathering, common prayer, hearing the word of God and responding; then presenting, blessing, breaking, and partaking? Finally, to what extent can all of these activities be deepened and enriched by faith?

In conclusion, there is the question of the role of ecclesiastical authority in the process of cultural adaptation of liturgical form. More than language was involved in the change to the vernacular, for language is the entrée to the whole culture, with its constant movement and subtle change. One would normally expect that once liturgical form has regained its relationship to culture, it would naturally participate in some of this movement and change. At any rate liturgical history gives abundant evidence of such slow processes. At times authority may have to introduce cultural adaptation formally. At other times authority may simply need to bless, perhaps with suitable refinement, what has already come about. There is no single path in the complex relationship between culture and liturgical expression.

Kenneth Smits

R. Kevin Seasoltz

Justice and the Eucharist

Monsignor Geno Baroni, who for almost thirty years ministered as a priest among the urban poor and ethnic groups of this country and developed into a national leader fighting for social justice, died of cancer at the age of 53 on 27 August 1984 in Washington, D.C. I met him for the first time in 1955 when we were enrolled in the graduate program in liturgical studies at the University of Notre Dame. We were both deacons studying for the diocese of Altoona–Johnstown. His funeral was a glorious celebration drawing church and government leaders, numerous family members and friends, both rich and poor, from all parts of the country. The place was St Augustine's Church where Baroni began to minister to Washington's poor in 1960 by developing parish programs for housing, education and health care. The community gathered not only to mourn the loss of a friend and leader but to thank God for the gift of the generous life of a man who raised human consciousness about social ills and built countless bridges so that the poor, the isolated and the alienated could cross over to conditions worthy of human persons. He brought compassion, healing and mercy wherever he found misery. Father Bryan Hehir's funeral homily aptly described him as an artist, a man who acted on instinct and intuition, whose solutions to complex problems were not always logical but were positive, energizing and creative. As Colman McCarthy noted in the obituary published in *The Washington Post*, among congressional and city officials Monsignor Baroni "became known as a general in the 1960s War on Poverty who lived among the troops, not at the officers' club in the suburbs." [1]

Geno Baroni was a man of deep faith whose driving passion was to bring the justice and love of God to bear on the brokenness of human hearts and on the structures of society. His memorial card carries a quotation from his last public homily given at the 1983 Labor Day Mass in Sacred Heart Church in Washington, D.C., during which he reviewed his own life of work for the rights and dignity

[1] 29 August 1984, p. C5.

of working men and women. In part he said: "I have learned by faith that in the final analysis of one's life there is only one final healing — death — and we know that final healing will be just."

In 1955 when Geno Baroni and I studied liturgy together, the link between social justice and the church's worship was affirmed by select leaders of the liturgical and social action movements, although there were really very few who moved comfortably in both circles and combined in their life of ministry an appreciation of the values of liturgical reform and renewal with a deep concern for social justice.[2] That helps us understand why the link was either understated or ignored in both the documents of the Second Vatican Council and the writings and teachings of those who assumed leadership roles in liturgical and social reforms in the postconciliar period.[3] Baroni was one of those who never forgot the link. His social ministry was rooted in the priesthood and in a prophetic and sacramental model of the church; his strength and nourishment were drawn from attentive listening to God's word in prayer, above all in the church's great eucharistic prayer.

Late on Holy Thursday evening in 1984 I visited him in Providence Hospital. We talked about many things that evening — of the meaning of Holy Thursday, of the priesthood, of the relationship between Christianity and the secular aspects of life. He commented on the ease with which one could divorce one's professional service from the gospel and how readily Christian ministry could degenerate into social service devoid of gospel significance. At the end of the evening he celebrated the eucharist from his bed. Sitting beside him I read John's Last Supper gospel telling how Jesus washed the feet of his disciples. I could not help but think of the appropriateness of the text at that time, in that place, with that remarkable priest, for it is this gospel text above all which forges the link between eucharist and social justice.

In recent years, the churches of South and Central America, as well as the Christian feminists in our own country, have asserted that there must be a congruence between liturgical celebration and

[2] John J. Egan, "Liturgy and Justice: We've Only Just Begun," *Pastoral Musician* 8 (December–January 1984) 36.

[3] The Constitution on the Sacred Liturgy affirmed the importance of liturgy for the life of the church but it failed to delineate the link between liturgy and social life or the role of the church in the world. Likewise the Constitution on the Church in the Modern World failed to mention the role of liturgy in forwarding the redemptive work of God in the world.

the practice of justice.[4] Increasing numbers of both liturgists and social activists as well as moral theologians are stressing the interdependence between the church's worship and responsible Christian life in the world.[5] Recent years too have witnessed a widespread awareness of the chronic ills of contemporary society — its violence, perversion and squalor — so that many people are prone to believe in the absence of God or the withdrawal of God from the modern world. The temptation on the part of liturgists is to retreat from the world's problems into a safe, comfortable, aesthetically pleasing past and to convert liturgical worship into thematic celebrations of abstract universals that supposedly please God but have little to do with responsible life in the world. The temptation on the part of social activists is to reject the liturgy as totally irrelevant, as a distraction of valuable time and energy which should be spent solving the world's problems. Discerning critics ask how Christians can "in truth celebrate eucharist after the Nazi holocaust and in face of an imminent nuclear holocaust, and in a world half-populated by refugees, in the same way as we did before the occurrence of such horrors."[6]

One respondent to that question asserts that Christians must

[4] Egan, "Liturgy and Justice." See also Rafael Avila, *Worship and Politics* (Maryknoll, New York: Orbis 1977); Leonardo and Clodovis Boff, *Salvation and Liberation* (Orbis 1984); Jon Sobrino, *The True Church and the Poor* (Orbis 1984); Richard Shaull, *Heralds of a New Reformation* (Orbis 1984); Sandra M. Schneiders, "Liturgy and Spirituality — The Widening Gap," *Spirituality Today* 38 (1978) 196–210; Mary Hunt, "Women Ministering in Mutuality: The Real Connections," *Sisters Today* 51 (1979) 35–43; Elisabeth S. Fiorenza, *In Memory of Her: A Feminist Theological Reconstruction of Christian Origins* (New York: Crossroad 1982).

[5] See Thomas E. Clarke, ed., *Above Every Name: Lordship of Christ and Social Systems* (New York: Paulist 1980); John C. Haughey, ed., *The Faith That Does Justice* (New York: Paulist 1977); Herman Schmidt and David Power, eds, *Politics and Liturgy* (New York: Herder and Herder 1974); Mark Searle, ed., *Liturgy and Social Justice* (Collegeville: The Liturgical Press 1980); William H. Willimon, *The Service of God: How Worship and Ethics Are Related* (Nashville: Abingdon 1983); Stanley Hauerwas, *A Community of Character: Toward a Constructive Christian Social Ethic* (Notre Dame: U.N.D. 1981); Enda McDonagh, *Invitation and Response: Essays in Christian Moral Theology* (New York: Sheed and Ward 1972) 96–108 and *The Making of Disciples: Tasks of Moral Theology* (Wilmington, Del.: Glazier 1982) 38–59, 99–111; Tissa Balasuriya, *The Eucharist and Human Liberation* (Maryknoll, New York: Orbis 1977); Monika Hellwig, *The Eucharist and the Hunger of the World* (New York: Paulist 1976); Christopher Kiesling, " Social Justice in the Eucharistic Liturgy" *Living Light* 17 (1980) 12–19; Roger Mahony, "The Eucharist and Social Justice," *Worship* 57 (1983) 52–60.

[6] David Power, "Response: Liturgy, Memory and the Absence of God," *Worship* 57 (1983) 328.

again create and maintain symbolic bondings "that acknowledge our dependence on a Creator God while clearly asserting our newly realized co-creational responsibilities."[7] That position would be in keeping with the contemporary reaffirmation of the importance of the creative imagination in human life, including the religious life of individuals and communities and their efforts to be socially responsible.[8] However, as Karen Laub–Novak has pointed out, "without . . . discipline of mind and memory, the imagination easily becomes self–pitying, sarcastic, helpless, passive; prefers fantasy; likes to wrap itself in its illusions. . . . Imagination likes to fling its clothes to the floor assuming that reason and discipline will come along later and pick up the pieces. Imagination is a wilful child, and at times a dangerous trickster. We often hear praise for the delightful side of imagination. We think of the imagination as angelic, holistic, and divine. We avoid the other side, the side that is obscure and vulnerable to self-deception."[9] It is not only a Creator God enabling us to envision and build alternate structures which assure us of a just future whom we need to welcome into our lives; above all we need to welcome a Redeemer God who will save us from that evil buried in human hearts and communities that empowers us to plan and execute the hideous crimes we perpetrate against each other. Sin has become so socialized that many of us forget our need for a personal Savior. The God who comes to us in the eucharist through Jesus Christ and in the power of the Spirit is surely the Creator God who enables us to take part in the creation of a new social order; he is also the Redeemer who saves us from our sin.

If we do not celebrate the eucharist, and celebrate it by acknowledging our absolute dependence on our just God who is both Creator and Redeemer, there will certainly be another holocaust. Not

[7] John T. Pawlikowski, "Worship after the Holocaust: An Ethician's Reflections," *Worship* 58 (1984) 329.

[8] See Kathleen A. Fischer, *The Inner Rainbow: The Imagination in Christian Life* (New York: Paulist 1983); Julian Hartt, *Theological Method and Imagination* (New York: Seabury 1977); Ruben Alves, *Tomorrow's Child: Imagination, Creativity and the Rebirth of Culture* (New York: Harper and Row 1972); Urban T. Holmes, *Ministry and Imagination* (New York: Seabury 1976); Faith and Imagination Issue, *Thought* 57 (March 1982); Religion and Imagination Issue, *New Catholic World* 225 (November–December 1982); Paul W. Pruyser, *The Play of Imagination: Toward a Psychoanalysis of Culture* (New York: International Universities Press 1983).

[9] "The Art of Deception," in *Art, Creativity and the Sacred: An Anthology in Religion and Art*, ed. Diane Apostolos–Cappadona (New York: Crossroads 1984) 17–18.

only must we learn to live justly with one another in order to celebrate the eucharist worthily, but in order to live justly with each other we must celebrate the eucharist with open minds and hearts, with lives wholly receptive to the powerful justice of God who alone empowers us to be just with ourselves and each other.

INCARNATION, CHURCH AND THE POOR

Eucharistic celebrations must grow out of life in the sense that they must express the faith in the Lord Jesus that is the basic commitment of those who celebrate, but they must also transform the celebrants and empower them to return to life with deeper understanding, renewed strength and invigorated hope. If Christian life is being lived with any measure of honesty, it does not lead us into narcissism but rather leads us to question and criticize the fundamental values of our lives as persons and communities. Christian life is surely not an escape from the implications of the incarnation and the outpouring of God's own Spirit on all of us, nor from the consequent responsibility to get involved in the ongoing redemption of the world. It implies deep confrontation with human alienation; its goal is to undermine illusion and falsehood so people might live honestly and justly.

In the eucharist we celebrate above all the life, death and resurrection of the Lord Jesus. His life sets the standard by which we live; he also empowers us to live according to that standard. We understand the life of the historical Jesus as one lived out in faithful willing service of God who revealed himself in the humanity of Jesus as both Creator and Redeemer. Day by day Jesus sought to do what the Father asked of him; his life involved responsible decisions taken and lived by until death. In seeking to do the Father's will, Jesus realized that part of that will was a commitment to his people, to bring them to fullness of life by empowering them to live as he lives — in unity, in peace, in justice and in love. This was the great vision of the kingdom which Jesus himself grasped and which he proclaimed in his preaching. Christian life, then, which is centered in hope for the coming of the kingdom, cannot be individualistic or escapist, for it is hope for both persons and communities created in the image and likeness of God who has revealed himself in Jesus as both personal and communal.

Union with God in Jesus through the power of the Spirit enables us both to live as God lives and to see as he sees. One of the great needs today is to recover the vision of Jesus. Seeing as Jesus sees is what Christian contemplation is all about. By sharing in his vision, we can see beneath the surface of events, see through the illusions and deceitful claims of many human systems, see beyond the transient and the immediate to what is ultimate and enduring. It is for this reason that genuine Christian contemplatives are a major threat to injustice. Unlike superficial activists who only see partial needs, Christians who struggle to appropriate the vision of Jesus become revolutionary in the sense that they see to the roots of the world's problems.[10] This contemplation is requisite for entering into the struggle against evil in the depths of human hearts and in the structures of society; it is requisite for the liberation of persons and communities. As Paul pointed out to the Philippians, resistance to evil can only grow out of breadth of knowledge and insight (Phil 1:9). Injustice and alienation are perpetuated through limited understanding, through an unwillingness or an inability to act.

Discovering the Christian vision, however, is not a purely theoretical enterprise. We also learn by doing. Following Christ involves following his way; believing in him implies our willingness to do his Father's will.[11] In the gospels obedience in suffering and action seems to take priority over a clear-sighted comprehension of theoretical vision.[12] It is only faithful discipleship which opens the way to a profound understanding of Jesus Christ and his revelation of God. One of the conditions that called forth scathing criticism from Christ was the human blindness about him, not the physical blindness that he cured, but the spiritual blindness that came from the failure to be converted. Such blindness was curiously related to deafness, the unwillingness to hear the word of God calling people to conversion. Conversion was not primarily a matter of espousing a new set of beliefs or executing new forms of worship; it rather implied a new way of relating to God in such a way that one also related differently to other people. Conversion was a matter of living justly.[13]

[10] Kenneth Leech, *Soul Friend: A Study of Spirituality* (London: Sheldon 1977) 192.

[11] David Morland, *The Eucharist and Justice: Do This in Memory of Me*, a document prepared for the Commission for International Justice and Peace of England and Wales (1980) 9. In this article I wish to express my special indebtedness to the insights of this author as well as to another Benedictine monk of Ampleforth Abbey in England, Thomas Cullinan, neither of whose works are readily available in this country.

[12] Thomas Cullinan, *The Passion of Political Love* (London: Catholic Institute for International Relations 1982) 3; Morland, 10.

[13] Cullinan, 5.

Justice in Scripture is not, as we might understand it, a matter of egalitarianism or fairness. In fact, God is not "fair," as the parable of the workers in the vineyard reminds us. The scriptural conception of justice implies community of life; it implies reaching out to all those who are excluded and sharing with them all that one has. In his justice God reaches out to all of us sinners who are excluded from his life and offers us communion with him. In turn he both empowers and requires us to do the same for all those who are excluded from our communion. "If God is God and is one, then his people cannot be divided without blaspheming the God who formed them into a people." [14] To follow Christ and to live through the power of his Spirit means that one must share his life not only with other committed disciples but with all those who are excluded from communion. The scandal of the rich in the gospel is not that they are rich and others are poor, implying that life would be just if everyone were equally well off. The scandal is that wealth gives the rich a false sense of security which walls them off from the demands of others, thus creating an essentially divisive situation. To attempt to live with the justice of God implies facing not only the problems of the poor but also the problems of the rich.[15]

We Christians can suffer from collective blindness as well as personal blindness. Institutional blindness makes it difficult for individuals to be converted and to hear the word of God calling them to conversion. Furthermore, clear vision is no guarantee of transforming action. There are those who see what must be done, who have deep insight into the world's problems, but fear, or lack of courage, or indifference keeps them from acting. Likewise there are those who see what should be done but in fact do not have the power to change the world because they only share to some degree in the justice of God; they are not God. The mystery of iniquity is stronger than they are. Isaiah proclaimed that the way of the just leads to a safe mountain where the Lord will provide fresh food and wine for his people and wipe away all their tears (Is 25:6–8), but there are faithful disciples who know no refuge here and now; their bodies are weary and their faces are worn. They are sensitive to the ways of God and the dream of justice and peace for the world that was entertained by Jesus, but they experience the pain of frustration because

[14] Cullinan, 5. See also John R. Donahue, "Biblical Perspectives on Justice," in Haughey, *The Faith That Does Justice*, 68–112; John Dalrymple, "The Cost of Justice," *The Way* 24 (1984) 198–207.

[15] Cullinan, 6.

of the intransigence of iniquity which continues to be rampant in human hearts and in the structures of the world. Galway Kinnell writes poignantly of such a person: "Each year I lived I watched the fissure / Between what was and what I wished for / Widen, until there was nothing left / But the gulf of emptiness. Most men have not seen the world divide, / Or seen, it did not open wide, / Or wide, they clung to the safer side. / But I have felt the sundering like a blade." [16]

The image of the kingdom of God as a banquet is tested and tried when injustice prevails in the world, even in the midst of those who claim to be disciples of Jesus. These are the times when honest Christians are tempted to cynicism and disillusionment because of institutional violence and benign indifference. Above all these are the times when they must be faithful to their consciences and continue to pursue their convictions. These are the times when the image of the kingdom must be reinterpreted because the bread of hope is all that one can eat and offer to others. Honest Christians are empowered to hope because they acknowledge that ultimately God saves the world from injustice, and God alone. The real test of Christian faith, then, is not so much what doctrines we believe but what we ultimately hope for.

Our Christian hope is to grow into the image of God by conforming our lives to the life of Jesus Christ through the power of his Spirit. This means we have to take the incarnation seriously and discover how Jesus Christ is for us not only the sacrament of God but also the sacrament of what it means to be human.[17] The New Testament is clear that in Jesus God assumed a human biography; he took on a human story which was concrete, specific and located in a particular socio-economic and political world. Contrary to the gospel teaching, we tend to locate Jesus in a separate world of priestly rituals far removed from political turmoil. But if we look closely at the gospels, we see that much of his life and teaching had little or nothing to do with religion in the narrow sense of the term.[18]

Jesus lived among people who were struggling under a heavy bur-

[16] "Conversation at Tea," *The Avenue Bearing the Initial Christ into the New World* (Boston: Houghton Mifflin 1974) 33.

[17] See Karl Rahner, "The Spirit That Is over All Life," *Theological Investigations* 7 (New York: Herder and Herder 1971) 193–201 and *Foundations of Christian Faith* (New York: Seabury 1978) 264–279; Jerome Murphy-O'Connor, *Becoming Human Together* (Wilmington, Del.: Glazier 1977) 33–55.

[18] Cullinan, 4.

den of taxes and subject to the repression of Roman authorities. In that context he spoke about power and possessions, about human sexuality and relationships, about ways in which community could be built or destroyed. One of the disturbing things he did was to lay bare the injustice and oppression within his own society.[19] He revealed God in the midst of his people, not primarily in the realm of religious rituals. If we identify our lives with Jesus by retelling and remembering his story, by opening our lives to his Spirit, we must do so with the whole of our lives, incarnate as they are in a social, economic and political situation. To follow Jesus is to take not only the stance that he took towards his Father but also the stance that he took in society and towards people. It implies being led by the Spirit into an identification with the poor, the oppressed and afflicted; it implies suffering with them and for them.[20]

One of the most crucial and yet most disturbing aspects of the incarnation is that Jesus identified above all with the poor; he designated them as the privileged heirs of his kingdom; he took their side and defended them against their oppressors. He promised them salvation — deliverance from sin and all the effects of sin. The poor included all those who were powerless and consequently marginal in an economic, political, social, cultural or religious sense. Jesus did not bring immediate relief to the poor but he assured them that their lives would be blessed and would have happy endings.[21] The foundation for his identification with the poor was that self-emptying whereby he himself left his divine power and self-sufficiency hidden so he could take on the likeness of a slave, the epitome of human poverty.[22] He became poor so the poor could become rich with the riches of God's life, so they could be raised up to experience communion with God and his people. Jesus came from the anawim, the poor of Yahweh whose portion was God, whose lives were open to that communion which God alone can offer. He identified with the poor so he could show both rich and poor alike that human fulfillment consists not in achieving human success as the world conceives success in terms of economic, political, intellectual and cultural prowess; it consists in realizing that unity that we all are because we are made in the image of God who is communion be-

[19] Cullinan, 5.

[20] Morland, 11; Cullinan, 8.

[21] Daniel Rees and Others, *Consider Your Call: A Theology of Monastic Life Today* (London: SPCK 1978) 209–211; Morland, 11.

[22] Morland, 11.

cause God is Trinity. Jesus came to reveal that "the fundamental reality about ourselves is that we are communion." [23]

Since Jesus identified with the poor, with those who acknowledged their isolation, their alienation, their lack of communion, their powerlessness and their failure in worldly terms, but who also recognized their total dependence on God as their true savior who could deliver them from their depravity into unity and peace, it follows then with inexorable certainty that the church which is to be the primary sacrament of Christ in the world must be a church of the poor, not primarily in the sense that it is a social servant bringing temporal relief to the suffering but in the sense that it is one with those to whom God has promised his kingdom. "The Church cannot afford not to be of the poor if it is to avoid the judgment of God and not be the object of woe rather than blessing." [24]

The identity of the true church with the poor has both theoretical and practical implications, especially in the northern hemisphere. For example, it helps us understand why the church in the north is beset these days with so much apathy, mediocrity and decline in numbers, whereas in the Third World countries, to the extent that the church is of the poor, there are centers of vitality and hope. [25] Unfortunately it is often those who are most closely identified with the church from a professional point of view, namely, the clergy and religious, whose lives seem so removed from poverty. Their way of life is often one of the most secure ways of life in our modern society, for the institution not only provides them with food, clothing and housing but also with education, employment, transportation, recreation and health care. Not only must ordained priests and professed religious critically scrutinize their own lives to see whether they have anything to do with the poor, but also candidates for the priesthood and religious life must be carefully screened so as to eliminate those who, consciously or unconsciously, are seeking the comfortable fringe benefits of a clerical or religious culture. Only those who are deeply committed to simplicity of life and sharing of goods should be admitted to ordination and religious profession in the church. Their commitment should not only affect their style of life in material terms but should also involve them in that risk, marginality and struggle with doubt which Christian faith always implies.

[23] Cullinan, 9.
[24] Morland, 12.
[25] Morland, 12.

One of the complex problems today is that in order to carry on its regular ministry of education, health care and social service as well as its specific ministry to the poor and outcast, the church is dependent on material resources. But the thrust of affluent societies is regularly towards a constant increase of what is thought to be essential for the efficiency of their work. Many Christians not only live and work in the midst of affluent societies but are in fact an integral part of such societies. They are apt, then, to raise their standard of living and working without adverting to the demands of the gospel. Furthermore, in order to secure funds to carry out their various ministries, church institutions, such as dioceses, parishes and religious communities, regularly court the wealthy capitalists in our society. Fund-raising techniques that are associated with big business are often uncritically adopted without bringing those methods and their implicit consumerist and competitive values under the judgment of the gospel. The church and its institutions then become indebted to the very rich. As history clearly shows, ecclesiastical institutions have often been closely associated with wealthy and rigidly conservative patrons who maintain reactionary views of social reality. In order not to lose the favor of their benefactors, Christians, especially those in leadership positions, have often assumed the same attitudes and have given way to what is simply an affluent style of life, thus betraying the gospel. Gospel poverty requires fidelity to God, not fidelity to wealthy patrons.[26]

There are many Christians — and their number is growing — who find themselves in middle class categories, who are keenly aware of the affliction of the poor and outcast in our world, but who feel there is little or nothing constructive they can do to share in the suffering and insecurity of the afflicted. That awareness in itself is a source of anxiety. But in that anguish there are ways in which God leads these people into the suffering of Christ and his poor ones. When Christians really absorb a sense of communion with the poor and afflicted, their lives are basically transformed. They will find themselves in many unexpected ways being a voice for those without a voice, speaking the truth when it is both awkward and unpopular, appearing to be a nonconformist. This is the kind of suffering that many people today experience when they undertake the work for justice and peace in its many forms. Fidelity to Jesus and his commitment to the poor and afflicted will affect every aspect of the

[26] Rees, 214–220.

church's life. It will affect the way Christians live, the way they embrace poverty, the friends they have and the friends they lose, the form of security they have or do not have, and the fundamental options they make about the kind of work they do and do not do.[27] Following Christ as the suffering servant, as the poor man from Nazareth, is a necessary condition for hearing the gospel as good news. We can understand the meaning of Christ's words, "Blessed are the poor" and "Woe to the rich," only if the church as a community and we Christians as individuals get involved in our contemporary world in the same way that Christ was involved in his world. Only then will we be heirs of his promised kingdom.[28]

EUCHARIST

What implications does all this have for the meaning and celebration of the eucharist? The Last Supper which Jesus celebrated with his apostles and during which he instituted the eucharist was a symbol of his whole life and mission. It was a prophecy of the meaning of his life, death and resurrection and the gift of God's Spirit to his people. The breaking of the bread and the drinking of the wine were for Jesus an expression of the new world, the new kingdom which would come into existence at the very moment when he appeared to be most powerless, when in a most devastating but eloquent way he bore witness to justice, truth and love in the face of evil and oppression. His death bore witness to the power of evil in the world, but his resurrection bore witness to God's victory over death and evil. At the Last Supper Jesus took over the old paschal meal of his people, a meal which symbolized their liberation from slavery in Egypt and their adoption as God's special people through the covenant. Jesus transformed the meal so it symbolized a new relationship between God and his people. The new covenant was established by God through the offering of his own life — his own flesh and blood — in Jesus; the offer was not limited to a single race but was given to all. Within the framework of the passover meal, Jesus took the old symbols of bread and wine and identified them with himself, with his life, death and resurrection. In sharing bread and wine with his disciples, he shared himself, thus incorporating those who took part in the meal into his own life and enabling them to relive his history and to reenact his story in their own lives.[29]

[27] Cullinan, 10–11.
[28] Morland, 12.
[29] Morland, 12–13.

In Jesus, God revealed that he lives for giving, for bringing people into union with himself and each other. Hence at the Last Supper, Christ constituted a new community based on faith in his own life and person. It was a community in which class distinctions were abolished and barriers were broken down with the result that people would not be classified as Jew or Greek, male or female, free or slave.[30]

In the eucharist, Christ made his life available to all those who would celebrate the eucharist in fulfillment of his words, "Do this in memory of me." Jesus promised that just as bread and wine become one with the person who consumes them, so those who shared in the eucharistic meal would become one with him. But the event that was memorialized in the eucharist was not simply the Last Supper. That meal in a real sense symbolized all the significant meals that Jesus had eaten during his life, especially those that are remembered in the gospels — the meals taken with Martha and Mary and Lazarus, his friends, but also those taken with tax collectors and sinners, who were the marginal people of his own society. It was reminiscent of the feeding of all those who were hungry and of the wedding feast to which those who were first invited refused to come so that others were brought in from the byways. It was also a prefigurement of the meals that Christ would eat with his disciples following his resurrection. The concreteness of these meals reminds us of the basic incarnational character of Christianity and prevents us from so spiritualizing the eucharist that its relevance is restricted to life hereafter and is divorced from life here and now. This all means that those who celebrate the eucharist in memory of Jesus, who follow his command to "do this," must feed the same sort of people and involve themselves with the same sort of dinner guests as Christ had at table. "It is perhaps a measure of the 'domestication' and 'ritualization' of the Eucharist that we in the west can celebrate a Mass without being confronted with the glaring scandal of world hunger for which with our diet of meat we are in part responsible."

The Last Supper was symbolic of Christ's whole life as a sacrifice, as something sacred, not in the sense that it was removed from the secular world but rather in the sense that he opened his whole humanity to the Father's life and will. Like the grain of wheat which is planted in the ground and then opens up to the soil and moisture

[30] Morland, 13.
[31] Morland, 13.

around it so that it might bring forth a rich harvest, so likewise Christ died to the human tendency toward isolation and self-sufficiency; he opened his whole life to the Father and so passed from death to the fullness of life. His whole life was sacrificial; it was holy. Jesus transformed the human understanding of the holy; it no longer refers to a separate sacred world but rather to the presence and power of God operating within humanity, saving men and women from the death of sin and reconciling them with God, with themselves and each other. For Christians, then, holiness refers to the Spirit of God abiding in the whole body of Christ, the community of believers, the communion of faithful saints. Through the eucharist which symbolizes the whole life and mission of Christ, holiness is communicated to Christians as they share in his body and blood. The body of Christ is not simply the resurrected body of the Lord Jesus; it is the body and blood of Christ communicated in the eucharist; it is the body of believers in union with Christ through the power of his Spirit.[32]

The Last Supper was a symbolic enactment of who Christ is, why he became incarnate among his people, what God becoming human really means. While sharing all that he is with his disciples, he commanded them to do what he did, to take on his life and history. He commanded them to become his body so they could be delivered from their sinfulness and come to fullness of life which they could share with others by healing wounds, saving people from isolation and alienation, giving life to the world and bringing people into communion with God and each other. Christ became incarnate primarily to free his people from slavery to sin and then from the other forms of slavery which find their roots in slavery to sin.[33] If the eucharist is to be celebrated with integrity, the church must be about the same sort of liberation. It has to be a suffering servant acknowledging its own need to be saved from sin. Like Christ, the church must lay down its life for others. Hence it must be unconcerned about its own prestige and prowess in the world; it must take its agenda, as Christ did, from the poor. The most important gift that the church can mediate to the poor is liberation from sin through the power of Christ's Spirit. Sin is the greatest evil since it strikes men and women at the heart of their humanity. Certainly this

[32] Morland, 14.

[33] Sacred Congregation for the Doctrine of the Faith, *Instruction on Certain Aspects of the 'Theology of Liberation'* (Vatican City 1984) 8–13.

liberation will have effects not only on the individual but also on the social levels.[34] It is a powerful thing to remember the Lord Jesus in the eucharist if that remembrance makes his presence real so that in the celebration he demands that those who partake of his body and blood become like him, other Christs. It means that they must become vulnerable; they must abandon their false securities which protect them from God and his people.[35]

In Luke's gospel the narrative of the Last Supper is followed immediately by the account of the disciples' dispute about power and prestige (Lk 22:24–30). Christ condemned their concern for greatness and instructs them: "Let the greatest among you become as the younger, and the leader as one who serves" (v. 26). The church as the community of disciples today cannot be committed to selfless service if it is simultaneously involved with structures of injustice and oppression in the world.

The implications of Jesus' teaching are brought out above all in John's gospel where the account of Jesus washing the disciples' feet appears where we would expect to find the institution of the eucharist. It has been suggested that the foot-washing is an "analogue of the institution narrative in the synoptic accounts of the supper." [36] It is John's vivid way of showing the connection between the eucharist and service; it is a symbolic expression of what the eucharist is all about.[37] John concludes the account with the command that his disciples should do for others what he has done for them (Jn 13:15), a command which parallels the eucharistic command in the synoptics, "Do this in memory of me." Instructive too is the fact that John concludes this section of his gospel by recalling Jesus' great commandment of love whereby we are to love one another not as we love ourselves but rather with that very love with which Jesus loves us. "It is only to the extent that the individual disciple has experienced the love of the indwelling Jesus that he or she can participate in the community experience of sharing that love." [38] The dynamic

[34] Ibid., 11.

[35] Morland, 15.

[36] Sandra M. Schneiders, "The Foot Washing (John 13:1–20): An Experiment in Hermeneutics," *The Catholic Biblical Quarterly* 43 (1981) 81; see also X. Léon-Dufour, "Faites cela en mémoire de moi," *Études* 354/6–VI (1981) 831–842.

[37] Dermot A. Lane, *Foundations for a Social Theology: Praxis, Process and Salvation* (New York: Paulist 1984) 149.

[38] Sandra M. Schneiders, "Christian Spirituality in the Gospel of John," in *Scripture and the Church*, ed. Robert Heyer (New York: Paulist 1976) 17.

effect of his love is symbolized by his act of washing the disciples' feet.

Walter Brueggemann has pointed out that the tools which Jesus left his disciples to carry out their mission of service were a towel and basin.[39] Tools determine and define one's trade. If Christ's disciples are left the tools of a servant, they can only do the work of a servant. Certainly a towel and basin are used to carry out the work no master would do. They are used to make contact with the soiled dimensions of humanity that call for personal attention.[40] The towel and the basin place heavy demands on Christians. We are commissioned to make contact with the soiled, sometimes unattractive dimensions of humanity and to carry out our ministry with loving attention. Such a mission can be fulfilled only by people who are not self-preoccupied, who can take their minds off themselves so as to focus on their ministry, on the poor and needy of the world in all their suffering and anguish.[41]

Brueggemann further highlights what a servant does in washing another's feet. The servant takes on a subordinate position while positioning the one whose feet are being washed in the place of a master. This is especially significant if the one who is set in the master's place is precisely the one who has been put down and excluded by society. In our contemporary world there are many who are lowered by society; those who are thought to be unworthy or inferior are pushed lower and lower in the community until their own sense of dignity and worth is decimated too. People can be rejected or excluded so long and so vigorously or perhaps so subtly that they perceive themselves as unworthy, inferior or excommunicated. But Christian ministry to these people must be ministry and service after the manner of Jesus. That means that the very ones who are pushed or kept down by society are the ones to be raised up so they achieve that sense of dignity and worth essential to the redeemed human condition. Likewise those who are excluded by society are the ones that should be included by the church. But the only church that can practice such a selfless ministry is one so secure in its salvation by Christ that it can confidently be a servant. The only church that can take on such a ministry is one that refuses to define itself in terms of secular competence and worldly achievement.[42]

[39] *Living toward a Vision: Biblical Reflections on Shalom* (Philadelphia: United Church Press 1976) 134.

[40] Ibid., 135.

[41] Ibid., 136.

[42] Ibid., 136–137.

That the early Christians understood the teaching and example of Jesus is clearly indicated in the Acts of the Apostles where concern for the poor and needy is asserted in the context of the eucharistic breaking of the bread (Acts 2:42, 44, 45). However, the most significant early example of the link between the celebration of the eucharist and social praxis is given by Paul in 1 Corinthians 11. He argues convincingly for social responsibility as a result of eucharistic celebration and then goes on to show how the social praxis is rooted in the organic unity that exists in the one body of Christ with its many members. When the Corinthians came together to celebrate the eucharist there were divisions among them which were wholly incompatible with an honest celebration of the eucharist. In his discussion of their celebration, Paul emphasizes not only the eucharistic species of the blessed bread but the new body of organic communion and fellowship effected by partaking of the eucharistic bread. It is this new corporate reality which Paul looks upon as the fuller real presence of the body of Christ. For Paul it is not just the bread alone which is the body of Christ. When he speaks of "discerning the body" (v. 29), he is not referring primarily to a recognition of the real presence of Christ in the eucharistic species but rather to a recognition of Christ in the organic unity that exists between the head and members of the body of Christ. To discern the body is to grasp the indissoluble link between the eucharistic action and the community that is created and sustained by that action.[43]

In his letter Paul was disturbed by the fact that the Corinthians divorced the presence of Christ in the eucharistic species from his presence in the community; they were in effect separating the head of the body of Christ from its members. Once that happens the basis for Christian social praxis within the community is eliminated. The reason why the Corinthians could make the dichotomy was that some of them tended to reduce faith in Christ to a form of gnosticism or esoteric saving knowledge; others focused attention on the glorified heavenly Christ to the neglect of his corporate presence in his community on earth. Still others over-spiritualized the doctrine of the divine indwelling so that the whole social dimension of the Christian faith was neglected. Perhaps above all there seemed to be a tendency toward individualism which made the Corinthians in-

[43] Lane, 164–165; see also John C. Haughey, "Eucharist at Corinth: You are the Christ," in *Above Every Name: The Lordship of Christ and Social Systems*, ed. Thomas E. Clarke (New York: Paulist 1980) 107–133.

sensitive to the fact that they were all one in Christ and therefore should act with love and concern for each other. False dichotomies between the spiritual and the social, between the sacred and the secular, between the private and the public, between the personal and the communal resulted in a neglect of the responsibilities of these Christian Corinthians in the world. Because of these aberrations, they could celebrate the eucharist while being oblivious of the social ramifications of what they were doing.[44]

The factors that were operative in Corinth are similar to the factors that are operative today, above all individualism, spiritualism, and the privatization of Christian faith. Hence it is all too easy for us today to eat the bread and drink the cup of the Lord in an unworthy manner, thus profaning the body and blood of the Lord and bringing judgment on ourselves (1 Cor 11:27–29). It is a perilous thing to remember the Lord.

The major issue today is not the matter of eucharistic ritual and the form it takes, but rather the nature of the community, with its vision, its goals and its praxis, which is celebrating the eucharist. Probably the greatest scandal of injustice in the world at the present time is the poverty, squalor and degradation of millions of human beings. If Christian communities are bound up in any way with structures of injustice which cause and maintain such a scandal or if they are indifferent to the problem, then they are colluding in evil; they must be converted and search for ways to oppose sin in both its personal and structural forms. Otherwise their celebration of the eucharist is hypocritical. The eucharist "cannot form the wellspring of vitality, hope and creative vision and energy which is contained in the 'real presence' of Christ. . . . Unless the Church is really being formed in its life, usually through suffering, into the body of Christ, then its celebration of the body and blood of Christ in the Eucharist brings judgment rather than blessing upon itself. There is no middle way: the meaning of Christ's death and resurrection cannot be reenacted without *some* effect; that is what is meant by the Catholic doctrine of *ex opere operato*. It does form a critical witness calling sinners to repentance and conversion; it does proclaim a sacrificial self-emptying which is not just a pious platitude or addressed to the individual communicant; it is a two-edged sword which cuts deep into the being of the Church."[45]

[44] Lane, 164–165.

[45] Morland, 16.

The church is a servant of Christ and as such is not the owner but the steward of the eucharist. It is always Christ who acts. In the eucharist, Christ's power is unleashed; it is a power over which the church has no control. His presence is dynamic and transforming; he is there as the Lord whose will is to shape the community celebrating the eucharist into his body, to make the community holy so it can proclaim good news to the world here and now in both word and deed.

There is a close relationship between the unity of the eucharist, the unity of the Christian community and the unity of humankind. In its Constitution on the Church the Second Vatican Council taught that "the Church is a kind of sacrament of the unity of humankind. She is also an instrument for the achievement of such . . . unity."[46] The eucharist nourishes the unity of the church, but the church must nourish the unity of the world. Both the church and the eucharist are grounded in the vision of promise and hope given to us by Jesus not only in his preaching but also in his own life and practice as he sought to establish the kingdom of God. Just as work for justice that neglects the unity of humanity or disrupts that unity by pitting one class of society against another cannot be called Christian, so neither can work for justice that overlooks the unity of the church be called Christian. In the same vein, any work for the unity of the church that overlooks the needs of the world is not in the tradition of Jesus. The eucharist is meant to mediate the unity of the church and the unity of humankind. It builds up the church but it also gives the church a missionary task which includes the ethical responsibility of taking liberating actions for justice in the world. The eucharist roots us in the just life of Jesus; it also thrusts us into the future where we will be one not only with him but also with each other.[47]

When Monsignor Baroni was working at the Department of Housing and Urban Development, he often showed his visitors a silk screen sent to him by an elderly woman who heard him speak on the importance of ethnic consciousness. The screen bore the words: "There are only two lasting things we can leave our children. One is roots, the other is wings."[48] In the eucharist, the Lord has left us, his children, both roots and wings.

[46] Art. 1: AAS 57 (1965) 5.

[47] Lane, 168–169.

[48] McCarthy, Obituary for Geno Baroni.

M. Francis Mannion

Stipends and Eucharistic Praxis

The analysis of the monetary transactions represented in the Mass stipend system as eucharistic praxis involves the assertion that these transactions are highly consequential and that they have played and continue to play a highly generative role in the formation of attitudes and ideas about the church, eucharist, and ministry. Without prejudice to the contemporary debates about the nature of praxis, I understand praxis as the dynamic by which action generates and shapes theoretical formulations, and is itself in turn modified by theory. Attention to Mass stipends as eucharistic praxis, then, means attention to the origin and evolution of monetary transactions in the eucharist with a view to ascertaining theological effects and consequences.

It is not possible, however, to isolate the practice of money in the eucharist from the larger complex of eucharistic transactions represented by the presentation, blessing, and sharing of gifts of bread and wine. The use of the language of transaction here represents an approach that seeks to highlight the relationship between the parts in a ritual complex, as well as the manner in which modifications and changes in one part of the ritual system affect and modify the whole, and consequently the activity and role of the participants.

This essay, then, seeks to situate the question of Mass stipends within two related perspectives: that of the generative relationship between liturgical practice and theological reflection; and that of the ecological relationship between money offerings and the whole complex of acts that go to make up the Christian eucharist. It will be suggested that these two contexts provide the only adequate criteria for a prospective evaluation of the Mass stipend system.

THE PAULINE MODEL AND ITS DEVELOPMENT

Edward Kilmartin has pointed out that "the meaning attached to the presentation of gifts at the Eucharist is determined by the basic idea that governs the understanding of the Eucharist in any

M. Francis Mannion

given period."[1] The same may be said for all eucharistic transactions. At the risk of oversimplification, it may be suggested that the early church had one eucharistic praxis, that is, one set of eucharistic transactions involving bread, wine, and money, with an attendant theology and ecclesiology, that stands in marked contrast to that of the medieval church. An analysis of the performance of bread, wine, and money in these transactions and of the movement from the one praxis to the other is the first task of this essay.

The fundamental economy of Christian eucharistic transactions is set forth in the New Testament texts that give an account of the Last Supper and the Christian eucharist. Attention is focused at once on a bread action and a wine action presented as ordinances for continuing discipleship in the memory of Jesus. The fundamental structure of these actions has been reduced to four in the classical analysis of Gregory Dix: *taking, giving thanks, breaking,* and *giving.*[2] It is Paul who provides an elaboration of the broader ecclesial dynamics of these eucharistic actions. In his First Letter to the Corinthians, we are given the fundamental outlines of an ecclesial act of tablesharing in which bread and wine are taken, blessed, and shared, and the poor are fed. Elisabeth Schüssler Fiorenza has succinctly encapsulated the significance of these acts, especially of care for the poor, in the assertion that tablesharing establishes tablecommunity.[3] In the transaction of the bread and the cup, there is established a *koinonia* in the body and blood of Christ. Eucharistic incorporation represents the fundamental definition of the church. Eating together at the common table actualizes the church and represents the fundamental paradigm for all transactions in the community, transactions essentially of *diakonia* and service: "The sharing of food and drink with each other, the celebration of a meal especially among those who are well-to-do and those who have nothing, is essential to the celebration of the Christian eucharistic meal."[4] For Paul, these eucharistic transac-

[1] Edward Kilmartin, "The Sacrifice of Thanksgiving and Social Justice," in *Liturgy and Social Justice*, ed. Mark Searle (Collegeville: The Liturgical Press 1980) 58. While the 1983 Code of Canon Law has replaced the term "stipends" with "offerings," the more familiar term is retained in this essay for clarity of subject matter.

[2] Gregory Dix, *The Shape of the Liturgy* (rpt; New York: The Seabury Press 1982) 48–50.

[3] Elisabeth Schüssler Fiorenza, "Tablesharing and the Celebration of the Eucharist," in *Can We Always Celebrate the Eucharist?*, ed. Mary Collins and David Power (Concilium 152, New York: The Seabury Press 1982) 9.

[4] Fiorenza, 10.

tions are made in the Spirit who is the life principle of the body (1 Cor 12:13; Rom 8:9–11), and they embody the church as a doxological sacrifice (Rom 12:1–12). A code of conduct is symbolized in the eucharist. A charge to share food and drink is intrinsic to the full reality of the eucharistic gathering. This explains why Paul rails against selfishness and factionalism in the assembly (1 Cor 11:17–34). Failure to share bread with the needy is an assault upon the eucharistic community and upon the Lord's body.

The most remarkable thing that emerges from a study of the Pauline assemblies is their profoundly inclusive ethos, that is, their profound sense of participation in the body of Christ. Every eucharistic act intensifies and radicalizes this communion in Christ, not least those acts expressive of care and concern for the poor and needy. This fundamental character of the Pauline eucharist is continued in the practice of the eucharist in the postapostolic and patristic periods. Gifts of bread, wine, and money are transacted in eucharistic communities deeply attentive to the charge of charity and *diakonia.* In the eucharist of Justin Martyr in the second century, the inclusive activity of the assembly in the various transactions of the gifts is clearly in evidence, and care for the poor is integral to the meaning of Christian assembly: "The wealthy who are willing make contributions, each as he pleases, and the collection is deposited with the president, who aids orphans and widows, those who are in want because of sickness or some other reason, those in prison, and visiting strangers — in short, he takes care of all in need."[5] In the baptismal eucharist of Hippolytus some generations later, the one who received gifts to bring to a widow or a sick person is exhorted to do so at once, or at least the next day, "adding something of his own, because the bread of the poor has stayed in his possession."[6] In the Syrian *Didascalia Apostolorum* from the early part of the third century, charity is placed so completely at the heart of the liturgical assembly that the bishop is exhorted to sit on the floor and give up his throne to a poor man when he welcomes

[5] *Apologia* I, 67, PG 6, 430; tr. Matthew J. O'Connell, in Lucien Deiss, *Springtime of the Liturgy: Liturgical Texts of the First Four Centuries* (Collegeville: The Liturgical Press 1979) 94.

[6] *La Tradition Apostolique de saint Hippolyte: Essai de reconstitution*, ed. Bernard Botte (LQF 39, Münster: Aschendorff 1963) 62; translation from Deiss, 145.

him into the gathering.[7] The Pauline ideal is eloquently expressed when Cyprian of Carthage chides a wealthy member of his congregation for offending against the ethics of the eucharist: "You should blush to come to the Lord's assembly without a sacrifice and to partake of the sacrifice offered by some poor person."[8]

An important aspect of the eucharistic *koinonia* of the early centuries was the offering of gifts in the name of the dead. In the words of Edward Kilmartin, "Since the dead were regarded as members of the Church, it was natural that they should be drawn into the fellowship of the earthly worshipers by gifts offered 'in their name.'"[9] The earliest references to this practice occur in the writings of Tertullian, where we learn of the custom of anniversary offerings for the deceased.[10] In Augustine's time, communion between the living and the dead was still practiced by means of memorial meals at tombs, at which the poor were often fed.[11] These eucharists and agapes represented acts of communion in Christ between the living and the dead, a communion deepened and solidified because the poor members of the community were fed by the offerings made in the name of the dead.

Was there anything akin to the Mass stipend as we know it today in the early centuries? The answer is yes. For one thing, the eucharist celebrated in small groups and involving special concerns seems to have been a feature of Christianity from the beginning.[12] Those involved in such eucharists provided the material elements for the occasion, and donations were often made to the one who presided.[13] We find figures such as Jerome preaching of the obli-

[7] *Didascalia et Constitutiones Apostolorum*, ed. F. X. Funk (Paderborn: Schoeningh 1895) 2, 58.

[8] *De opere et eleemosynis*, PL 4, 612–613.

[9] Kilmartin, 57.

[10] *De corona* 3, PL 2, 79.

[11] See the chapter entitled "The Feasts of the Dead," in F. van der Meer, *Augustine the Bishop: The Life and Work of a Father of the Church*, tr. Brian Battershaw and G. R. Lambe (New York: Sheed and Ward 1961) 498–516.

[12] Joseph Jungmann, *The Mass of the Roman Rite*, tr. Francis A. Brunner (New York: Benziger Brothers) 1, 212–233.

[13] There is no significant distinction between food offerings and money offerings in this early period. Some anthropologists have concluded, in fact, that shared food represented the earliest form of money, and that money itself had a fundamental link with ancient food rituals. See William H. Desmonde, *Magic, Myth, and Money: The Origin of Money in Religious Ritual* (New York: Free Press of Glencoe 1962).

gation to support the church's ministers who live from the altar in terms derived from the Old Testament: "The tithes and first fruits, which were once given by the people to the priests and levites, apply also to the people of the church."[14] Jerome is quick to follow up this appeal, however, with the important qualification that the Christian obligation to charity extends to all goods and properties, not just to the tithe.[15]

It is this qualification, more than anything else, however, that warns against an easy appeal to the practice of the early centuries in support of the full-fledged Mass stipend system. The Mass stipend does appear, on the surface, to have some precedent in the practice of early Christianity, but the similarities amount only to evidence of special prayers sought by individuals, gifts provided by the people, and the support of the church's ministers derived from these gifts. The difference between the early practice and that of the developed Mass stipend system is the difference between the eucharistic praxis of early Christianity and that of the medieval and post-medieval periods.

In the Pauline eucharistic model and its practical and theological elaboration in the postapostolic and patristic periods, the eucharistic transactions of bread, wine, and money took place *out of the fullness* of the church's communion in Christ and gave expression to the bounty of the church. Eucharistic *koinonia* involved the care of the poor and the dead; offerings of food and money found their radical identity in this involvement. In the dynamics of the eucharist in this early period, there was operative what might be called a *principle of inclusion,* by which Christians acted not *in order to* gain access to sacred realities, but rather *on the basis of* their inclusion through the Holy Spirit in the communion of Christ. Gifts and money were transacted in the fullness of communion and flowed from this communion as its embodiment and expression.

The early Christian eucharist differed essentially from the manner in which pagan sacrifices and offerings were made in order to gain divine favor. Christian eucharistic transactions were not envisaged within the categories of pre-Christian sacrifice; neither was the *sacrum commercium,* the holy exchange, interpreted in any way that suggested contingency upon ritual priesthood and temple cult. The Christian eucharist was a radically different affair: the act

[14] *In Malachiam* 3:7, PL 25, 1571.

[15] On this point in general, see H. Leclercq, "Dime," DACL 14, 995–1003.

of a transformed people embodying a living cult in its common life.

We cannot go into the question here of the relationship between the Old Testament practice and conception of priesthood and sacrifice and the New Testament early Christian notions of liturgy and priesthood.[16] However, the fundamental transformation that took place in the Christian order cannot be underlined enough. We may characterize this as a spiritualization — indeed, more suggestively, as a *pneumaticization* — of sacrifice and priesthood in the Christian dispensation. Worship in the Spirit transformed the whole of Christian life into a living sacrifice. The temple became the people; priesthood was appropriated by the Spirit-filled body of the baptized; worship was no longer cult, but *koinonia* in the Spirit.[17]

It was precisely this transformed, inclusive sense of Christian life and liturgy that began to be reversed in the self-understanding of the church in the medieval period, when a principle of exclusion came into play, largely through the reassertion of pre-Christian ideas of sacrifice, liturgy, and priesthood. Thereafter, liturgical acts would be seen as a means of gaining temporary access to sacred realities to which the baptized had no constitutional access.

THE STIPEND AND THE DYNAMICS OF EXCLUSION

It would not be correct to romanticize the patristic period or to set it in opposition to the medieval. Indeed, significant modifications in ecclesiastical structure and liturgical practice had already begun to take place by the end of the patristic period. These found expression in the increasing exclusion of the people from the transactions of the liturgy and their marginalization in the structure of the church. Clericalization was quickly established as the church began to be reconceived structurally according to the imperial model. Increasingly the ministry of the ordained ceased to be understood as a charism within a community of believers, and appeared instead as a personal authority complete in itself,

[16] This vastly complex area is introduced in Robert J. Daly, *The Origins of the Christian Doctrine of Sacrifice* (Philadelphia: Fortress Press 1978); see also David N. Power, "Words that Crack: The Uses of 'Sacrifice' in Eucharistic Doctrine," *Worship* 53 (1979) 386–404.

[17] On this, see John Hall Elliott, *The Elect and the Holy* (Leiden: E. J. Brill 1966); Raymond Corriveau, *The Liturgy of Life: A Study of the Ethical Thought of St Paul in his Letters to Early Christian Communities* (Studia 25, Brussels/Montreal: Desclée 1970).

ecclesiastically absolute, with ordination seen as accession to hierarchical power and official status.

The liturgy itself had unwittingly provided some internal impetus in this direction when it began to appropriate the style and ethos of imperial ceremonial. This gave rise to a set of symbols that would result in the transference to Christ of regal categories, and thus to a changed relationship between Christ and believers. The latter began to be seen more as servants and unworthy dependents, and there arose as a result a growing sense of unworthiness and awe in the face of the *mysterium tremendum,* as the eucharist was increasingly called.[18]

The most significant expression of this was the decline in congregational communion. The seriousness of this development was recognized at once by such eminent bishops as John Chrysostom and Ambrose of Milan, both of whom campaigned against this trend.[19] The decline was not reversed, however, but only deepened in succeeding centuries.

The withdrawal of the people from communion may be regarded as the first of a series of radical shifts in the church's eucharistic transactions. The gifts were still prepared and offered by the people, *but no longer shared in communion.* This established a serious break in the giving and sharing of the gifts of the eucharist. The result was a profound modification not only of the dynamics of eucharistic participation, but of the manner in which access to the sacred would be perceived thereafter.

Increasingly, penitential supplicatory elements came to dominate the older ones of thanksgiving and communion; the spiritual sacrifice of the common life gave way to ritualism. There emerged a growing sense of the eucharist as a privileged act by which God's aid might be sought for various personal favors, as well as for the benefit of others, living and the dead. This resulted in a conception of the priest as the subject of the eucharist, and on his act of offering and consecration as *the* central dynamic of eucharistic transactions.

The significance of this shift in the Christian praxis of the eucharist can hardly be exaggerated. The eucharist no longer appeared to believers primarily as expressing Christian identity in

[18] On this, see Joseph Jungmann, *The Place of Christ in Liturgical Prayer,* tr. A. Peeler (New York: Alba House 1965) 245–255.

[19] See Jungmann, *Mass* 2, 339–367.

Christ, but as a privileged mode of *access* to divine favors and sacred realities to which there was virtually no other means of access. The subsequent history of eucharistic transactions may be read as the elaboration of this principle. Gifts and offerings were no longer transacted *out of* the fullness of eucharistic *koinonia* in the body of Christ, but *in order to* gain access to eucharistic realities extrinsic to the self-definition of Christian believers. The priest was increasingly seen as the mediator, as having power over the blessings of the eucharist. Thus, offerings and gifts were no longer given to the clergy because the latter were servants of the eucharistic community, and worthy of a living thereby, but because they were custodians and dispensers of eucharistic grace. The praxis of a priestly people was replaced by the praxis of a hierarchical society; a dynamic of inclusion was replaced by a dynamic of exclusion.

From the seventh century onwards, the offering of money came increasingly to the fore and the offering of bread and wine was discontinued. There was the practical consideration that the decrease in congregational communion led to a curtailment of the bringing of the gifts for communion. The more significant reason for this development, however, was the transition from the use of leavened to unleavened eucharistic bread. It was this development, more than anything else, that signified the reemergence of Old Testament ideas about priesthood and liturgy.[20] The motivation behind this change was to remove eucharistic bread and its production from the sphere of the earthly and the profane and to ensure it worthiness for the Christian cult. The result was the ritualization of the process of producing eucharistic bread and the restriction of its production to the clergy and to monasteries. With this development, the people's role was curtailed once more, this time at the level of the originating action which the preparation and provision of material gifts for the eucharist represented.

This change had greater significance than might appear at first sight, as Mary Collins has shown in her exploration of the profound interplay between restrictions in the matter of eucharistic bread and restrictions in ecclesial roles and theological conceptions. The emergence of a new set of restrictive choices about eucharistic bread and the qualifications of those who produce it

[20] Jungmann, *Mass* 2, 33–41.

could not but shape and effect restrictive conceptions about redemption, holiness, and access to God.[21] With this further exclusion, then, came the second major shift in the practice of the eucharist, and the emergence of a set of conceptions that further contributed to a restrictive and exclusive eucharistic praxis.

By the twelfth century, the presentation of bread and wine by the people took place only on a very small number of occasions, and, when practiced, had little more than dramatic value. Where the collection of money continued, it no longer had intrinsic connection with the eucharist or with alms for the poor.[22]

It was against this background that the practice of the Mass stipend had begun to emerge from the eighth century onwards. Significantly, as Joseph Jungmann has shown, the point at which the Mass stipend proper emerged was the point at which the connection between eucharistic participation and the presentation of the gifts finally broke down. The particular character of the Mass stipend was of an honorarium paid in advance to obligate a priest to celebrate exclusively for the intention of the donor.[23] It was, thus, an *extra-eucharistic* transaction directed toward *obtaining* a special benefit available only through the exclusive mediation of the priest.

The earliest regulated accounts of Mass stipends are found in the eighth century Rule of Chrodegang of Metz, in which it was granted that a priest might accept a stipend in return for a Mass celebrated for a donor and his intentions.[24] By the ninth century,

[21] Mary Collins, "Critical Questions for Liturgical Theology," *Worship* 53 (1979) 302–317.

[22] Jungmann, *Mass* 2, 12–13; 25–26.

[23] Jungmann, *Mass* 2, 23–24.

[24] *Regula Canonicorum* 43, PL 89, 1076; cf. 32, PL 89, 1117. Historical and canonical studies of the Mass stipend system are available in the following: Adalbert Mayer, *Triebkräfte und Grundlinien der Entstehung des Messstipendiums* (Münchener theologische Studien III: Kanonistische Abteilung 34, St Ottilien: Eos 1976); Charles Frederick Keller, *Mass Stipends* (St Louis: Herder 1926); Klaus Mörsdorf, "Erwägungen zum Begriff und zur Rechtfertigung des Messstipendiums," in *Theologie in Geschichte und Gegenwart*, ed. J. Auer and H. Volk (Munich: Karl Zink 1957) 103–122; id., "Mass Stipends," in *Sacramentum Mundi: An Encyclopedia of Theology*, ed. Karl Rahner et al. (New York: Herder and Herder 1968) 3, 429–431; A. Meunier, "Les offrandes des messes," *Revue ecclésiastique de Liège* 43 (1956) 107–116; T. Ortolan, "Honoraires de messes," DTC 7-1, 69–94; also, Colum Kenny, "Mass Stipends: Origin and Relevance," *The Homiletic and Pastoral Review* 64 (1964) 842–850; C. Edward Gilpatric, "Mass Stipends and Mass Intentions," *Worship* 38 (1964) 190–201; Joseph A. Jungmann, "Mass Intentions and

it was understood that such stipends were accepted in an exclusive way, as we know from the revisions undertaken by that time on the Rule of Chrodegang.

The practice was not adapted without some reserve and even opposition, however. The ecclesial sensibility of many ecclesiastics led them to recoil from the exclusive, extra-eucharistic nature of the transaction. The Synod of Rome held in 826 rejected the practice, declaring that priests should not be allowed to take offerings from some persons, to the exclusion of others.[25] As late as the twelfth century, the privatizing tendency of the Mass stipend practice was rejected by the Synod of York, which allowed priests to receive stipends only during the Mass.[26] However, by that time, the Mass stipend system was firmly established throughout the Western church. Stipends were given more and more outside the liturgy, and were increasingly attached in a permanent way to benefices of various kinds.

With the growing organization of the stipend system came the multiplication of votive Masses for various needs and an enormous increase in the number of priests whose sole duty was the celebration of Masses to fulfill the numerous requests. In this way, there was firmly established the practice of private Masses and the principle that the giving of a stipend was effective even without the physical presence of the donor. The eucharist was increasingly removed from its ecclesial context and the manner of its performance and effectiveness was defined without reference, except in the most minimal way, to the eucharistic congregation. In effect, the eucharist could now be transacted from beginning to end without the participation of the people. The congregation, when present, involved itself in the eucharist in a drastically curtailed manner, if at all.[27] In this exclusive and restrictive eucharistic

Mass Stipends," in *Unto the Altar: The Practice of Catholic Worship*, ed. Alfons Kirchgaessner (New York: Herder and Herder 1963) 23–31; Edward Kilmartin, "Money and the Ministry of the Sacraments," in *The Finances of the Church*, ed. William Bassett and Peter Huizing (Concilium 117, New York: The Seabury Press 1979) 104–111.

[25] Canon 17, Mansi 14, 1005.

[26] Decretum 3, Mansi 22, 653.

[27] Two further expressions of the growing alienation of the people from active participation in eucharistic transactions were represented in the practice from the ninth century onwards of giving communion to the people on the tongue, rather than in the hand, and from the twelfth century onwards of withholding the chalice from the people. See Jungmann, *Mass* 2, 381–386.

praxis, the Mass stipend became virtually the only ritual means for the people to gain access to the most cherished graces of the eucharistic sacrifice.

It is not difficult to see that monetary transactions of this sort were related to the eucharist in quite a different way than were those of the postapostolic and patristic periods. Because of the curtailment of the people's role in providing the elements for the eucharist and their exclusion from communion, as well as the many other manifestations of ecclesiastical and clerical exclusivism, the Mass stipend system of the medieval period had only a surface similarity to the offering of gifts in the early Christian eucharist. There is a world of difference between gifts transacted within the fullness of an inclusive Christian eucharist, and gifts transacted in an attempt to gain access to a eucharistic and ecclesial system from which ordinary Christians are, in fact and theory, excluded. The offering of gifts was no longer a *symbol of participation* as it was earlier, but rather a *symbol of access.* Because of this, the medieval Mass stipend stood only in apparent continuity with the original practice of the offering of gifts. The whole ritual complex of the eucharist within which monetary transactions originally operated had been radically changed and modified, and thus such transactions operated differently as a result, departing radically from their original meaning and function.

The dynamics represented in the movement from the early form of the offering of gifts to the medieval Mass stipend system bear comparison with what the anthropologist Schlomo Deshen has referred to as *profanation* in the process of change in symbolic operationality. Profanation occurs, according to Deshen, when a symbol is separated from the range of experience within which it originally operated, and when a new range of experience becomes operative to the effect of violating the original integrity of the symbol.[28] This is precisely what happened in the shift of modes of offering in the eucharist from the patristic to the medieval periods. The whole ecclesial and liturgical ethos within which the eucharistic offerings operated was no longer that of an inclusive, participatory order but of a clerical and exclusive order to which the people

[28] Schlomo Deshen and Moshe Shokeid, *The Predicament of Homecoming: Cultural and Social Life of North African Immigrants in Israel* (Ithaca, N.Y.: Cornell University Press 1974) 162.

had access only in the manner of outsiders. As a consequence, the popular modes of offering lost their original character and integrity.

AN ECONOMIC THEOLOGY OF THE EUCHARIST

If praxis refers to the process by which practice shapes and generates theoretical understanding, then it should not be surprising that the medieval theology of the eucharist arose to a great extent out of the Mass stipend system, given the prominence this system had achieved by then. Nor should it be surprising that the language of economics and commerce should have entered into the conceptualization of eucharistic operationality and efficacy.[29]

Edward Kilmartin describes the results in the assertion that "the history of theological opinion concerning the value and fruits of the Mass is intimately associated with the history of the system of Mass stipends."[30] The fundamental issue for eucharistic theology in this regard was established by a practical consideration: if something may be gained from the Mass by one who offers a stipend to a priest which is independent of the donor's own attendance or nonattendance, then that gain must be in the objective order. Theologians affirmed the existence of such an objective quantity, and thus was established the theory of the fruits of the Mass.

Amalar of Metz in the ninth century had suggested a threefold distinction that was now taken up and elaborated upon as a way of explaining how these fruits might be applied. The Mass, according to Amalar, is offered for the holy universal church; for those who offer alms and gifts; and for the priest.[31] Duns Scotus in the thirteenth century developed this scheme, asserting the existence of three distinct fruits of the Mass, applicable as follows: to

[29] This development was represented in the use of ambiguous expressions such as *comparatio missae* and *missam comparare.* See Jungmann, *Mass* 2, 24, n. 133. For a study of monetary factors in the formation of philosophical ideas in general, see March Shell, *Money, Language, and Thought: Literary and Philosophic Economies from the Medieval to the Modern Era* (Berkeley: University of California Press 1982).

[30] Edward Kilmartin, "The One Fruit or the Many Fruits of the Mass," *Proceedings of the Catholic Theological Society of America* 21 (1966) 37–38. On the development of theological ideas in this area, see Erwin Iserloh, "Der Wert der Messe in der Diskussion der Theologen vom Mittelalter bis zum 16. Jahrhundert," *Zeitschrift für Katholische Theologie* 83 (1961) 44–79.

[31] *De ecclesiasticis officiis* 3:23, PL 105, 1138.

the priest (*specialissime*); to the universal church (*generalissime*); and to the one who is the subject of the special intention (*specialiter*).[32] With this scheme came a set of assertions that were widely accepted thereafter: that the fruits available from each Mass are limited; that they are produced in an objective fashion independent of the dispositions of the priest and the participation of the people; and that the priest has the power to apply these fruits.

Here we have the logical conclusions to a practice of the eucharist that was restrictive, nonparticipatory, and pointedly clerical. These principles also logically coincided with a disintegration of the profound sense of the unity between Christ, the church and the eucharist that had characterized the postapostolic and patristic periods. It is telling, for example, that in the medieval church, "body of Christ" no longer referred to the communion of the church in Christ, but only to the eucharist itself in a restricted fashion, while the church was regarded as the body of Christ only in a vague sense.[33] But if the church is separated from Christ, then great difficulty arises in maintaining the sense of how Christ and the eucharist are united. Indeed, it was only by an appeal to nominalism that theologians were able to affirm how it is that Christ is present in the eucharist. In other words, only by an artificial principle was theology able to maintain eucharistic orthodoxy in the face of a set of ecclesiological and liturgical fragmentations and countermovements.

We see this problem of disintegration operative also in medieval discussions about how the fruits of the Mass could be limited. The limitations can be accounted for, according to Scotus, by the fact that it is the church and not Christ which is the immediate subject of the eucharist.[34] This thinking gained wide currency in the thirteenth century and after. It is significant, as Kilmartin points out, that such considerations in the fourteenth and fifteenth centuries arose less from theological speculation than from "the practice of the Church which allows Mass to be offered for an individual and often forbids the acceptance of more than one stipend for a single Mass."[35] A restrictive practice of the eucharist gave rise to a re-

[32] Duns Scotus set out his thought on this matter in *Quaestio* 20 of the *Quaestiones Quodlibetales*. See *Opera Omnia* 26 (Paris: Vivès 1895) 298–331.

[33] See Henri de Lubac, *Corpus mysticum: L'eucharistie et l'église au moyen âge* (Paris: Aubier 1944).

[34] *Opera Omnia* 26, 298.

[35] Kilmartin, "The One Fruit," 53–54.

strictive theology; in turn, a eucharistic theology that distanced Christ from the church's eucharistic operationality shaped a eucharistic practice that was self-centered and introverted.

It was only in the sixteenth century with Cardinal Cajetan that a new conceptualization of the question of limited fruits in the Mass was brought forward.[36] According to Cajetan, the Mass is of infinite value in itself because in it the sacrificial offering of the cross is present. At this level the Mass is unlimited. Where the limitation enters in, according to Cajetan, is at the level of the devotion of Christians. This position did not alter the practice of the eucharist in any way, but it did provide a more adequate account of the relationship between the infinite value of the Mass and the limitations that were at the same time thought to attend its efficacy. The position of Cajetan became the dominant one and was widely held in the seventeenth century and after.

The question of the relationship between the stipend and the fruits of the Mass was not so easily resolved, however. A feature of this question was the necessity of distinguishing the stipendiary transaction from simony. Scotus' approach was to insist that the priest does not accept payment for the Mass, but only a gratuitous donation.[37] Thomas Aquinas interpreted the stipend in broader terms as a contribution to the priest's support.[38] A number of theories were presented during the medieval and post-medieval periods, each seeking to avoid, on the one hand, the danger of simony, and on the other, the notion that the acceptance of a stipend involves no more than a nonbinding promise on the part of the priest. A primary consideration in these theories was to preclude any impingement of the stipendiary transaction upon the essence of the eucharistic sacrifice and its fruits.[39] But it is precisely in this necessity that the ultimate irony of the whole stipendiary system appears. For theology's final defense against simony was to exclude the stipend from any intrinsic role in the eucharistic act. Considering the original form and conception of monetary

[36] *Opuscula Omnia* 2 (Lyons: Tinghi 1585) 147–149.

[37] *Opera Omnia* 26, 324.

[38] On this, see Kilmartin, "The One Fruit," 43–44.

[39] For a historical study of this problem, see Thomas McDonnell, "Stipends and Simony," *The Irish Ecclesiastical Record* 54 (1938) 593–612; 55 (1939) 35–57, 159–175. On the notion of the stipend as an ecclesiastical tax, see R. G. Renard, "Les honoraires de messe," *Revue de sciences philosophiques et théologiques* 28 (1939) 222–227.

transactions as a mode of participation and communion in the eucharist, we are thus given a signal of the extent of the problem that the final evolution of the Mass stipend represented. Within the early practice of the eucharist, monetary transactions were intrinsic expressions of *koinonia* and of care for the needy in the community (including the church's ministers); within the medieval eucharistic context, these monetary transactions bordered dangerously on the buying and selling of spiritual goods from a priest conceived as the exclusive subject of the church's power.

We can see, then, that from the medieval eucharistic praxis in which the stipend came to play such a prominent role there was derived a theology of the monetary gifts as a ritual means of obtaining rights over eucharistic fruits; an ecclesiology and a theology of orders that placed the ordinary Christian outside the realm of eucharistic subjectivity; and a popular spirituality concerned to a great extent with personal gain conceived in overly commercial terms.

TOWARD A RENEWED EUCHARISTIC PRAXIS

The modern liturgical movement has had as one of its primary concerns the revitalization of the subjectivity of the baptized in the liturgy. Apart from the restoration of frequent communion during the pontificate of Pope Pius X, one of the earliest practical expressions of greater participation was the restoration of the offertory procession. The success experienced with this practice no doubt generated further interest in the achievement of a more profound theology of the role of the baptized in eucharistic offering and consequently of the Mass stipend.

In the twentieth century, two theologians have had much influence in developing such a theology: Maurice de la Taille and Karl Rahner. De la Taille approached the question of eucharistic sacrifice and stipends by situating it in a biblical context. In his view, the stipend should be viewed as providing the material elements for the sacrifice, thereby drawing the donor into the role of active offering in the eucharist. In de la Taille's conception, while the power of eucharistic consecration belongs to the priest, the act of offering belongs to the one who provides the elements for the eucharist.[40] To support this view, he returned to the early practice

[40] Maurice de la Taille, *The Mystery of Faith and Human Opinion Contrasted and Defined* (New York: Longmans, Green and Co. 1930) 108ff. See also *The Mystery of Faith* (New York: Sheed and Ward 1950) 2, 223–283.

of the offertory and from this drew the conclusion that "the authors of the sacrifice, in a manner which is proper and personal to them, are the faithful whose gifts are by the priest's hands addressed to God under the form of the Body and Blood of Jesus Christ."[41] This principle, he asserted, provides the only proper interpretation of the Mass stipend.

While de la Taille's approach would be faulted today on a number of grounds, not least because of the analogies he drew between Old Testament sacrifices and the Christian eucharist, as well as his interpretations of patristic thought, he did provide a strong impetus toward the restoration of popular eucharistic subjectivity.

In a controversial essay published in 1949, Karl Rahner developed the general approach of de la Taille and attempted a reinterpretation of the question of the fruits of the Mass and their relationship to active participation.[42] Rahner's fundamental concern was to remove the Mass from the domain of mechanical and impersonal operation and to establish as a primary principle the efficacy of the Mass within the categories of active participation and *devotio*.[43] At the outset, Rahner proposed as the norm for the frequency of Masses that they be celebrated as often and only as often as *devotio* would be increased, and he contested the notion that the Mass gives glory to God by the simple fact that it is celebrated.[44] While at pains to insist that *devotio* is not the cause and origin of eucharistic operationality, he nevertheless made clear his conviction that the *effects* of the Mass are contingent completely upon personal *devotio*.

As regards the fruits of the Mass, Rahner proposed that "union by grace in faith and love with Christ's sacrifice is the *one* effect of the sacrifice itself, the essentially single fruit of the sacrifice issuing from the sacrifice itself."[45] In applying this principle, Rahner

[41] De la Taille, *Mystery of Faith and Human Opinion*, 134.

[42] Karl Rahner, "Die vielen Messen und das eine Opfer," *Zeitschrift für Katholische Theologie* 71 (1949) 257–317. This essay has been incorporated in a modified form into Karl Rahner and Angelus Häussling, *The Celebration of the Eucharist* (New York: Herder and Herder 1968). Quotations are from this latter work.

[43] See David B. Burrell, "Many Masses and One Sacrifice: A Study of the Thought of Karl Rahner," *Yearbook of Liturgical Studies* 2 (Notre Dame: Fides Publishers Association 1961) 104.

[44] Rahner and Häussling, *The Celebration of the Eucharist* 1–12; 34–38; 91–96.

[45] Rahner and Häussling, 78.

denied any radical division in the fruits of the Mass. There is no *fructus specialissimus* acquired by the celebrant that is independent of his devotion; nor is there a *fructus specialis* that accrues to the one for whom the Mass is offered that is not dependent upon the *devotio* of the donor.[46] The Mass stipend, in Rahner's view, has no meaning apart from the quality of active participation in the eucharist by the person who makes the offering. It is, in effect, nothing other than a mode of participation in the Mass.

Rahner could be criticized for having put too much emphasis on eucharistic *devotio* and not enough on the eucharist as sacrament. It would be argued that it is the latter and its ecclesial authenticity that properly determines the frequency and operationality of the eucharist. Nevertheless, Rahner did advance theological understanding on a number of important points: namely, that the eucharist operates primarily as an act of communion in Christ; that the priest who presides has no more access to eucharistic realities than does the devout believer; and that the stipend has its fundamental validity as a symbol of eucharistic participation.[47]

At this point, the fundamental question of this essay may be introduced: does the Mass stipend have a future? To follow through a fundamental principle of this essay — that the stipend system cannot be dealt with apart from considerations about its operationality within a larger complex of eucharistic transactions — means that the answer cannot be a simple one; neither can it be given apart from wider considerations about the church, ministry, and the nature of liturgy. However, the conclusion cannot be avoided that the Mass stipend in its medieval and post-medieval form is a highly problematic institution. Its emergence to prominence in the Middle Ages was contingent upon a number of distorted factors in the church's ecclesial and liturgical praxis, and its subsequent evolution gave rise to a fractured, exclusive, and alienating theology of worship, church, and ministry.

[46] Rahner and Häussling, 79–84.

[47] Rahner's views did not go unchallenged by the Roman magisterium at the time. See Pope Pius XII's address of 2 November 1954, AAS 46 (1954) 313–317; and his address of 22 September 1956, AAS 48 (1956) 711–725. That Rahner's positions are compatible with the magisterial positions set forth in *Cum Semper Oblatas* of Benedict XIV (1744) and *Auctorem Fidei* of Pius VI (1794) has been argued by Colum Kenny in "Mass Stipends: Doctrinal Problems," *The Homiletic and Pastoral Review* 66 (1966) 306–311.

The Mass stipend system, then, can only have an acceptable future within a liturgical and ecclesial environment in which there is vigilance about the problematic features of the history identified in this essay. The system must find fresh theological reformulation by contact with the original and most authentic role that monetary transactions performed in the early Christian eucharist. This, in turn, will mean a careful and intelligent practice of the Mass stipend system which avoids the dangers of commercialism, the improper multiplication of Masses, and the encouragement of an individualistic piety impervious to the communal nature of the liturgy.[48]

In order to propose a way forward here, three elements of the postconciliar praxis of the eucharist may be invoked. The first of these elements finds expression in the principle of the *ecclesial subjectivity of the eucharist.* According to this principle, the primary subject of the eucharist is the church, not the ordained minister. While no local eucharistic assembly is valid in isolation from the catholicity and apostolicity of the church, sacramentalized and verified in the episcopal and presbyteral orders, it is nevertheless clear from the ancient tradition and its modern appropriation that the primary eucharistic subject is the congregation of the baptized.[49] It is within this primary ecclesial subjectivity that the subjectivity of the ordained minister is properly situated and understood.

Those ordained to official ministry, then, may not be regarded as the primary eucharistic subjects, celebrants, or agents of offering. Though indispensable for eucharistic validity, they are to be properly conceived as sacramental ministers of the celebration and offering that is founded in the subjectivity of the ecclesial Body of Christ, in which all share equally by baptism.[50]

[48] The 1983 Code of Canon Law incorporates a vigilant attitude regarding the proper theological understanding and pastoral practice of Mass stipends. See Code of Canon Law, canons 945–958. See also John M. Huels ''Stipends in the New Code of Canon Law'' in this book (pp. 347–356).

[49] On the ecclesial subjectivity of the eucharist, see Yves M.-J. Congar, ''L 'ecclesia' ou communauté chrétienne, sujet intégral de l'action liturgique,'' in *La Liturgie après Vatican II,* ed. J.-P. Joshua and Y. Congar (Paris: Cerf 1967) 241–282. See also Kenneth Smits, ''A Congregational Order of Worship,'' *Worship* 54 (1980) 55–75.

[50] See Hervé-Marie Legrand, ''The Presidency of the Eucharist According to the Ancient Tradition,'' *Worship* 53 (1979) 413–438. This essay provides a useful summary of early evidence on the corporate understanding of eucharistic celebration and

Accordingly, liturgical or pastoral practices which appropriate the eucharist to individuals or special groups, or remove it from its public, communal context, are offensive to the ecclesial constitution and purpose of the sacrament. Similarly unacceptable is the suggestion that the one who presides has fuller access to the eucharistic reality than is available to the liturgical assembly at large.

Since the Mass stipend system has contributed to these and similar theological distortions in the past, the continuance of the system can only be justified within a theological and pastoral framework careful about the reemergence of these problems. This will mean, for example, vigilance about the celebration of the eucharist in private with little consideration given to the role of the community, and with a special intention attached to a stipend as the dominating concern.[51]

What is being suggested here is that the stipend system be so modified in its practical elements that it will never appear merely as a private transaction between an individual and a priest, but always have a communal orientation. For instance, the intention for which a stipend is given should be incorporated carefully into the eucharistic liturgy (in the general intercessions, for example), so that it will be not only the priest, but the whole assembly, that prays for the intention. The appeal is not only to the private prayer of the priest, but to the public prayer of the whole assembly.

Similarly, the stipend should be seen not as a commercial, remunerative transaction between an individual and a priest, but as an expression of care for the church and its ministry on the part of the person requesting prayers. This point could be given effective expression in the creation of a pastoral system wherein the priest receiving the stipend places it in the charity fund of the

offering. A valuable historical study on the question is also provided in Benedicta Droste, *"Celebrare" in der Römischen Liturgiesprache. Eine Liturgie-Theologische Untersuchung*. (Munich: Max Hueber Verlag, 1963.)

[51] The more questionable practices generated in this regard are among religious congregations that operate mail-order Mass associations and purgatorial societies. Some of these even advertise for Mass stipends through Catholic periodicals. Such practices fall very short of exemplifying the qualities of ecclesial and liturgical integrity promoted in postconciliar renewal. There is also the troublesome practice of priestly concelebrations at which all or some of the priests present accept stipends for individual intentions. On this see Kevin Seasoltz, *New Liturgy, New Laws*. (Collegeville: The Liturgical Press, 1979) 88–91.

parish or ecclesiastical institution. In this way, there would be restored a more intimate connection between the monetary transaction and the eucharist. The model here would be that of the Pauline tradition in which the eucharist and communal charity are inseparably connected.

The second element in the postconciliar liturgical praxis which it is appropriate to call upon here is represented in the ongoing reconstitution of the *participatory dynamics of the eucharist.* This finds expression in the recognition that the eucharistic liturgy is primarily an *action* that unfolds in hearing the Word and participation in the communion of the Lord. This active process unfolds in a set of dynamics that are intelligent, formative, and graceful. This participatory conception of the liturgy stands in contrast with those phases of history in which the liturgical assembly was perceived in a passive and purely receptive mode vis-à-vis the sanctifying action of the priest. Recent renewal emphasizes that the eucharist sanctifies not in an automatic or mechanical way, but in and through the very dynamics of the act of participation. This sanctification comes not from any intention of the priest to direct eucharistic graces to individuals or groups, but from the fact that the people themselves participate in an intrinsically sanctifying action.

What this implies is that the liturgical assembly is itself the primary recipient of the operations and effects of every eucharistic celebration. No psychological intention on the part of the priest is necessary or able to open to the people more intense levels of grace or benefit.

It follows from the participatory dynamics of the liturgy that prayer for the absent and the dead is not efficacious in a mechanical or automatic way. The eucharist does not assist such persons in the manner of legal transactions. Thinking in this way fails to respect the proper dynamics of eucharistic sanctification and it depersonalizes the process by which the absent and the dead are recipients of the grace and blessedness of the eucharist.

Historically, the Mass stipend system has offended against the participatory operationality of the eucharist by generating the notion that active participation need not be the primary consideration in receiving eucharistic grace. It has encouraged the view that an absent person may actually gain more from the eucharist than one who is present but not included in the primary intention of the Mass. This has found expression in the notion that while the eucharist is always *celebrated* for the congregation present, it may be *offered* for another intention, often one known only to the priest and involving an absent donor.[52] Some corrective to this has been enshrined in the traditional requirement that the Mass be offered *pro populo* at least once a week.[53] However, the theology and practice of the ancient liturgical tradition, as well as the principles of postconciliar praxis, imply that the Mass is always and unavoidably *pro populo,* and that the benefit to the absent and the dead arises from this foundational reality.

If the restoration of the participatory dynamics of the eucharist remains one of the primary tasks of ongoing renewal, then the practice of prayer for the absent and the dead in the liturgy will be reconceived and enriched by this restoration. This means a recognition that such prayer has a deeply personal basis in the devotion and care incumbent upon the eucharistic community. Prayer of this kind will be conceived properly as an outpouring of love on the part of the church for particular persons and groups, living and dead, and for particular conditions of the church and the world. It will be understood as a conscious expression of love and solidarity founded in the requirements of true Christian conversion. The dynamics of the efficacy of this prayer will not be understood in terms of a private, legal transference of grace, but will be recognized to have the shape of a loving act arising out of the edifying role of the eucharist within the communion of saints. As already suggested, the stipend attached to the request for such prayer will be seen properly as a material expresssion of the charity that flows from authentic Christian prayer.

The final element of the church's eucharistic praxis here concerns the *intrinsic economy of the liturgical order.* By economy is meant the mutually complementary manner in which all the elements of the church's liturgy (the eucharist, the other sacraments, the liturgy of the hours, and so forth) are interrelated and unfold according to a calendar of days, times, feasts, and seasons. In this economy, different features of the mystery of faith come to the fore at different times and the church participates in the mystery of faith according to a carefully moderated understanding of the gradual processes of sanctification and edification. There is an in-

[52] On this see George St Hilaire, "Eliminating Mass Stipends," *The Homiletic and Pastoral Review* 66 (1966) 845–852.

[53] The requirement finds expression in the 1983 Code of Canon Law in canon 534.

ner rhythm and timeliness in the unfolding of the liturgy that is measured and wisely calculated.

That the stipend system habitually cuts across this liturgical economy is evident within the broad lines of the present analysis. We have already observed that this system offended against the communal nature of worship by separating the special intention of the Mass from the public prayer of the people. It offended similarly by ignoring the manner in which prayer for the living and the dead arises out of the prayer of the eucharistic assembly. The further problem that needs identification here is the tendency of special intentions and the transaction of stipends to take on an autonomy of their own unrelated to the economy of the liturgy. This problem is acutely represented, for example, in the popular premium placed on the multiplication of Mass intentions and in the view that the graces and benefits from such multiplication are cumulative and quantitative.

It is evident, for instance, that the multiplication of Masses for the dead impedes the proper integration of prayer for the dead into the whole structure of the eucharist and the liturgical year. Accordingly, the practice of prayer for the dead would gain greatly from a scheme based on the intrinsic economy of the liturgical year. It might be suggested, for instance, that the number of Masses for the dead be limited. An historical scheme worth recovering would be that of early Christianity, when Masses were celebrated on the third, seventh, and thirtieth days after burial.[54] This scheme was not primarily concerned with the accumulation or multiplication of the benefits of the eucharist, but, rather, served to symbolize, in a public and processual way, the desire of the church to accompany and be in solidarity with the dead in their continuing pilgrimage toward blessedness in God's Kingdom. In a similar way, Masses for the living could be carefully regulated and moderated to avoid any implication of intrinsic value in multiplication.

In general, all special intentions, supported by stipends, might be considered more suitable for weekday Masses. This would al-

[54] On this see Geoffrey Rowell, *The Liturgy of Christian Burial: An Introductory Survey of the Historical Development of Christian Burial Rites.* (London: Alcuin Club/S.P.C.K., 1977), esp. 12–13. Rowell shows how the schematization of post-burial observances varied from place to place. See also Robert J. Hoeffner, "A Pastoral Evaluation of the Rite of Funerals," *Worship* 55 (1981) 482–499.

low the preeminence of Sundays, major solemnities, and feasts to be celebrated with a more universal and ecclesially inclusive outlook, with concern for all God's people and every condition of humanity and human need.

The emerging liturgical praxis of the eucharist, then, as outlined in this essay, would seek to reshape the practice of Mass stipends and special intentions by contact with the Pauline eucharistic model. In this model, gifts and money are brought to the eucharist, collected for the poor, and distributed out of the bounty of the church. It is a model that is ecclesially and liturgically inclusive. The modern basis for this conception and practice of the gifts is established in the General Instruction of the Roman Missal of 1969 which speaks of the preparation of the gifts at the eucharist as "the time to bring forward or collect money for the poor and the church."[59] This involves a theological and pastoral conception of the gathering and presentation of the gifts as a transaction of liturgical *diakonia* that flows from the very nature of the eucharist. It involves a corresponding movement away from the superficial view that the eucharistic collection has no more significant value than the utilitarian necessity of raising funds for the maintenance of ecclesiastical institutions. A richer understanding of the intrinsic eucharistic nature of the collection of the gifts is already being set in place in many congregations and Christian communities by the advancement of a theology of stewardship. In this perspective, the offering of money within the eucharist is seen as an integral feature of liturgical spirituality. By the same process, the stipend system can be purified and enriched by contact with the same rich and traditional theology and practice of eucharistic *diakonia*.

In short, the Mass stipend system can have a suitable future only if it continues to be subjected to the same critical scrutiny and positive theological and pastoral enrichment to which the liturgy in general has been subjected in the renewal advanced by the Second Vatican Council.

[55] The General Instruction on the Roman Missal, no. 49. Text in *Vatican Council II: The Conciliar and Post Conciliar Documents*, ed. Austin Flannery (Collegeville: The Liturgical Press, 1975) 175.

M. Francis Mannion

John M. Huels

Stipends in the New Code of Canon Law

A course on sacramental law which I teach to ministry students includes a lecture on Mass stipends or, more properly, "Mass offerings,"[1] and to stimulate their thinking I open the lecture with a question: "When you buy a Mass card, what are you getting for your money?" Admittedly the question is provocative and perhaps even offensive, but in truth it speaks to the experience of a great many Catholics who, when offering a donation for the application of Mass, frequently ask how much a Mass costs. Moreover, the question achieves the desired objective because the students for the first time must wrestle with the troublesome theological and pastoral issues connected with this longstanding custom. Their answers are slow in coming, confused and tentative, some trying to find genuine good in the practice, others simply dismissing it as an antiquated and curious holdover from the Middle Ages or even rejecting the whole system because of its simoniacal associations. A few students share their view that the Mass card is primarily a way of expressing a message of sympathy to the bereaved, or it provides an opportunity to highlight the intention in the eucharist so that the whole community might pray for the deceased. Others respond more cynically that the only thing they get for their money is a card and, as one student put it, "it's a lot cheaper than sending flowers." Interestingly, not one of these young people has ever said that the deceased or other intention receives any additional graces, any "special fruits of the Mass" which the celebrant or concelebrant applies. Yet since the time of Duns Scotus this had been the dominant theological rationale, and I suspect it is still the motivation of a good many Catholics who have Mass celebrated for particular intentions.

Certainly it is not my aim to promote this traditional theory whose weaknesses have been so thoroughly exposed by contemporary theologians, including M. Francis Mannion in this issue. The real questions I want my students to understand are: How does the

[1] The significance of this terminological change will be discussed below.

church justify the perpetuation of the Mass offering system, and how can these values best be fostered in pastoral practice? As a canonist I look for my answer to the first question primarily in legal texts and their historical and theological contexts, and in fact it is in the law where the Apostolic See treats the issue of Mass offerings. Church law as a rule tends to avoid giving reasons or favoring particular theories but aims to provide clear norms for the regulation of systems and groups. This is largely true of the treatment of Mass offerings both in the former Code of Canon Law and in the new Code promulgated by John Paul II on January 25 of this year.[2] Nevertheless, a careful analysis of the texts and the context of the new law reveals a certain rationale for the practice. By such an analysis I intend to show here: [1] that the principal justification given for Mass offerings is the fact that the practice has a long tradition; [2] that the Apostolic See has implicitly rejected the traditional theological rationale for Mass offerings; [3] that the chief motive for maintaining the system of Mass offerings is financial; [4] that the church considers Mass offerings to be wholly gratuitous donations given by the faithful out of concern for the church's ministry and not payments for services rendered.

The discussion will begin with an overview of the reactions of canonists to the treatment of Mass offerings in the drafts of the Code, and will note what impact these critiques had on the final text. Next there will be an examination of the more important norms and significant changes in the section on Mass offerings in the revised Code. Following the conclusions I will address briefly the pastoral question by suggesting some alternatives to the Mass offering system which are in accord with canon law.

CRITIQUES OF THE SCHEMAS

The norms on Mass offerings in the 1975 schema,[3] or draft, of the revised Code of Canon Law were a disappointment to many canonists and others who questioned the adequacy of the institute in light of Vatican II and postconciliar theology and the emphases of the liturgical reform. Schema norm 69, adopted as canon 901 in the re-

[2] *Codex Iuris Canonici,* auctoritate Ioannis Pauli PP. II promulgatus (Libreria Editrice Vaticana 1983).

[3] Pontificia Commissio Codici Iuris Canonici Recognoscendo, *Schema Documenti Pontificii quo Disciplina Canonica de Sacramentis Recognoscitur* (Vatican City: Typis Polyglottis Vaticanis 1975).

vised Code, states that a priest may apply the Mass for anyone, both living and dead. This suggested to some an unacceptable theology of merit and the fruits of the Mass.[4] A report on the schema sponsored by the Canon Law Society of America raised fundamental questions about the whole institute of Mass offerings, as did a critique prepared by the department of canon law at The Catholic University of America.[5] Reports of other canonical societies, including those of Canada[6] and Great Britain and Ireland,[7] questioned whether the Code is the proper place for such detailed regulations, and noted the disproportionate number of canons in the schema. There were more norms on stipends in the draft sent to the pope in 1981 than there were on the entire sacrament of confirmation!

The critical views on the schema expressed in the evaluations of professional canonical societies and canon law faculties were not without representation on the Pontifical Commission for the Revision of the Code of Canon Law. Before its final plenary session in October 1981 there were eleventh-hour attempts to remove the whole section on stipends from the Code. Two petitions sought a radical reduction in the number of canons because they smack of "casuistry" and "commercialism." Two proposals suggested that the entire practice be left to the competence of the episcopal conferences. One prelate, representing one of the largest episcopal conferences in the world, proposed that the whole stipend system be abolished and some other way be found to provide for clerical support without any connection between the celebration of the eucharist and an offering of money.[8] None of these petitions was accepted and the

[4] A more complete synopsis of reactions to the initial schema is provided by T. Green, "The Revision of Sacramental Law: Perspectives on the Sacraments other than Marriage," *Studia Canonica* 11 (1977) 261–327, esp. 294–297 on stipends.

[5] T. Green, Task Force Chairman, "Reflections on Other Parts of the Proposed Draft *De Sacramentis*," *Proceedings of the 37th Annual Convention of the Canon Law Society of America* (1975) 201. The *Animadversions on the Schema de Sacramentis*, prepared under the direction of J. Lynch, chairman of the department of canon law, is unpublished.

[6] The report of the Canadian Canon Law Society was endorsed substantially by the Canadian Catholic Conference. It was dated 22 January 1976 and is C.C.C. Official Document no. 401. See p. 10.

[7] The Canon Law Society of Great Britain and Ireland, *Report on the Schema Documenti Pontificii quo Disciplina Canonica de Sacramentis Recognoscitur* (October 1975) 31.

[8] Pontificia Commissio Codici Iuris Canonici Recognoscendo, *Relatio* (Typis Polyglottis Vaticanis 1981) 220–221. The names of these cardinals and archbishops are withheld since the *Relatio* is labeled *Patribus Commissionis stricte reservata.*

Code Commission made no substantial changes in the section on Mass offerings in the final draft sent to the pope.

MASS OFFERINGS IN THE NEW CODE

When the approved version of the canons appeared following their January 25 promulgation, a number of revisions mostly of a stylistic nature could be detected in the section on Mass offerings, canons 945–958. Some changes already were foreseen in the previous schemas. Four canons from the 1917 Code were suppressed, canons 825 and 826 which forbade abuses and distinguished the three kinds of stipends, and canons 833 and 834 which had strongly contractual overtones with their provisions for the stipend donor to stipulate conditions such as the time of the celebration of the Mass. One new canon (946) and one new paragraph (945,2) were added, and these will be discussed below. The pope's advisors reduced the total number of canons on Mass offerings from the nineteen in the 1980 schema to fourteen in the 1983 Code. This was accomplished not by making any substantive changes but simply by consolidating several short canons into longer ones, especially canon 955 which is based on five different canons of the 1980 schema. Thus, while the number of canons in the final version is smaller, there is no diminution in actual content.

The first paragraph of the initial canon on Mass offerings, canon 945, is quite similar to its counterpart in the 1917 Code: "In accord with the approved usage of the church, it is lawful for any priest who celebrates or concelebrates Mass to receive an offering to apply the Mass according to a definite intention." In both the former and the revised Codes, "the approved usage of the church" looms large in the mind of the legislator as the principal justification for the practice. In response to the prelate who sought the abolition of the stipend system, the 1981 *Relatio*, or report, of the Code Commission, then under the presidency of Cardinal Pericles Felici, countered that this "discipline is rooted in the very ancient tradition of the church."[9] Mass offerings in one form or another have been a part of the life of the Western church at least since the Carolingian period, and church authorities seem to find this sufficient reason, or the principal reason, to justify the continuance of this custom. The argument from tradition was the first to be mentioned by Paul VI in

[9] *Relatio*, 221.

his 1974 apostolic letter *Firma in traditione*,[10] the only important contemporary legal document of the Apostolic See other than the Code to deal with Mass offerings. The very title of this motu proprio reveals how much weight tradition alone has with the Holy See even when convincing theological arguments are lacking.

The second paragraph of canon 945 is new to the revised Code: "It is strongly recommended that priests, even if no offering has been received, celebrate Mass for the intention of the faithful, especially of the needy." This paragraph implies that there is some benefit to be gained from the celebrant's praying for a specific intention at the eucharist over and above the financial benefit that accrues to the church from the offerings. The Code gives no explanation of what this benefit might be, but one need not infer that the traditional theory is intended. Although the first paragraph speaks of "applying the Mass according to a specific intention," it does not suggest any particular theological explanation of the phrase, so one need not assume the "fruits of the Mass" theory is implied. On the contrary, *Firma in traditione* indicates that the "special fruits of the Mass" theory may be in disfavor not only among theologians but also with the official magisterium. Paul VI offered two reasons of a quasi-theological nature in his justification of Mass offerings: [1] the practice is a kind of sacrifice made by the faithful so that they might more actively participate in the eucharistic sacrifice; [2] it is a sign of the union of the baptized with Christ and of the donor with the celebrant. While the pope also mentions "a more abundant supply of fruits" which comes to the faithful in virtue of giving a Mass offering, it is not stated that it is any "special fruit of the Mass" but rather a grace which apparently is the result of the donors' faith and devotion as they "associate themselves more closely with Christ offering himself as victim and thereby they reap a more abundant supply of fruits."[11] It should be noted, moreover, that the beneficiary of this fruit is not the *intention* for which the priest prays, but the Mass offering *donors* themselves. Neither the pope nor the Code claims that the offering of Mass for a certain intention produces any benefit at all for that intention.

Since the traditional explanation of the special fruits of the Mass is no longer fostered by the church, what is the purpose of the cele-

[10] June 13, 1974, AAS 66 (1974) 308.

[11] Ibid.

brant's praying for a specific intention during the eucharist as canon 945,2 recommends? Whatever the answer, there is no need to suggest that this prayer is any more or less efficacious than other intercessory prayers made by the eucharistic assembly. Indeed, the liturgy itself expressly states that the eucharist is offered for many intentions. The eucharistic prayers speak of offering the sacrifice for the church, the pope, bishop, clergy, faithful, and other intentions. Thus, the intention of the celebrant, whether or not it is conjoined with an offering, can be viewed as simply one more intention which may be prayed for in the eucharist. The official documents of the contemporary magisterium make no claim that there is any particular efficacy in the priest's remembering this special, additional intention.

A second significant change in the revised Code's treatment of Mass offerings is the inclusion of a new norm, canon 946, which is the only attempt the law makes at a rationale for the institute: "The faithful, who give an offering that Mass be applied for their intention, contribute to the good of the church and by their offering participate in its concern for the support of its ministers and works." This canon justifies Mass offerings for the opportunity they provide the donors to participate in the work of the church, and in so doing it indirectly promotes the financial motive as paramount. The financial considerations were more pronounced and explicit in Paul VI's 1974 motu proprio *Firma in traditione.* The several theological and anthropological reasons given by the pope for continuing the Mass stipend system are tersely expressed in the apostolic letter, but somewhat more space is devoted to the financial motive than to any of these others.[12] From canon 946 and *Firma in traditione* one might conclude that the church sees itself as the chief beneficiary of the Mass offering system because of the added revenue it receives from such offerings, and this financial consideration is a major factor for the perpetuation of the practice.

Although critics of Mass offerings sometimes downplay their financial impact, statistics indicate the contrary. An unpublished report of a province of one religious order listed more than $700,000 in annual receipts from Mass offerings, with over a quarter of a million dollars coming from a single parish. Although no actual figures exist for the national or international levels, if one takes the sum of $1800

[12] Ibid.

as conceivable annual income for each priest from Mass offerings, then the priests in the United States alone earn over $105 million each year.[13] Since the salaries of priests are frequently budgeted at a low scale to account for stipend income, the institutional church has that much extra money at its disposal.

Of the substantive changes from the former Code, perhaps the most significant is the change in title of the section. The 1917 Code spoke of "Mass alms or stipends" whereas the new Code uses the term "Mass offerings." This change was proposed originally by the Code Commission *coetus* (committee) on the sacraments in 1972 because the word "stipend" (*stipendium*) has connotations of a mercantile transaction and the remuneration owed for the performance of some service. By contrast, the *coetus* report says the word "offering" (*stips*) properly signifies a donation made for the honor of God or to the poor and thus is a more fitting term for use in connection with the eucharist.[14] The change also suggests that the church considers the donation for the application of Mass to be wholly gratuitous and not the payment due on a *do ut facias* contract. Thus, Mass offerings can be understood correctly in a way similar to other kinds of bequests. When one gives a Mass card to the bereaved or has a Mass applied for the intention of anyone living or deceased, the offering of money involved is given to the church *in the name of* the intention, just as a donation to any charitable institution or foundation is made in the name of, or as a memorial of, some person. A Mass offering is a freewill donation to the church which expresses the donor's desire that the church remember in prayer the requested intention, but it is not payment which can require in justice such prayer. Canonically, the application of Mass for the donor's intention means only that there can be but one offering accepted for each Mass (canon 948), and therefore only the donor's intentions can be conjoined with that offering. Canon law does not specify that the priest must actually pray for that intention, and in practice the priest often does not know the precise offering-intention of the Mass which he is celebrating. This is not to say that praying for the intention is not a worthy

[13] The figure of $1800 is based on five-dollar stipends, which are about average today, for 360 Masses. The figure of $105,116,400 is derived from $1800 times the total number of U.S. priests, given as 58,398 in the 1982 *Catholic Almanac* (Huntington, Indiana: Our Sunday Visitor). Even if the actual total may not be quite this high, it is evident that the amount is substantial.

[14] *Communicationes* 4 (1972) 57.

practice, but rather that the offering is totally gratuitous and cannot require in justice such prayer.

CONCLUSIONS AND PASTORAL SUGGESTIONS

From the foregoing analysis of the treatment of Mass offerings in the revised Code of Canon Law and other legal sources, one can discern a rationale offered by church authority for the continuance of this custom. The principal justification for the practice is its long tradition, and the chief motive for perpetuating this tradition is financial. The Code provides no theological justification for the practice, nor does it presume any particular theory such as that of the special fruits of the Mass applied by the priest for the donor's intention. Indeed this theory is conspicuously absent from Paul VI's brief treatment of the issue in *Firma in traditione*, which may mean that the Apostolic See has rejected or at least no longer fosters the traditional theological explanation.

In effect, it is difficult to find any statement on Mass offerings in the new Code which is not open to broad theological interpretation. Furthermore, the important terminological change from "Mass stipend" in the old Code to "Mass offering" in the new Code signifies the church's understanding of the practice as wholly gratuitous and not a payment for services rendered. Nearly all the evident contractual connotations of the practice in the former Code have been removed. Instead the revised Code chiefly offers straightforward disciplinary norms to regulate the practice in order to avoid the appearance of simony and to prevent abuses.

The chief problem with Mass offerings is not truly theological anymore, for the concept of a freewill donation to the church without contractual obligations does not offend against good theology. The problem with Mass offerings now is principally a moral one because many of those who "buy Masses" are being deceived. They think they are getting something for their money, some spiritual favor or grace which benefits their intention. In reality, contemporary church documents indicate that the principal beneficiary of the Mass offering is the institutional church and the secondary beneficiary is the donor, but (fortunately) no claims are made of any benefits accruing to the donor's intention. While the new Code may have made significant progress in removing contractual and simoniacal associations from its treatment of Mass offerings, the perpetuation of the old system with a new rationale and vocabulary could leave the church vulnerable to the charge of creating a deception as long as the Catholic people do not understand this new rationale and vocabulary.[15]

Several practical alternatives arise from these conclusions: [1] Catholics should be reeducated on the meaning of Mass offerings in light of the church's new discipline, its reformed liturgy, and sound theology; or [2] the Mass offering system should be abolished altogether; or [3] it should be altered radically to prevent continued deception or misunderstanding. The first alternative would require a massive effort and likely produce total confusion on all sides. The second option is perhaps the ideal and could be accomplished legally. Canon law does not impose the Mass offering system, but only seeks to regulate it where it exists. The Code says that *it is lawful* for a priest to accept Mass offerings, but the inverse is not excluded. Nothing in the law prevents individual priests from refusing to accept Mass offerings, or even whole groups of priests such as those of a diocese or a province of a religious institute. Canon 952 allows the provincial council or the meeting of bishops in an ecclesiastical province to define the amount of the offering. This council or meeting also could become a forum for a local church to reexamine thoroughly its position on Mass offerings, notwithstanding their total abolition voluntarily accepted by all priests in the province.

While this second alternative might be the ideal, it may not be pastorally or financially wise as an immediate solution. The third possibility of radically altering the system may be the best way to preserve its benefits while eliminating misconceptions. It also could allow wide latitude for local creativity and initiative. For example, in some places priests already refuse to accept particular stipends and

[15] The possibility of misconception or deception is increased by commentators and others at eucharist who announce that the Mass is being offered or especially offered for some intention, and by priests who remember aloud the intention at the memento during the eucharistic prayer in violation of the rubrics which reserve this memento to Masses of the dead. Such practices not only are outside the requirements of church law, but they border on simony by giving someone special consideration in the eucharist in exchange for the payment of money. On the other hand, there is nothing offensive to the contemporary understanding of Mass offerings in such common practices as listing the intention in the parish bulletin, or mentioning it in the prayers of the faithful without the phrase "for whom this Mass is offered." As noted above, the eucharist is expressly offered for many intentions and cannot be "especially offered" for one intention without reverting to a eucharistic theology which is ill-suited to the reformed liturgy.

intentions but instead furnish a special box for donations and a book for intentions at some place in the church. The members of the parish who desire special prayers write their intentions in the book and freely place a donation of any amount in the box. The offerings and book are brought forward at the offertory procession to symbolize the prayers of the whole worshiping community for these special intentions.

In the same vein local churches should reconsider the so-called "Mass card." Since Mass cards provide a pastoral service especially as an expression of sympathy to the bereaved and of the church's prayer for the deceased, they could be redesigned to highlight these values without perpetuating bad theology. The content of the card could be worded something like this: "A donation to St Joseph Church has been made by John Smith in the name of Jane Doe who will be remembered in the prayers and worship of this parish community."

Obviously such changes might necessitate an adjustment in the salaries of priests who depend on income from stipends. There also may be other pastoral and liturgical difficulties arising from well-intentioned but misguided initiatives. However, if uniform practices are recommended at the level of the ecclesiastical province referred to above, these risks would be minimized and pioneering local churches could pave the way for the elimination of all deception, misunderstanding, and outdated theology in connection with the practice of praying for special intentions in the eucharist.

John M. Huels

Acknowledgments

The articles of this collection were published in the following issues of *Worship*:

Jerome Murphy-O'Connor, "Eucharist and Community in First Corinthians," vol. 50, no. 5 (September 1976) 370–385; vol. 51, no. 1 (January 1977) 56–69.

Aidan Kavanagh, "Thoughts on the Roman Anaphora," vol. 39, no. 9 (November 1965) 515–529; vol. 40, no. 1 (January 1966) 2–16.

Robert J. Ledogar, "The Eucharistic Prayer and the Gifts over Which It Is Spoken," vol. 41, no. 10 (December 1967) 578–596.

Thomas J. Talley, "From *Berakah* to *Eucharistia*: A Reopening Question," vol. 50, no. 2 (March 1976) 115–137.

Aidan Kavanagh, "Thoughts on the New Eucharistic Prayers," vol. 43, no. 1 (January 1969) 2–12.

James Dallen, "The Congregation's Share in the Eucharistic Prayer," vol. 52, no. 4 (July 1978) 329–341.

Philippe Rouillard, "From Human Meal to Christian Eucharist," vol. 52, no. 5 (September 1978) 425–439; vol. 53, no. 1 (January 1979) 40–56. The French original of this article appeared in *Notitiae,* nos. 131–132 (1977). This English translation was prepared by the *Worship* staff.

David Power, "Words That Crack: The Use of 'Sacrifice' in Eucharistic Discourse," vol. 53, no. 5 (September 1979) 386–404.

Edward Schillebeeckx, "Transubstantiation, Transfinalization, Transignification," vol. 40, no. 6 (June–July 1966) 324–338.

Donald Gray, "The Real Absence: A Note on the Eucharist," vol. 44, no. 1 (January 1970) 20–26.

Hervé-Marie Legrand, "The Presidency of the Eucharist According to the Ancient Tradition," vol. 53, no. 5 (September 1979) 413–438.

Jean Leclercq, "Eucharistic Celebrations Without Priests in the Middle Ages," vol. 55, no. 2 (March 1981) 160–168.

John Quinn, "The Lord's Supper and Forgiveness of Sin," vol. 42, no. 5 (May 1968) 281–291.

Robert Taft, "*Ex Oriente Lux?* Some Reflections on Eucharistic Concelebration," vol. 54, no. 4 (July 1980) 308–325.

R. Kevin Seasoltz, "Monastery and Eucharist: Some American Observations," vol. 54, no. 6 (November 1980) 512–537.

Kenneth Smits, "A Congregational Order of Worship," vol. 54, no. 1 (January 1980) 55–75.

R. Kevin Seasoltz, "Justice and the Eucharist," vol. 58, no. 6 (November 1984) 507–530.

M. Francis Mannion, "Stipends and Eucharistic Praxis," vol. 57, no. 3 (May 1983) 194–215.

John M. Huels, "Stipends in the New Code of Canon Law," vol. 57, no. 3 (May 1983) 215–224.

Index